THE INTERNATIONAL RELATIONS OF THE MIDDLE EAST IN THE 21ST CENTURY

For Shareen
who carries the
torch for us

The International Relations of the Middle East in the 21st Century

Patterns of continuity and change

Edited by
TAREQ Y. ISMAEL
University of Calgary, Canada

Ashgate

Aldershot • Burlington USA • Singapore • Sydney

Published by
Ashgate Publishing Limited
Gower House
Croft Road
Aldershot
Hampshire GU11 3HR
England

Ashgate Publishing Company
131 Main Street
Burlington
Vermont 05401
USA

Ashgate website: http://www.ashgate.com

British Library Cataloguing in Publication Data
The international relations of the Middle East in 21st
century : patterns of continuity and change
1. Middle East - Foreign relations 2.Middle East - Politics
and government - 1979-
I. Ismael, Tareq Y., 1939-
327.5'6

Library of Congress Control Number: 00-134006

ISBN 0 7546 1506 5

Printed in Great Britain by
Antony Rowe Ltd, Chippenham, Wiltshire

Contents

PART THREE: THE GLOBAL CONTEXT

List of Contributors

Hilal Elver was formerly UNEP Chair at the Mediterranean Academy of Diplomatic Studies at the University of Malta where she taught environmental diplomacy and prior to that, a member of the faculty at University of Ankara Law School and head of the Legal Department, Minister of Environment. She is currently writing books on transboundary rivers and international law, and collaborating with Richard Falk on a book dealing with the public order of the ocean.

Richard Falk is Albert G. Milbank Professor of International Law and Practice at Princeton University. He is the author of *Revolutionaries and Functionaries: The Dual Face of Terrorism* (E.P. Dutton, 1988); *Explorations at the Edge of Time* (Temple University Press, 1992); and *On Humane Governance: Toward a New Global Politics* (Pennsylvania State University Press, 1995). His concerns with the Middle East include being vice chairman of the MacBride Commission, which investigated Israeli violations of international law during the 1982 invasion of Lebanon, and serving as a member of the International Peace Research Association's Commission on a Peace Process for the Middle East.

Jeffrey W. Helsing is Program Officer for Education and Training at the United States Institute of Peace in Washington, D.C. He has written on American foreign policy making, the Arab-Israeli peace process and conflict resolution. Most recently, he authored the forthcoming *Johnson's War/Johnson's Great Society: The Guns and Butter Trap* (Praeger Publishers). Helsing was Assistant Professor of Political Science at the American University in Cairo and has also taught international relations and American politics at Swarthmore College and the University of Pennsylvania.

Jacqueline S. Ismael is a Professor of Social Work at the University of Calgary and an adjunct Professor of International Relations at Eastern Mediterranean University. She has published a number of articles and monographs on social change in the Middle East, as well as several works on Canadian social policy. She is co-author with Tareq Y. Ismael of *The People's Democratic Republic of Yemen: The Politics of Socialist*

Transformation (1986); *Middle East Studies: International Perspectives on the State of the Art* (1990); *Social Policy in the Arab World* (1995); *Government and Politics in Islam* (1986); *Politics and Government in the Middle East and North Africa* (1991); *The Gulf War and the New World Order: International Relations of the Middle East* (1994); *The Communist Movement in Syria and Lebanon* (1997); and is also the author of *Kuwait: Dependency and Class in a Rentier State* (1993).

Tareq Y. Ismael is a Professor of Political Science at the University of Calgary and President of the International Center for Contemporary Middle East Studies at Eastern Mediterranean University (TRNC). He has written extensively on the politics and international relations of the Middle East, and ideology in the Arab world. Besides the works he has co-authored with Jacqueline S. Ismael, his publications include *International Relations of the Contemporary Middle East* (1986); *The Communist Movement in Egypt* (1990); *Canada and the Middle East: The Foreign Policy of a Client State* (1994); and *Civil and Political Rights in the Arab World* (1995).

Andrej Kreutz is Professor of International Relations and Middle Eastern Politics at the Institute of International Studies, University of Lodz (Poland). He also teaches on a part-time basis at the University of Calgary (Canada) and is an Associate of the Centre for Russian and East European Studies, University of Toronto. He is the author of *The Struggle for the Holy Land* (Greenwood Press, 1990) and numerous papers and articles. His research interests include: Vatican and Russian politics toward the Middle East, and the political role and importance of religion and the post-Cold War international political system and culture.

Philip Marfleet is Lecturer in Development Studies and Director of the Refugee Studies program at the University of East London. He has published widely on globalization, religious activism, and on refugee issues. His recent publications include (with Ray Kiely) *Globalization and the Third World* (Routledge 1998).

Ali A. Mazrui is Director of the Institute of Global Cultural Studies, State University of New York at Binghamton. He is also professor at Cornell University, Ithaca, New York, and at the School of Islamic and Social Sciences in Leesburg, Virginia. Dr. Mazrui has published more than twenty books and hundreds of articles. He is best known for his television series *The Africans: A Triple Heritage* (BBC and PBS, 1986).

He is a former Vice President of the International Political Science Association and a former President of the African Studies Association of the United States.

Adel Safty is a visiting Professor and Director of International relations at Eastern Mediterranean University. He has been director of the United Nations University's International Leadership Academy in Amman, Jordan since 1996. He is author of *From Camp David to the Gulf: Negotiations, language & propaganda, and war* (1996).

John Strawson teaches law and Middle Eastern studies at the University of East London, where he is also a member of the Center for New Ethnicities Research. He writes on law and postcolonialism with special reference to Islam and the Middle East. He is also member of the European Consortium supporting the Birzeit University Institute of Law in Palestine.

Paul Sullivan has been teaching courses on the Middle East and Central Asia at the American University in Cairo since Fall 1993. His reasearch and writing have been almost exclusively on the economics and political economy of the Middle East and Central Asia. Recently, however, he has begun writing on US diplomacy in the Middle East, especially US policy towards Iraq. The economies of Iraq, Palestine/Israel, Syria, Jordan and Egypt are his main foci. He is currently in the process of completing a book on The Economics of Peace in the Middle East, two papers on the Iraqi economy, and two comparative papers on the developments in Syria, Egypt and Jordan since Camp David. Dr. Sullivan has often been a commentator on issues related to the Middle East for the Egyptian national press and the international press based in Cairo. He obtained his Ph.D. in economics from Yale.

Foreword

Historically embedded in the context of confrontation, political dynamics in the Middle East today threaten to spin out of control at the international level. *International Relations of the Middle East in the 21st Century: Patterns of Continuity and Change* is an effort to provide an in-depth analysis by specialized scholars of the inter-related dimensions of confrontation that have entangled almost every aspect of contemporary politics in the region. The sustained confrontation between dominant external interests and regional politics is the common theme across the twelve chapters that comprise the book. These chapters are organised into three sections based on subdivisions of this common theme.

The two chapters in the first section, "The Regional System," situate the context of the Middle East in terms of historical and contemporary global dimensions. Chapter One, "Regional Dynamics in Historical Perspective" by Jacqueline S. Ismael and Tareq Y. Ismael, schematizes the changing contours of the Middle East over the last millennium in terms of changing patterns of co-operation and conflict. Within this framework of periodization, four different phases of Middle East regional dynamics are identified – Islamic, Ottoman, nationalist, and post-nationalist. A systematic description of political dynamics in the region over the 20th century provides the basis for delineating changes in patterns of co-operation and conflict in the transition from the 20th to the 21st century.

Chapter 2, "The State: Globalization and the Middle East" by Richard Falk, maintains that of all the non-western regions of the world, the Middle East has suffered the most at the hands of Western inspired ideals and development efforts, as well as having been politically "internationalized" during the 20th century. Crises in the region are thought of in geostrategic terms and international powers tend to intervene rather than waiting for the evolution of any political settlement. As well, the region has clearly been deficient in the sort of indigenous capabilities needed to transform political independence (and in some instances, exceptional resource endowments) in directions that bring happiness and prosperity to the peoples of the Middle East. The importance of the region to the main geopolitical forces in the world has led to persistent disruption in the form of a variety of hegemonic efforts to intervene and exert influence. With the exception of the European heartland, no part of the world has been perceived as so important as the Middle East to the established geopolitical order. Further, the West has stereotyped the region by way of "orientalism" to provide a continuing foundation for asserting its superiority and justifying various modes of interventionary diplomacy. Finally, the region has been kept in constant tension as a result of the establishment of Israel.

In the face of this array of problems, the region has been unable to evolve a constructive response. Authoritarian governments have proven to be oppressive toward their own people and irresponsible in dealing with others. Despite the vast extra-regional intervention into Middle Eastern politics, Professor Falk argues that the pattern of state formation in the Middle East is not so seriously affected by the dynamics of globalization, as is the case in other regions. In this respect, the states in the Middle East have managed to retain a relative degree of autonomy in relation to the world economy, although they remain vulnerable to the old geopolitics of international rivalry and Western hegemony. It is likely that the region will be severely tested in the decades ahead by water shortages, and its future will be shaped by the extent the responses are co-operative or conflictual. Beset by degenerative tendencies, states in the region are manipulated by geopolitical forces because of the region's energy resources, its strategic position, and out of fear that it might mount a formidable extra-regional challenge if states who are "unfriendly" acquire weaponry of mass destruction. The region has been effectively stigmatised as the main springboard for international terrorism, and as a zone where intervention remains a plausible geo-political option.

The second section, "The Regional System After the Gulf War", composed of four chapters, examines the major sources of inter-state rivalry and tension in the region. Chapter 3, "Hydropolitics in the Middle East" by Hilal Elver, argues that environmental conflicts, especially in relation to transboundary waters, are emerging as an important dimension of peace and security for the Middle East. There are four major, unresolved regional disputes over the distribution and management of waters; one is a complex controversy over water allocation rights in the Euphrates/Tigris River basin among Turkey, Syria and Iraq; two involve the Jordan River basin and West Bank groundwater. The last one involves the Nile. These complex freshwater resources reflect the interplay of environmental, economic, cultural, political and ethnic factors that in their aggregate pose a severe threat to peace and security in the region. On this basis, Dr. Elver argues that there is a correlation between environmental security and transboundary water conflicts. The Tigris/Euphrates conflict is examined as a case study of the complexity of regional hydropolitics.

Chapter 4, "The Gulf War, Economic and Financial Linkages, and Arab Economic Development: Iraq - The Pivot?" by Paul Sullivan, investigates the nature of Iraq as a pivotal state in the Middle East. The pivotal effects of the Gulf War and of the fall of Iraq on some of the remittance sensitive (RS) countries and some of the oil sensitive (OS) countries in the Arab World are analysed. Pivotal states are hot spots that could not only affect the fate of the region but also affect international stability. Could Iraq be a good example of a country that proved it was a pivotal state through its collapse? Professor Sullivan examines the economic pivotalness of Iraq and the political fallout of the war.

Chapter 5, "Balance of Power and Nuclear Deterrence: The Middle East after the Gulf War" by Adel Safty, argues that the Nuclear Non-Proliferation Treaty regime has codified nuclear inequality but has stopped neither vertical proliferation nor discriminate horizontal proliferation of nuclear weapons. It has not brought nuclear disarmament any closer to reality and nuclear powers continue to prize the value of nuclear weapons in preventing wars and even in war fighting strategies. There is no reason why the nuclear deterrence logic, which worked successfully between nuclear powers, cannot apply between regional nuclear power.

In the absence of a just and comprehensive integrated peace environment in the Middle East, balance of power calculations will continue to characterise political and defence relations in the region. The deteriorating balance of power in the Middle East is creating a situation where the national defence of the Arab countries of the Middle East, especially Egypt, may be inadequate. Given that conventional military parity with Israel, the dominant military power in the region, is out of the question, a credible nuclear-weapon strategy may be the most credible defence option in the 21st century.

In Chapter 6, "Some International Law Implications of the Oslo/Cairo Framework for the PLO/Israeli Peace Process," Richard Falk notes that at this stage, from the perspective of international law, it is difficult to provide any clear guidelines as to the likely reception of the Palestinian/Israeli peace process under international law, especially as it pertains to the protection of human rights of Palestinians subject to the authority of the Palestinian Authority and with respect to final status arrangements. In the end, the role of international law is likely to relate to the mobilization of world public opinion in support of Palestinian nongovernmental efforts to achieve constitutional democracy, including human rights, especially the core struggle for statehood and the full exercise of self-determination. No matter how one-sided the agreed texts, Palestinian rights of self-determination are intrinsic and inalienable. Despite Israel's retention of security rights and settlements, the Palestinian reality has been strengthened, at least temporarily, by these developments to the point where the operational situation is increasingly one of a Palestinian state, although qualified as to the exercise of sovereign rights, vulnerable to intervention, and not able yet to assert itself formally in many international arenas including the United Nations. If such arrangements turn out to be the end-point of "the peace process" it is not to be confused with the realization of Palestinian rights of self-determination. The change in Israeli government from Labour to Likud (and back to Labour again, as Chapter 10 by Jeff Helsing makes clear in its update of the Israeli regime) changes little, while exposing the pre-existing inadequacies of the Oslo/Cairo framework from the Palestinian viewpoint. As such, it may have the positive effect of clarifying the work that remains to be done if the Palestinian struggle is to be carried eventually to a successful end.

Section three, "The Global Context," composed of five chapters, expands the focus to include those international actors and historically rooted issues that continue to have a profound impact on the region. Chapter 7, "Britain's Shadows: Post-colonialism and Palestine" by John Strawson, proposes that Britain's colonial past has created a postcolonial present which complicates Tony Blair's new Labour ethical foreign policy project. Nowhere is this clearer than in the case of Palestine. Pronouncements on human rights do not place Britain automatically on the side of self-determination and statehood for the Palestinians. British Mandate land law continues to provide Israeli occupiers with weapons to establish settlements and alienate the Palestinian people from their land. British policy on Palestine cannot begin anew as it is anchored to this imperialist past. English legal discourse disrupts Palestinian claims to their own land half a century after the departure of the British occupation. Postcolonial theory provides an effective way of revisiting this legal occupation of Palestine and illuminates the bonds that still remain to be broken. New Labour looks promising as a post-postcolonial government, but Palestinians are entitled to a more thorough break with postcolonialism than a Foreign Office mission statement video. In visiting this site of legal occupation we can begin to deal with the subtle ways in which postcolonial thinking has secreted itself in the modern British polity.

In Chapter 8, "Post-Communist Eastern Europe and the Middle East: The Burden of History and New Political Realities" by Andrej Kreutz, divides Eastern Europe into three parts, each of which has a different history and a different current political orientation. He describes how the nations of the southern part of East-Central and Eastern Europe, especially the Balkan Peninsula, have for centuries been submitted to Ottoman rule, and how their cultural links with – and understanding of – the Middle Eastern peoples are consequently strong and often articulated. Due to the weakness of these nations, however, their political, economic and international importance is currently quite negligible. He then demonstrates how the north western part of the region has traditionally been integrated with and/or submitted to the West and how the nations there are now also following Western leadership, sometimes even showing a particular lack of sympathy and understanding toward the dark-skinned Middle Easterners and their painful political and social problems. Russia itself, and in the future perhaps also an independent Ukraine, he feels have a marked interest in the Middle East which is based on their entire history as Eastern Orthodox and even partly Muslim countries, their geographical proximity to the region, and the subsequent numerous political and economic links with its peoples.

Despite all their differences, Professor Kreutz believes the people of Eastern Europe and the Middle East have some common features: when compared with the West they are relatively backward in industrial development, they still have a largely traditional character to their societies. Both regions grapple with the lack of stable legal and political institutions as well as the consequent and often heightened importance of religious belief and religious institutions, and perhaps most importantly a marked proneness toward populist demagogy and authoritarian regimes. Kreutz feels that coping with the difficult tasks of modernization and development, the peoples of both regions can learn much from each other and thus create a firm basis for better and closer relations in the future.

In Chapter 9, "A New Orientalism: Europe Confronts the Middle East," Philip Marfleet observes that recent collaborations between the European Union (EU) and countries of the Arab world have been hailed as marking "a new beginning" in relations between these regions. Diplomatic ties have been strengthened and a vast new European aid program has been created to speed development of the Maghreb and the Arab East. But to what effect? Within a few years, the program had faltered and allegations of bad faith had been directed at the EU and at European governments. This chapter examines "Club Med" - the new

Euro-Arab dialogue - and asks whether it marks a new era of amity, or a renewal of old regional hostilities.

Chapter 10, "The American Shadow: U.S. Foreign Policy and the Middle East" by Jeffrey W. Helsing, maintains that as the worlds sole remaining superpower, the United States clearly has a major impact on economic, political and even social issues throughout the world, including the Middle East. The shadow of the United States permeates the region. Yet, the impact of America's role in the region is tempered in a number of ways: U.S. foreign policy actions do not match American rhetoric; there are too many raised and unfulfilled expectations throughout the Middle East; and global U.S. leadership has been considerably weakened over the past decade. As a result, U.S. foreign policy in the Middle East has become quite muddled and the region more unstable.

The United States claims the mantle of leadership and has a vision of a new order in the Middle East that encompasses traditional U.S. foreign policy themes of economic liberalism, the promotion of democratic values and the rule of law, and an enhanced regional security. The American vision reflects much of the view articulated by many in Israel's Labour Party, particularly Shimon Peres. This reflects a rather idealistic or moralist foreign policy agenda, one that is premised on a belief that the Middle East can be re-made through an American-sponsored peace process into a peaceful, more democratic and more economically prosperous place. This will occur through economic integration, arms reduction, and regional co-operation. But U.S. actions do not match the rhetoric.

In Chapter 11, "The United Nations and the Muslim World: Allies or Adversaries?," Ali Mazrui maintains that the United Nations and Islam constitute a tale of two kinds of universalism. Islam has envisaged the universalism of people, the *ummah*; the UN has envisaged the universalism of states. Samuel P. Huntington's thesis about a "Clash of Civilizations" has its equivalent in traditional Islamic international law which saw the world divided into *Dar el Harb* (the Abode of War), *Dar el Islam* (the abode of Islam) and *Dar el Ahd* or *Dar el Sulh* (the Abode of Contractual Co-existence).

In the second half of the 20th century the West evolved a similar tripartite view of the world. To the West, the Abode of War was the world of communism, and the equivalent of *Dar el Islam* was what the West called "the Free World" under Western leadership. The Abode of Contractual Co-existence was the world of non-aligned states. As the Cold War ended what was *Dar el Islam* to the Muslims became *Dar el*

Harb to the West. Adversarial relationships often developed between the West and Islamic movements.

The United Nations represented all states but did not represent all civilizations. Of the five original languages of the UN, four were European languages. Four of the five permanent members of the Security Council are primarily white countries (France, Britain, USA and Russia). Six out of the last seven Secretaries-General of the UN have come from Christian traditions. There has been no Hindu, Muslim or Confucian Secretary-General – although there has been one Buddhist one (U Thant). The United Nations is one more arena of Western dominance. The Muslim world is often marginalized when the oil-weapon is weak. But there are times when the UN is an ally of Muslim causes – ranging from such political causes as Palestine and Kashmir to such humanitarian ones as relief for refugees in Afghanistan and Somalia.

In Chapter 12, "The Global *Ummah* and the British Commonwealth: Four Ethical Revolutions," Ali Mazrui argues that member nations of both the United Nations (which was born out of the ravages of war) and the British Commonwealth (which was born out of the ravages of imperialism) experienced four ethical revolutions in the last hundred years. The first was a revolution against laissez-faire economics and in favour of morally accountable economies. This influenced the emergence of left wing parties and welfare states, including such concepts as Arab socialism and Islamic modernism.

The second ethical revolution of the 20th century was the racial revolution against imperialism, racism and apartheid. Much of the Muslim world was a victim of Western imperialism. Islam became an ally of nationalists and anti-colonialists in Asia, Africa and the Middle East. The *Ummah* and the Commonwealth were seeking a new racial order. The third ethical revolution of recent decades had been the gender revolution – redefining the rights and roles of women world-wide. In the second half of the 20th century the Muslim world produced four women prime ministers in three different countries (Pakistan, Bangladesh and Turkey). Pakistan and Bangladesh are in the Commonwealth. The struggle for the wider rights of women has continued into the 21st century. Specific gender reforms are needed in the Muslim world and the Commonwealth.

The fourth ethical revolution of recent decades has been the green revolution with its concern for the environment and the ecology. Issues of population growth and population policy are also involved. The *Ummah* has been slow to respond to the green revolution, but Islamic environmentalism has now begun. The more industrialised members of the Commonwealth have had stronger green movements. Does the Muslim world face a fifth revolution in the 21st century – the search for a more balanced cultural order? The Commonwealth is a union ultimately based on language (English). The *Ummah* is a solidarity ultimately based on religion (Islam). A cultural interaction enters a new phase in the new millennium.

Not sacrificing depth of analysis for parsimony, this collection endeavours to highlight the importance of historical influences and the patterns of extra-regional influence so predominant in the Middle East. Doing so without collapsing under the weight of historical samples and illustrations is a difficult task given the wealth of opinion and data available. It is that depth which allows for the understanding that the politics of the region today, and indeed in the future, are shaped by the historically intrusive devices outlined in the text.

This book was a collective effort, and I would like to thank the authors for their forthright analyses and patience with the revision process. Many took valuable time from already overburdened schedules to revise and update their chapters several times. The good humour and dedication to provide such excellent work speaks to their commitment and credibility. I would also like to thank my research assistant John Measor who examined and clarified often-obscure footnotes and prepared the manuscipt with a smile and increasing ability.

Tareq Y. Ismael
Calgary, March 1, 2000

Part One:

The Regional System

1 Regional Dynamics in Historical Perspective

JACQUELINE S. ISMAEL and TAREQ Y. ISMAEL

The Middle East has long held an important place in world affairs, as reflected in the attention given to the region in the Western press, both scholarly and journalistic. However, both have tended to view the area through the prism of great power politics. This chapter examines regional dynamics in the Middle East from a historical perspective in order to focus on historical patterns of regional interaction rather than on regional problems or issues in international relations. Our purpose is to outline successive stages of development in the regional dynamics of Middle East politics over the millennium and identify patterns of continuity and change.

From this perspective, the Middle East is approached as a somewhat fluid unit of analysis in international politics. At any given time, in other words, the parameters of the region are a function of historical context and are delineated in terms of core and peripheral areas.[1] The core, defined as the political centre of the region, is characterized by "a relatively regular and intense pattern of interactions, recognized internally and externally as a distinctive arena, and created and sustained by at least two generally proximate actors."[2] Patterns of cooperation and conflict constitute the significant dimensions of core interactions. Actors proximate to the core, but with irregular or less intense involvement in core patterns of interaction, are classified as the periphery. Another category of important actors in Middle East politics are from outside the region altogether and are classified as intrusive forces.

Thus, the concepts of core and periphery provide the basis for outlining the general geographic contours of the Middle East at any given time. The concepts of patterns of cooperation, patterns of conflict and intrusive forces provide the dimensions for examining regional dynamics in Middle East politics at different historical periods. In different historical stages, the dimensions of the region may have been changing, but the dynamics of change were a function of historical context that is, a function of the regional dynamics driving change in a stage. These are developed into four periods: Islamic, Ottoman, nationalist and post-nationalist. Although these periods are sequentially related, they are not bounded in time with distinct beginnings and endings. Rather, they tend to blend one into another, with patterns emerging, more or less becoming dominant, and then submerging as new patterns come to the fore. The designation of a phase is simply a heuristic label used to connote the central political dynamic through which a period is being viewed.

Islamic Phase

The Islamic phase covers the period from the 7th through the 13th centuries. The emergence of Islam in Arabia in the 7th century and its rapid expansion outward from Arabia across southwest Asia and North Africa encompassed the central political dynamic of this period. With the expansion, the political centre of gravity shifted from Arabia to the Fertile Crescent (first Damascus under the Umayyad Dynasty, 661-750 A.D.; then Baghdad under the Abbasids, 750-1258 A.D.). It then began to fragment into regional dynasties: in Spain, the Umayyad, 756-1031 A.D.; in Egypt, the Tulunids, 868-905 A.D.; the Fatimids, 969-1171 A.D.; the Ayyubids, 1171-1260 A.D.; in Morocco and Tunisia, the Idrisids, 788-922 A.D.; the Aghlabids, 800-909; the Murabids, 1062-1145; and the Muwahhids, 1145-1223 A.D. The socio-political character of the Islamic stage emerged in the context of the process of accommodation and integration of different socio-cultural realities that the spread of Islam presented to civil decision-makers and administrators who constituted the ruling class in conquered territories. Composed of courtiers, clerics, artisans and jurists, the urban based ruling elite adopted Arabic as the language of culture, law and politics, and linked the ruler and ruled in what came to be called Islamic civilization.[3]

Islamic civilization, at its zenith by the 10th century, engendered bonds of solidarity among the diverse ethno-cultural groups that were encompassed within its boundaries. Economic prosperity, catalysed by the long distance trade made possible by an alliance between nomadic tribes and urban-based merchants, contributed to the social stability and cultural accomplishments of Islamic civilization. In 10th century Islam, the dominant worldview of a balance between the state and the individual was manifested in a strong sense of political and public conscience.[4] This worldview fostered the recirculation of economic surplus (a surplus made possible by the combination of expanding markets due to territorial expansion and increasing exchange between productive centres in the region)[5] for the benefit of socio-cultural diversification in the framework of Arabization and

Islamization; and this, in turn, cultivated social solidarity within the framework of Arab-Islamic culture.

The decline of the Islamic stage coincides with the successive incursions of the Crusades throughout the 11th and 12th centuries, which marked the initiation of foreign intrusions and encroachment. Catalysed by the Crusades, and initiated with the expedition of Marco Polo in the 13th century, European mercantilists began the process of exploration that ultimately diverted virtually all of the trade routes of Africa and the Far East away from the Middle East. In the same period, Mongolian armies overran the region, ravishing the physical environment in their wake. Only Egypt was spared their devastation. Successive waves of Mongolian incursions culminated in the Ottoman capture of Constantinople in the 16th century.

Over the course of the Islamic stage, the political centre or core of the Middle East encompassed the Arabized lands of the expanding Islamic world. Its periphery covered the non-Arabized lands of the Islamic world. During the first several centuries of this period, the region's elastic boundaries expanded westward across Arabia, the Fertile Crescent, and North Africa; and eastward across Persia, Afghanistan and the northern Indian subcontinent. Commerce provided the axis for patterns of cooperation; and territorial expansion was the focal point for patterns of conflict. The Crusades, in effect, provide a marker for the cessation of territorial expansion. Thereafter, patterns of conflict centred on forestalling the territorial incursions of intrusive forces from the West and from the East, and the commercial inroads of the West. Under sustained attack, the vibrancy and buoyancy of the Middle East attained in this stage went into decline.

Ottoman Phase

With the collapse of Constantinople in 1453, the Ottomans unified the Middle East under their dominion. With this, the centre of gravity of Middle East politics shifted from the Fertile Crescent and North Africa to Istanbul (the Ottoman Empire's capital). Under the banner of Islam, the empire not only brought political unity to the region, but also spread Islam into Eastern Europe, territorially expanding the empire into the Balkans. Ottoman expansion into Europe in effect triggered the initiation of the so-called

Eastern Question[6] (a metaphor for European preoccupation in international affairs with the Middle East).

Confrontation with the West constituted the dominant pattern of conflict in the Middle East throughout the Ottoman stage. It was manifested not only in military confrontation over territorial incursions and excursions, but also in the economic struggle for supremacy over world commerce, and in the political struggle for suzerainty over the Middle East. The confrontation triggered by Ottoman encroachment into Europe was incarnated as the Eastern Question by historical context. This included the emergence of capitalism, nationalism and nation-states in Europe, which synergized into the industrial revolution. The insatiable appetite of the industrial revolution for raw materials and markets fuelled Europe's onslaught on the rest of the world, known as the age of imperialism.

The penetration of capitalism into the Ottoman Empire disrupted the traditional economy and resulted in lop-sided development. This was marked by the expansion of cash crops and improvement of transportation and financial industries to service the export of cash crops. Alterations in legal and administrative systems were also made to favour the agricultural export economy to the detriment of subsistence agriculture and community economic activity. A grave consequence of the changes ushered in by the penetration of capitalism was the dislocation of the traditional industrial sectors. In effect, artisans, craftsmen, small merchants and the guilds were economically marginalized, while clusters of petit bourgeoisie formed in urban enclaves in association with foreign economic penetration.[7] By the turn of the 20th century, the Middle East was economically integrated into Europe's imperialist system, and the traditional economic infrastructure (comprised of local economies and regional exchange networks) was fragmented and impoverished.[8] The First World War resulted in the demise of the Ottoman Empire and the dismemberment of its dominions.

In the Ottoman phase, the political centre or core of the Middle East encompassed not only the Arab world of the Fertile Crescent and North Africa but also the non-Arab domains of the Ottoman Empire. Ruled from its capital in Istanbul, this huge empire was administered by a vast and complex civil service. Contiguous Islamic lands in the Middle East and south eastern Europe constituted the periphery. Islam provided the framework for the emergence of cultural patterns of cooperation among diverse peoples. Fuelled by the rich cultural diversity encompassed within the empire, the era spawned distinctive music, art and architecture. Islamic centres of learning (Al-Azhar in Egypt; Qayrawan in North Africa; Najaf in Iraq) became hubs of intellectual exchange between scholars, jurists and artists from different regions in the empire.

Diversity, however, was not only a source of cultural enrichment. It was also a source of political tension (and often, conflict) in an empire held together by an elaborate decentralized administrative-military apparatus. In other words, the empire lacked a sufficient economic infrastructure to transcend local interests and loyalties. In this context, Western economic penetration faced little resistance and increased fragmentation. In response to the challenge posed by the West, the Empire initiated a process of economic and administrative modernization, known as the Tanzimat. Up to the Tanzimat period of administrative reform (1839 through 1876), Ottoman administration was based on the maintenance of the status quo among autonomous ethno-religious communities that maintained their economic viability through specialization of production (professions and crafts). Within the framework of the empire, an inter-communal pattern of life emerged around a form of community-centred corporatism. The political interests of the community vis-à-vis the empire were mediated by the community's notables, who formed a coalition of local forces. The Tanzimat represented an effort to centralize administrative control in the state and threatened the autonomy of the ethno-religious communities and the viability of their corporatist economies. Thus, state organizational reform became an issue of intense conflict for important segments of Middle Eastern society. With the emergence of Turkish nationalism by the turn of the century, the political dynamic in the region had three inter-related dimensions: the threat of centralization to the corporatist formula; the threat of pan-Turanianism or Turkification to the Arabs; and Western political and economic inroads into the Ottoman Empire.

Nationalist Phase

With the collapse of the Ottoman Empire in the aftermath of the First World War, the core of the Middle East reverted to its contours in the Islamic phase; that is, to the Arab lands of Southwest Asia and North Africa. Islamic countries contiguous with the Arab world constituted the periphery. However, the political character and dynamics of the core were very different. In 1922, at the conference of al-Aquir, the boundaries between

Iraq, Kuwait and Nejad were drawn by the British. With these boundaries, the Western concept of sovereignty was introduced into the political lexicon of the region. This concept was not only culturally alien to the tribal character of the area but also incompatible with the nature of the interior land trade economy. Borders were unknown, as the area was "a sea of sand that caravans, much like ships on water, crossed without a trace."[9] The borders were not based on natural geographic, ethnic, linguistic or religious cleavages; they were political facts, not geographic or demographic, and were part of Britain's grand design to preclude any unity of Arabs by creating rival but pro-Western regimes in Iraq, Kuwait and Saudi Arabia. In effect, the borders set the stage for the two themes of regional political dynamics that played counterpoint to each other throughout this phase: pan-Arab nationalism and nation-state nationalism; that is, regionalism vs. localism. The counterpoint played in a context orchestrated by the big powers whose own strategic interests vis-à-vis the Middle East became a driving force in regional political dynamics in this period.

After World War I, Britain, in effective control of Egypt and the Gulf since the turn of the century, gained control over Palestine and Iraq through a mandate granted by the League of Nations. France, already with colonial control over Morocco, Tunisia and Algeria, was granted mandatory powers over the major portion of Greater Syria (modern day Syria and Lebanon). While ostensibly mandate powers were to shepherd a country to independence, in effect the mandates provided little more than an international legalization of colonial exploitation.

The mandate system constituted a Western scheme for dividing the occupied territories of the defunct Ottoman Empire into political entities with boundaries designed and drawn to perpetuate political fragmentation in the face of Western economic and strategic interests. Within the political systems of these fragmented political entities, governments were installed, the management of which was given over to indigenous elites already strongly oriented to Western interests. The petit bourgeoisie, what Samir Amin identified as the "Third Estate"[10] championed the struggle against the physical presence of the occupying forces by adopting, quite ironically, Western notions of self-determination and nationalism. National liberation movements were spawned throughout the Middle East, and in the interwar period (between WWI and WWII), regional political dynamics in the Middle East were fragmented by the multiplicity of inward directed struggles for national independence.

In 1945, under British tutelage, the Arab League was established in an effort to coordinate the efforts of Arab governments to stave off the rising tide of popular resistance to neo-colonial exploitation and to manage the transition to nominal independence.[11] Thus, the end of the Second World War marked the emergence of nominally independent states throughout the region. However, the loss of Palestine to Zionist occupation, a struggle that spanned the decades of the thirties and forties, disconcerted the Arab peoples and undermined the legitimacy of the regimes in power. The partition of Palestine in 1948, and the routing of the Palestinian population in the aftermath of the war that followed partition, resulted in a profound public reaction to Western sponsorship of Zionism. By the early sixties, most of the states were governed by nationalist military regimes that had wrested control from the overtly pro-Western elite set up by Western powers. Only the sheikhdoms of the Gulf remained under the control of such regimes.

With sovereignty embedded in the state, political power was rooted in the institutions of state. The political elite of the region, ideologically bound to the political identity of their respective states, had a vested interest in the entrenchment of the state's identity. In this way, the political borders imposed by Western powers on the Middle East in the first quarter of the 20th century had become tangible artifacts in the construction of political identity by the middle of the century.

In contrast to this concrete institutional framework for national identities, pan-Arab nationalism – the sense of common identity and common destiny of the Arab people – represented little more than an intangible though popular sentiment by mid-century. In terms of the strategic interests of the big powers in the Middle East, pan-Arab nationalism was hardly a relevant factor in the geopolitical intrigues of the Cold War. Then, in 1952, Colonel Gamal Abdul Nasser overthrew the Egyptian monarchy; and pan-Arab nationalism became personified in Nasser's leadership. With Nasser as its principle narrator, pan-Arab nationalism quickly became a dominant theme in regional political dynamics, manifested in the rapid emergence of the Arab cooperative core.

The Arab cooperative core represented efforts to institutionalise pan-Arabism in regional politics. Composed of the official bilateral and multilateral relations between Arab states, as well as non-governmental agencies and popular organizations across Arab states, the Arab cooperative core's most important formal organizations were the League of Arab States, established in 1945, and the Organization of Arab Petroleum Exporting Countries, formed in 1968.[12] They were complemented by the existence of councils of Arab ambassadors in every major foreign capital, as well as by Arab caucuses in the United Nations and other international agencies.

Arab heads of state (or summit) conferences, initiated in January 1964 and convened irregularly thereafter (as the following list indicates) in response to crisis, constituted another significant pattern of Arab cooperative core interaction:

January 1964 in Cairo
September 1964 in Alexandria
September 1965 in Casablanca
August-September 1967 in Khartoum
December 1969 in Rabat
November 1973 in Algiers
October 1974 in Rabat
October 1976 in Cairo
November 1978 in Baghdad
November 1979 in Tunis
November 1980 in Amman
November 1981 in Fez
September 1982 in Fez
August 1985 in Casablanca
November 1987 in Amman
June 1988 in Algiers
May 1989 in Casablanca
May 1990 in Baghdad
August 1990 in Cairo

As well, there were regular multilateral meetings held between Arab cabinet ministers of various portfolios, including foreign affairs, justice, health, housing, development, and education. Furthermore, a careful examination of the nature of high-level intergovernmental visits within the Middle East in the period 1946-1975 reveals a clear pattern of intense political interaction between Arab states.[13]

The establishment and operation of national and multi-national Arab aid agencies throughout the 1960s and 1970s was another manifestation of the Arab cooperative core. These agencies functioned to redistribute wealth from the oil-rich to the poorer Arab states on a regional basis. The Kuwait Fund for Arab Economic Development, established in 1961, was the first such agency, and represented the largest regional fund. The Arab Fund for Economic and Social Development, established by the

Arab League in 1968, did not actually become operational until 1972. The Abu Dhabi Fund for Arab Economic Development was set up in 1971; and was followed by the Saudi Fund for External Development in 1974. The Iraq Fund for External Development and the Arab Monetary Fund followed. Between 1963 and 1974 such agencies disbursed bilateral and multilateral development loans to Arab countries with a value in excess of $507 million. For the period 1975-80, the total rose to over $6.6 billion. The total of all inter-Arab economic assistance, including funds bilaterally disbursed outside of the major development agencies, was much higher still. While some of this increase was attributable to growing capital surplus on the part of the Arab oil-producing states, it was nonetheless a clear manifestation of Arab cooperative interaction.

Yet another pattern of Arab cooperative interaction is reflected in the repeated attempts of many states in the area to realize some form of Arab unity. The formation of the United Arab Republic in 1958 was the most conspicuous attempt, not only because it was first, but also the most enduring as it lasted for more than three years. Other less successful examples were the Arab Hashemite Union (Jordan and Iraq) of 1958, the tripartite federal union of Egypt, Iraq and Syria in 1963; the Iraqi-Egyptian union of 1964; the Egyptian-Sudanese-Libyan federation of 1970; the federation of Arab Republics (Egypt, Libya, and Syria) in 1971; the Egyptian-Libyan and North Yemen-South Yemen unity agreement of 1973; the 1974 Arab Islamic Republic (Libya-Tunisia); the Syrian-Jordanian Supreme Command of 1975; the Syrian-Egyptian United Political Leadership of 1976; and the Syrian-Iraqi unity agreement of 1979; the Gulf Cooperation Council (Saudi Arabia, Kuwait, United Arab Emirates, Bahrain, Oman, Qatar) in 1981; the Pan-Arab Command (Syria, Algeria, South Yemen) in 1985; the Maghreb Consultative Council (Algeria, Morocco, Tunisia) in 1987; the Maghreb Union (Algeria, Morocco, Tunisia, Mauritania, Libya) in 1989; and the Arab Cooperation Council (Iraq, Jordan, Yemen, Egypt) in 1989.

George Lenczowski identified four major issues that fostered the development of these instruments of cooperative interaction: issues related to the struggle against imperialism; issues involving Israel and Palestine; issues of cooperation and coordination in oil affairs; and issues related to the peaceful resolution of inter-Arab conflicts and disputes.[14] The issue of Arab unity must be added to this list. While the institutionalisation of the Arab state system made unity increasingly difficult to realize in practice, the issue remained a cardinal principle of Arab political culture and one of the most powerful political symbols in the Arab world in the 20th century. In one-way or another, the goal of Arab unity was enshrined in the constitution of every Arab state as a primary responsibility of government. Pan-Arab groups and political parties (most notably the Ba'ath, the Arab Nationalist Movement, the Nasserties, and the New Left groups)[15] formed a nongovernmental, transnational dimension of the cooperative core. Pan-Arab professional and academic associations, as well as business, labour, educational, sports, and cultural organizations (such as the Union of Arab Chambers of Commerce, the Union of Arab Universities, the Union of Arab Artisans, the Union of Arab Broadcasters, the Arab Literary Union, and so forth) all represented manifestations of Arab cooperative interaction at the nongovernmental level.

Playing counterpoint to the Arab cooperative core was the Arab-Israeli conflict core. This pattern of regional interaction was focussed around the conflict between Israel, the Palestine Liberation Organization (PLO) as well as other Palestinian resistance groups, and the Arab states bordering Israel – Egypt, Syria, Jordan, and Lebanon – which all had concentrations of Palestinian refugees within their borders. The entire Arab world was symbolically engaged in this conflict core; but practically, actual conflict was for the most part confined to the interactions of Israel, Palestinian resistance groups, and the Arab states bordering Israel. For Israel and the Palestinians, the issue at stake was fundamental to national survival. For the Arab states bordering Israel, the geopolitics of Zionism made the conflict a vital strategic concern. For the rest of the Arab world, historical, cultural, religious and political factors rendered the Palestine question important through the 1948 and 1956 wars. The 1967 Arab-Israeli War and the Israeli occupation of the West Bank, Gaza Strip, Sinai, and Golan Heights raised the confrontation from strategic to national importance for border states. Other Arab states were peripheral to this core in the sense that their interaction in the conflict was not based on direct military confrontation. However, some of the Arab states – notably Iraq, Saudi Arabia, Kuwait, Libya, and Algeria – had considerable involvement in the issue (despite their geographic and political distance from it), and virtually all of the other Arab states showed some degree of indirect involvement.

In the aftermath of the Second World War, regional political dynamics unfolded in the international context of the Cold War. This ideological conflict within the advanced industrial world not only set the stage for the political dynamics driving inter-state relations in the Middle

East, but also directly intruded into the region. Intrusive powers were involved in regional politics primarily through bilateral relations. In the fifties, there were attempts by the West (primarily Britain and the U.S.) to involve Middle East states in military alliance systems (most notably the Baghdad Pact). However, these caused such a political uproar in the Arab world that all attempts were forestalled. As a result, the Cold War was increasingly played out by proxy through bilateral relations with states in the region. An arms race, triggered by the Arab-Israeli conflict core, provided the venue for strategic alignments in the international arena.[16]

By the mid-sixties, all of the states in the region were identified ideologically with one side or the other in the Cold War. Hence, two ideological camps were apparent in Middle East politics: the radicals, spearheaded by Egypt, represented forces for socio-political change and were supported by the Soviet Union and its allies; the conservatives, spearheaded by Jordan and Saudi Arabia, and supported by the United States and its allies, represented the political status quo of monarchy and the economic status quo of neo-colonial exploitation of oil wealth. In addition, both Israel and Iran (until the Islamic revolution in 1979) were staunchly supported and fully armed by the United States.

Tendencies toward political fragmentation and integration constituted conflicting patterns of development in regional politics. On the one hand, the Arab-Israeli conflict core contributed to the tendency toward fragmentation of the Arab world by rendering the Middle East more permeable to outside influence and exasperating inter-Arab conflicts. On the other hand, the Arab cooperative core served to reinforce the pan-Arab nationalist dynamic by providing mechanisms for inter-Arab conflict management, rendering the region less permeable to outside influences.[17]

By 1970, with Egypt in the role of vanguard Arab nation and Nasserism as the dominant expression of Arab nationalism, the Arab-Israeli conflict core and the Arab cooperative core were fully integrated in an essentially dialectical relationship. The 1967 Arab-Israeli war had contributed significantly to this integration by intensifying contradictions between the two cores. The most apparent contradiction was the U.S. role in the conflict core – both as Israel's main ally and as an important influence in neighbouring Jordan. Another contradiction between the cooperative and conflict cores was revealed in the relationship between Saudi Arabia and the United States on the one hand, and on the other, U.S. support for Israel in the 1967 war and continued occupation of Arab lands seized in the war.

Nasser's strategy of counterbalancing opposing forces relied on the contradictions implicit in the dual role played by conservative regimes in both cores. Caught between the forces of Arab nationalism on one hand and their strong ties with the United States on the other, these regimes were in effect forced to participate in the cooperative core to protect their own interests (both symbolic and strategic). The progressive and anti-imperialist thrust of Nasserism highlighted their reactionary role and forced their increased participation in the cooperative core in order to play a moderating role. Nasser's rapprochement with Saudi Arabia and Jordan after 1967, and his acceptance of the Rogers Plan in 1969 in exchange for a collective front against Israeli aggression and continued U.S. support for it were evidence of the dialectic between conservative regimes and Arab nationalist forces.

Pan-Arab nationalism came to the fore in Middle East politics in the aftermath of World War II as a result of the problems left behind by colonialism: the political, social and economic fragmentation of Arab society; an aggregation of weak national governments dependent upon external powers; an ever-increasing subpopulation of Palestinian refugees; and an expansionist Israeli state. The dominant patterns of cooperation and conflict evolved in the post-war period from the efforts of national governments to deal with these problems as they threatened the sovereignty, legitimacy, and/or capability of the state itself. Thus, ironically, Arab nationalism was sponsored by nationalist regimes to serve the interests of the state. The ideology of Arab nationalism helped to mobilize the Arab people in a common struggle against the problems threatening the sovereignty of the state. This resulted not only in the increasing integration of the dominant patterns of cooperation and conflict but also in the increasing concentration of sovereignty in the hands of the political elite throughout the region, in both the core and periphery.

By increasing Arab cohesion – that is, by enhancing the probability of concerted Arab action on common problems – the power of Arab states was essentially aggregated at both the regional and international levels. Concerted Arab action in the October 1973 Arab-Israeli War and the Arab oil embargo of 1973-74 illustrated the impact of cooperative and collaborative interaction on regional and extra-regional relations. During the peak of collaboration in the early 1970s, the Arab world was able to exert significant influence on the policies of external actors. In Africa, for example, Arab policy succeeded, both bilaterally and multilaterally, in displacing a significant Israeli influence and securing African support for the Palestinian cause. Much the same thing occurred in Asia. In the developed world, the relative cohesion of Arab countries facilitated their pursuance of linkage politics. The Arab economic boycott of Israel, the oil embargo, and the Euro-Arab dialogue all demonstrated this. In a different vein, inter-Arab collaboration on the Arab-Israeli conflict facilitated regional cooperation on different international issues. Such cooperation was particularly evident in 1971-74 concerted actions that culminated in breaking the power of the multinational oil companies in the Middle East and bringing about a transformation of the global petroleum market.

In contrast to the patterns of increasing cooperation, however, the 1970s encompassed several developments that set in motion significant changes in regional political dynamics. The first of was the weakening of the driving forces behind pan-Arab nationalism: Nasser, Nasserism and Egypt's vanguard role among Arab states declined. These forces worked to concentrate the attention of regional actors on the Arab-Israeli issue, and their decline presaged a decline in the integration of the cooperative and conflict cores. The death of Egyptian President Gamal Abd al-Nasser on 28 September 1970 in effect initiated this process. With Nasser gone, the region lacked a popular, charismatic spokesman for Arab nationalism. Nasser's successor in Egypt, Anwar al-Sadat, did continue Nasser's effort to maintain inter-Arab cohesiveness in the face of Israel for the first few years following Nasser's death; however, he lacked Nasser's pan-Arab appeal and vision. More important, he set Egypt on the path of unilateral settlement with Israel after the 1973 Arab-Israeli War, a process that culminated in an Egyptian-Israeli peace treaty of 1979, the Camp David Accords. In effect, Egypt's vanguard role as a driving force in Arab nationalism was eclipsed.

Sadat's actions had a dramatic impact on the region. At first, it appeared that a new reactive Arab cohesion would be forged in opposition to Sadat's moves. At the Ninth Arab summit conference in Baghdad in 1979, twenty Arab League members condemned Sadat's policies and took action to isolate Egypt. However, this was short-lived. Nasser's death and Egypt's subsequent defection deflated the ideological force of Nasserism. The weakening of Nasserism both reflected and hastened the decline of pan-Arab ideologies during this decade. Practically speaking, Nasser's death deprived Nasserism of its charismatic core. The man was a particularly important element of the doctrine's appeal, as Nasserism had failed to create any meaningful organizational structure whereby it might be perpetuated. At an ideological level, the appeal of pan-Arabism was essentially populist, while the state itself became increasingly authoritarian in the very states that championed Arab nationalism – Egypt, Syria and Iraq.

As the 1970s progressed, the Palestine Liberation Organization (PLO) was seriously weakened by external and internal difficulties. In the autumn of 1970 (called Black September), Jordan clamped down on the PLO, essentially ejecting the organization from its territory. Saudi Arabia and the Arab states of the Gulf, which all had large numbers of Palestinians in their labour forces, clamped rigid controls on their political activity. Syria, too, significantly reduced the freedom of action of its large refugee population. In addition, the PLO was weakened by internal dissension over matters of strategy and objectives; by external interference by some Arab states in its internal affairs; by the Lebanese civil war (1975-1990); and by serious conflicts with Syria (1976-77), Egypt (1975-1982), and Iraq (1978).

These contrasting tendencies represented manifestations of the counterpoint themes of pan-Arab nationalism and nation-state nationalism in regional politics. The pan-Arab nationalist theme was the dominant voice in the first quarter of the century; and the nation-state theme dominant in the second quarter. In the third quarter, the nation-state theme did not subside in any respect but the pan-Arab voice re-emerged above it. Finally, in the last quarter of the century, the relationship between the themes reversed again. Nasser's death in 1970 earmarked the beginning of this shift with the significant weakening of the forces of political integration of the Arab world. The proliferation of regional conflicts accelerated the arms race and overloaded the conflict management capacity of the cooperative core: the Lebanese civil war (1975-90); Maghreb-Saharan war, (1976-88); Libya-Chad war, (1973, 1981, 1982-87); Sudanese civil war, (1955-72, 1983-present); the Iraqi Kurdish wars (1961-69; 1973-75; 1982-present); and the Iraq-Iran war, (1980-88).

In particular, the Camp David Accord of 1979 and the Iraq-Iran war of 1980-88 significantly bolstered the forces of political fragmentation. The identification of the Egyptian position with the American-Israeli position, manifested in the Camp David Accord, was the outcome of a process of ideological reorientation initiated by President Anwar Sadat shortly after Nasser's death. The process culminated with the signing of a separate peace agreement with Israel sponsored by the United States, the Camp David Accord. In accepting the logic of the Camp David treaty, Egypt effectively subscribed to American political and strategic priorities in the Middle East, as is demonstrated by Cairo's support for American policies in the region in the post-nationalist phase. Contrary to conventional analyses, the Camp David Accord led inevitably to the subordination of

Egypt's role in the region to Washington's two priorities: a dominant role for Israel in the region and American access to the region's resources and strategic facilities.[18] Sadat's successor, Hosni Mubarak, attempted to reconcile the political order imposed on the region through the Camp David Accord with his effort to regain for Egypt a leading role in the Arab world. The Gulf crisis, however, forced American priorities to the fore, priorities that placed Egypt firmly on the side of the oil rich, conservative, anti-democratic Gulf states. The Iraq-Iran War brought the superpowers directly into the region and essentially turning the Gulf into an American military zone. By the end of the war, the political identity of the region was firmly rooted in the narrow self-interests of nation-states. Inter-regional relations, dictated by the strategic interests of the state, were determined in the context of dependence upon extra-regional powers. Intrusive powers had a vested interest in intensifying regional conflicts, not ameliorating them, both for pragmatic reasons (such as increases in arms sales) and for ideological reasons (such as increasing dependency on external political support). By the end of the Iraq-Iran war in 1988, the political core of the Middle East – embodied in patterns of cooperation throughout the millennium – ceased to have a determining influence on political developments in the region. Rather, the interaction of actors in the region with intrusive powers was more significant. In this context, regional dynamics of Middle East politics were driven more by patterns of conflict than patterns of cooperation.

Post-Nationalist Phase

By the end of the Iraq-Iran war in 1988, the political dynamic driving both the cooperative and conflict cores of Middle East politics was severely diminished. Furthermore, new patterns of interaction, set in motion by the Soviet military incursion into Afghanistan in 1979, emerged in Middle East politics. In response to the Soviet military adventure, in support of the Marxist government in Kabul, Saudi Arabia spearheaded the mobilization of volunteers from all over the Islamic world to assist the feudal forces in Afghanistan in waging a civil war against the government. The United States armed and helped train the guerrilla fighters, called Mujahidiin. The guerrilla war that ensued not only brought down the Kabul government in 1992, but also devastated Afghanistan and turned the majority of its population into refugees; and debilitated the Soviet Union (much as the Vietnam war had debilitated the U.S.). With the collapse of the Marxist government in Kabul, Saudi and U.S. support were withdrawn, and the rabidly fanatical and well-trained and well-equipped *Mujahidiin* volunteers left Afghanistan to pursue violent Islamic activism throughout the Middle East.

Coterminous with events in Afghanistan, throughout the Middle East, disillusioned populations, abused by authoritarian regimes and disenchanted with materialist doctrines of social progress, turned to religion in reaction to the increasing alienation of their societies. As an alternative vision of social progress, Islam offered a culturally legitimate worldview.[19] Iran, though not universally accepted in the Muslim world as a model for this worldview, nevertheless was a symbol of its viability and vitality.[20] It was to this context that the Mujahidiin volunteers returned and spawned the fanatical and violent fringe of the Islamic revival that was already gaining momentum in virtually every country of the Middle East.

The 1991 Gulf War, precipitated by Iraq's invasion of Kuwait in August 1990, constitutes a watershed in the transition of the political dynamic propelling Middle East politics into the 21st century. While the nationalist dynamic was already waning, and new patterns of cooperation and conflict were already emergent, the 1991 Gulf war in effect shattered the fundamental principle of sovereignty that constituted the very core of this dynamic. Iraq's violation of Kuwait's sovereignty, followed by the progressive violation of Iraq's sovereignty (by a U.S. led coalition) in the decade following the war in effect changed the basic rules of the game of nations. This occurred in the context of a unipolar world where one superpower – the United States – functions as the primary arbiter of law and order in the international community.[21]

In the post-nationalist era, patterns of cooperation and conflict in Middle East politics seem to be emerging around two independent (and interrelated) themes: the nature of relations between Middle East governments and the U.S.; and the nature of relations of Middle East governments with politically active forces in the Islamic movement. On the first theme, three groupings of Middle East states may be identified:

1. Oil rich states with regimes that maintain either:
   (a) Foreign policies closely aligned with U.S. interests; this category constitutes a cohesive sub-grouping in the Gulf Cooperation Council (GCC) organized in 1981 (composed of Saudi Arabia, Kuwait, Qatar, Oman, U.A.E., Bahrain), which functions as a sub-

regional alliance that in effect coordinates their regional and international patterns of interaction; or

(b) Antagonistic relations with the U.S.: Iran, Iraq and Libya; U.S. policy has effectively isolated these states and marginalized their role in regional politics.

2. Poor states with regimes that are either:
   (a) Dependent on U.S. goodwill for their economic and/or political survival: Jordan, Egypt, and Yemen;
   (b) Not dependent, but accommodating to U.S. policy: Morocco, Tunisia, Algeria, Sudan; together with Libya and Mauritania, they form a sub-regional alliance in the Arab Maghreb Union (AMU), established in 1989 to coordinate their regional and international patterns of interaction, but has been largely dysfunctional. These states align their foreign policies with the U.S. In regional politics, category (a) states tend to play surrogate roles to U.S. policy; while category (b) states maintain accommodative external policies when they act regionally at all.
3. States that have a special geopolitical relationship with the U.S.: Israel and Turkey. In 1996, they established a military alliance and in effect constitute the only power bloc in the region; in the context of their special relationship with the U.S., Israel and Turkey are able to aggressively pursue their own national interests in the region with great impunity.[22]

The first two groupings generate patterns of functionally localized cooperation (GCC, AMU) and patterns of geographically localized isolation in regional politics. The third grouping generates patterns of conflict: Israel's stalling of the peace process; Turkey's incursions into Iraq and threats to Syria; the over-exploitation of shared water resources by both. The common denominator of all these patterns is the relationship with the U.S.

On the second theme (the nature of relations of Middle East governments with politically active forces in the Islamic movement), patterns or trends are not readily discernible given the shadowy character of the Islamic movement. The notion of movement perhaps connotes more coordinated action than actually exists. In fact, the Islamic movement is made up of a large number of diverse groups that vary by scope and nature (location of operation, sect affiliated to, organizational character and socio-political propensities). As non-governmental voluntary associations, they constitute an important segment of civil society. However, many of the Islamic groups are clandestine or quasi-clandestine, either because they espouse political action or because they are officially suppressed by the government. The participation of Islamic groups in the socio-political spheres is actively suppressed in Algeria, Egypt, Tunisia, Bahrain, Kuwait, U.A.E., Saudi Arabia, Turkey, and Syria. In most other countries in the region, they are passively suppressed. Only in Jordan, Lebanon and Yemen has there been effort to accommodate their participation in the socio-political life of the country.

In this context, any cross-national or regional interaction within the Islamic movement is likely to be subterranean. Whether founded or not, however, the movement poses an ideological challenge to established power structures in the region; and fear of it has generated regional as well as national responses. The entire movement has been vilified with the terrorist label; and in April 1998, all of the Arab governments signed a protocol against terrorism, a directive clearly designed to forestall cross-national interaction and legitimate suppression. The patterns and contours of this phase are not yet in focus. The trends identified above may signify emergent patterns; or they may merely be trends that dissipate in the face of new forces. The case studies in the next section may help to fill in the picture and provide a concrete basis for prediction.

Notes

1 The concepts of core and periphery are borrowed from systems theory but are used here only for heuristic descriptive purposes, and are not intended to signify systems' theoretic properties. For an examination of the Middle East from the perspective of systems theory, see Tareq Y. Ismael , *The International Relations of the Middle East* (Syracuse University Press, 1986), pp. 41-67.

2 William R. Thompson, "Delineating Regional Sybsystems: Visit Networks and the Middle East Case," *International Journal of Middle East Studies*, Vol. 13, No. 2 (May 1981), p. 213.

3 Samir Amin, *The Arab Nation*, (London: Zed Press, 1978), p. 21.

4 Mohammad Dhia'a al-Din El-Rayes, *al-Nadhariyyat al-Siyasah al-Islamiya*, 7th ed. (Cairo: Dar al-Turath, 1977), pp. 216-220.

5 Samir Amin, *The Arab Nation*, (London: Zed Press, 1978), pp. 22-99.

6 L. Carol Brown, International Politics and the Middle East: Old Rules, Dangerous Games (Princeton University Press, 1984).

7 Charles Issawi, *An Economic History of the Middle East and North Africa* (Columbia University Press, 1982), pp. 1-14.

8 Samir Amin, *The Arab Nation*, (London: Zed Press, 1978), p. 23.

9 Mohammad H. Heikal, *Harb al-Khaliej* (Cairo: Markaz al-Ahram lil Tarjama wa al-Nashr, 1992), p. 67.

10 Samir Amin, *The Arab Nation*, (London: Zed Press, 1978), p. 31.

11 Egypt and Iraq had gained formal independence earlier: Egypt in 1922 and Iraq in 1932.

12 For a list of the specialized agencies of the League and joint projects of OAPEC, see Yusuf A. Sayigh, *The Economics of the Arab World: Development Since 1945* (London: Croom Helm, 1978), pp. 692-693.

13 William R. Thompson, "Delineating Regional Subsystems: Visit Networks and the Middle East Case," *International Journal of Middle East Studies* Vol. 13, No 2 (May 1981) pp. 213-35.

14 George Lenczowski, *The Middle East in World Affairs*, 4th ed. (Ithaca: Cornell University Press, 1980), pp. 749-751.

15 Tareq Y. Ismael, *The Arab Left* (Binghamton: Syracuse University Press, 1976).

16 Fawaz A. Gerges, *The Superpowers and the Middle East: Regional and International Politics: 1955-1967*. (Boulder, CO: Westview Press, 1994), pp. 175-204.

17 See Tareq Y. Ismael, *International Relations of the Contemporary Middle East* (Syracuse University Press, 1986).

18 See Adel Safty, *From Camp David to the Gulf* (Montreal: Black Rose Books, 1992) for a detailed analysis of the nature and impact of the Camp David Accord; see also Avraham Sela, *The Decline of the Arab-Israeli Conflict: Middle East Politics and the Quest for Regional Order*, (Albany, New York: State University of New York Press, 1998).

19 Jacqueline S. Ismael and Tareq Y. Ismael, "Cultural Perspectives on Social Welfare in the Emergence of Modern Arab Social Thought," *The Muslim World*, Vol. 135, No. 1-2 (January-April 1995), pp. 82-106.

20 Tareq Y. Ismael and Jacqueline S. Ismael, *Government and Politics in Islam* (London: Frances Pinter, 1985).

21 Tareq Y. Ismael and Jacqueline S. Ismael, "Cowboy Warfare and Biological Diplomacy: Disarming Metaphors as Weapons of Mass Destruction," *Political and the Life Sciences* (March 1999).

22 Alain Gresh, "Turkish-Israeli-Syrian Regions and their Impact on the Middle East," *The Middle East Journal*, Vol. 52, No. 2 (Spring 1998).

2 The State: Globalization and the Middle East[1]

RICHARD FALK

It is a complex matter to appraise the state in the Middle East at this stage in world history, and it is equally difficult to evaluate the Middle East as a region of the world system as the 20th century draws to a close. These regional concerns are set in a broader sweep of macro-historical developments that are changing the overall interaction between market forces, governmental authority, and the peoples of the world. Among many trends that of economic integration is among the most significant, especially to the extent that it is being shaped by the ascendancy of neo-liberal ideas about state/society relations. In this chapter, against the background of these concerns, a general assessment will be made, followed by some specific remarks directed at the specific circumstances of the Middle East. It should be appreciated that despite the effort at an overview, the unevenness of conditions throughout the world, on a state-by-state and region-by-region basis both make generalization necessary and hazardous.

The State in an Era of Globalization

For reasons of clarity, I would like to ground the inquiry of this chapter in the work of Hedley Bull and John Vincent as representative of the British version of realism in international relations. It is a convenient generalization to suggest that both Vincent and Bull felt conceptually, and, what is more significant, normatively, committed to an outlook that accepted "a society of states" as the only viable foundation of world order. As such, they were variously suspicious, and even somewhat scornful, of my more sceptical attitude towards statism, regarding my level of criticism as "utopian" or "Salvationist" because it seemed to them to be advocating a post-statist type of world order as more desirable than the world of states that existed and – what was worse in their eyes – implying that a differently constituted and better world order might even be attainable in the near future under certain conditions.[2]

My concern is to use this realist backdrop as the basis for commenting upon the dubious triumph of globalization and its somewhat ironic implications for the future of the states system. I believe that the states system as the self-sufficient organizing framework for political life on a global level is essentially over: "it is history." Let me explain. The state remains the pre-eminent political actor on the global stage; but the aggregation of states, what has been called "a states system," is no longer consistently in control of the global policy process. Territorial sovereignty is being diminished on a spectrum of issues in such a serious manner as to subvert the capacity of states to govern the internal life of society, and non-state actors hold an increasing proportion of power and influence in the shaping of world order.

I am not celebrating these results as a vindication of my earlier views; far from it. In this respect my focus on the ascendancy of globalization is deeply ironic, because the post-statist world order that is increasingly becoming dominant even as we speak is not at all what I had earlier favoured as an alternative to statism. It is, rather, a new alignment of forces that is being crystallized by a constellation of market, technological, ideological, and civilizational developments that have nothing in common with the alternative world orders that I and others had earlier proposed as normative projects, put forward in the form of rooted utopias within the framework of the *World Order Models Project*, and elsewhere.[3] The core of this normative project had been, in contrast, based on embodiments of human aspiration responsive to world order values specified so as to emphasize the interplay of peace, economic well being, social justice, and environmental sustainability. Instead – and this is part of the irony – the globalised world that is taking shape makes me, in central ways, nostalgic for the realities and potentialities for moral evolution of a society of states in the spirit of Hedley Bull: an orientation that Andrew Linklater has imaginatively interpreted in a recent paper devoted to matters of sovereignty and citizenship.[4] It should be realized that there is little, or no, normative agency associated with this emergent world order: it is virtually designer-free, a partial dysutopia that is being formed spontaneously, and in the process endangering some of the achievements of early phases of statist world order.[5] I acknowledge that this emergent globalised world order is not altogether regressive in its effects; its operative logic is fashioning several dramatic improvements on what previously existed globally, especially through the remarkable transformation of a series of Asian societies as a consequence of sustained high economic growth and social orders that have been impressively redistributive as their economic pies have grown.

However, even here the unresolved Asian economic crisis casts doubt on the durability of these gains. It no longer seems the case that these countries are achieving benefits for an expanding proportion of their respective societies so that poverty and unemployment are contained, and gradually, eliminated. Globalization also gives rise to a levelling dynamic that is making it possible for portions of North and South to cooperate and negotiate on the basis of far greater parity than in the past. Further, the weave of global economic interdependence works against the type of intense geopolitical rivalries among leading states that have accounted for most of the serious international wars that have occurred in the last several centuries.

Perhaps it would clarify matters at this stage if I refer more explicitly to the chapter title. I am contending that "globalization" has already won out in the sense that the language and imagery of a state-centric world have become anachronistic in crucial respects. At the same time, as is common with obsolete paradigms it is the professional observers of international affairs who appear to be the last to know, and resist stubbornly the mounting evidence that contradicts their "realist" world view. In this regard, it is almost amusing to note that realism has never been so professionally robust and ideologically dogmatic as now, when it appears to be languishing on its deathbed. How else to account for the seemingly endless fascination with the structural framework set forth by Kenneth Waltz or the ultra-realist constructions of reality by his star student and exponent, John Mearsheimer?[6] Much more than when I started out in academic life, it is difficult these days for young specialists in international relations to get past the academic gatekeepers at leading American universities unless they can demonstrate their unconditional, unto death, adherence to the outmoded postulates of realist orthodoxy. By comparison, at least in the United States, earlier academic resistance to Marxists during the Cold War era was mild. These days Marxism has virtually disappeared as a serious strand of academic inquiry, and liberalism has become "a gentler realism," offering a pale, pacified, and generally contained "other," whether liberalism's gloss on realism is formulated by reference to human rights or support for somewhat stronger international institutions.[7] The most serious non-realist mode of inquiry these days is contained in the various strands of critical theory, which has been essentially deconstructive in its preoccupations, but is as agonistic as its realist adversaries to reconstructive thought or normative theorizing, especially by way of its rejection of meta-narratives as such.[8]

What I am concerned about is the widespread reluctance at present to give academic credibility to those forms of inquiry that are dedicated to preferred futures for the organization of political life on the planet. The normative horizon of what is treated as serious inquiry into the future is foreshortened by realist orthodoxy, unless it happens to be presented in the shape of a challenge to geopolitical stability, as in the case of Samuel Huntington's *Clash of Civilizations* thesis. If conflict is highlighted, then an assessment of the future will be discussed endlessly, almost regardless of how thin the argument that is put forward.[9]

Of course, such attentiveness to conflict scenarios signals the degree to which realism (and its recent applications) remains, as always, a surrogate for geopolitics, and specifically diverts attention from the continuing hegemonic project to extend Western, and in most instances American, dominance into the next century. Revealingly in the Huntington instance, what provokes discussion is the substance of the alleged challenge of Islam to the West, not the more fundamental contention being made in the article that a state-centric world order is being superseded by an emergent inter-civilizational world order. Taking Huntington's own words more seriously, "It is my hypothesis that the fundamental source of conflict in this new world will not be primarily ideological or primarily economic. The great divisions among mankind and the dominating source of conflict will be cultural."[10] It is essential to depict the ideological underpinnings of Huntington's conceptually presented argument, especially considering his earlier prominence in the Vietnam era as a counterinsurgency apologist and his continuing presumed closeness to the American foreign policy establishment.

It may help to situate Huntington's emphasis on the Islamic threat to realize that only a year before his notorious *Foreign Affairs* article, Huntington gave a lecture at Princeton insisting on the inevitability of an imminent strategic clash with Japan that was posited at the time as almost certainly leading to a future war, although possibly of the cold, rather than hot, variety.[11] In effect, Huntington has, over the years, been operating as a geopolitical therapist on special call to the Pentagon, and has since 1989 been responding to the dangerous climate of depression that gripped the upper echelons of the American national security establishment when the full impact of the end of the Cold War began to sink in, and the loss of a credible enemy was perceived as debilitating, both to professional identity and to budgetary support. In effect, the extraordinary impact of Huntington's clash thesis was not a result of questioning world order fundamentals, but rather reflected the frenzied search for a new enemy of sufficient magnitude to fill the void created by the collapse of the Soviet Union and revolutionary Marxism. The specific policy implications drawn by Huntington have been widely criticized as irresponsibly encouraging the outbreak of culture wars. The amazing response to his article – a truly worldwide phenomenon – can be attributed partly to the sensitivity of his geopolitical proposals to the displacement of the states system, couching the emergent rivalry within an inter-civilizational rather than an interstate matrix.

The complementary side of this post-statist geopolitics is a renewed confidence in the capacity to project Western power successfully in relation to potential adversaries, and here one encounters not an acknowledgment of civilizational pluralism but an extension of the "unipolar moment" that was proclaimed in the aftermath of the Gulf War. Also writing recently in *Foreign Affairs*, Joseph Nye reaffirmed the hegemonic vision of world order on the basis of American mastery of the military applications of cyberinformatics, as follows: "In truth, the 21st century, not the 20th, will turn out to be the period of America's pre-eminence. Information is the new coin of the international realm, and the United States is better positioned than any other country to multiply the potency of its hard and soft power resources through information."[12] What is being claimed for the United States is an overwhelming military capability that can be used with little risk and almost no human costs, explicitly invoking the Gulf War as a rudimentary foretaste; a similar, gentler version of this hegemonic interpretation of the future was expressed by Bill Clinton's former National Security Advisor, Anthony Lake, in a short essay, "For a Second American Century."[13] Returning to my main line of inquiry, there is present in this Huntington/Nye view of the future a geopolitical translation of the realist tradition in world order thinking into the idiom of the post-Cold War world. Expressing this assessment differently, what is being advanced, partly analytically, partly ideologically, and partly normatively, is a dogmatically modernist view of international political reality.[14]

Let me briefly clarify what I mean by "modernist" in this setting of emergent globalization. I refer to the framing of international political life that was associated with the Enlightenment, broadly construed and somewhat over-generalized as resting on three pillars of interconnected ideas and convictions: the primacy of the territorial state; the secularization of political relations among states, including the prospect of technological innovation as enhancing the quality of life; and the globalising mission by the West to dominate the non-Western world.[15] I am contending that each of these three pillars of modernism has been eroded in such a way as to deprive that statist orientation as a whole of its explanatory and structural authority in relation to world order theorizing.[16] The state persists as an important actor, of course, as indicated earlier, especially as the repository of ultra-modern military technologies, and as such retains a crucial ordering role in most conflict situations. Increasingly, however, the state has itself been "globalised" or "internationalised," that is, the policy orientation of the state has been pulled away from its territorial constituencies and shifted outwards, with state action characteristically operating as an instrumental agent on behalf of non-territorial regional and global market forces, as manipulated by transnational corporations and banks, and increasingly also by financial traders.[17]

Appropriately, these days it is business elites that are declaring themselves most ardently to be citizens of Europe, or even global citizens, and thereby apparently most willing to forego the specific identities of the nation-state; unlike more idealistic and cosmopolitan shifts in loyalty, which in the past have been associated with the advocacy of world government, this new type of global citizenship is pragmatic, and has grown up without accompanying feelings of regional or global solidarity of the sort associated with a sense of community. It is questionable whether such globalist sentiments should be confused with traditional notions of citizenship, which implies a commitment to the well being of the relevant community.[18] This new global orientation reflects mainly a cold, practical calculation of interest, reinforced by the capacity of franchise capitalism to light up the urban landscape throughout the world with McDonald's golden arches, a worldwide continental cuisine, five-star hotel chains, Benetton stores, homogenous casual and formal dress codes, MTV, global internet access, real-time uniform news dissemination by CNN and Sky News, and a capacity to be understood and entertained everywhere in the English language.

This partial instrumentalization of the state was evident in the Gulf War, properly regarded as the first post-modern war, where the extraordinary mobilization of military capabilities was responsive to severe global market anxieties about the price of oil and the future control of Gulf oil reserves. The visual portrayal of the war in real time made the war into a kind of simulation exercise that resembled a sophisticated arcade game in its early stages. Other relevant modernist concerns, such as the security of Israel, the stability of the region, and non-proliferation of nuclear weapons were also present, but the financing and scope of the war, including especially its self-limitation that allowed Saddam Hussein to survive while the social and military capacities of Iraq were devastated, reflected the primacy of a new set of largely hidden transnational factors associated with sustainable and profitable economic growth for an integrated world economy, but also a growing strategic indifference to state-society relations that belies and is at odds with pretensions to a serious foreign policy commitment to human rights and democracy.[19]

This indifference was underscored by the extent to which these same countries that had moved mountains to restore sovereign rights to the neo-feudal rulers of Kuwait waited near the sidelines ever so patiently for several years while ethnic cleansing and horrifying crimes against humanity were being committed in Bosnia, or while genocidal turmoil overtook Rwanda. The steps that were eventually taken as a result of public pressures were gestures of an ambiguous character rather than serious political military initiatives: ambiguous sanctions, loosely implemented embargoes on arms, an under funded war crimes tribunal; more responses to public pressure than efforts to protect the victims of gross abuse.[20]

The same line of argument can be approached from other angles. John Ruggie has noted that the dynamics of globalization are gradually disembedding the domestic social contract between the state and society, which had become integral to the program of welfare capitalism and social democracy.[21] In effect, there is currently no sufficient countervailing power to offset the drive of business and finance to subordinate social policy to economistic criteria of profitability and efficiency in the use of capital. As a result, international corporations and banks report profits while downsizing and outsourcing operations, shifting production units to the Pacific Rim and elsewhere. It is a pattern that causes the stock market to rise to record or near record levels while the life of lower – and middle – class people in many settings continues to stagnate, or even deteriorate, with reduced wages and salaries along with cutbacks in public services. In this process, structural pressures of regional and global scope shape national policy to such an extent that credible political parties in democratic states adopt convergent party platforms that are all variations on the single theme of "neo-liberalism." This convergence of pressures on the state is particularly damaging and discrediting for those who favour the type of compassionate forms of governance associated with American liberalism or European social democracy. What this means is that, temporarily, at least, in such a world order, Sweden can no longer be Sweden! The humane or compassionate state is being phased out, although unevenly and incompletely.

Let us consider this altered character of the state from one further angle, continuing the focus on this eroded pillar of territorial sovereignty.

In his important book on sovereignty and the modern state, *The Sovereign State and Its Competitors*, Hendrik Spruyt concludes that the statist world of modernity arose out of an organizational competition between states on the one side and city-leagues and city-states on the other. The state won out over these rivals for organizational pre-eminence in late medieval Europe. According to Spruyt's well-argued and documented appraisal, "[s]tates won because their institutional logic gave them an advantage in mobilizing their societies' resources."[22] I think we are living at a time when states are losing their organizational advantage in the provision of public goods, with the revealing exception of security, and only then if security is conceived in the narrowly artificial terms of military/police activities.[23] Elsewhere the pressure on public goods, whether involving labour rights, health care, social safety nets, higher education, support for the arts, or environmental protection, is prompting fiscal reductions, resulting in societal atmospheres of increasing austerity, despite overall indicators of continuing prosperity as measured by share prices, salaries for media celebrities and sports stars, and end-of-the year bonuses for CEOs. Indicative of this new era has been a new pattern of labour relations, with traditional areas of industrial activity being mainly on the defensive, while worker militancy and "strikes" occur sporadically in privileged domains: millionaire athletes in soccer, baseball, and hockey seeking larger portions of the revenue pie from billionaire team owners, a result that arises not from the money paid by sporting fans in the stands, but mainly from the sale of national and international TV rights. Those sectors of labour that have been most afflicted by globalization in the form of layoffs and stagnant wages, victims of corporate restructuring to sustain profitability and competitiveness in this global era, have been surprisingly passive, undoubtedly reflecting their feelings of impotence, a sensed inability to mount effective challenges due to their declining political strength and economic leverage.

This loss of territorial focus by the state is reinforced by the manipulation of financial traders by the flows of ideas and information, migrants, popular culture, drugs, lifestyles, pollution, and organized crime. In this fluid setting, various transnational networks of social activists exhibiting a generally diminishing regard for the boundaries of sovereign states have also taken shape.[24] The rejection of these globalizing tendencies in its purest form is associated with and expressed by the resurgence of religious and ethnic politics in various extremist configurations. Revealingly, only by retreating to pre-modern, traditionalist orientations does it now seem possible to seal off sovereign territory, partially at least, from encroachments associated with globalized lifestyles and business operations, and even then only with considerable materialist sacrifice and, for this reason, probably in a manner that is sustainable only for brief periods. Even in the setting of religious and ethnic resurgence the primary identification is more often civilizational than territorial. Ayatollah Khomeini was emphatic in his insistence that the movement he was leading was an "Islamic revolution," and not an "Iranian revolution." But elsewhere, as with the BJP in India and Likud in Israel, the religious vision is bound up with strong versions of statist nationalism. In other words, the territoriality of religious and ethnic nationalism is itself anti-modern in other respects, rejecting the second pillar of modernism, namely its secularism, expressed by way of the separation of church and state, through its liberation of reason and science from any kind of accountability to and regulation by religious authority, and its strong affirmation of the individual as the primary repository of socially constructed, as distinct from natural, rights.

There is also less operational content associated with the application of the doctrine of sovereignty to the practice of politics on the global level.[25] States, conceived as governmental units rather than as territorial entities, have increasingly been challenged from within and below, as well as from without and above.[26] The rise of identity politics associated with ethnic and religious affinities has recently challenged the authority and legitimacy of many secularist traditions associated with multi-ethnic states. Separatist tendencies operating under the rubric of "the right of self-determination" have been threatening the perception and reality of the state as a single unified actor at home and abroad, and have had divisive impacts on even such a supposed bastion of moderation as Canada. Instead, a kind of neo-medievalism in international society, of the sort that Hedley Bull briefly anticipated two decades ago, has made claims of sovereignty less descriptive of the way problems are solved and social aspirations achieved.

Robert Jackson wrote a provocative book some years ago in which he contended that many of the ex-colonial states, especially those in Africa, were in effect unrealised, non-autonomous actors; he downgrades these with the epithet of "quasi-state," arguing further that these quasi-states are hopelessly seeking to make their way in interaction with "real" states.[27] My argument carries this logic of quasi-states further in both directions: all states, no matter how militarily potent and economically formidable, have become to a significant degree, "quasi-states," while "real states," if these persist at all, are a hopelessly endangered species of political animal whose reality is subject to various forms of doubt.

Turning now more directly to the second pillar concerns of the modern with the dynamics of secularization, here too significant challenges are evident, although not so dramatically and self-evidently as in relation to territoriality and sovereignty. This is a complicated area, partly reflecting the widespread and variegated religious resurgences occurring in virtually every important civilizational space. There are crucial elements in this mixture. The development, and use of, and reliance on, the atomic bomb, nuclear weaponry and nuclear powers (especially in the aftermath of the Chernobyl meltdown) have raised deep and persisting questions about whether science and technology, unmediated by some kind of spiritual tradition, were after all benign vehicles for innovation and progress, and even whether over time technological innovation linked to the market was compatible with the security and well being of peoples. Culturally, the 1960s raised the question whether the machine was not gradually impairing the quality of individual and collective life, setting a large question-mark against the word *modernity*, politically, ethically, and philosophically. In the 1990s these issues remain on the agenda of social concerns, but tend to be phrased more powerfully in relation to computers, the emergence of super-human artificial intelligence, the almost limitless claims made on behalf of virtual reality and genetic engineering, and the blurring of the line between human activity and machine mechanism, a process that Mark Dery summarized effectively as "cybergorging the body politic."[28]

Another challenge came from nature, no longer merely a backdrop for human adventure and conquest, but a realm to be brought under progressive domain so as to minimize danger and maximize control. The modern thrust was in the direction of limitless growth and exploitation; but nature has revealed a formidable ability to hit back against human society in devastating ways, disclosing limits to the carrying capacity of the earth. In addition to the emergence of severe uncertainties about social risks, long-term effects are casting dark shadows over the future by way of unchecked global warming, expanding ozone depletion, water contamination, polluted commons, demographic pressures, and an array of specific environmental breakdowns producing immediate and local harm.

For several decades it has been evident that environmental consciousness has the capacity to generate mitigating policies and adjustments, but does not possess the leverage to induce drastic modifications in human behaviour if such turn out to be necessary to achieve sustainability. The modernist confidence in human autonomy is thus deeply challenged by environmental risks; but also the sustainability of a world order that lacks strong governance capacities and a collective will based on feelings of human solidarity is drawn into question in relation to ultimate concerns about survival. These structural difficulties are now accentuated by the influence being exerted by neo-liberal tendencies to downsize government, rely on the rationality of the market to signal social and physical dangers and induce corrective action, and trust in the enlightened self-interest of the private sector to protect the global commons and preserve the earth as a going concern.[29] In these domains, sovereignty, in the sense of a refusal to be accountable on a supranational level, imposes additional difficulties for any sort of global standard-setting, allowing lifestyle orientations and economic development choices to proceed without external accountability and beyond the reach of any regulatory authority, even if the implications for the world over time appear to be ecologically catastrophic. Such risks are not figments of a doomsday imagination, but arise from such concrete occurrences as the presence of extensive radioactive waste dumps, the destruction of portions of the Amazonian rain forests, and the early stages in populous Asian countries of mass introduction of automobiles relying on internal combustion. The probable scale of these activities is so great, and the means of control so trivial and belated, that there is little that can be done beyond the fervent prayer that warnings will somehow be heeded and curative steps taken early enough to prevent full-scale bio-regional collapse. In effect, neither rationality, so prized as an attribute of the modern sensibility, nor reliance on secular politics provides any solid ground for hope about the human capacity to deal successfully with a range of unmet, mounting world order challenges.

Despite widespread psychological denial, the subliminal recognition of these vulnerabilities partly explains a widespread malaise among Western youth expressive of feelings of helplessness. The apocalyptically pessimistic lyrics of Nirvana's Kurt Cobain, coupled with his suicide, are best understood as a cultural scream of anguish in reaction to this disturbing prevalence of collective mechanisms of denial and escape in the face of continuing and mounting planetary danger. As a result, the modernist belief in the future, especially in the West, is disappearing as a cultural dimension, and seems to be giving way to an array of postmodernisms and fundamentalisms that call into question the very possibility of coherent understanding or disinterested public action. Under these conditions various states are responding with differing degrees of success to the challenges arising from religious resurgence, identity politics, regional and global market forces, transnational cyberpolitics, and the accelerating mobility of capital, people, and images.

The third pillar of modernity was its implicit civilizational arrogance in privileging the West in relation to non-Western societies. This has been most dramatically evident in the essentially genocidal meeting between European settler migrants and the indigenous peoples situated throughout the non-Western world. In the Americas alone the most reliable assessments now suggest that as many as 50 million natives died during the first century of large-scale European settlement. Zygmunt Bauman writes relevantly that "[m]odernity was not merely Western Man's thrust for power, it was his mission, proof if moral righteousness and cause of pride. From the point of view of reason-founded human order, tolerance is incongruous and immoral."[30] Modernity induced confidence, even arrogance, as it spread its influence around the world. The dynamics of de-Westernization that started with the collapse of the formal colonial system, but are going forward now in the shape of the assertiveness of non-Western civilizational claims, particularly those being made on behalf of Islam and Asia, have undermined the universalism of the modern era. As a result, globalization coexists with civilizational pluralism and various forms of political fragmentation, superficially contradictory pressures that have in common a move away from centering political action on the control of government in sovereign states.

To summarize, globalization has undermined the certitudes associated with proclamation of a state-centric world. At the same time, globalization has helped to conceal the emergent locus of real power in relation to the shaping of global economic policy. Leaders of states are constrained by these structural forces, although to varying degrees, and seem to be receptive to the interpretation of global market priorities as perceived through the prism of neoliberal ideas. In paradoxical fashion, the Marxist account of the relation between economic and political power seems persuasive only after Marxism has lost its capacity to win adherents to its worldview.

These developments pose a series of dangers that can be understood societally, politically, and ecologically, as well as ethically and cognitively. There is a loss of democratic control over the course of history. Polarization of society tends to deepen, and there are many victims who are left in the cold, ranging from the homeless in the streets of affluent societies to virtually the whole of sub-Saharan Africa. Beyond this, the creative and empathetic sides of governance are challenged, and in retreat.

Responding to the Challenges of Neo-Liberal Globalization

To avoid any impression of determinism arising from this analysis, it may be useful to take brief note of three directions of response that could avoid many of the negative policy implications of the argument:

- A global social contract that provides for basic human needs and regulatory uniformity, resembling the achievements of social democracy and the labour movement at the level of the state. The social agencies capable of bringing about such results are the backlash in Western societies experiencing rollback and downsizing and the greater social flexibility of Asian countries that have reached thresholds of development that give a higher priority to social demands.
- The strengthening of tendencies connected with world order values, transnational social forces dedicated to human rights, environment, gender consciousness – and peace – what I have called globalization-from-below, with an emergent capacity to balance the influence of globalization-from-above through the regulation of the global economy and by way of accountability for those beyond the reach of the regulatory operations of states; also the opening of pathways towards cosmopolitan or transnational democratic ethos of renewal.[31]
- The inevitable push towards law and governance on regional and global levels as a result of greater complexity, interconnectedness, and fragility of human activity. Such tendencies could be accelerated by environmental breakdowns and failures of technology that rouse public consciousness.

The normative possibilities for international society that John Vincent and Hedley Bull foresaw and helped nurture are now more compelling than ever, but the substantial displacement of a statist world makes it necessary to recast such aspirations, as well as to rethink our conceptual tools for the framing of world order. Globalization has intermingled our categories of thought, discouraged the projection of "imagined communities" on a global scale, and eclipsed the image of global governance by way of a society of states. At this point, what we require minimally are visions of the present and future that can better encompass reality than "realism," as well as proposals and tactics for bridging the normative and ideological gaps between the ascent of economic globalization and the descent of human well being in established societies.

On the Middle East: Region, State, and World

Of all regions of the non-Western world, that of the Middle East has been the scene of the most intense and continuous geopolitical contestation during the entire century. Unlike developments in other regions, the outcomes of many political conflicts in the Middle East have been treated globally as matters of strategic concern. Also, the region has not been very successful in its effort to create modernizing and dynamic state structures or in its capacity to absorb Western ideas about constitutional democracy to which it has subscribed. As a result, its contemporary experience has veered between poles of disappointment and poles of tragedy, with very little sense of achievement. Of course, there are crucial variations over time and through space, with some highs as well as many lows, but the overall experience has been generally negative and there is no end in sight.

In reaction to such negative history it is not surprising that the region has given rise to a variety of extremist religious and political movements that are regressive from the perspective of a modern secular value scale. Thus, it seems to be the case that the region has been a pawn in the geopolitical chess game. As well, it has been deficient in the sort of indigenous capabilities needed to transform political independence (and in some instances, exceptional resource endowments) in directions that bring happiness and prosperity to the peoples of the Middle East.

There are several lines of explanation. To begin with, the importance of the region to the main geopolitical forces in the world have led to persistent disruption in the form of a variety of hegemonic efforts to intervene and exert influence. The Middle East has been regarded as the bridge between Europe and Asia, but also Africa; this bridge is important for trade and investment, and for the projection of power throughout the non-Western world. Further, the West has stereotyped the region by way of "orientalism" to provide a continuing foundation for asserting its superiority and justifying various modes of interventionary diplomacy. At the same time, the region has both provided the inspirational point of origin for the entire Judeo-Christian trajectory and has periodically challenged the West most harshly by mounting radical movements of a military, religious, and cultural character.

In this century, the presence of a large portion of the world's oil in the region has made it a strategic priority to avoid having the main oil-producing countries, especially those in the Gulf, fall into hostile hands. With the exception of the European heartland no part of the world has been perceived as so important as the Middle East to the established geopolitical order. The Carter presidency made clear in the aftermath of the Soviet invasion of Afghanistan in 1979 that nuclear weapons would be used if necessary to avoid any military threat to the Middle East. The Gulf War reinforced the view that major strategic interest were at stake whenever Western access to Gulf oil at roughly current prices were put at risk, but also added the concern with weaponry of mass destruction falling into unfriendly hands and the overall stability of the region.

Finally, the region has been kept in constant tension as a result of the establishment of Israel. For fully a half century this development has been both resisted and associated with the parallel frustration of the Palestinian people who have not been able to exercise their own right of self-determination. Israeli success on the battlefield and with the US Government, especially with Congress, has aligned the world's strongest state with the main adversary of the countries in the region. The more hopeful initiation of a peace process in the 1990s has not resulted in any solution to the Israeli/Palestinian conflict, and none is in sight.

In the face of this array of problems, the region has not demonstrated the capacity to evolve a constructive response. Authoritarian governments have proved to be oppressive toward their own people and irresponsible in dealing with others. The effort to achieve Arab unity has never yielded important positive results despite the unifying presence of Islam throughout the region. The resurgence of religion, beginning with the Iranian Revolution, has brought additional tensions to the region and to relations with the world. Those states endowed with vast oil wealth have not produced democratic societies, and have invested heavily in modern military hardware without exhibiting much capacity to use it effectively. Saudi Arabia is prime example, being the world's leading arms purchaser by far, and yet seemingly without the ability to uphold its sovereign rights on its own in relation to its neighbours or in the setting of the conflict with Israel.

In some respects, Turkey has avoided some of the worst regional tendencies. It has managed to achieve and sustain its independence in a manner that has constructed a strong modern state, but there are also serious unresolved problems. It is allied with the United States in ways that defy regional priorities, and it has failed to resolve serious internal problems, including the Kurdish struggle, hyper-inflation, and civil/military relations. It has also not yet succeeded in combining secular democracy with religious freedom. Serious problems remain about the role of Islam in Turkish society and in relation to the continuing relevance of the legacy of Kemal Ataturk. Turkey seeks acceptance as a European power, which would involve a partial disaffiliation from the region, and Turkey flirts with the possibility of leading a commonwealth of Turkic-speaking peoples consisting of itself and the countries in Central Asia that emerged out of the collapsed Soviet Union. In this respect, as a secular, non-Arab country situated at the gateway to Europe and with ties to Asia, Turkey is the least Middle Eastern of Middle Eastern countries, a reality reinforced by its explicit strategic cooperation with both Israel and the United States.

It is probably the case that as oil diminishes in importance during the next century, the Middle East will gradually be able to achieve greater autonomy as a region. Aside from being a major oil supplier, the countries of the region have not managed to be important or particularly successful players in the global market. At the same time, these countries seem less vulnerable to currency volatility and to domination by the Bretton Woods institutions, especially the IMF and World Bank, than do other non-Western regions. It may be that if the Palestinian struggle can be successfully resolved, economic cooperation could bring benefits to the peoples of the region, as well as more moderate patterns of government that were respectful of human rights. Trends in Iran suggest the possibility that Islamic rule may turn out to be compatible with most practices associated with constitutional democracy.

In conclusion, the pattern of state formation in the Middle East is not so seriously affected by the dynamics of globalization, as is the case in other regions. In this respect, the states in the Middle East have managed to retain their relative degree of autonomy in relation to the world economy, although they remain vulnerable to the old geopolitics of international rivalry and Western hegemony. It is likely that the region will be severely tested in the decades ahead by water shortages, and its future will be shaped by the extent the responses are cooperative or conflictual. The prognosis is not very optimistic as the main states in the region are governed in a manner that relies very much on coercive relations to society, either by using the military as an instrument of political rule or by situating real power in the military despite a façade of civilian rule. It would seem, then, that the Middle East is not likely to experience important reform in the foreseeable future, beset by degenerative tendencies within its constituent states and manipulated by geopolitical forces because of its energy resources, its strategic position, and out of fear that it might mount a formidable extra-regional challenge if it acquires weaponry of mass destruction. The region has been effectively stigmatised as the main springboard for international terrorism, and as a zone where intervention remains a plausible geopolitical option. In relation to Iran and Iraq the policy of "dual containment" has been employed by the United States in a thinly disguised adaptation of cold war era thinking. It is possible that the "hard" approach of the United States to the region, as exemplified by sanctions imposed on several countries, will create deep enough divisions among the main extra-regional states as to create some political space for a more imaginative relationship between the region and the world, but such a path has not yet been cleared and is not easily discerned at present.

Notes

1 Parts of this chapter were published in an article under the title "State of siege: will globalization win out?" *International Affairs*, Vol. 73, No. 1 (January 1997), 123-136. Another version of that article will appear as a chapter in my book entitled Predatory Globalization: Critique and Response, to be published by Polity Press in 1999.

2 For Bull's criticisms see *An Anarchical Society: A Study of World Order in World Politics.* (London: Macmillan, 1977); the criticisms are directed against Falk, i.e. *This Endangered Planet: Prospects and Proposals for Human Survival.* (New York: Random House, 1971); and *A Study of Future Worlds.* (New York: Free Press, 1975); for Vincent's most characteristic work see John Vincent, *Nonintervention and International Order.* (Princeton, NJ: Princeton University Press, 1976).

3 For the range of earlier proposals of the World Order Models Project, in a series called "Preferred Worlds for the 1990s," see Saul H. Mendlovitz, ed., On the Creation of a Just world Order (New York: Free Press, 1975).

4 "Citizenship and Sovereignty in the post-Westphalian Age," *European Journal of International Relations* 2: 77-103 (1996).

5 Such an interpretation is strongly argued by Ulrich Beck in "The Reinvention of Politics: Towards a Theory of Reflexive Modernization," in Ulrich Beck, Anthony Giddens, and Scott Hash, *Reflexive Modernization: Politics, Tradition and Aesthetics in the Modern Social Order* (Cambridge: Polity, 1994), 1-55, esp. 1-5.

6 For Mearsheimer see "Back to the Future: Instability in Europe After the Cold War" in Sean M. Lunn-Jones, ed., *The Cold War and After: Prospects for Peace* (Cambridge, MA: The MIT Press, 1991), pp. 141-192, (first published in *International Security*, Vol. 15, No. 1, Summer 1990). For more theoretically oriented Waltzian analysis see Barry Buzan, Charles Jones, and Richard Little, *The Logic of Anarchy: Neorealism to Structural Realism* (New York: Columbia, 1993); Hidemi Suganami, *On the Causes of War* (Oxford: Oxford University Press, 1996).

7 For an application of liberal perspective to the current international agenda see the report of the Commission on Global Governance published under the title *Our Global Neighbourhood* (Oxford: Oxford University Press, 1995). For a critical assessment of this report and its liberal orientation see Richard Falk, "Liberalism at the Global Level: The Last of the Independent Commissions?" *Millennium* Vol.24 (1995), pp. 563-576; for the argument that the liberal option was ended by the events of 1968, and after, see Immanuel Wallerstein, *After Liberalism* (New York: New Press, 1995), esp. pp. 1-7.

8 R.B.J. Walker, *Inside/Outside: International Relations as Political Theory* (Cambridge: Cambridge University Press, 1993); but see normative theorizing in Drucilla Cornell, *The Philosophy of the Limit* (London: Routledge, 1992).

9 For Huntington's reconsidered position see *The Clash of Civilizations and the Remaking of the World Order* (New York: Simon & Schuster, 1996); for a more inclusive view of inter-civilizational relations on the basis of a legitimate world order see Falk, "False universalism and the geopolitics of exclusion: the case of Islam," *Third World Quarterly*, Vol. 18, No. 1 (March 1997), pp. 7-23.

10 Samuel Huntington, "The Clash of Civilizations?" *Foreign Affairs* Vol. 72 (1993), pp. 22-49.

11 For the published text of this lecture see Huntington, "Economic Power on International Relations," *Research Program in International Security*, Monograph Series, No.1, 1993, Center of International Studies, Princeton University; see also Samuel Huntington, "Why International Primacy Matters," *International Security* Vol. 17 (1993), pp. 68-83.

12 See Joseph S. Nye Jr. and William Owens, "America's Information Edge," *Foreign Affairs* Vol. 75 (1996), pp. 20-37, at 35. (where near the beginning of the article it is written that "[t]he one country that can best lead the information revolution will be more powerful than any other" (p. 20)). A companion article, more technical in nature, proceeded along the same lines: Eliot A. Cohen, "A Revolution in Warfare," *Foreign Affairs* Vol. 75 (1996), pp. 37-54.

13 *International Herald Tribune*, May 6, 1996.

14 The normative dimension of the Nye/Lake conviction that American leadership, which is not presented as hegemonic, is a global public good.

15 An excellent depiction of modernism as constitutive of world order is contained in Stephen Toulmin, *Cosmopolis* (New York: Free Press, 1990.

16 See Beck, Giddens, and Lash, Reflexive Modernization, note 5, for a different appreciation of the restructuring of world order in the present period.

17 For several arguments along these lines, see essays in Yoshikazu Sakamoto, *Global Transformation: Challenges to the State System* (Tokyo: United Nations University Press, 1994); see also Richard Falk, "An Inquiry into the Political Economy of World Order," *New Political Economy* Vol. 1 (1996), pp. 13-26.

18 For a range of views see Martha C. Nussbaum and others, *For Love of Country: Debating the Limits of Patriotism* (Boston: Beacon Press, 1996); Bart von Steenbergen, ed., *The Condition of Citizenship* (London: Sage, 1994).

19 On interpretations of the Gulf War see Tareq Y. Ismael and Jacqueline S. Ismael, eds., *The Gulf War and the New World Order* (Gainesville, FL: University of Florida Press, 1994); Victoria Brittain, ed., *The Gulf Between Us: The Gulf War and Beyond* (London: Virago, 1991); John Gittings, ed., *Beyond the Gulf War: The Middle East and the New World Order* (London: Catholic Institute of International Relations, 1991).

20 See especially, David Reiff, *Slaughterhouse: Bosnia and the Failure of the West* (New York: Simon & Schuster, 1995); also Susan L. Woodward, *Balkan Tragedy* (Washington, DC: The Brookings Institution, 1995); Richard H. Ullman, ed., *The World and Yugoslavia War* (New York: Council on Foreign Relations Press, 1996); see also illuminating paper by Mahmood Mamdani, "From Conquest to Consent as the Basis of State Formation: Reflection After a Visit to Rwanda", unpublished paper, dated February 1996.

21 John Gerard Ruggie, "At Home Abroad: International Liberalization and Domestic Stability in the New World Economy," *Millennium* Vol. 24 (1995), pp. 507-526; see also Stephen Gill, "Globalization, Market Civilization and Disciplinary Neoliberalism," *Millennium* Vol. 24 (1995), pp. 399-423.

22 Hendrick Spruyt, *The Sovereign State and Its Competitors* (Princeton, NJ: Princeton University Press, 1994), p. 185.

23 For discussions of a people-oriented approach to security, specified as "human security," see the various volumes of the *Human Development Report*, published annually since 1990 under the auspices of the United Nations Development Programme, but especially the 1994 volume, *Human Development Report 1994* (New York: United Nations, 1994), pp. 1-107; see also Majid Tehranian and Laura Read, "Human Security

and Global Governance: The State of the Art," *Prospectus for a Collaborative Research Project*, Toda Institute, Honolulu, Hawaii (1996).

24 For a spirited assessment, yet somewhat exaggerated along these lines, see Jean-Marie Guihenro, *The End of the Nation State* (Minneapolis, MN: University of Minnesota Press, 1993); a more careful and convincing analysis along similar lines is to be found in Joseph A. Camilleri and Jim Falk, *The End of Sovereignty?* (Aldershot, Hants, United Kingdom: Edward Elgar, 1992).

25 A balanced account of the decline of sovereignty is offered by James N. Rosenau in "Sovereignty in a Turbulent World," in Gene M. Lyons and Michael Mastanduno, eds., *Beyond Westphalia? State Sovereignty and International Intervention* (Baltimore, MD: Johns Hopkins University Press, 1995), pp. 191-227.

26 For theoretical background see Walker, Inside/Outside, note 8.

27 Robert H. Jackson, *Quasi-states: Sovereignty, International Relations and The Third World* (Cambridge: Cambridge University Press, 1990.

28 Mark Dery, Escape Velocity: *Cyberculture at the End of the Century* (London: Hodder & Stoughton, 1996), pp. 226-319; see also Kevin Kelly, *Out of Control: The Rise of Neo-Biological Civilization* (Reading, MA: Addison Wesley, 1994).

29 My discussions of these structural aspects of world order can be found in Falk, note 2, and more recently in Falk, *On Humane Governance: Toward a New Global Politics* (Oxford: Polity Press, 1995) and "Environmental Protection in an Era of Globalization," *Yearbook of International Environmental Law*, Vol. 6, 1995 (1996), pp. 3-25.

30 Zugmunt Bauman, *Imitations of Postmodernity* (London: Routledge, 1992), xiv.

31 For two important and quite different recent efforts in this direction see Martha C. Nussbaum "Patrioitism and Cosmopolitanism," in Nussbaum and others, *For Love of Country*, note 18, 2-17, 131-144 and David Held's *Democracy and the Global Order: From the Modern State to Cosmopolitan Governance* (Oxford: Polity Press, 1995), esp. pp. 219-286.

Part Two:

The Regional System After The Gulf War

3 Hydropolitics in the Middle East

HILAL ELVER

Part One : Hydropolitics and Environmental Security in General

I. Concept of Environmental Security

Environmental conflicts, especially in relation to transboundary waters, are emerging as an important dimension of peace and security for the Middle East. There are four major, unresolved regional disputes over the distribution and management of waters, one is a complex controversy over water allocation rights in the Euphrates/ Tigris River basin among Turkey, Syria and Iraq, the other two involving the Jordan River basin and West Bank groundwater. The last one is despite having the agreement between some riparian countries, the biggest river in the region, Nile and conflict over some other riparians. These complex freshwater resources present the interplay of environmental, economic, cultural, political, and ethnic factors that in their aggregate pose a severe threat to peace and security in the region.

On this basis, first we will try to explain the correlation between environmental security and transboundary water conflicts, and second we will locate the complexity of this particular case study in the framework of the Middle East and provide guidelines for a peaceful resolution of the Tigris/Euphrates conflict in a manner that is mutually beneficial for the three countries (Turkey, Syria and Iraq) principally involved.

Environmental security is becoming a key element in long-range government policy. Historically, security analysts have paid little attention to environmental issues. In recent years, however, the role of environmental degradation as a generator of local and international conflict has been widely recognized. The fast rate of global environmental change, on the one hand, and the signs of exceeding the earth's carrying capacity by humankind, on the other, are now increasingly considered in relation of human security and viewed as an urgent and important future challenge comparable to the issue of war and peace. This development is especially evident since the end of the cold war.[1]

The post-Cold War period has changed the international security agenda and given greater attention to such previously neglected sources of conflict as international migration, nationalism, population pressures, and environmental problems, including access to scarce resources. It is tragically apparent that these factors can give rise to political disputes that lead eventually to violent conflict. The security of individuals, communities, nation-states, and global community as a whole is increasingly jeopardized as a result of environmental non-military threats. Of course, most environmental problems are of a character that is not relevant to international security. Nevertheless, environmental problems are definitely becoming a more serious source of political conflict between states in a series of circumstances that is contributing to violence within and between states.[2] In the meantime, the environment, in particular its purposeful modification has been used recently to gain battlefield advantages. The environment can become both a target and a weapon in military action. In reaction, international legislation has been enacted in order to discourage military uses of the environment.[3]

Environmental changes are likely to cause shifts in the regional and global balance of power between states in a manner that will produce the sort of instabilities that could easily lead to conflict even war. Indeed, global environmental vulnerabilities increase the disparity between North and South. Poor countries will generally be more adversely affected by environmental deterioration than rich ones. Because of this sensitivity, environmentally induced conflicts are more likely to arise and to be severe in the developing world. Economic decline, population displacement, and disruption of regular and legitimised social relations give rise to various forms of acute conflict, including scarcity disputes between countries, clashes between ethnic groups, and civil strife and insurgency. Each category of environmental conflict has potentially serious repercussions for the overall security interests of the developed world.

Natural resources are spread around the world in a manner that is independent of national borders. Many natural resources and problems associated with their use are shared with neighbour countries. Despite the fact that the state sovereignty principle is still very crucial, states need to become more sensitive to the mix of local, regional and international conditions and concerns in developing their resource policy. States no longer have the exclusive discretion over the use or protection of the world's resources. New environmental law principles, such as equal access to natural resources, sustainable development, common heritage and common concerns of mankind, intergenerational equity, impose to varying degrees, significant limitations on traditional absolute sovereignty and are by stages shifting this principle to one of "responsible sovereignty".

According to Homer-Dixon,[4] there are at least seven major environmental problems that have the potential to cause violent conflict: greenhouse warming, stratospheric ozone depletion, acid deposits, deforestation, degradation of agricultural land, overuse and pollution of water supplies, and depletion of fish stocks. In this array of problems, the one that seems most immediately important, is the struggle to maintain or gain control over high-quality fresh water resources. The scarcity and limitation of these water resources is one of the main reasons for regional conflicts. Especially as the scarcity of water and increasing demands for water are aggravated by an expanding third world population that are making it more and more difficult to develop water resources on a renewable basis. As far as international rivers are concerned, categorizations of potential sources of conflict emphasize: access and control over water flow; uses of river system itself that negatively affect other present and future uses; and activities beyond the river system per se, but that adversely affect it.[5] While the first category is concerned primarily with issues of water quantity, the latter two are focused on water quality.

As indicated, access to water as a vital resource has often been an objective of military action, and given the population increase this could be even more true in the future if and as fresh water becomes increasingly scarce relative to demand.[6] Upstream states can manipulate shared river basins to the detriment of other riparian states; further, dams, desalination and purification plants, and irrigation systems provide serious potential targets in the event of war and the water supplies of enemies can be poisoned. Since water is an essential element of life, and disruption of access to adequate supplies of unpolluted water can have dramatic political and strategic impact, as well as can greatly magnify the human suffering associated with war. This occurred during and after the Gulf War of 1991. Many civilian casualties resulted from the destruction of Iraq's highly centralized water purification facilities, resulting in many deaths that occurred months and years after the cease-fire had put an end to active combat.

The use and misuse of water resources have been concerns of civilization since ancient times.[7] Historically, this was a source of concern in arid and semiarid regions alone; today it is a concern everywhere. Increasing populations, compounded with rising standards of living, lead us to rapidly reach the limit of finite resources.

There are major reasons that make water likely to be a source of conflict are: (1) the degree of scarcity, (2) population growth and migration, (3) unsustainable agricultural practices and irrigation, (4) the extent to which the water supply is shared by more than one region or state, (5) the ease of access to alternative fresh water resources, (6) conflicting development strategies and objectives, (7) the relative power of the basin states, (8) political and attitudinal factors, and (9) environmental concerns.[8]

II. Conflicts Over the Fresh Water Resources in General

Water is a fundamental substance, making life possible on our planet. While most resources have substitutes, water fulfils a number of functions for which there is no substitute. In every conceivable life form, the global circulation system down to the individual cell, water is present. Furthermore, although water is a renewable resource, it is at the same time finite. Water stores redistributes and releases about thirty per cent of the total amount of solar energy that comes to the Earth. But it is also a fragile resource, and for people, in large parts of the Third World, in particular, it is increasingly a scarce resource. Its degree of availability is largely dictated by climate.

The scarcity and limitation of water resources exists in the face of constantly increasing demands for water by industrializing third world countries whose populations are growing. This background reality makes it more and more difficult to utilize water resources on a renewable basis. Of course, the struggle for water is not a new subject for human history. For six millennia, the human race has been involved in various struggles to control water resources.[9] Every project and almost any process in society and in nature need water. Nevertheless, there is little mention of water, and its role in human destiny, invariably, water is taken for granted. A kind of water blindness has become common in discussions about development projects and even in relation to policy documents about our future.[10]

Water shortages are also a potential problem, and not only for developing countries, but also for many developed countries. However, industrial nations can usually resort to buying their way out through the use of expensive energy, expensive technology and expensive investments.

They can install the wherewithal to recycle their water, or even to desalinate seawater. Developing countries, trapped in poverty and debt, have no such option. Those who suffer from serious water shortages are faced with a cruel dilemma: they must either confine their use to available water reserves, or they must rely on untreated water. To choose to reuse untreated water is an open invitation to disease. In developing countries, most drinking water is contaminated to some extent and sewage is often left untreated. A survey by the World Health Organization (WHO) showed that only 35 per cent of the world's population had access to relatively safe drinking water, and 1.4 billion people lacked sanitation.

During recent decades, much progress in the efforts to improve living conditions all over the world has been achieved through technological solutions. Parallel to these developments, total water use in the world has quadrupled during the last fifty years. Therefore, for the future, efficiency in water handling and its allocation for productive and optimum use are crucial. New approaches are needed for the proper management and use of water resources. Instead of asking how much water we need and where to get it, we should ask how much water there is and how we can best benefit from it.[11]

In a United Nations study international river and lake basins are estimated to comprise about 47% of the world's continental land area.[12] In Africa, Asia and South America this proportion rises to at least 60%. Many of the world's river and lake basins and groundwater aquifers are shared by two or more countries. Of the 200 international rivers, 148 are shared by two countries, 30 by three, 9 by four, and 13 by five or more countries as many as ten.[13]

The allocation of water among riparians is fraught with considerations, historical, legal, moral, social and environmental, other than considerations aspects of economic efficiency. These are political considerations, or politics of water allocation. Each region, and each state has their own priorities and understandings. Contrasting economic, social, and political differences among neighbouring countries, price equalization across the region would not meet each nation's goals. Also, the social welfare implications of water policies in separate countries that share the same resources are different than each other. Each country has an individual incentive to subsidize water use and, thus, lessen water availability to the other party.

On the other hand, water resources abound with uncertainty. Rainfall or snowfall that feeds streams, recharges aquifers, or irrigates crops entail spatial and temporal variability; the size of many aquifers and their role of replenishment are incompletely known. Salinization and other quality degradation processes, for example, due to seawater intrusion, are not completely understood. These several uncertainties and unknowns affect the management of water resources.[14]

Water is a resource with many uses, but each use can change the characteristics of the water available for subsequent uses. For many years, ecologists and hydrologists have argued for a watershed scale to managing river resources. Economists also have described the systems approach to resource allocation. Political or institutional boundaries, however often overlap within a river basin, which can lead to the inefficient use of resources.

Differences in religious, political, and cultural beliefs may make negotiations difficult without participation of third party. The transactions costs involved in negotiating complex agreements governing water flows and uses may be prohibitively high for many countries. Income constraints may also limit offers poorer countries can make in water resource negotiation.

In recent years, water management issues have come to the forefront of policy discussion in many countries, as well as international development agencies. The reasons for the increased interest are apparent when one observes the 21 countries around the world have renewable water resources of less than 1000 cubic meter per capita, a level commonly taken to indicate a severe water stress. Another 18 countries are within the range of 1000-2000 cubic meters per capita, which is associated with periodical stress. In many other countries the problems are concentrated in specific regions or certain times of the year. With world population expected to grow by some 55 per cent over the next generation (mostly in developing countries), problems are likely to become even more acute. The demand for food and hence for irrigated agriculture will increase, as well as the demand for water for domestic consumption and industry. The growth in income, and the consequent changes in consumption patterns in ways that further increase the demand for water, are other likely developments. A re-examination of the ways in which water is allocated and managed is thus warranted, and indeed, has been the topic of a bargaining literature.[15]

Part Two: Emerging Water Conflicts in the Middle East

I. Overview of Hydropolitics in the Region

The Middle East is one of the most arid and water scarce regions in the world where the history of water related conflicts extend back 5000 years. Control, use, share, and management of water produces great tensions and underlies various types of conflict between sovereign states and peoples of the region. Despite the size of the Middle East, there are only three rivers that can be classified as large by world standards: the Nile, the Euphrates, and the Tigris rivers. These rivers provide relatively extensive water resources for the region. Except in Turkey and a few mountainous areas, rainfall is generally inadequate and is unable to support regular water needs and agriculture without irrigation.

The flow of major Middle Eastern rivers such as Nile and the Euphrates comes to a large extent from rain and snow that falls outside the region. The geopolitical importance of the region, as well as ethnic and religious controversy, aggravates the usual problems of sharing natural resources such as oil and water in many different settings. One of the new agenda items of security studies, environmental security, particularly natural resources conflicts gives serious attention to water disputes. According to these various studies, there are major reasons that make water likely to be a source of military or political action, such as, the degree of water scarcity, the extent to which the supply is shared by two or more groups, the relative power of those groups, and the ease of access to alternative fresh water resources.[16] In the Middle East region, besides these general reasons, we can categorize several other factors that create particular obstacles.

Transboundary character: Every major river in the region crosses one or more international border and 50% of the population in the region depend on water flowing from another sovereign State(s).[17] Political borders of sovereign states exert a major influence on individual policies on water and in general, often lead to impractical and unpredictable water management systems, which pose a serious threat to security of the people.

Geography and climate: The Middle East is the most arid region in the world. Moreover, the rivers of the region possess a volatile character. The net result of these conditions is that the management of such rivers is extremely difficult even if they were to be confined within the borders of a single nation. This is particularly true when the history of land use along the rivers is taken into account. In almost every case, these rivers and their flood plains have been settled and utilized first in their lover reaches. The upstream area has been the last to be developed, and is generally used for hydroelectric generation as well as agriculture. This geographical setting contributes to tension between upstream and downstream countries.

Population, environment and economy: Increasing population, poverty, and inefficient use of water accentuates the existing problem of water. The level of economic development, increasing pressure from population growth, irresponsible patterns of urbanization and industrialization, lack of environmentally sensitive technology adversely affects the quality and quantity of available water. The main disputes in the region are over the use of fresh water as a resource for consumption, whether in relation to agricultural, domestic or industrial activity. Transboundary pollution will become part of this picture soon, if it does not already exist. Navigation and fisheries disputes are minor issues in the region at this point.

Political uncertainty: The region is a politically turbulent area of the world. The various societies in the region were greatly affected by the two world wars. During the last 50 years, the region has been the scene of half-a-dozen substantial outbreaks of armed conflict, two of which involved intervention by forces from outside the region. None of these conflicts was directly about the control of water resources. Nevertheless, the character of these disputes has made it difficult for governments to co-operate over water. There is a severe lack of confidence among the states, and their leaders. There is no regional institution that is capable of bringing together countries over the economic and political issues. The only organization, the Arab League, does not include Ethiopia, Turkey, and of course, Israel. Even among the members of Arab League there are significant differences over a series of regional problems and issues. It is very hard to predict the future of the region given the fast and dramatic changes of the past three decades. The regions most important natural resource, oil reserves, was an immense attraction for Western countries, especially during the late 19th and 20th century. Outside powers have been playing an important role in the past, and this will be the case in the future.

Uncertain databases: The last obstacle to establish a policy in the region is a lack of reliable and agreed information about the overall inventory of water resources. The vital statistics of Middle Eastern rivers and aquifers are often incomplete and unreliable. There are several reasons for this uncertainty. First, the water resources have not been fully studied over a sufficiently long period for reliable results. Second, figures for the same watercourse may vary because different 'runs' of the year have been used to establish an average. Third, data may be presented in different ways for a variety of political reasons. For example, while an upstream state may wish to show a high figure for the river's average annual flow to show that there is ample water in a shared river to enable a proposed project and to satisfy the needs of downstream states. A downstream state however may demonstrate that the average flow was likely to be much lower if the project goes ahead and thus deprive it of the water that it needs. The difficulty of obtaining precise agreed data hinders scientific work on rivers and aquifers in the region.[18]

II. The Case of the Euphrates and the Tigris Rivers Basin

In the Middle East region, the Euphrates and Tigris river basin conflict involving Turkey, Syria and Iraq, is considered one of the three major water conflicts in the region. The others are the Jordan river basin conflict engaging Israel, Jordan, Syria and the Palestinians; and the tension concerning access to West Bank groundwater that has caused a conflict between Israel and the Palestinians.[19] Nevertheless, these conflicts have to be understood independently and dealt with differently from each other, in review of the complexity of political, social and environmental facts.

The longest inter-state river, the Euphrates, has been developed since 4000 BC. Several ancient civilizations in Mesopotamia were supported by irrigation from the Tigris and Euphrates river basin. Thousands of years ago, water from these two great rivers helped create the "fertile crescent" giving rise to the first civilization in the Middle East. Forty-five hundred years ago, the control of irrigation canals vital to survival became the source of conflict between the states of Umma and Lagash in the ancient Middle East.[20] Having an extremely arid climate, however, the farmlands on the Mesopotamian alluvial have suffered from salt accumulation and water logging problems since 2400 BC, the Sumerian age.[21] Throughout history, this ancient civilization disappeared and many others were devastated by the abandonment of irrigation systems. Twenty-seven hundred years ago, Assurbanipal, King of Assyra from 669 to 626 BC, seized control of wells in the course of waging strategic warfare against Arabia. Over the course of human history different factors have come together many times to produce a wide range of disputes over access to shared freshwater resources in Mesopotamia.

The Mesopotamian waters, the Euphrates and the Tigris, rise in the mountains of eastern Turkey; the Euphrates flows through Syria to Iraq before emptying into the Persian/Arab Gulf. The Tigris flows to Iraq and joins with the Euphrates in Iraq before reaching the Persian/Arab Gulf to Shatt-al Arab. Until the end of World War I, these rivers were under the control of the Ottoman Empire, and little international importance was attached to the river basin.

The Euphrates River: The Euphrates River consists of two main tributaries, the Karasu and Murat rivers, both originating in the Eastern Anatolia, as well as numerous smaller tributaries. 88.7% of the water potential of the Euphrates is derived from snow and rain that falls in Turkey, and only 11.3% from rainfall in Syria.[22] During its passage through Syria (675 km) and Iraq (around 1,200 km.), the Euphrates receives only negligible amounts of water. The Euphrates has only one third the volume of the Nile River with an average flow of 32.5 bcm2, but it is the longest river in East Asia (2700 km). Although the longer of the two, the Euphrates is smaller than the Tigris in volume. Table 1 indicates the three riparian countries contribution and demands respectively.

The Tigris River: The Tigris River, originating from Lake Hazer became the border between Turkey and Syria for a distance of 40 km, and border between Turkey and Iraq (7km.), as it flows into Iraq. So, the Tigris is divided only between Turkey and Iraq. Its main tributaries are Botan, Batmansu, Karpansu and the Greater Zap rivers emerging from Turkey, the lesser Zap, and the Diyala emerging from Iran, and finally Uzayam whose

Table 1: Water Potential of the Euphrates Basin

Countries	Water	Potential	Consumption	Target
Turkey	31.58	88.7%	18.42	51.80%
Syria	4.00	11.3%	11.30	31.80%
Iraq	0.00	0.0%	23.00	64.60%
Total	35.58	100.0%	52.92	

Source: "Water Issues Between Turkey, Syria and Iraq"; Ministry of Foreign Affairs Department of Regional and Transboundary Waters, June 1996, Ankara, Turkey

source is in Iraq's northern mountains. The Tigris receives 50% of the water in Iraq, and the other half in Turkey. While the river receives virtually no additional water after entering Iraq, the tributaries, which join the Tigris in Iraq, add a significant amount of water to the Tigris below Baghdad. As a result, Iraq's supply of water from the Tigris is much less vulnerable to developments upstream than is its supply from the Euphrates. Iraq also has an opportunity to obtain water from Tigris. Iraq has the physical means to do so, having constructed canals linking the two rivers. However, like the Euphrates, the volume of the Tigris also varies greatly from year to year and season to season. This may limit Iraq's opportunities for substituting water from the Tigris for that of the Euphrates, or vice-versa, when the flow in one river is low.[23] Table 2 indicates water potential of the Tigris River basin and consumption targets of the riparian countries.

Table 2: Water Potential of the Tigris Basin

Countries	Water	Potential	Consumption	Target
Turkey	25.24	51.90%	6.87	14.1%
Syria	0.00	0.00%	2.60	5.4%
Iraq	23.43	48.1%	45.00	92.5%
Total	48.67	100.0%	54.47	

Source: "Water Issues Between Turkey, Syria and Iraq", Ministry of Foreign Affairs, June 1996, Ankara, Turkey

The Euphrates and Tigris rivers have possessed a distinctive character. They receive all their waters near their sources and grow, and then become smaller as they flow to the sea. They have extremely high seasonal and multi-annual variances in their flow (between 10.7 bcm – 63.4 bcm.). Seasonal changes are also remarkable in terms of the volume of water. The river's peak flow is in spring and early summer, and it is almost eight times bigger than low period flow from July to October.[24]

III. The Development of Water Management Projects and Emerging Conflicts over the Euphrates-Tigris Rivers

Until 1970: The use of these rivers by the three respective countries has been the subject of diplomacy and commentary ever since the dissolution of the Ottoman Empire and the consequent disruption of the political unity that had previously inhibited conflict with respect to the Euphrates Tigris Rivers basin. However, until the 1970's, there was no significant complaint or conflict. Iraq, as a downstream country, was the earlier developer and user of these waters flowing between the riparian countries. Turkey and Syria, as upstream countries, were not active in using the water in the Euphrates and the Tigris river basin. In Iraq, large-scale irrigation did begin late in the 19th century, when a number of the ancient irrigation canals were cleaned and opened again for use. In the years just before World War I, while Iraq was still a part of the Ottoman Empire, a dam was constructed on the Euphrates at Hindiya, to divert water for irrigation. Later Iraq sought to control the two rivers for other end as well. Barrages were built on the Tigris to produce hydropower, and a barrage was constructed on the Euphrates at Ramadi to protect areas further downstream from flooding.[25]

The diplomatic effort to specify respective legal rights was contained in three international legal documents. First, the 1921 Ankara Treaty with France that formalized the Turkish-Syrian border, second the 1923 Lausanne Treaty, that established the new State of Turkey, and third the 1946 Friendship and Good Neighbour Treaty with Iraq.[26] These agreements worked as long as the waters were being used at minimal level. The real problem emerged when the midstream and upstream countries, Syria and Turkey respectively, initiated projects for developing the waters of the Euphrates in the 1960's. Turkey decided to build Keban Dam on the Euphrates River, and made arrangements for financing on conditions that the World Bank has imposed on similar projects. According to the terms of the agreement,[27] Turkey would try to make the necessary arrangements with Syria and Iraq with regard to an initial filling of a reservoir.

First Crises: In 1968, Syria started to build the Tabqa (later renamed al-Thawra) Dam on the Euphrates with Soviet assistance. Iraq too, had undertaken the Gharraf Project between the lower reaches of the Tigris and Euphrates rivers. Al-Thawra and Keban dams were both completed in the period between 1973-1975, when particularly dry seasons had been experienced, making the operation of both dams generative of a crisis. Iraq accused Syria of reducing the river's flow to intolerable levels, while Syria transferred blame to Turkey. The water shortage brought Iraq and Syria to the brink of armed hostility.[28] In 1974, Iraq threatened to bomb the al-Thawra dam in Syria; Iraq massed troops along the Syrian border, alleging that the dam had reduced the flow of water to Iraq. Water war was averted through the frantic efforts of Saudi Arabia, which mediated the dispute, urging that Syria release additional amounts of water so that they would flow into Iraq. According to the agreement, that was not made public, Syria will keep 40% of water and will allow 60% through to Iraq.

One year after the crisis, Turkey laid the foundations of the Karakaya Dam and accompanying hydroelectric power plant, further downstream from Keban. This was a second major step in the development of water resources, financed by the World Bank. Turkey unilaterally guaranteed a minimum flow of 500 cum/s to downstream countries. The Karakaya Dam entered service in 1987, while work on the Ataturk Dam had been under way since 1983. During these years, Syria was studying the feasibility of another major work upstream from al-Thawra, the Tishrin Dam. Thus, successive water development projects upstream became nightmares for downstream states throughout the 1970s and 1980s.

Southern Anatolia Project (GAP): Meanwhile, since the 1970s all these dam projects like Karakaya, Ataturk and many others built and plant, was part of the big integrated water development project initiated by Turkey in upper Mesopotamia, Southern Anatolia Region. The target of this ambitious project, so called GAP (Southern Anatolia Project), one of the largest of its kind in the world, to increase its hydroelectric production and to irrigate an additional two million hectares of land by early in the next century. The Keban and the Karakaya were designed solely for hydroelectric power generation, but the centrepiece of GAP, the Ataturk Dam and hydroelectric power plant, also included a major irrigation scheme, with a secondary network planned to follow. Thus, for the first time, Turkey was engaged in consumptive use of waters, and doing so in huge quantities. Turkey proved that it could proceed far into the project relying on its domestic resources, without giving any further concessions to downstream neighbours in return for conditional loans.[29] This $32 billion project, GAP, will consist of 22 dams, 19 hydroelectric power plants, and the irrigation network for 1.7 million hectares of land schemes of various scales in 13 different locations.[30] Table 3 represents the groups of projects in Euphrates and Tigris Rivers.

Table 3 : The GAP Projects on the Euphrates and Tigris Rivers

Project Area	Installed Capacity	Energy Produced	Irrigated Land	Planned Projects	Dams	Planned Work
Euphrates	5304MW	20 billion kWh	1 million ha.	7	14	11 HPW
Tigris	2172MW	7 billion kWh	700 000 ha	6	8	8 HPW
Total	7476MW	27 billion kWh	1 700 000 ha.	13	22	19 HPW

The project covers an area of 75 000 square kilometres in southeast Turkey, 9.5% of the national land area. Approximately 6 million people live in the region, which represents 9.1% of Turkey's population. The Tigris and Euphrates Rivers represent over 28% of the national surface water supply, and the total economically irrigable area in the Project Region accounts for over 20% of that for the Country. This area is equal to 26% of Iraq, 42% of Syria, 1.1 times the size of Israel and 1.25 times that of Jordan. When completed, the project will achieve full development of over 1.7 million hectares of land through irrigation that the ratio of irrigated land to the total GAP area will increase from 2.9% to 22.8% while that for rain-fed agriculture will decrease from 34.3% to 10.7%. 27 billion kWh of hydroelectric energy will be generated annually with an installed capacity of 7500 MW. When GAP is fully implemented, it is expected that the national average of energy use will more than double.[31]

The work, which was originally planned as a water resources development package, was later transformed into an integrated, multisectoral, regional development program. According to Turkish authorities, GAP, a regional development project carried out with the human elements at its focus, aiming at the comprehensive development of a whole region offers a significant example for the world.[32] The project is socially essential as it is intended to significantly improve the living standards and quality of life of the local people, increase their per capita income, create new employment opportunities, and protect the environment. Also economically viable as it will radically change the economic structure, increase production and more than quadruple the GRP. As a direct result of the GAP investments, the living standard of many inhabitants have already started to increase.[33] The population is expected to increase from six million in 1998 to 9 million by 2005, with 66% living in urban centres. Urbanization in the region has received a boost, and rural migration should slow down considerably.

The Second Crises: Syria and Iraq fear that Turkey's use of the Euphrates waters will disrupt both their current consumption patterns and future development plans. The GAP project created anxiety for Turkey's downstream neighbours even before starting any kind of adverse effect. After the first crises between Syria and Iraq, in 1990, when Turkey finished construction of the Ataturk Dam, the largest of the twenty-two dams proposed for the Grand Anatolia Project, and interrupted the flow of the Euphrates for a month partly to fill the reservoir, the second crises happened. Despite an advance warning and given more water before and after this period from Turkey the temporary cut-off of river waters created high tension over the downstream. Syria and Iraq both protested that Turkey now had possessed a water weapon that could be used against them. For one month Turkey held back the main flow of the Euphrates River, which cut the downstream flow in Syria to about a quarter of its normal rate. Syria is already desperately short of water, and much of the water for its towns, industries, and farms comes from the Euphrates.

Beyond this dependence, the country has been chronically vulnerable to drought. Furthermore, Syria's population growth rate, at 3.7% per year, is one of the highest in the world, constantly adding to the scale of Syria's demand for water. Turkey and Syria have exchanged angry threats arising from this situation. Syria has been giving sanctuary to guerrilla separatists of the Kurdish Workers Party (the PKK), a movement that has been waging a war of insurgency against the Turkish government in eastern Anatolia.

Diplomatic Attempts: Meanwhile, diplomatic meetings have been taking place among the three countries. In 1980, the Turkish-Iraqi Mixed Economic Commission agreed upon the formation of a Joint Technical Committee (JTC), to study matters relating to regional waters, in particular the Euphrates and Tigris rivers basin. In 1983, Syria joined the meetings and from then on the JTC convened its sessions on a trilateral basis. But after sixteen technical and two ministerial meetings, the JTC talks reached a deadlock, having failed even to produce an outline for a report.[34] However, bilateral talks continued and further initiatives were put forward. In 1987, two protocols were signed simultaneously between Syria and Turkey in Damascus. The first was an agreement on economic cooperation, Article 6 of which contained a commitment by Turkey to release a minimum annual average of 500 cum/s from the Euphrates waters "until the ultimate allocation" of the river's waters between the three countries could be agreed upon.[35] The second protocol was an agreement on security cooperation. The contents of the protocol were an outgrowth of Turkey's pressure on Syria to end its support for PKK operations. Syria was allegedly using the PKK as a way to induce Turkey to release additional waters. As a result, it seemed natural to assume that the political and resource controversies were inescapably connected to each other.[36] At every opportunity, Turkey unequivocally declared that it would not use transboundary waters for political purposes, whereas Syria denied any connection between its relations to the PKK and water issues. Nevertheless, in October 1989, late Prime Minister Turgut Ozal indicated that Turkey might impound the river's water if Syria failed to restrain the PKK operating from its territory. Although Ozal later withdrew this threat, the underlying tensions have not been resolved, and there are currently no significant high-level talks on water sharing. The most recent negotiations concerning the Euphrates and Tigris Rivers basin was held three times first two with Syria and the last one with Iraq bilaterally, in 1993.

Political Obstacles between Syria, Iraq and Turkey: The issue of Euphrates water is also entwined with concerns about territorial integrity and relations with ethnic minorities for these countries. Consequently, although water scarcity is a source of serious tensions between Syria and Turkey, and may trigger interstate violence in the future, the dispute is not a pure example of a simple-scarcity conflict.[37] Syrian officials argue that Turkey has already used its power over the headwaters of the Euphrates for political goals and could do so again. On the contrary, Turkey is blaming to support PKK against Turkey's national security and unity.

The ability of Turkey to shut off the flow of the Euphrates, even temporarily, was noted by political and military strategists at the beginning of the Gulf conflict. In the early days of the conflict during the crisis preceding the war, there were behind-the-scenes discussions at the United Nations about using Turkish dams on the Euphrates River to deprive Iraq of a significant fraction of its fresh water supply in response to its invasion of Kuwait. While no such action was ever taken, the threat of the "water weapon" was again part of the diplomatic setting. Turkey has never yet used water as means of political pressure and it declined to do so during the Gulf War.[38]

According to some interpretations, there is a link between the Middle East Peace agreement and the tension between Syria and Turkey with regard to the Euphrates River. If Syria is obliged to give up water sources on Golan, and then it will need to extract more water from the Euphrates.[39] This way of thinking creates more conflict than cooperation. In terms of hydrology, it is difficult and also not feasible to establish comprehensive and sustainable water management system larger than river basin principle.

Peace Pipeline Projects: Turkey's late president Turgut Ozal championed the concept of a "peace pipeline" that would transport water from two western Turkish rivers, the Seyhan and Ceyhan, southward to Syria, Jordan, Saudi Arabia, and the other Gulf States. A Canadian company has been trying to market a highly imaginative project: the transfer of as much as 250 mcm of water from Turkey to Israel in enormous containers - referred to as "Medusa bags" - that would be floated across the Mediterranean. At the same time the "Peace Pipeline" project has been trumpeted by the Turkish government as one of the best hopes for lasting peace in the Middle East region because if fully implemented, it could effectively end regional states' competition and anxiety over this scarce resource. The project, however, has not been so warmly received by several states in the region, partly because of its high estimated cost of $21 billion - a figure believed by some to be "grossly underestimated,"[40] and of the length of time (ten years) projected as needed for the operationalization of the pipeline. However, the most important concern is that the pipeline, as currently conceived, would pass through a number of downstream countries that do not trust each other (e.g., Syria/Jordan; Syria/Turkey), or that recently were in an official "state of war" posture with one another (e.g., Israel/Jordan; Israel/Syria). Moreover, the downstream Arab states, especially the oil-rich ones, would be reluctant to grant any further advantage to the militarily, politically and hydrologically stronger upstream state of the "Ottoman/Turks".[41]

Recent Situation: In 1995, a new storm over water supplies broke out as a result of the finalization of a credit agreement for the new Birecik Dam on the Euphrates River. The dispute has led Syria to start lobbying against Turkey, not only in the Arab League, but also in Western countries. The latest broadside in the bitter war of words over Middle East water resources has come from an unlikely cross-border alliance: Two states that have had no diplomatic relations for 15 years, Syria and Iraq. There are governments in which their respective leaders hold each other in mutual contempt and the enemy of one is a close ally of the other. Nevertheless, they have somehow managed a common stand, Syria and Iraq agree absolutely only on one thing – the threat to their future that is being posed by Turkish action to harness the resources of the Tigris and the Euphrates under its predominant control. Despite their deep patriarchal divisions, officials from both states, along with other Arab countries, endorsed a Damascus Declaration accusing Turkey of releasing contaminated water downstream to Syria. Ankara, responded by dismissing the attacks as "a storm in a teacup", insisting that Syrian claims of polluted water flowing downstream to Syria along the Euphrates, "were not taken seriously by experts." According to Turkish experts, the Birecik Dam is a regulation dam that aims to monitor the flow of water from the Ataturk Dam with the objective of providing a more regular supply of water to downstream countries. At present, GAP is irrigating less than one-tenth of the area that it plans to irrigate. The Turkish side has also denied that Syria was uninformed on the construction of Birecik Dam, saying that all technical information has been provided to Syria since 1983.

As the positions of the three countries have remained essentially unchanged for years, the Turkish press assumes that the latest diplomatic fuss over the water is linked to the latest round of peace talks between Israel and Syria. The former Israeli Prime Minister, Shimon Peres, had proposed that Syria obtain water from Turkey, thereby allowing Israel to keep all the water sources that are currently under its authority today. Ankara insists categorically that the waters of the Euphrates have nothing to do with the Middle East peace process.[42] Indeed, the 1996 agreement between Turkey and Israel represents one further aspect of the search for a new balance in the region against other neighbouring countries. As this controversy continues to unfold, it is evident that access to water is a crucial element in any viable system of comprehensive security for the region.

In September 1998, the latest crisis between Syria and Turkey was the serious one. Turkish leaders have adopted a new, harsh tone with Syria. Prime Minister Mesut Yilmaz accused Syria of being "the headquarters of terrorism in the Middle East" and reportedly warned Damascus that the Turkish army is on standby, "awaiting orders" to attack.[43] Ten thousand Turkish troops have moved to the Syrian border and have been prohibited from taking leave. The Turkish air force is on red alert. And Egyptian President Husni Mubarek has spent the week shuttling between Ankara and Damascus. Finally, the agreement reached between Syria and Turkey, unlike previous talks between the two countries, water issue is not included to commitments. This tendency indicates that Turkey is clearly differentiating these two issues and seems to be successful at this point.

Part Three: Institutional and Legal Responses

There is a large and growing literature warning of future "water wars" that point to water not only as a cause of historic armed conflict, but also as the resource which will bring combatants to the battlefield in the 21st century.[44] Water disputes more often produce political friction rather than violent conflict and this, fortunately, encourages the parties to have recourse to international negotiations and means of cooperation rather than to embark upon military action.[45] Over 3,600 treaties have been signed historically over different aspects of international waters, 145 in this century.[46] There are a number of legal institutional means available to help reduce the risk of water related conflicts and to provide for fair and reasonable international management of rivers and other transboundary water resources. The prominent international lawyers NGO, International Law Association (ILA),[47] and the United Nations institution, International Law Commission (ILC)[48] has been working for three decades on this issue, seeking to develop a treaty structure for the non-navigational uses of international watercourses. The United Nations General Assembly adopted the Convention on the Law of Non-Navigational Uses of International Watercourses, based on general principles of various draft articles prepared by the ILA and the ILC, on May 21, 1997.[49] The convention is divided into seven parts containing thirty-seven articles: Introduction; General

Principles; Planned Measures; Protection, Preservation and Management; Harmful Conditions and Emergency Situations; Miscellaneous Provisions; and Final Clauses. An annex sets forth procedures to be used in the event the parties to a dispute have agreed to submit it to arbitration. During the negotiation period, some parts of the Convention created some conflicts and argued by the states. The vote was 103 in favour, 27 abstentions and 3 against (Burundi, China and Turkey). The Convention will enter into force after thirty-five ratifications. This level of ratification will probably not be achieved easily. Many states already have treaties governing their international watercourses with which they are satisfied and may perceive little to gain in the Convention. Others may believe they are better off not being a party because of ongoing dispute. Some others are island states or otherwise lack international watercourses and therefore may have little or no interest in becoming a party to the Convention.[50]

International rivers, lakes and aquifers are a unique type of natural resource. Unlike territorial resources, controlled by single state, they are not fully subject to national appropriation, and yet such resources are not an aspect of the global commons to which all states enjoy potentially unrestricted access, like the high seas, the mineral resources of the deep seabed, and outer space. Aside from their navigational uses, freshwater resources that traverse political boundaries are a collective good to which only the riparian states enjoy rights of use and access. Even though non-riparian states are excluded from using such water resources, riparian states still need to regulate their respective rights and obligations with one another.

International environmental law, a new branch of international law, despite its fast and comprehensive development, is not effective in promoting environmental security as broadly conceived. Traditional international law remains focused principally on the territorial interests of states, giving relatively little attention to efforts to accommodate the widening range of ecological interests and needs. The first important principle of international environmental law is "territorial sovereignty" and an unrestricted right to use natural resources as qualified by an obligation not to cause significant harm to the environment of other states.[51] This principle has found application in the context of transboundary freshwater pollution, and has found expression in a series of multilateral freshwater agreements.[52] A second cornerstone of international environmental law is the obligation of riparian nations to share equitably the beneficial uses of transboundary freshwater resources.[53] Considering customary international environmental law principles, as ensuring equitable use and prevention of transboundary harm, states in these settings are subject to rules governing prior notification, information, consultation, and negotiation. However, these principles do not effectively address environmental security concerns. First, given their focus on territorial interests and uses rather than environmental needs, the rules cannot ensure ecological balance. Second, such principles are ultimately incapable of preventing conflict over degraded resources. Third, because of the division of water resources into territorial segments and the focus on competing state interests, customary law is inherently confrontational and does little to promote cooperation on behalf of the common environmental interests of all states.[54]

Interpretations of rights can be more beneficial if we define water resources management as "the art of matching supply of water demands while controlling quality." In other words, water quality and quantity issues are complementary each other. It is by now accepted that water resource development projects create some environmental problems. The goal of "no damage to nature" while developing water resources is not realistic. However, intelligent planning, sustainable economic development, and environmental management can be concordantly pursued to minimize negative effects.

The complexity of the relations between the two legal principles of "reasonable and equitable utilization" of transboundary watercourses and "not causing appreciable harm" to neighbours should be reconciled to the extent possible by means of well-mediated technical approaches. The new framework convention of the United Nations on transboundary waters (1997) tried to compromise these two principles in order to establish a balance between downstream and upstream parties. While downstream countries are favour of "not causing appreciable (or significant) harm principle", the "equitable utilization principle" is favourable for upstream states.

Conclusion

The hydropolitics of the Euphrates and Tigris dates back at least until 1920s, and will be on the agenda of future relations irrespective of whether a solution is found for the political and ethnic problems of the region. The greatest obstacle arises from the differences in the approach taken by Turkey, Iraq and Syria. Iraq and Syria insist that an agreement on the water issues is necessary, while Turkey, on the contrary, is favourably disposed toward international negotiations on the sharing of the water between the three countries. Iraq claims "historical rights" over the rivers, and presupposes that two rivers, have to be tackled separately. However, Turkey considers that the two rivers are part of the same water basin, and insists on an "integrated river basin management system" in the region covering the Euphrates and the Tigris. This approach also defined and accepted by the new framework convention of the UN.

Turkey supports a three-stage plan to be realized through the cooperation of the three parties, which basically proposes the distribution of water according to the needs of each country, and technological cooperation between the parties to promote rational use. This plan presupposes a long-term convergence of interests in the region, but the short-term degenerates into a series of crises due to the presence of distrust and tension between these countries. To identify the reasonable and appropriate amount of water each country needs from both rivers depends upon the use of complete and accurate information on land water resources of the Euphrates-Tigris basin. It should be noted that in many countries institutional mechanisms to merge available water supplies with competing demands are absent or are very weak. Collecting data on water is not an easy task in the Middle East, where information on available resources can be a powerful bargaining chip in negotiations. The establishment of a joint data bank could help build the trust that will be required to move the affected governments towards a comprehensive agreement or to resolve disputes as they arise.[55]

The three riparian countries, during the past two decades, have engaged in aggressive political attacks upon each other. For instance, Turkey, against Syria claiming that "we will dry them up" or "they need additional water to wash the blood of terrorism from their hands."[56] Syria did not hesitate to use PKK and support Kurdish movement not as a whole on behalf of humanitarian reasons, but only against the Turkish State as a negotiation chip in order to get more water from Turkey. However, it is inconceivable that given the actual or potential ethnic turmoil and separatism in the region that the problems with Turkey, Syria and Iraq would simply disappear if water disputes are solved. That is, the water dimension has become implicated in the ethnic conflicts, but it doesn't fully account for their existence.

Instead of emphasizing these political factors, Turkey needs to demonstrate that it is not a water rich, water surplus country. Although Turkey has sufficient water resources for the time being, it may find itself in the near future faced by a situation in which it will not be able to meet all of its water needs. Due to the imbalance in the geographic distribution of existing water resources, topographic and technical limitations, the water potential of Turkey cannot be fully utilized. Particularly the western regions of the country are even now faced with serious problems of water storage. For instance, Istanbul will be seriously short of water until a huge water transfer project comes on stream early in the next century.[57] In the Euphrates and Tigris basin, the following points concerning water resources management and allocation should be addressed:

- Conflicting data on the irrigation potential of the Euphrates and Tigris river needs to be resolved.
- The tendency to base assessments solely on the Euphrates River and the neglect of water diversion possibilities from the Tigris should be overcome by estimates of the resource potential of the whole Euphrates-Tigris basin.
- The allegations over the causes of water quality changes along the Euphrates River must be more objectively evaluated.

The diverse and opposing nature of ethno-religious groups in the Middle East, which include Turks, Kurds, Arabs, and Israelis, makes the management of scarce water resources a precarious venture in diplomacy, and adds to the difficulty of achieving cooperation. Moreover, shortages of water, mismanagement of natural resources, and the notion of sovereignty exert a set of negative pressures on the foreign policy of Middle Eastern countries. At this point, calculating a nation's short-term benefits will not overcome the challenge. Regional problems can only be solved through common supranational approaches. Only supranational solutions offer some prospect of conflict-resolution. The European Union's approach to solve environmental conflicts is the best example as such by far. The International Court of Justice has solved the conflict between Hungary and Slovakia over the Danube River.[58] The reason was, the European Union put pressure on the countries that was the precondition being in the list of prospect members of the EU.

What kind of strategies can be developed to reduce the intensity of conflict and the danger of outright violence arising from these states that are competing for access to transnational water resources within the Middle East region? Confidence building measures, conflict-resolution techniques will be needed to address this urgent challenge. Preventive diplomacy, in international relations and confidence building techniques are elements of an emerging diplomacy for the world. Resource management diplomacy is one form of preventive diplomacy that holds out great promise. The idea is to agree upon sustainable uses of natural resources so as to reach a sensitive balance between economic development and environmental protection. It is a precondition of arriving at stable solutions that mutual interests and benefits are taken into consideration and realized. The best solution of such a deep conflict, as in the Middle East, is to establish a good faith bridge between countries, relying on confidence building and preventive diplomacy, in the one hand while, preparing a long term sustainable water management plan that considers on the other hand, prospects for economic growth, as well as takes account of the agricultural and environmental situations of the three countries and on these bases specifies reasonable requirements for water. For such an approach to succeed, upstream countries have to show utmost forthcoming in making water available to downstream countries within the limits of fairness.

In sum, this multi dimensional and multiphase controversy over water allocation rights, with its complex interplay of environmental, economic, cultural, political, and ethnic aspects, poses a severe threat to peace and comprehensive security in the region. To remove this threat peacefully calls for imaginative reliance on resource diplomacy in which the respective governments of the affected states act in a manner that recognizes the interests and needs of the other as well as safeguards its own position.

Notes

1 Renat Perelet , "The Environment as a Security Issue," *The Environment: Towards a Sustainable Future* Ed: Dutch Committee for Long Term Environmental Policy. (Kluwe Academic Publishers, 1994), p. 147.

2 Sean Lynn-Jones & Steven E. Miller (eds.), Global Dangers. Boston: The MIT Press, 1995, pp.5-6.

3 Gaps in international law arose as a result of the use of oil for marine and air pollution in the Gulf war and blowing up a dam protecting a pond with hazardous chemicals during the Moldavia ethnic military conflict to pollute a nearby river that was a fresh water supply source. For latter example see: Arthur Westing (ed.), *Global Resources and International Conflict*. (Oxford: Oxford University Press, 1986), pp.85-113.

4 "On the Threshold: Environmental Changes as Causes of Acute Conflict," in Lynn-Jones & Miller, note 2, pp. 43-83.

5 Jon Martin Trolldalen, International Environmental Conflict Resolution: The Role of the United Nations. (Geneva: UNITAR, 1992), p. 63.

6 During World War II, Korean War, Iran-Iraq War, Vietnam War, Middle East War, Gulf War and, in the wars in former Yugoslavia water supplies were threatened or militarily targeted and bombed. For more information see: Mladen Klemencic; "The Effects of War on Water and Energy Resources in Croatia and Bosnia," The Peaceful Management of Transboundary Resources, (London/Dordrecht/Boston: Graham Trotman/Martinus Nijhof , 1995), pp.167-174.

7 Code of Hammurabi is the oldest legal source that dealt with water allocation: "If anyone be too lazy to keep his dam in proper condition, and does not so keep it. If then the dam break and all the fields be flooded, then shall he in whose dam the break occurred be sold for money, and the money shall replace the grain which he has caused to be ruined. If he be not be able to replace the grain, then he and his possession shall be divided among the farmers whose corn he has flooded."

8 See Peter H. Gleick; "Water and Conflict" Note 2, p. 90; Jutta Brunnee & Stephen Toope, "Environmental Scarcity and Freshwater Resources" *Yearbook of International Environmental Law*, V.5, (1994), p. 41.

9 See: Karl A. Wittfogel, Oriental Despotism: A Comparative Study of Total Power, (New Haven and London: Yale University Press, 1957).

10 Robin Clark, Water: The International Crisis, (Boston: The MIT Press, 1993).

11 Further information about water demands and the human carrying capacity of the earth see: Joel E. Cohen., How Many People Can the Earth Support?, (New York - London: W.W. Norton & Company, 1995), pp.329-355.

12 Register of International River and Lake Basins; United Nations, 1978. (Pergamon Press: Oxford, U.K.).

13 Barret; Conflict and Cooperation in Managing International Water Resources, Policy Research Working Paper 1303, 1994, The World Bank: Washington D.C.

14 Douglas D. Parker & Yacov Tsur (eds.); *Decentralization and Coordination of Water Resource Management*, (Kluwer, 1997), p. 2.

15 K. William Easter & Gershon Feder; "Water Institutions, Incentives, and Markets" p. 261 in *Decentralization and Coordination of Water Resource Management*; Douglas D. Parker & Yacov Tsur (Eds.), 1997.

16 Peter H. Gleick: "Water and Conflict." (*International Security*,Vol.18, No.1), pp.79-112.

17 John Kolars "Hydro-Geographic Background to the Utilization of International Waters in the Middle East," (American Journal of International Law: Proceedings of the 80th Annual Meeting, 1986), pp. 249-50.

18 Greg Shapland: Rivers of Discord (St. Martin Press: New York, 1997).

19 Miriam R. Lowi: "Political and Institutional Responses to Transboundary Water Disputes in the Middle East'" (Environmental Change and Security Project Report, Woodrow Wilson Center Publication, 1996), p.5.

20 Peter H. Gleick : The World's Water, The Biennial Report on Freshwater Resources 1998-1999 (Island Press: Washington D.C., 1998) p.108; see also Appendix A and B Chronology of Conflict Over Water in the Legends, Myths, and History of the Ancient Middle East. pp.125-130.

21 Masahiro Murakami: Managing Water for Peace in the Middle East- Alternative Strategies (United Nations University Press, 1995), p. 34.

22 According to Kolars and Mitchell these figures 98% for Turkey, and only 2% for Syria. See: The Euphrates River and the Southeast Anatolia Development Project (Carbondale, IL, 1991).

23 Greg Shapland: Rivers of Discord,(St.Martin Press: New York, 1997), p.106.

24 *Ibid.* p. 106.

25 *Ibid.* p. 107.

26 Huseyin Pazarci: "Su Sorununun Hukuki Boyutlari," (Orta Dogu Ulkelerinde Su Sorunu, Tesav Yayinlari: Ankara, 1994), p. 52.

27 Turkish Official Gazette, (*Resmi Gazete*) October 15, 1966. According to this agreement, initially Turkey agreed upon release a minimum of 350 cum/s of water. This formula became the basis for a tense modus vivendi among all three countries.

28 Thomas Naff & Ruth Matson: Water in the Middle East; Conflict or Cooperation? (Westview Press, 1984), p.42.

29 Gun Kut; "Burning Waters: The Hydropolitics of the Euphrates and Tigris," *New Perspectives on Turkey*, 1993, p.6.

30 Ali Ihsan Bagis: G.A.P. Southeastern Anatolia Project, The Cradle of Civilization Regenerated. (Istanbul: Interbank, 1989).

31 "Water Wars in the Middle East," *The Economist*, (May 12, 1990), pp. 54-59.

32 Olcay Unver: "Regional Socio-economic Development and Water: The South-eastern Anatolia Project of Turkey", (Unpublished paper presented in Workshop held in Paris March, 1998: Averting a Water Crisis in the Middle East: Make Water a Medium of Cooperation Rather Than Conflict).

33 *Ibid.* p. 103.

34 Gun Kut; Note 18, p. 8.

35 Resmi Gazete, Turkish Official Journal, December 10, 1987.

36 See David Kushner; "Conflict and Accommodation in Turkish-Syrian Relations," in *Syria Under Assad* (Moshe Ma'oz & Avner Yaniv (Eds.), 1993), pp. 85, 95-97; H.J. Skutel; "Turkey's Kurdish Problem," *Conflicts in the Middle East*, (1993), pp.3-5.

37 Thomas F. Homer-Dixon; "On the Threshold: Environmental Changes as a Causes of Acute Conflict," in *Global Dangers,* Lynn-Jones and Miller (Eds.), (Boston: The MIT Press, 1986) Note 2, p. 75.

38 See Peter H. Gleick; "Water and Conflict: Fresh Water Resources and International Security," *International Security*, Vol.18, No.1, p. 94, footnote 30.

39 *Turkish Daily News*, January 13, 1996.

40 Chris Cragg, "Water Resources in the Middle East and North Africa," *Middle East and North Africa*, (1993), pp. 177-180.

41 Hussein A. Amery & W. Andy Knight, "Confidence Building Measures and the Management of Scarce Water resources in the Middle East," (Unpublished discussion paper); *Turkish Daily News*, February 14, 1996.

42 *The Wall Street Journal*; October 9, 1998.

43 Aaron T. Wolf and Jesse H. Hamner; "Trends in Transboundary Water Disputes and Dispute Resolution," (Unpublished paper presented at workshop, Green Cross International, March 1998, in Paris).

44 Peter Gleick; "Water and Conflict: Fresh Water Resources and International Security," Note 2, p. 117.

45 Aaron T.Walf & Jesse H.Hamner; p. 120.

46 The ILA has been very productive and influential in the clarification and development of this law. See: "Helsinki Rules," 52 ILA Conference Report 484 (1966), and "Seoul Rules," 62 Conference Report 251, 1986.

47 The ILC adopted 33 "draft articles" on the law of non-navigational uses of international watercourses and resolution on confined transboundary ground water. The ILC submitted these instruments to the United National General Assembly and recommended the elaboration of convention on the basis of the draft articles. (See: Report of the ILC on the work of its forty-sixth session, UN GAOR, 49th Session Supplement No.10, at 195, UN Doc. A/49/10 (1994).

48 For the Convention, see GA Res. 51/229, annex (May 21, 1997), 36 (ILM) 700 (1997).

49 Stephen C. McCaffrey and Mpazi Sinjela; "Current Developments: The United Nations Convention on International Watercourses", (American Journal of International Law, Vol.92, 1998, p.97-102).

50 Principle 21 of the Stockholm Declaration on the Human Environment (1972), and Principle 2 of the Rio Declaration on Environment and Development (1992).

51 See Patricia Birnie & Alan Boyle, *International Law and the Environment* (Oxford: Oxford Press, 1992), p.230.

52 Article IV, V of the ILA Helsinki Rules; Article 5,6 of the ILC 1994 Draft Articles.

53 Jutta Brunnee & Stephen J. Toope, "Environmental Scarcity and Freshwater Resources," (*Yearbook of International Environmental Law*, V.5, 1994), p. 41.

54 Peter Kemp, "Special Report: Water," (*Middle East Economic Digest*, 27 January 1995).

---

55 *Turkish Daily News*, January 5, 1996.

56 Water, MEED Special Report, January 26, 1996.

57 Water, MEED Special Report, January 26, 1996.

58 See Gabcikovo-Nagymaros Project , Judgement. <hhtp://www.icj-cij.org>. International Court of Justice, September 25, 1997.

4 The Gulf War, Economic and Financial Linkages, and Arab Economic Development: Iraq – The Pivot?*

PAUL SULLIVAN

Introduction

A. *Levels of Pivotalness*

This paper will investigate the nature of Iraq as a pivotal state in the Middle East. The pivotal affects of the Gulf War and of the fall of Iraq on some of the remittance sensitive (RS) countries and some of the oil sensitive (OS) countries in the Arab World will be analysed.

It is important to clarify what are pivotal states.[1] Often the description of these countries revolves around their future importance. Kennedy calls them hot spots "that could not only determine the fate of [their] region but also effect international stability."[2] Could Iraq be a good example of a country that proved it was a pivotal state through its collapse? Pivotal states are those states that are regionally and globally vital. Events that change these states often have significant effects on other states. That is, shocks to these countries can cause something similar to the old "domino theory," but in more subtle and complex ways.[3] For the Middle East the pivotal states are often considered to be Egypt, Turkey and Algeria.[4] However, even though Iraq has a much lower population than these states it could be considered a pivotal state – as should Saudi Arabia. But then why should such states be considered pivotal or not? One could set up general degrees such as slightly pivotal, moderately pivotal and highly pivotal. Slightly pivotal states could effect strongly in the short-term neighbouring countries and send some minor shockwaves beyond its region.[5] A moderately pivotal state could effect strongly in the medium run regional states and send some significant, but short to medium run, shock waves outside of its region.[6] A highly pivotal state could have extreme and long-term effects on its region and send strong, and long term, shock waves well beyond its region. These are three general states of pivotalness.[7] However, the pivotalness of a state can be seen as a continuum. There are infinite degrees of pivotalness. Politically, via the Iran-Iraq war, the invasion of Kuwait, the Gulf War, and the subsequent sanctions period, Iraq has shown to politically and militarily moderately pivotal.

In this paper the economic pivotalness of Iraq will be the focus. There will be commentary on the political fallout of the war, but a full analysis of political pivotalness is not within the scope of this paper. It is understood that there have been complex interactions of economics and politics, and significant shifts in intrastate and interstate relations in the Middle East due to the Gulf War. For reasons of consistency, focus and compactness of argument these issues will be excluded from this work, but will be covered in a future publication.

Iraq has clearly proven to be a moderately economically pivotal state. It had strong effects on the MENA region in the medium run and sent some short to medium run economic shock waves outside of its region. Part of the reason why it was moderate rather than slightly is the importance Iraq had in the regional labour markets, and international oil and financial markets. It is not highly pivotal because even in the MENA region most of the states (outside of Iraq), excepting Yemen and the Occupied Territories, have nearly fully recovered from the effects of the war and the collapse of Iraq by 1998. Its importance in the oil markets gained it a moderate stature because of the shock waves it sent out from the region. Iraq had about 10% of the world's reserves in 1989. International financial markets were affected in the medium run because of the liquidation of Gulf Assets and the cross-border movement of funds to pay for the war. However, compared to the size of the world foreign exchange and capital markets these movements were relatively small. They were smaller than the billions in assets held by Arabs outside of the region.

B. Trade and Investment

The MENA region takes up a lot of ink in the press. That the MENA region is important strategically and economically for both the West and the East is undeniable. However, economically, politically and demographically, its importance often seems exaggerated. It is important to put things in perspective. If the Gulf War were in China then we would have a more highly economically pivotal war. China's GNP was about $1.2 billion in 1989. If such a war were in Japan then clearly we would have one of the extremes of economic pivotalness. The Japanese GNP was about $3 trillion+ in 1989. Japan and China were also significantly more connected to world trade markets than Iraq was. A collapse of Japan or China to the extent that Iraq collapsed during and after the Gulf War would have been catastrophic for the world economy. Iraq's GNP in 1989 was only about $66 billion.[8] This was about the same as the gross state product of Kentucky in the USA.[9] Internationally it was on par with Poland – that is pre-reform Poland before the fall of the East Bloc.

When it comes to the Middle East and West Asia's[10] (MENA plus some minor changes) position in FDI stocks and flows, both inward and outward the regions were a tiny part of the whole world's FDI in 1990. FDI inflows to North Africa and West Asia were $886 million and $1.9 billion respectively.[11] This was about 1.7% of the World FDI inflows of $160 billion. FDI outflows to the two regions were $138 million and $332 million. This was about .2% of the FDI outflows for the world of $200 billion. FDI outward stock of the two regions were $882 million and $6 billion. This was about .4% of the FDI outward stock for the world of $1.7 trillion. FDI inward stock was $15 billion and $48 billion for North Africa and Western Asia. This was about 3.6% of the total world inward stock of $1.73 trillion.[12] It seems investors had gone elsewhere. Because of this the ripple effects from the Gulf War in FDI circles were subdued.

For FDI the EU, North America and other parts of Asia are the pivotal regions. In 1990 FDI inflows were $97.4 billion to the EU, $55 billion to North America, and $19.8 billion to South, Southeast and East Asia. In 1990 FDI inward stocks were $227 billion in the EU, $250 billion in North America, and $64 billion in South, Southeast and East Asia.[13]

The value of oil exports from Iraq in 1989 was about $15.5 billion out of total OPEC exports of $107.4 billion.[14] The exports of the United Kingdom were around $155 billion in 1989,[15] more than all oil exports from OPEC. The exports from the State of Louisiana in the USA were about the same as the oil exports from Iraq in 1990.[16] The combined exports of California,[17] Florida, New York , and Texas were a bit more than the value of all OPEC oil exports in 1989.[18] The only things Iraq seemed to be "world class"[19] in were oil reserves[20] (10% of the world total), military personnel (1 million), and military expenditure ($12 billion). It was the largest importer of military weapons in the world for most of the 1980s.[21]In 1989 Iraq had just 18 million persons in a world with about 5.2 billion.

Demographically, Iraq was about on par with the population of Seoul, South Korea in 1990.[22] In 1989 the Middle East and North Africa was just 5.5% of the world's population. China had 20%.

The entire Middle East's share in world merchandise exports was just 5.3% in 1985 and 2.9% in 1995.[23] Exports from Asia increased from 20.8% to 28.6% during the same time period. Exports from Western Europe and North America thoroughly dominated world markets at 56.1% in 1985 and 60.7% in 1995. Overall fuels exports as a percentage of all exports dropped from 18.2% to 7.1%.[24]

The share of all world merchandise imports into the Middle East dropped from 4.5% in 1985 to 2.6% in 1995. The Middle East's shares of world exports and imports were about 11% and 5% respectively, in 1980. In world trade, one of the major linkages that would give leverage to a region for its pivotalness, the Middle East has been a declining player.

These small and declining percentages belie the fact that the MENA region has been highly dependent on international markets. On average the MENA countries trade/GDP ratio from 1976-80 was 84.2, from 1981-8 it was 72.8, from 1986-1990 it was 60, and from 1991-1995 it increased again to 70.5. Those countries in the region with the highest trade to GDP ratios were most often the GCC states, that is, oil exporting and oil-dependent states.[25] Even the "openness" of these economies seems to be determined by oil revenues over time. The times when the oil revenues were in decline were also the times when the "openness" of the MENA economies was in decline. The "openness" of the MENA economies is also determined by the importation of foodstuffs and manufactured goods. For the entire MENA regions from 1990- 1994 mineral fuels accounted for 68% of all exports, and manufactured goods and food accounted for 67.8% and 14.7% of imports respectively.[26] These ratios, however, are more a reflection of relative resource allocations, such as high oil reserves, low water and human capital and skills reserves, as well as low technological capital stock, than on the "openness" of the region to international markets. Because of the relatively high tariff barriers this "openness" is a false one based on the weights and importance of these three trading items. Tariffs and other non-tariff barriers have been declining recently, but still there is a long way to go toward real openness and real competitiveness. On the other side of the trade equation, the MENA region has also been a marked failure in its attempts to increase non-oil, manufactured exports. On per capita terms East Asia exports of manufactures increased from $1,000 in 1980 to $3,500 in 1992. The GCC remained at around $500 from 1980 to

1992, with a short upward swing from 1980 to 1982. Non-GCC MENA barely shows up on the chart.[27]

Being a trade-dependent economy may be good if trade is diversified and competitive, and the domestic economy is on solid ground and it also diversified and dynamically disposed to respond properly to changes in the international and domestic environments. Most of the MENA economies have shown little solidity or resiliency in responding to sharp changes in the international and domestic environments until just recently. Many of these MENA states have been protecting industries and industrialists that were uncompetitive for reasons of politics, cronyism and just plain corruption. What the Middle East has been lacking most of all were sustainable economic development policies and good economic leadership.

Iraq was one of these trade-dependent Middle Eastern states. Before the war it imported about 70% of its food needs, most of its weapons and manufactured products, and almost all of its technology. Its exports were mostly oil. The import trade of Iraq was dominated by the industrialized countries, which were around $6.6 billion in 1989.[28] Total imports from developing countries were $3.25 billion in 1989.[29] Trade with European developing economies in 1989 was in the $2 billion range with Turkey trading the most. Exports from Iraq to Turkey, mostly oil, dropped from $1.5 billion in 1988 to $951 million in 1990 and then to almost nil until the oil-for-food deal went through. Now most of the oil being exported from Iraq under this deal goes through Turkey. Turkey's exports to Iraq were about $1 billion in 1988. The dropped by around 50% in 1989, another 50% in 1990, and still another 50% to $145 million in 1991. They remained at around $100 to $200 million until 1996.[30] Even though data are not yet available for the recent trade between the two countries one can easily conclude that it has increased since the oil started to flow out of Iraq into Turkey under the "oil-for-food" deals. After the war Turkey, along with Jordan, handled most of Iraq's legal, and possibly also illegal, trade during the time of sanctions. Iran and the UAE do not show up in the official statistics, but their illegal smuggling activities, especially of oil from Iraq and food and other items into Iraq, are well known.

Before the war, imports from the Middle East to Iraq were a relatively paltry $1.1 billion in 1989 and $824 million in 1990. Kuwait, Jordan, Saudi Arabia, and Egypt were the ones who lost the most trade. In 1989 Egypt's exports were just $69 million – out of its total exports of over $3 billion. In 1989 Iraqi imports from Kuwait were $426 million, from

Saudi Arabia $180 million, and from the UAE $101 million. These are a pittance in comparison to these countries total exports in that year. Nevertheless, Kuwait was Iraq's largest Arab trading partner before the Iraqi invasion of Kuwait. It exported about $430 million in goods to Iraq in 1989.[31] After the invasion by Iraq, Kuwait had shown no interest in resuming trade with its nemesis.

The country in the region[32] that may have been affected the most by a cutting off of trade with Iraq was Jordan. Jordan's total worldwide exports were just $1 billion 1990. $179 million went to Iraq. In 1989 they sent $233 million to Iraq. [Turkey had $236 million in exports to Iraq in 1990, but out of a total of $13 billion.][33] After the war Iraq's "legal" trade with the Middle East almost ceased, except with Jordan and Turkey. Exports from Iraq to Jordan were $374 million in 1990, $251 million in 1991, and $405 million in 1993. Imports from Jordan to Iraq were $233 million in 1989, $196 million in 1990, $79 million in 1992, and $124 million in 1993. By 1995 exports from Jordan to Iraq increased to $300 million, and imports increased to $411 million.

Syria and Iran, although neighbours of Iraq, had, predictably, no real legal trade with the country. These two countries had been at odds, and at war in the case of Iran, with Iraq for years. Economic contacts between these two countries and Iraq had been pretty much severed more than a decade before the Gulf War.

Total imports from industrialized countries to Iraq dropped from $6.6 billion in 1989 to $114 million in 1991. They have been at low levels since the war. In 1996 imports from industrialized countries into Iraq were officially $85 million. Even the "oil-for-food" deals had not increased them to pre-war levels. Imports from non-oil developing countries dropped from $3.3 billion in 1989 to $356 million in 1993.[34] By 1996 they were just $142 million.[35] Iraq's imports from the entire world dropped by 93.4% in 1991. The largest drop was from the Western Hemisphere, 99%. Imports from the Middle East dropped 82% in 1991, 47% in 1992, increased by 57% in 1992, but dropped by 44% in 1994. Iraqi exports to the entire world dropped by 95% in 1991.[36]

Part of the economic pivotalness of Iraq due to the Gulf War is based on its invasion of Kuwait. Kuwait, which disappeared from the map for a little while, was an important trade player. In 1989 it had $11.5 billion in exports and $6.3 billion in imports. By 1991 the figures were $1.1 billion and $4.8 billion respectively. Imports in 1990 were only $4 billion. Exports in 1990 dropped to $8 billion. Imports from industrialized countries dropped from $4 billion in 1989 to $2.5 billion in 1990. By 1992, however, they were over $5 billion. Imports from the Middle East dropped from $829 million in 1989 to $12 million in 1990. This trade did not start to fully recover until 1993. In 1994 they were $882 million, but by 1996 they dropped to $87 million. Imports from all developing countries dropped from $2.5 billion in 1989 to $417 million in 1991. "Full recovery" took until 1994. Kuwait's exports to the world dropped by 91.4% in 1991. Its imports dropped by only 14% in 1990. But they dropped by 31% in 1991.[37]

Clearly these full-year figures for 1990 and 1991 mask the full short-term shocks to trade. There must have been considerable periods of time in late 1990 and early 1991 when Kuwaiti trade ceased entirely. It was not until 1993-1994 that significant imports from other Arab countries started again. These were mostly from the UAE and Saudi Arabia. Trade with the other Arab countries remains tiny. This is, of course, fitting with Kuwait's trade history. Most of its imports before the war, 70-80%, had been from the Industrialized countries or with developing countries outside the Middle East. The pivotal nature of the merchandise trade of Iraq and Kuwait with the Middle East seems to have no real foundation, except for trade between Jordan and Iraq and trade between Iraq and Kuwait, which is clearly now a moot point. The trade shock waves sent out when the initial invasion of Kuwait happened, and then again with the Gulf War, affected the industrialized countries and some Eastern European countries the most. These trade shock waves proved to be short term because of the liberation of Kuwait, and the small proportion of all trade of the industrialized countries and of Eastern Europe that Kuwait and Iraq represented.

C. Oil, The Military, Economic Stagnation, and Vulnerability

The economic effects of the long term drop in the real price of oil (combined with the fall of the volume of oil exports from MENA producers) from 1980 to 1988 had a much greater effect than the Gulf war on investment, growth and development in the Middle East. Kuwaiti oil export revenues dropped from $18 billion in 1980 to $6.2 billion in 1988. Libyan oil export revenues dropped from $21 billion in 1980 to $5 billion in 1988. Saudi Arabian oil export revenues dropped from $106 billion in 1980 to $21 billion in 1988. Oil export revenues from the UAE dropped from $20 billion in 1980 to $7.3 billion in 1988. Iraq's[38] oil revenues dropped from $26 billion in 1980 to $15 billion in 1989. Iran's dropped from $19 billion in 1979 to $12 billion in 1989.[39] If we added up these revenue losses over this 9-year period the overall financial losses and the multiplier effects on these economies would far outweigh the costs of the Gulf War to these oil-exporting countries.

The economy of the MENA region is mostly built on oil, either directly or indirectly. The following chart from the World Bank gives us an indication of the direct power oil and the oil trade have had over many of the economies of the Middle East:[40]

Country/ Region	Trade in fuels as % of GDP in 1984	Trade in fuels as % of GDP in 1993	Share of oil in total exports in 1993
GCC	35	35	95
Bahrain	72	67	90
Kuwait	47	40	80
Oman	47	30	95
Saudi Arabia	37	33	99
UAE	39	40	95
Others in MENA	10	10	85
Algeria	22	20	85
Egypt	6	7	45
Iran	7	15	90
Iraq	9	23.5	90
Syria	7	14	42
Total	20	30	90
MENA Exports (billions USD)	100	110	80

Unfortunately, during the 1980s the spending sprees of the GCC states were beginning to be firmly in the non-sustainable category. Some of the oil states, which had been awash in petrodollars, were now borrowing on the international financial markets. The average annual real GDP growth of GCC countries from 1980-85 was -21.36%, from 1985-89 it was -3.79%.[41]

Intimately connected with the shocks to the Middle East due to the Gulf War is the idea of the "Dutch Disease" or the "Arab Syndrome."[42] As oil money and remittance money pour in a country often becomes too reliant on these unstable sources of income. Economic incentives are often distorted away from balanced and sustainable development. Economic security can sometimes be weakened in an ostensibly paradoxical manner. More money does not always mean better economic development. More weapons do not necessarily mean more defensive capabilities. More buildings and infrastructure do not necessarily mean more development. During the "holiday period" in the 1970s and very early 1980s government spending skyrocketed.

Currencies appreciated well over what they would have been without the dollar-denominated oil exports. Agriculture and industrialization were neglected, with few exceptions. Cheap imports took the place of indigenous production. Consumption and income had little to do with production and productivity – except in the production of one major commodity. Economic diversification was postponed. Non-tradables took on a high, and distorted, percentage of the economies. Wages increased drastically without concomitant increases in overall productivity. There were massive expenditures on public works projects, infrastructure, and building. Subsidies and grants were handed out without any real long-term perspective in mind. Some clearly uneconomic projects, like the Saudi wheat fields, were pushed through without much thought of their financial sustainability. Budgets could be balanced when the oil price was high. When the price of oil fluctuated wildly so did the budget balances. Massive amounts were spent on militaries, which proved more often than not to be sinkholes for oil revenues rather than bastions of national security.

Such overmilitarism is quite clearly the case in countries such as Saudi Arabia, the U.A.E., and Kuwait. For Kuwait the massive expenditures put into the military before the invasion by Iraq proved useless. Yet, from 1992-1994 they spent $25.6 billion on the military.[43] During 1990 and 1991 they spent close to $30 billion.[44] From 1990-1994 they spent $55 billion. Saudi Arabia had spent some $131 billion on the military from 1990-1994. Close to $73 billion had been spent from 1992-1994.[45] The U.A.E. had spent some $13.6 billion since 1990, and almost $6.1 billion since 1992.[46] In 1995 Saudi Arabia spent over $13 billion, Kuwait $3.2 billion, the UAE around $2 billion, and even Oman spent $1.8 billion. Arms imports into Saudi Arabia from 1990-1994 were $28 billion, into Kuwait about $2.8 billion, and into the UAE about $2.8 billion. Arms imports into Saudi Arabia in this period were about 25% of all imports into the country.

What might be the motivations behind such huge military expenditures by the Gulf States when the Gulf War showed that they could not defend themselves and that they needed outside interventions to protect themselves? It seems to be a mixture of the end of illusions and the beginning of hope. These countries live in a dangerous neighbourhood. They also live near a militaristic country that they helped to destroy, Iraq.

Logically, they surely consider, some day the resentments held toward them will cause another war with Iraq. They also have to keep an eye, and a threat, directed toward Iran. The GCC still considers Iran to be a major threat to security and stability – and for good reason. There may be a short-term thaw in relations between the GCC and Iran recently, but this could freeze up fairly quickly with a change in administration in Iran or further attempts by the Iranians to destabilize the GCC. Then again, GCC-Iran relations improve for years to come. However, the GCC countries are hardly convinced on this one.

The GCC countries may be hoping that someday they could defend themselves in a war similar to the one that happened in 1991. There have been indications of better training of troops, improvement in military infrastructure, etc. These, of course, lead to a heightened capacity for national defence. Even these improvements and significant arms imports may not be enough. The larger hope may be that with the right quality and quantity of domestic military personnel, equipment, hardware, software, and infrastructure combined with the threat of the military of the USA pouring in to help them it will be less likely that others would want to attack them. Much of this weaponry may be considered as pre-positioned, or potentially there for pre-positioning, for use by U.S. or other Western forces. The defence of tiny Kuwait is still very much dependent on the looming power of the United States keeping Kuwait's more powerful neighbours away. A country such as Kuwait with such a small population and a tiny military compared to Iraq would not have much of a chance in another Iraqi invasion without help from the outside – unless of course they had non-conventional weapons and Iraq did not. Then the military scenarios would change entirely.

The GCC countries also see internal threats to their security and stability. The bombings in Saudi Arabia, and the fires, riots and bombings in Bahrain, are some indication that these perceived threats are real. The now-famous Osama Bin-Laden's policy of trying to rid Saudi Arabia of American troops is another result of the Gulf War. The troops would not be there if the Gulf War had not happened. Bin laden may also have remained an obscure personality if he had not made the USA his bogeyman.

The Gulf War may have also compounded and magnified the significant internal political problems facing Saudi Arabia. This is a difficult country to understand. It is often secretive and unpredictable, somewhat like the former USSR, but different, obviously, in many ways. In any case, bombings and mass arrests can lead one to conclude that there are some serious problems. Other indications are also present, such as the political tensions not only in the Shi'a East, but also the very conservative Nejad.

Usually, weapons purchases and military expenditures are based on perceived and actual threats to a country. There are other reasons, such as pork-barrel politics, political inertia, and corruption, but these seem to be not the most important factors determining military expenditures in the GCC – although they seem to be still important influences on what is bought and when.

Even with the burst in military expenditures in the immediate post-war environment, military expenditures, in nominal dollar terms, as a percentage of GDP, and per capita, have dropped for all of the GCC countries excepting Kuwait between 1985 and 1995.[47] This is a reaction to the end of the Iran-Iraq War. This may also be a result of the realization that such wild spending sprees simply cannot add up to solvent (or even fully defensible) countries. It may also be that some of the defence expenditures are buried elsewhere in the budgets.

Whether we are talking about the 1980s or the 1990s the GCC countries are hardly in a position to defend themselves even with such expenditures. They must still rely on the United States.[48] As with their expenditures on construction and other government projects in an earlier time, the GCC has been spending money, but has not been planning for a sustainable, or a defensible, future. Such military spending is not compatible with the vulnerable economic environment of the countries, especially considering their reliance on a commodity that has such high price and revenue volatility – oil.

The stagnation of economic growth in real terms in the Arab world has a lot to do with the pivotalness of the Gulf War and the Fall of Iraq. Such stagnation lent weakness and inflexibility to many Arab economies. If we were to look at a chart of real per capita GDP for the Arab countries from 1970 to 1996 there would be a steady growth from 1970 to 1980 and then a rapid decline from 1980 to 1990. There is a small upswing in 1991, the time of the Gulf War, followed by more stagnation. The real GDP per capita of Arab countries in 1996 was about the same as it was in 1972. A major determinant of real GDP per capita seems to be the real oil price.[49] As the real oil price drops, so does real GDP.[50] The real GDP of the Arab world has been on average (over time and across countries) stagnant over the time period 1972-1996 – with just brief bursts of positive growth during the time periods between the 1973 and 1979-80 oil shocks. Comparatively, the Asia region has seen real GDP increase by 250% and all developing countries on average have seen an increase of over 100%.[51] For the MENA region, if we look at the long-term trends in macrodata, the period of the Gulf War hardly seems to matter in comparison to the period of the slide in the price of oil.

Since the early 1980s, there has been a sharp reduction in the real price of oil. The spill over effects from the oil to the non-oil economies worked in a contradictory manner at a time when labour demand subsided in the region's major external markets. Concurrently, the return from earlier investment surge declined rapidly, leaving many non-oil Arab economies with a growing problem of external indebtedness, financial imbalances, and an aging capital stock.[52]

Investment performance[53] rapidly fell in the Arab countries in the 1980s.[54] Investment was 32% of GDP in 1978. It dropped to about 20% in the mid-1980s and remained thereabouts. The period just after the war saw an increase in investment to about 22% of GDP. This could be due to the rebuilding of Kuwait and the new investments in Saudi Arabia and the UAE directed toward economic diversification. Still this is hardly to be compared with the drop from close to 30% in 1980 to 21% in 1989. There were further drops in 1993-1996 leading one to conclude that the post-war investment "boomlet" was over relative to GDP. As the Arab countries saw their investment as a percentage of GDP fall the Asia region saw it increase from 22% in 1986 to 31% in 1996. Comparatively, all developing countries on average increased their investments as a percentage of GDP from about 20% in 1987 to 26% in 1996.[55] There was a peak followed by a temporary decline for both Asia and all developing countries on average in 1991 that may have been the result of the Gulf War, but this was a short-lived decline.

On average total factor productivity has also been in decline for most Arab countries since the end of the short-lived oil boom.[56] The only countries to show positive growth in total factor productivity on average during the entire period 1971-1996 were Egypt, Syria, Oman, and Tunisia. The total factor productivity growth in these countries was positive, but hardly impressive.[57]

The impressive working paper by Bisat, El-Erain et al comes to some thoughtful conclusions.[58] Three factors emerge from the analysis. First, that the investment process was not accompanied by sufficient improvements in total factor productivity. Second, that the disappointing evolution of total factor productivity was compounded [in the period after the fall of the oil prices] by declining investment rates. Third, that the funding of investment activities was overly dependent on volatile external sources [that is, oil].

The Middle East was in the main, an economy in a moderate free fall (or at best stagnation) in the time period 1980-1990. Even the diversified economies like Egypt, Syria and Iraq were heavily dependent either directly or indirectly on oil revenues, or income associated with other countries oil revenues. If the Middle East economy was built on solid ground then it could have withstood the shock of the war much better. However, it was built too much on oil and the military, and too little on diversified development, human capital formation, technological change, education, and solid and strong intra-Middle East and international trade patterns.

Looking in the longer run we can see that the average real GDP growth rate per annum in the MENA region was 2% in the period 1980-89 and 3.6% in the period 1990-99 (est).[59] The real GDP growth rates of the region were 4.2% in 1990, 3.9% in 1991, and 5.6% in 1992. These are not the real GDP growth rates of a region that as a whole is severely, and reparably, damaged by the Gulf War.

D. Recent Signs of Recovery

1996 was a good year and showed that possibly the medium term effects of the war were winding down. The gross domestic product (GDP) of the ESCWA region, excluding Iraq, is estimated to have registered a 4.8% growth rate in 1996, compared with 2.2% in 1995. The region's GDP per capita registered a 2.1% growth rate, the first positive growth recorded in several years. This was mainly due to the performance of the economies of the Gulf Cooperation Council (GCC) countries. The GDP of the GCC countries as a group is estimated to have grown by 4.9% in 1996, more than four times the 1.1% growth rate is achieved the previous year. Among the regions more diversifies economies, only Egypt and the Syrian Arab Republic achieved GDP growth rates in 1996 that were higher that there 1995 respective levels.[60]

The main reason for this increase seems to have been the increase in the price of oil and the increase in oil revenues by almost $17 billion to $96.5 billion.[61] These were the highest oil revenues since 1985.[62] Even so, unemployment has remained a major problem in the region. The worst hit are still Yemenis and the Palestinians, erstwhile supporters of Saddam Hussein. Debt rescheduling for Yemen and Jordan has helped take the economic pressures off these countries, but the labour problem still persists.[63] The demise of the peace process, Israel's attacks on Lebanon, closures in the Occupied Territories, sanctions on Iraq, and the slow pace of reforms have tended to slow the post-war recovery.[64] With attempts at diversification the GCC's GDP is still 35-40% dependent on oil. Oil revenues still account for about 80% of government revenues, and about 80-90% of export revenues. For Egypt, Yemen and Syria oil revenues have respectable percentages in their GDPs, government revenues and export revenues.[65] Hence, even in the more diversified economies a shift in the price of oil can have significant impacts on economic growth. The long-term structural economic and political issues of the MENA region are still in need of reform, repair, and reorganization.

Now that we have put some qualifications and limits on the pivotalness of Iraq, mostly from the macro side, let us now turn to a more detailed review of the pivotal effects of the Gulf War and the collapse of Iraq on remittance sensitive and oil sensitive countries. Along with the description of the effects of these shocks to the chosen economies will be analyses of why one country seems to have recovered fully and another has not.

Pivotal Effects on Remittance Sensitive (RS) Countries: Case Studies

A. Labor Gets Hammered

For remittance sensitive countries (RS) the export of labour is seen as a way to vent surplus labour and to get hard currency flowing into the country. It is also a way for the unemployable and women, children and the elderly or infirm back home to be taken care of. Instead of investing in productive employment back home remittance labour is sent abroad. There is a brain and skill drain.

Remittances like oil and because they are linked to oil, can be a highly unstable source of income. When this income is closed off then there are major shocks to the RS economies, i.e., in Jordan, Yemen, Egypt, and the Occupied Territories. These shocks can also be translated into societal shocks, i.e., civil strife in Yemen and the Occupied Territories after the Gulf War. Remittance money can also be seen as a windfall. Windfall moneys can lead to relative revaluations of currencies of the RS countries. This can lead to an increase in relatively cheap imports, a neglect of agriculture, and a loss of incentives to invest in manufacturing. Add to this that most of the remittance money in many of these countries went to buying consumer goods, land, or small "garage" businesses. We can see that the benefits of remittance moneys exist, but these benefits are often minimized. Furthermore, if the remittances are "wasted" then when the remittances eventually dry up these countries will be almost back to step one.

Yemen is a case in point on this. The Yemenis were thrown out of Saudi Arabia after the war. This was a major shock to the Yemeni economy and its society. Not only was the expected money not to be there, but also many of the expatriate Yemenis had not been to Yemen for years, if ever. They considered the GCC States, especially Saudi Arabia, as a place of permanent residence. Saudi Arabia did not even require work permits or visas for Yemenis up to the time of the invasion of Kuwait. To be fair, Yemen was in the process of reuniting its country as the Gulf crisis was in effect. This is a very costly and risky process under any circumstances. The Yemenis were doubly hammered.

The Jordanian/Palestinians and Palestinians of the Occupied Territories found themselves in a similar position. They had established themselves in almost a permanent fashion in Kuwait. When they were ejected many of them lost savings, stores, financial and physical assets, housing, and more. Their return to Jordan and the Occupied Territories was not at all that smooth, either economically or socially. The Intifada had only ended just recently before the eruption of the war. The Palestinians in the Occupied Territories were shattered by the Gulf War. Many of the Palestinians throughout the Middle East saw remittance income and other support cut off during and after the Gulf Crises of 1990-1991. The Yemenis and the Palestinians had years of collecting remittance funds. It seems that much of this money went to things other than economic development. Both peoples were hardly prepared financially or otherwise for the consequences of the Gulf War.

The reliance of many of the Arab countries on remittances can be seen in the following chart for total cumulative remittances by country from 1973 to 1989.[66]

Country	Net Worker's Remittances (NWR)/$billion	NWY/Imports	NWR/GNP
Arab Middle East	21.457	5.6	2.0
Bahrain	(2.18)	(5.1)	(6.1)
Iraq	0.004	n/a	n/a
Jordan	10.14	29.2	20.3
Lebanon	n/a	n/a	n/a
Oman	(6.53)	(22.7)	(7.8)
Syria	4.535	9.1	2.2
Yemen A.R.	10.836	54.6	18.0
Yemen P.D.R.	4.653	38.2	34.9
Arab Africa	65.576	16.9	4.4
Algeria	4.648	3.4	0.8
Egypt	38.85	32.5	10.8
Mauritania	(0.4)	(11.0)	(3.5)
Morocco	14.64	24.2	6.0
Somalia	0.45	11.1	1.8
Sudan	2.51	13.9	1.8
Tunisia	4.88	10.8	4.1
Total	87.00	11.3	3.4

Quite clearly the countries that relied most on remittances were Jordan, the two Yemens, Morocco and Egypt.[67] There weren't that many Moroccans in Iraq and Kuwait during the 1980s and before August 1990, so we can rule out the direct labour market pivot effects on them. So the countries whose labour we would expect to be affected most from the fall of Iraq would be Jordan, the Yemens and Egypt. Their remittance workers tied their future to work abroad, mostly in the Gulf, and many of them were to be found in Iraq and Kuwait. So any massive shock to these two countries would transfer to the labour markets of these three countries. There were also citizens of other countries, especially in Asia, who also were effected by the crisis. The following charts indicate how many persons were in Iraq and Kuwait from various Arab and Asian countries just before the invasion of Kuwait by Iraq.[68]

This totals out at close to 2 million economically active "guest workers" plus 713,000 or so of their dependents. Both groups were directly, and sometimes brutally, affected by the crisis. It may be very surprising to some how many dependents were involved. The Jordanians, read that mostly Palestinians, had established families and businesses while in Kuwait. That they seemed to be the most settled of these groups is shown by the percentages of their populations that were dependent in both countries. In Iraq 81% of the Jordanian/Palestinians were dependents. In Kuwait the figure was 78%. Egyptians did not bring many dependents with them, but they had the highest proportion of the population of guest workers plus dependents in the two countries, about 1,115 million people or about 42% of the total "guest" populations. The next largest group was the Jordanian/Palestinians at 537,000 or 20%. Then came the Sudanese, at 115,000 or 4.3%. All three of these countries had, and still have, economies struggling to develop. The total Arab presence in the two countries at the time of the crisis was closes to 2 million persons – about half the population of Libya at the time.

Many of them stayed even after the crisis hit with the Iraqi invasion of Kuwait. After two months there were still 795,000 Egyptians, 317,000 Jordanian/Palestinians and 90,000 Sudanese in Iraq and Kuwait. Most of the remaining Sudanese and Egyptians were in Iraq (740,000 and 80,000 respectively), whereas most of the Jordanian/Palestinians were in Kuwait (300,000).[69] By the end of 1990 most had left because it was clear that the situation would become very deadly very soon. Others also left the nearby Gulf States, either voluntarily for fear of their safety, or by force, as was the case with the Yemenis. 880,000. Yemenis[70] were essentially thrown out of the GCC states, mostly from Saudi Arabia and the U.A.E., because of Yemen's alleged support of Saddam Hussein's invasion of Kuwait.

For the non-oil Arab world, already facing employment crises back home, these were difficult times. Over 700,000 returned to Egypt, while Jordan saw 220,000 return, Lebanon had 60,000 return, Sudan saw 30,000 return, Syria had to accommodate 110,000 returnees, most of whom fled or were thrown out of Kuwait (by the Iraqis when Kuwait was "part of Iraq") due to Syria's bellicose stand toward Saddam Hussein.[71] For Egypt this was about 7% of its economically active population and for Jordan this was an astonishing 11.6% of its economically active population.[72] Yemen's population increased by 8% with its returnees and unemployment in increased by over 15 percentage points. Furthermore:

> Like those Kuwaitis who stayed behind, many Palestinians had their property confiscated and bank savings rendered almost worthless when Iraq converted Kuwait dinars into the much over-valued Iraqi dinars.

> Banking sources from Kuwait estimate the Palestinians lost between $4 to $5 billion in the value of their deposits in Kuwait banks. When this value is added to the depreciation in the value of properties, securities, stocks and other assets owned by Palestinians in Kuwait, total economic losses for Palestinians from Kuwait are conservatively estimated at $10-$12 billion.[73]

The countries that seemed to be most affected by the crisis in the medium and long runs were Jordan, the Occupied Territories, Egypt, Yemen, and Syria. That is, those that were to feel the brunt of the moderate pivotalness of Iraq.[74] Jordan, Syria, Yemen, Egypt, and the Occupied Territories-Palestine all have excess labour (read that as high underemployment and/or unemployment rates) and all rely on remittances as a major source of foreign exchange. The following chart from Sadek Wahba shows remittances as a percentage of merchandise exports for these countries.[75]

Year	Gaza and West Bank	Jordan	Syria	Egypt	Yemen
1988	58	79	27	136	70
1989	88	51	13	113	40
1990	55	n/a	9	119	n/a
1991	60	n/a	n/a	n/a	n/a

Importantly, there were significant differences (between those who seemed to have supported Saddam Hussein and those who joined the multinational coalition) in the treatment by the GCC states and by others involved in the multinational coalition.

> Workers from countries that were perceived to have sided with Iraq during the crisis (Jordan, Sudan, Yemen and the Palestinians) have typically been denied entry to GCC labour markets. Replacement workers were hired from the Arab countries that were members of the alliance against Iraq, particularly Egypt, Lebanon, and the Syrian Arab Republic. For example, following the expulsion of Yemeni workers during the Gulf Crisis, over one million Egyptians received Saudi work permits as a reward for their government's anti-Iraq positions. Similarly, the Kuwait labour market attracted workers from Egypt, Lebanon and the Syrian Arab Republic to replace the Arab workers who, in the aftermath of Kuwait's liberation, had lost their jobs because of their citizenship.[76]

This different treatment economically, of course, was mirrored in political change. There was a political cooling, and in some cases freezing, between the GCC states and the states (and the Palestinians as a group) that seemed to have supported Saddam Hussein. In some cases things have thawed slightly, such as relations with Jordan. In other cases the freeze is still very much on, like the Saudi relations with Yemen. The Palestinians are still viewed with considerable suspicion, and sometimes-outright hostility, by the Kuwaitis. The GCC states have been slow to bring back the economic and political support they gave the Palestinians before the Gulf War. They have also been slow to reemploy them or pay them back their wages, bank accounts and other assets lost because of the conflict. The Jordanians, Palestinians and Yemenis lost considerable political as well as financial and economic capital because of their alleged support of Iraq.

B. Palestinians[77] *(referencing the economies of the West Bank and Gaza)*[78]

The Gulf War seriously damaged the Palestinians.[79] There is talk now of their being rehired to some extent, albeit in very small groups in Kuwait, but in Iraq they lost out totally, as did everyone else. Other Arab labour and Asian labour are replacing most of them in Kuwait. Other GCC countries have not treated them as harshly, but have not exactly placed the red carpet out for them. Since the Gulf Crisis workers remittances to Egypt increased to $5.6 billion in 1993 from about $3.293 billion in 1989.[80] Syrian remittances went up from $350 million in 1991 to $600 million in 1993.[81] These two countries supported the multinational coalition against Iraq. Their labour has a warmer welcome mat out in the GCC than do the Palestinians. Any increase in the current remittances going to Egypt and Syria may have gone to Palestinians and Jordanians if they had not supported Saddam Hussein, [Sudanese remittances increased from $45.4 million in 1991 to $123.7 million in 1992,[82] but it is nearly impossible, given the state of the country, to figure out where, why and how this happened]. Palestinians had a rough time of it, especially after the liberation of Kuwait. According to Ann Lesch, in 1991:

> In addition to the pervasive fears of arrest, which keeps many Palestinians close to their homes, the government has instituted widespread restrictions on the Palestinian community. Some appear designed to punish alleged collaborators during the occupation and others appear intended to pressure Palestinians to leave the country. Virtually no Palestinians have been reinstated in their posts in government, including teaching. Civil servants

> have lived virtually without pay since August 1990, aside from those who received the now-worthless Iraqi dinars during the fall. They lack the cash to meet their daily needs, much less pay rent. Moreover, they fear that the government is recruiting Egyptian teachers to replace Palestinians. Such measures appear to be an explicit collective punishment for the fact that some Palestinians continued to work during the Iraqi occupation.[83]

They lost billions in potential remittances[84] that would have been sent back to the Occupied Territories and Jordan (or elsewhere) to support their families. Nazem Abdalla estimates that they may have also lost from $1.4 to $1.5 billion in deposits in Kuwait banks.[85] It is unknown how much they may have lost in Iraq in bank accounts. Bishara Bahbah reported in 1990 that "...[R]emittances from individual Palestinians living in Kuwait to their relatives in the Occupied Territories have completely stopped. They were estimated at $120 million in 1989.[86]

Total remittances to Palestinians in Kuwait could have been as much as $550 million per year. This, of course, had the potential to increase over time due to either inflation or the increase in the real demand for Palestinian labour. This, unfortunately for the Palestinians, is a counter-factual world. This $550 million per year figure is taking Bahbah's estimate of $5000 per labourer in Kuwait in 1989[87] and Nazem Abdalla's estimate of 110,000 workers who were Palestinians.[88] Nazem Abdalla also estimates that there were some 5,000 Palestinians in Iraq before the war.[89] If we assume a $3,000-4,000 average income then that means an opportunity loss of some $15-20 million per year - not including the other lost assets and their revenues. There were also partial expulsions from other Gulf States. The Gulf States also cut off most aid to the Palestinians. One consequence of the Arab states' displeasure with the PLO was the suspension of all financial support for the organization, which from Saudi Arabia and Kuwait alone exceeded U.S. $100 million per year.[90]

Total aid to the PLO from all Arab Gulf Countries before the war was about $480 million per year. Also, the "liberation contribution," 5% from Palestinian's wages given to the PLO, completely stopped from Kuwait and Iraq. This was a loss of about $37.5 million from the Kuwaiti Palestinians alone. PLO donations from other Gulf Palestinians also dropped. Losses over the last seven years have certainly been in the billions for the PLO/PNA.[91] On a positive note: some of the financial support from the GCC has subsequently been at least partially restored. The Palestinians, however, had their vulnerability on this issue more than clarified. The Kuwaitis are still keeping a distance from the PNA and the Palestinian cause. The Kuwaitis were also upset with the PLO's constant attempts to link the Gulf War with the Palestinian issue.[92] Furthermore, Kuwait supported the ensuing Arab-Israeli peace process. It was encouraged to that position by the US sponsorship for the process, Egyptian and Syrian participation, and the possibility of stabilizing the Arab-Israeli arena, which would, in turn, helps stabilize the Gulf region. Moreover, either because of Israel's support of the anti-Iraqi coalition and/or its anti-PLO attitude, Kuwait somewhat improved its attitude toward Israel. The media remained critical of what they considered Israel's stubbornness, but encouraged the start of negotiations. In mid-November [1991], after continuous denials, its director-general of customs and excise, Ibrahim Ghanim, admitted that Kuwait had eased the Arab boycott on Israel.[93] After the war, Israel was to be the most significant and powerful modern strategic power in the region. It became much more difficult for the Palestinians to bargain from a tough position given that Israel's only real threat in the region was just neutralized. The Palestinians position in Israel significantly changed after the Gulf War.

The Gulf War marked a turning point for Palestinians working in Israel. What were already difficult employment conditions were further worsened by the return of approximately 25,000 Palestinian workers; most having lost their savings, from the Gulf to look for work in the Occupied Territories or Israel. During the war Israel imposed a blanket curfew on the whole of the Occupied Territories for 45 days, and since the war, travel restrictions have been, and continue to be enforced on Palestinians throughout the West Bank and Gaza Strip. For Palestinians whose jobs were in Israel these were disastrous. Between 15,000 and 25,000 Palestinians lost their jobs. Others as a result of the severe economic crisis in the West Bank and Gaza Strip were forced to look for additional jobs in an increasingly hostile labour market.[94]

Also, the Jordanian dinar has been the currency of choice of the Palestinians in the Occupied Territories. The devaluations of the dinar due the war and its aftermath harmed them directly. Much of their savings had been in dinars. Remittances sent to the Occupied Territories from Kuwait in 1989 were about $120 million. These were also lost. The potential increase in these has also been lost over the last seven years. Such losses will likely continue. Remittances from Palestinians in the other GCC countries also most likely declined over the last seven years from what they would otherwise have sent to the Occupied Territories. About 40,000 Palestinians with Israeli travel documents returned to the Occupied

Territories after the war. This worsened employment stress in the Occupied Territories.[95] Israel has also tightened controls over exports going across to Jordan from the Occupied Territories. Closures of the border have been common.

The West Bank and Gaza economics also used to get aid directly from Arab agencies. Kuwaiti agencies have cut the aid off entirely. Other GCC Arab aid agencies also cut back on aid.[96] The Economist Intelligence Unit Country Reports and Country Profiles on the Occupied Territories do not mention any recent aid from the GCC states. If it does exist it is likely to be insignificant beside the large aid donors such as the EU. If not for the war things could have been much better. Could things be worse?

Remittances to the West Bank and Gaza after 1991 were almost all from labour working in Israel. These remittances dropped from $930 million in 1992 to $218 million in 1996.[97] Data on remittances from the very few let back into the GCC countries seems unavailable. When adding in the lost remittances which would have been coming via Jordan to the Occupied Territories one gets a horrific picture of a Palestinian economy that lost 1/2 of its GNP per capita in a matter of months.[98] Agricultural exports to the Gulf states and other Arab states from the West Bank and Gaza were to be cut off for some time to come.[99] Many of the crops were also damaged because the curfew was not only from moving to Israel but also within the West Bank and Gaza. Lands not tended were ruined. The olive, citrus and other crops were badly damaged. Estimates for the total loss to the Palestinian agriculture sector as a direct result of the [Gulf-War related] curfew were $45 million per week in the West Bank, and $15 million in the Gaza Strip. Some areas were totally devastated. In the Tulkarem region, for example, thousands of dunams of citrus fruit rotted, resulting in a total loss of approximately $4.5 million per week.[100]

Previous to the Gulf War, the Intifada caused employment and economic growth problems for the Palestinians. As soon as this situation seemed to have cooled down the Gulf War happened. At about the same time he USSR collapsed and 600,000+ of its former citizens immigrated to Israel from 1990-1995. These new immigrants have been, and will obviously continue to, compete with the Palestinians and Israeli Arabs for land, housing, jobs, and so forth. The labour force of Israel has also been augmented by labour imported from Asia and Eastern Europe. The amount of Palestinians from the Occupied Territories working in Israel has plummeted from well over 100,000 in 1990 to often zero during closures. On average the numbers are now somewhere around 20,000 to 30,000 per day over the last three years. The Palestinian labour force in the Occupied Territories has increased from 313,000 to over 350,000 from 1990 to 1994.[101] It may be well over 400,000 by now. The Palestinian population growth rate in Gaza was 4.6% and in the West Bank 3.4% in 1995.[102] The population of Gaza is expected to double in 15 years. The population of the West Bank is expected to double in 20 years. It is hard to imagine that a large proportion of these new labour force entrants will find jobs in Israel or anywhere else in the MENA region. Libya had ejected them. Lebanon now requires hard to-get work permits. Syria has its own employment problems. Egypt competes with the Palestinians for jobs, as Egyptians have taken many of the jobs lost by Palestinians in Kuwait. Considering the difficulties Palestinians have in finding and retaining jobs anywhere in the Arab World since the Gulf war it is even harder to imagine the millions of new Palestinians to be born in even the next ten years to find employment easily. The Palestinians were hammered by the Gulf War. The ensuing peace process and its "peace dividends" have not alleviated the ongoing costs of the Gulf War to these people:[103]

The average Palestinian in the Occupied Territories is in horrid shape. The "peace process" seems to have brought more economic strife, not less. The peace dividend has so far been considered a net negative in the extreme. But the fact that the economic troubles followed the "peace process" does not mean that it is the cause of them. The Gulf War contributed mightily to the vulnerability of the Palestinian economy, as did the fall of the USSR, which caused an inflow of new settlers to Israel.

Is there any good news recently? The GDP of the West Bank and Gaza declined by 5% in 1996. This was due to frequent closures and much lower economic aid and foreign and domestic investment than expected. The demise of the peace process has added to the demise of the Palestinian economy in the West Bank and Gaza Strip. The Gulf War was a shock. The election of Netanyahu and the policies that he has followed since then have proven to be an additional, and significant, shock. Nevertheless, for the Palestinians the Gulf War was highly economically and politically pivotal. One sign of hope is that the peace process is not yet completely dead. Also, the world outside of the Middle East seems to be getting a bit more sensitive to the plight of the Palestinians. Since 1992 about $2.95 billion in aid has been pledged. Most of this is from the EU. About $2.91 is pledged to go toward investment. As of mid-1997 about $1.78 billion has been disbursed. In 1994-1996 the EU disbursed $172 million, European countries $318 million and the USA disbursed $225 million.[104] This aid has been helpful during these difficult times, but it is not even nearly sufficient to get the Occupied Territories to recover fully from the Gulf War and the collapse of the peace process - and all that has followed from that.

C. Jordanians

King Hussein's "neutral stance" was interpreted by the coalition partners and others to be pro-Saddam Hussein and this cost Jordan dearly, but mostly in the medium run. It seems that Jordan has started on the road back to post-war recovery. This road was solidly paved with economic diplomacy. During the early war-and-post-war periods the unemployment creep due to the crisis was extreme. In March 1990, several months before the crisis began, between 17 and 20% of all Jordanians were unemployed. By November, the unemployment rate was reported to be 20%, and by December it had hit 25%. In September 1991, the Jordanian Statistics Department reported unemployment had risen to 33%, to a total of one-third of the work force.[105] Remittances to Jordan dropped from $1.2 billion in 1986 to $447 million in 1991, but increased to $1 billion in 1993.[106] In human terms, Jordan and its Palestinian majority are suffering tremendously. A survey conducted by UNICEF in November/December of 1990 showed that because of the crisis in the Gulf, the number of Jordanians (many of whom are Palestinian) living below the poverty line ($120 of income per month) rose from 600,000 in 1988 to one million in 1990.[107] 1993-1994 seemed to be a turning point toward the recovery from the war in terms of remittances anyway. But in real terms the remittances were still lower than in 1989. It is difficult to judge how many of these post-war Jordanian remittance workers in the GCC were Palestinians.[108] These new groups could include non-Palestinian Jordanians who were responding to the more difficult times that Jordan was going through in 1991-1993. It could also be that the increase in remittance was due to the increase in oil production in the GCC states as they took up the "missing oil" from Iraq. This was especially so in the over 3-mbd increase for Saudi Arabia from 1988 to 1992. That is, there could be both push and pull effects to get more Jordanians to work in the Gulf – even under somewhat hostile conditions.

In any case, it seems that some Palestinians and other Jordanians are making their way back to the Gulf. However, it may be a long time before Kuwait accepts them in any large number again. Other GCC countries may not have much choice but to employ Jordanians because of the special skills many have built up over many years in these countries.[109]

The U.A.E relies on many Palestinians and Jordanians for their civil service and other government positions. For Jordan 85% of those working abroad were employed in Saudi Arabia and Kuwait before the Gulf War in August 1990. While the numbers of Jordanians in Kuwait has fallen dramatically since the Gulf War, the vast majority of migrant workers from Jordan are still employed in the Gulf region.[110] Jordan was initially economically slammed by the Gulf War. There were some 5,000 Jordanian workers with their 22,000 dependents in Iraq just before the Gulf Crisis started in 1990.[111] There were some 110,000 workers and 400,000 dependents from Jordan in Kuwait just before the crisis.[112] Close to 400,000 of these persons found their way back to Jordan.

Though this had long-term political and economic ramifications, in the short term the main problems were the extreme pressures that the returnees imposed on Jordan's expatriate workers. Their remittances had formerly buoyed the country's economy. Only about 10% of them were said to be reasonably well off. The rest were in "dire need."[113] Housing and other prices skyrocketed. Medical and other services were put under great strain. There was a great need to build new schools. The resources of Jordan could hardly keep up with its pre-war population. This sudden increase in 10-12% of the population was a massive short to medium term burden.[114]

Jordan also had to pay for some of the costs of other remittance workers transiting across its territory. Jordan was the only way out for many of them. The Iraqi and Kuwait borders were closed in all other directions. Jordan also had to pay for absorbing the dependents of its returning remittance workers. It is not easy for a country of just over 4 million to absorb over 500,000 people in such a short period. The shock of this exodus still remains. Even so, there may be a positive twist to all of this for Jordan:

> The economic pressure of the returnees on Jordan was mitigated by the accompanying return of their savings, including severance pay, particularly after the liberation of Kuwait. Most Jordanian returnees invested their repatriated savings in small business..., creating their own employment in the informal sector. Initially Jordan's unemployment rate increased as a result of the relatively large number of returnees, but then, as the returning migrants started investing their repatriated savings in housing and businesses, the economy witnessed a mini-boom and the rate of unemployment actually declined in 1992.[115]

Also,

> Part of the damage done to Jordanian exports by the loss of markets in Iraq, Kuwait, and Saudi Arabia was redressed by an agreement to sell phosphates to Iran worth $66m. Simultaneously, imports declined as a result of uncertainties over the Gulf situation and problems arising from the blockading of Aqaba. The gross domestic product (GDP) for 1991 increased by 1% in comparison to the 8% decline in GDP in 1990.[116]

Japan, The European Community, Canada, Taiwan, and the World Bank gave considerable aid, low-cost loans and grants to Jordan, all totalling about $1.85 billion, in 1990 and1991. This helped Jordan stabilize its economy beyond all previous expectations.[117] In 1992 and 1993 the total grants and loans dropped to around $600 million. Others, including the USA, after the signing of the Israeli-Jordanian Peace Treaty, have helped Jordan adjust to the post-war environment. The lead in to the peace agreement also showed some increases in loans and grants. Total grants and loans to Jordan were about $2.2 billion in the 1994-1996 period.[118] These extraordinary grants and loans proved to be very important. All of the GCC countries had cut off bilateral grants to Jordan. The grant from Iraq has been in terms of concessionary oil sales from 1991-1996.[119] Without these outside grants, especially in the 1990-1996 time period, Jordan would have had a much worse time.

Having borne the brunt of the oil counter shock, the Jordanian economy recorded a 13.5% fall in GDP in 1989. With the advent of the Gulf crisis, Jordan felt that it could not allow itself to abandon Iraq: the latter country was, after all, its main partner, taking up one quarter of its exports, and its sole oil supplier. The conflict resulted in a fall of nearly 50% in Jordan's exports to Iraq and led to the repatriation of 500,000 emigrant workers in the Gulf. While well trained and in many cases bringing substantial wealth with them, they nevertheless had to integrate into a working population of 580,000. However, Jordan recovered quickly from this triple external shock, growth reaching 1.7% in 1991 after a 2% downturn in 1990. Debt reduction and grants and low-interest loans that Jordan has accrued since the peace treaty have helped. Potential joint ventures with Western, as well as other Arab and Israeli investors, are being discussed. Some have been signed, such as the deal on natural gas with Qatar, but some of these are now in abeyance because it the uncertain situation with Israel. Even in this fragile environment some Israeli-Jordanian joint ventures continue to be developed. Examples are the joint water and potash programs with Israel and the joint industrial park on their border, which are still in the works. Again, politics rules economics in the

Middle East. Jordan's economy lost in 1990-1991 through politics and may be turning the corner after its peace treaty with Israel and other reconciliation gestures because of politics. The recent tensions between the Arab States and Israel may, however, make many of these reconciliation moves considerably more complicated.

On the other hand, Jordan has gained by an increase in trade with Iraq. According to the *Star*[120] of Jordan in the first seven month of 1995 Iraq imported JD 97.4 million from Jordan.[121] In the full year 1994 Iraq imported JD 105.2 million. Jordan had also been getting much of its oil from Iraq. During the multinational invasion and for couple of months after it Jordan imported oil from Yemen and Syria, but that was soon stopped once Iraqi supplies started up again.[122] There have been some rather drastic changes recently. Since the war Jordan has signed a peace treaty with Israel. It is also getting some oil and other supplies from elsewhere. Saudi Arabia has even mentioned that it will repair the Tapline for oil that used to go through Jordan. It was the major source of oil for Jordan's power station at Zarqa. Jordan has also been patching relations with other GCC States and has to some extent succeeded.

Jordan's unemployment rate as late as of 1994 was still close to 20%.[123] In 1996 it was about 15-20%. Its GDP per worker has not been at competitive growth rates to say the least. Its debt is nearly double its GDP. Real wages have been in decline over the last decade or so. The percentage of persons below the poverty line tripled from 1985 to 1990.[124] Recent reform, like removing subsidies from bread, caused riots in Karak and Amman. The Jordanian economy is still fragile. Its labour force growth rate is expected to be almost 4% per year on average until 2025.[125]

Signing the peace treaty with Israel has brought little in return so far.[126] Nevertheless, there may be some regional economic benefits flowing into Jordan sometime in the future based on the new potential for a Middle East Market. Jordan has had some success in increasing tourism. Construction and agriculture have had some recent successes as well. Jordan has had some success in keeping inflation much lower than it might have been since the war. Also, total reserves and foreign reserves have almost doubled since 1992.[127] Investment as a percentage of GDP has been kept at over 20% per year since the war. Considering the drain on resources due to the war this is fairly impressive for this small country – even if much of the investment has been in housing.

The dinar has lost some value in the last couple of years, but this is expected, especially with the IMF conditional ties that have been imposed.

As with Egypt, the Gulf War was a watershed for Jordan when it came to facing up to its economic difficulties and putting efforts into getting them solved. The IMF, of course, stepped in with its usual prescription. The IMF conditional ties have made Jordan's political economy a bit more fragile. Since 1991 the figures for the growth rates of real GDP at market prices have greatly improved. In 1992 it was 16.1%. In 1994 it was 8.1%. The IMF estimate for 1996 was 5.2%.[128] The budget deficits as a percentage of GDP have been in decline on average since 1991. In 1991 it was 17.4%, by 1996 the IMF estimate was just 4.6%. External debt has declined from 176.6% of GDP in 1991 to about 100% of GDP by 1996.[129] The external debt in absolute nominal terms, however, was at about the same level in 1996 as it was in 1991, $7.3 billion. The current account balance has improved from a $646 million to -$217 million in 1996. The large net imports of Jordan still remain a problem. Jordan's terms of trade have increased slightly since 1991.[130] Gross official reserves increased from $221 million in 1990 to $825 million in 1991 mostly due to foreign aid and suspension of debt service. But by 1996 it had dropped to under $700 million, with a period low of about $420 in 1995.[131] But workers' remittances have almost tripled since the very low year of 1991. About 80,000 Palestinians have been let back into Kuwait.[132] Most of these are likely coming from Jordan. Jordanian expatriate workers were estimated to have remitted to Jordan $1.54 billion in 1996, a 25.2% increase above the 1995 level of $1.23 billion.[133]

So it seems that Jordan had it pretty rough in 1990-1991. However, these tough times were alleviated by foreign grants, *inter alia*. The economic diplomacy efforts of King Hussein should not be underestimated. As time went on and the adjustments to the shocks were made, with considerable outside help, Jordan has started to get back on its feet again. Signing a peace deal with Israel has helped a bit, but not as much as the King would have hoped. Jordan has proven to be more flexible than most would have imagined. Its leadership, especially its economic and diplomatic leadership has proven remarkably adept under tough circumstances. Even so, Jordan has a long way to go yet. The political environment in the Middle East is also getting tenser. There are also the crises and opportunities available to Jordan when Iraq comes back on line with the world economy. As with many other countries in the MENA region Jordan had some good news in 1996 that signalled some further recovery from the effects of the Gulf War.[134] Nevertheless, the sanctions placed on Iraq are still stifling trade growth for Jordan. The peace treaty with Israel has not given the returns that the Jordanians had hoped for. The collapse of the peace process and intermittent closures and partial closures of the Occupied Territories, as well as Israeli restrictions on Jordanian trade with the West Bank, have also hampered growth. The Gulf War's effects on the Jordanian economy and polity may have contained some of the reasons behind Jordan going to the negotiation table with Israel, and why it ultimately signed a peace treaty. The Jordanians may have expected more debt to be written off, more aid to pour in, and more trade, joint ventures and other investments with Israel and others than actually occurred since the peace treaty was signed. Many Jordanians feel that the results of the peace treaty are minimal. Yes, there are joint ventures and investments. As with the peace between Egypt and Israel, Jordan's peace with Israel is a cold one. The economic, political and social returns may, hopefully, be found in the future.

Associated with the peace with Israel is the newfound warming of relations between Turkey and Jordan. Turkey has also been getting closer to Israel, much to the chagrin and consternation of Turkey's Arab neighbours. A future building of economic, technical and political linkages between Turkey and Jordan may help Jordanian development. It may also, possibly ominously, distance Jordan from its Arab neighbours.[135] The GCC and Jordan have improved relations – albeit slowly, cautiously, and without some of the warmth that existed in the past. Jordanians have been coming back to the GCC, but their stay seems less welcoming than before the conflict.

Jordan is progressing with its needed economic reforms – albeit with many difficulties.[136] The bottom line is that Jordan seems to have recovered from much of the shock of the Gulf War even with the lingering adjustment issues related to the return of at least 400,000 persons, but still has to tackle many non-Gulf-War related economic and social problems. Its major international economic problems include its long-term debt, which is about two times GDP, a growing unease in the country about the IMF reforms, nagging unemployment, and the potential and actual fallout from the failed peace process. It also has to deal with the problem of repairing its relations with its wealthier and more powerful neighbours in the Gulf.

D. Egyptians

Some Egyptians probably were happy to leave Iraq given that they were under threat by the Hussein regime for Egypt's support of the multinational coalition. Many Egyptians were also threatened, or even killed, after the

Iran-Iraq War when the Iraqi soldiers came back to their farms to see Egyptians tending them. They have not been happy about the massive losses they initially[137] had due to the invasion of Kuwait and the Gulf War. There were some 850,000 Egyptian remittance workers and 50,000 of their dependents in Iraq just before the invasion of Kuwait. There were also 180,000 Egyptian workers and 35,000 of their dependents in Kuwait before August 1990.[138] Almost all of these persons left. The Egyptians who fled both countries left behind approximately $18 billion in property.[139]

The Egyptian economy in 1990 was in pretty bad shape. Real wages had been declining rapidly for the previous decade: 65% for agriculture, 50% for manufacturing, and 50% for government labour.[140] Budget deficits were close to 18% of GNP. Unemployment was close to 20%. The only reliable sources of venting this surplus labour was either in the informal sector or remittance work in the Gulf. Yet, each year unemployment seemed to grow with some 1.4 million new Egyptians that year and 400,000 new job seekers in Egypt, the last thing Egypt needed was for these 1.115 million persons, 1.030 million workers, to be sent back from Kuwait and Iraq.

Foreign debt in 1988 was an astonishing $52.7 billion, or about 140% of the GNP. Debt service was crushing this $38 billion dollar economy. The public sector had proven to be mostly an industrial failure. Its burden on the economy could have been as much as $2 billion in subsidies per year. Agricultural production was not keeping up with population growth. Food imports were growing to close to 1/2 of the import bill. More loans had to be taken out to feed the population. The import bill was nearly three times its export revenues. Egypt's balance of payments was way out of sync with its development objectives[141] when the war hit.

The IMF had estimated in 1991 that the Gulf War cost Egypt $27 billion: $12 billion in lost remittances, $2 billion in tourism, $500 million from lost revenues of the Suez Canal, and $7,500 per person to support each unemployed returnee.[142] Iraq was also in debt to Egypt by $1 billion[143] which Egypt should hardly expect to be paid back anytime soon. Fortunately, later it became apparent that the tourism losses due to the war might have been a bit less than the 1991 estimate. Unfortunately the terrorist attacks from the Egyptian militants picked up pace in 1991-1995. Thus, there were internal as well as external reasons behind tourism's fall. It was also found that Suez dues actually increased in 1990-1991. War ships also pay dues and many of them passed through the Canal on their way to the Gulf. Income to the Canal increased by over 18% from 1990-1991.[144] Egypt lost out on overland

and other trade with the Gulf countries during the war, but made up for this by the 200% increase in oil revenues due to price and output increases in 1990-1991.[145] The $7,500 figure on returnee support seems unjustifiable. President Mubarak supported the multinational coalitions attack on Iraq. With the invasion of Kuwait by Iraq the diplomatic and strategic equations for Egypt shifted dramatically. They shifted again when the multinational forces invaded Iraq and liberated Kuwait. Mubarak's decision to support the multinational coalition made certain that the Egyptian economy had been saved for the time being.

In 1990-1991, France, Germany, Denmark, the Netherlands, Switzerland, Finland, the UK, the EC and others agreed to debt reduction and special grant agreements for Egypt. They also more or less agreed to increase investments in Egypt. The Paris Club, after prompting from US Treasury Secretary Nicholas Brady, soon agreed to reduce Egypt's debt in stages over the next several years.[146] 15% of the estimated Paris Club debt of $27-28 billion was written off in July 1991. Another 15% was written off with the completion of the IMF program (in 1993). Another $4 billion was written off in 1996, and 30% of interest payments were cut by the Paris Club in 1991. 50% of the Paris Club debt that was remaining after the write-off was rescheduled. Debt service/merchandise exports dropped from 22.7 in 1990 to 14.6 in 1995. Debt service was $3.1 billion in 1990. In 1995 it was just $2.4 billion.[147] A further $7 billion in debt was written off by Arab countries, and $7.1 billion in US military debt was also written off.[148]

Aid from Arab countries was $2.2 billion in 1990, $510 million in 1991, $408 million in 1993 and $380 in 1993.[149] Arab Agencies gave some $50 million in aid from 1990-1994. A remarkable thing about this is that it is the first significant aid to Egypt from Arab Agencies or Arab States since Camp David was signed. DAC aid increased from $3.2 billion in 1990 to $4.2 billion in 1991. It was significantly cut after that, but that initial boost after the war was a significant help. US Aid was also a significant factor in Egypt's recovery from war-related problems.[150] Through these debt reductions and rescheduling, and with the help of significant aid, Egypt was given more economic breathing space to get on with its Economic Reform and Structural Adjustment program, which, coincidentally, started in 1990. These reforms were pushed strongly by the IMF, the World Bank, USAID, and so on. The write-offs of the debt and further grant, loans and investment agreements allowed Egypt to move more smoothly and quickly on its reforms. For a country that has such a fragile political landscape this was an important respite. Even with some of the implicit and explicit economic and political pressures attached to these agreements they have proved to be good for Egypt so far.

Egypt's economy has made some positive strides since the war. This is clearly the case in the last couple of years. Economic reform and structural adjustment and its new energies put toward privatisation and getting foreign investment into Egypt could bode well for the future. Insha'allah, things will go well for this country that will have a labour force growth rate of over 2.5% until 2025 and not nearly that many jobs being produced in the country each year. Many of the jobs that were held by Jordanians and Palestinians in Kuwait have been taken by Egyptians and remittances to Egyptian workers increased from $3.293 billion in 1989 to $5.664 billion in 1993.[151] In 1992 they were about $6.1 billion[152] by 1994 they had dropped to $3.6 billion and in 1995 they were just $3.3 billion. Part of the explanation is found in the fact that the Egyptian government started new rules for the calculation of remittances in 1994. Also, in 1992 and 1993 the figures may have been that high because of persons in the Gulf sending back their savings to Egypt because of the increasing uncertainty in the Gulf. By 1995 that uncertainty may have abated. In 1986 there were 2.25 million Egyptians overseas. In 1996 there were 2.18 million.[153] There may be less working in the GCC than during the heyday of oil revenues and remittance labour, but it is also clear that many of the jobs that may have been there for the Palestinians (there being less jobs available in the GCC anyway) went to Egyptians. Official estimates released in early 1996 suggest that Arab nationals make up at least 61% of the non-Kuwaiti population, with 220,000 Egyptians, 80,000 Palestinians, 80,000 Lebanese and 57,000 Syrians. Before the war about 450,000 Palestinians and Jordanians lived in Kuwait.[154]

Some of the excess labour is being vented. Real GDP per capita growth rates have been turning toward the positive side. Government deficits are getting under control. Inflation has dropped form its pre-war highs. Foreign exchange reserves have increased from just about $1 billion before the Gulf War to over $16 billion in 1995. Egypt was under pressure before the war to significantly devalue the pound. That pressure has eased lately. That is good for the food bills to Egypt. Egypt imports 65% of its people's food needs. The results of the war for Egypt were, in the short run, a big remittance shock, a small trade shock, followed by foreign aid, debt reduction, oil prices increasing, and a great increase in remittances coming into the country from 1993 to 1995.

The Luxor massacre of November 1997 and its effects on tourism and other parts of the Egyptian economy aside things are going fairly well for the country. The structural adjustment programs, as well as other things, have reduced inflation, increased real GDP growth, and increased slightly foreign direct investment. The private, non-oil manufacturing sector has been growing much quicker than it was previous to the reforms. New labour and investment laws are just now starting to have some positive impacts. Privatisation has been moving slowly, but not altogether unsuccessfully. Foreign reserves have been pouring into the banking system. Egypt has made real positive strides toward becoming a more solid and better developing economy. It still has a long way to go. The Gulf War may have helped Egypt on the road to change and recovery with the debt write-offs, the short run unemployment shock, and the indirect effects the Gulf War had on the peace process in the short run.

In other words, Iraq was a moderate economic pivot for Egypt at first, but outside influences and significant internal policy changes, seemed to have not only nullified many of the negative macroeconomic effects of the war, but also improved the Egyptian economy tremendously. Even so, Egypt could benefit from the return of Iraq (under a new Iraqi leadership) and the jobs and trade growth that it may indirectly and directly produce. It has definitely been helped with its new closer ties to the GCC and its full acceptance back into the fold of the Arab states after years of partial embargo due to its signing of the Camp David Accord and a peace treaty with Israel. Its trade and other forms of economic cooperation with the rest of the Arab world, in particular the GCC, have improved considerably since the Gulf War. Aid from the GCC in the billions helped Egypt to more smoothly move from the post-war environment to structural adjustment and economic reform.

Egypt is also now considered the political leader of the Arab world. It has been more active in Arab issues than before the war. The GCC and other Arab states have more often than not supported Egypt on the major issues facing the Arab world since the Gulf War. Supporting the multinational coalition was a very wise political and economic decision. The negative fallout from this had mostly been internal. The "fundamentalists" did not appreciate such support for the West and the movement of Western "infidel" troops to Saudi Arabia. Some of the internal terrorism has been based on this disagreement. Most of it, however, is still based on the power struggle between the "fundamentalist" minority and those who are perceived as supporting the Mubarak regime.

E. Yemenis

Yemen was one of the countries that were hardest hit by the war. Its losses were due mainly to catastrophic evaporation of remittances and foreign aid and the return of 850,000 persons from the Gulf. Beginning in September 1990 about 70,000 Yemenis were forced to leave Saudi Arabia and return to Yemen. With about one-third of the workers taking their families with them (58% of Yemenis in Saudi Arabia were actually dependents). In November 1990 the Saudi government allowed work permits for Yemenis only for nurses and teachers, effectively expelling the rest of the Yemenis who might still have remained in the country. Other Gulf countries also forced their Yemeni emigrants to leave (and 45,000 Yemenis had fled Kuwait and Iraq with the 1990 invasion). At least 850,000 Yemenis from all the Gulf States were forced to suddenly return home in late 1990, increasing the population of Yemen by 8%.

Most Yemenis who were in Saudi Arabia suffered sizable financial losses, because they were forced to sell their property at extremely low prices. The returnees lost an estimated $7.9 billion in assets.[155] These persons poured into poor Yemen and the unemployment rate rapidly shot up from 4% to 25%. Remittances coming into Yemen before the war were $600 million in 1988 and $500 million in 1989. After that they were nil in the official figures.[156] Yemen, like Jordan, but in more extreme circumstances, had to absorb hundreds of thousands of dependents and take care of them. This was very costly for such a poor country. What made things worse was that all aid from the Gulf was cut off.[157] From 1992 to 1994 real GDP growth was in the 4-6% range. Thereafter it has dropped. 1995 was a particularly bad year, because of the uneven real GDP growth rates and Yemen's high population growth rates (and a civil war and many other political and other problems in the country) real GDP per capita has dropped since the Gulf War.[158] Inflation has been unusually high in Yemen since the Gulf War. The oil and agricultural sectors have been doing fairly well at times. Most others have done fairly poorly.[159] The capital and financial account of the country had been in decline from 1990 to 1994.[160] The current account was $460 million in the positive direction for the Republic of Yemen in 1989. By 1993 it was -$1.3 billion. There was a significant improvement in 1994,[161] but this may have been due to changes in demand patterns during a civil uprising rather than a long-term improving trend.

Total reserves in the country were on a steep decline in the 1990-1994 period.[162] Foreign exchange reserves, even while being boosted up by the oil industry and agriculture, still could not keep up with the many problems the country was facing. These reserves declined to less than 1/4 of their 1991 level by 1993.[163] The Yemeni riyal has been losing value regularly since the Gulf War. Unemployment is still a major issue in the country, as well as illiteracy. Over 60% of the adult population is illiterate. The average annual growth of the labour supply is expected to be 4.25% from 1995 to 2025.[164] The unemployment rate in Yemen has been around 25% in recent years.[165] About 70% of the labour force in Yemen is still in agriculture, while only about 10% is in industry.[166] Where this labour is going to find jobs is an important and vital question for Yemen.

Yemen is a poor country. Its GNP per capita in 1996 was only about $380, while it had been $420 in 1991.[167] This makes it clearly the poorest country within the scope of our study outside of Iraq. Remittance funds used to pour into the country. Now capital is flowing out of the country. Aid remains at a paltry 4.6% of GNP. The average annual growth rate of the population was 5% from 1990-1995. A considerable amount of this increase was from the returning expatriates. The labour force growth rate during the same period was 4.9%. The overall deficit as a percentage of GNP was 17.5% in 1995. This is the highest recorded by the World Bank in its *World Development Report, 1997*. External debt is nearly twice export revenues.[168] Yemen is in rough shape and a good part of this is due to the Gulf War.[169] The good news found in much of the MENA region in 1996 seems to have bypassed Yemen:

> Yemen, the region's least developed country, has been confronted by severe internal and external imbalances. It began implementing economic and structural reforms in 1995, under the auspices of the World Bank and IMF. After registering a GDP growth rate of 8.5% in 1995, the economy was estimated to have grown by 3% in 1996. Owing to Yemen's relatively high population growth rate, it's GDP per capita declined by an estimated 0.7% in 1996. Although Yemen's economy benefited from higher oil prices and revenues, the country suffered considerably from the June 1996 floods, which had a severe impact on the important agricultural sector.[170]

The debt rescheduling by the Paris Club in 1996 has helped give the country some breathing space toward recovery. However, the IMF/ World Bank structural adjustment and economic reforms package has resulted in sporadic violence in Yemen associated with the ending of subsidies and price increases in basic items. In June 1998 more than 50 people were killed and 200 wounded in the Ma'rib Al-Jawf region. This has turned out to be a mini-war between the Government and tribesmen. The tribesmen are protesting the increases in petrol, wheat and flour prices. Trade unions have called for general strikes.[171] Yemen has yet to recover from the effects of the war. It also has many non-Gulf-War related, mostly long running and long term, economic, social, political, tribal, and international problems to solve.

F. Republic of Syria

According to Nazem Abdalla in 1991: "It is reported that about 110,000 Syrians returned home owing to the Gulf Crisis. Immediate impact of the influx of returnees has been the significant strain imposed on the already fragile and overstretched social services and infrastructure facilities in the country, particularly in health and education. In addition, the returned migrant workers have led the unemployment rate to jump by 4%, thereby reaching a socially and economically detrimental level of 14%.[172]

The Syrian economy was adversely affected by the Gulf crisis in many other ways. These losses include: (1) fall in remittances, (2) loss of exports to Kuwait and other Gulf countries, (3) loss of most tourism revenues, (4) decease in transit revenue on overland shipments headed for the Gulf region, (5) losses of in-kind transactions from Syrian expatriates in Kuwait, (6) loss of poll tax and (7) losses due to suspension of Iraqi transit agreement.

These are real shocks to Syria. However, with the help of some grants, loan guarantees, and other benefits from the coalition states, including increased foreign aid from the GCC, Syria was able to considerably reduce the damages of the war. Syria received about $2 billion in aid in 1990-1991. From 1992 to 1997 $4 billion in aid from Arab Governments and Arab agencies, such as the Arab Fund for Economic and Social Development, the Kuwait Fund for Arab Economic Development, and the Saudi Fund for Development poured into Syria.[173] Syria also got the benefit of the neutralization of its bitter rival, Iraq. Syria supported Iran in the Iraq-Iraq war.

Many of its remittance workers have been able to return to the Gulf, especially Kuwait. There were about 57,000 Syrians in Kuwait in 1996. Syria's remittance income has increased considerably since the liberation of Kuwait from $300 to $600 million from 1991 to 1993. It was estimated to be about $910 million in 1994.[174] The EIU believes that remittance income for Syria has increased significantly since 1994. But this is complicated by the fact that Syrian remittances don't just come from the GCC. There are about 300,000 Syrians in Lebanon as part of the rebuilding program of that country. There are also many Syrians in Latin America.[175] But those 57,000 Syrians in Kuwait certainly help.[176] The Syrian labour supply growth is expected to be 4.46% per year to the year 2025.[177] The growing oil industry may help to finance employment growth in the medium run. But Syria does not have that many years left to its oil – about 8 by recent estimates. Syria's unemployment rate is one of the lowest in the Middle East, at about 5-7%. However, its GDP growth per worker was from 1985-1993 was in the range of negative 2% per year.[178] Real wages, as in the rest of the Arab world, have been dropping over the last decade or so. More Syrians have been seeking work outside of the country.

The Syrian Government claims an 8% growth rate in 1994 and 1995.[179] This may be a bit of a stretch. If it is accurate, then it is questionably sustainable. The oil will run out in a few years. Population pressures are expected to increase. Investment as a percentage of GDP has dropped recently after a big increase just after the war. Its balance of payments situation recently has been uneven at best. Imports more than doubled from $2.5 billion in 1990 to $5.3 billion in 1994.[180] It helped that most of these exports were paid for by aid. But after this Syria may have to deal with an imports expectations problem. Exports dropped by $500 million in the same period. Yet, inflation has been in control and the currency seems relatively strong. If peace breaks out in the area then some of the flight capital – equal to 161% of the present value of its debt – may return.[181] Also, in the short run, its nascent energy industry, which, accounts for some 85% of its exports, could produce more employment either directly or indirectly. The economy is still run by something of an iron first of government control. Its public sector firms are a drain on the economy and the budget. They produce debt. There have been attempts lately to reform the economy through structural adjustment and privatisation. Syria, like Egypt, made a rebound after the war. Part of this is due to its political position to support the multinational coalition during the war. Part is due to both countries attempting to reform their economies during difficult times and against difficult odds.[182]

Syria's historical entrepreneurial spirit, its energetic people, and the opportunities that may open to it with peace and the development of a regional common market may bode well for the future. In 1996 Syria benefited from rising worker remittances and the increase in oil prices. Oil prices, however, have been in decline in the first half of 1998. Remittances for Syria are tied to oil revenues for the GCC. Also, oil reserves in Syria are limited and may run out within a decade or so. Syria, like Egypt is in need of economic reform. The debt rescheduling that occurred after the Gulf War and more recently have helped the Syrian economy. This debt rescheduling, however, is just bandage measures on an economy that is in serious need of reform. The Gulf War had a strong impact on Syria, but it was only in the short run.

The real problems for the Syrian economy are in the long run, independent of the Gulf War, and require tough, long-term solutions on the part of the Syrian Government and private sector. They may also push Syria to the bargaining table with Israel. Syria may not have a choice to continue its warlike stance with Israel to the detriment of its economic and political development.[183] Sometimes internal economic and political problems in Syria translate into external aggression. Fortunately, all indications point to the opposite presently. With the fall of the USSR, Syria's major patron, the new "warmth" between Syria and the USA, the certain betterment of ties between Syria and the GCC, along with the maturation of its political elite, one could see hopeful signs for peace. Nevertheless, Syria holds significant grudges against Israel. It still may also have ambitions for a greater Syria. There are also long-standing tensions between Syria and Jordan, Turkey, and Iraq. Many of the GCC leaders have also not forgotten the support Syria gave Iran in the Iran-Iraq War. In the Middle East, a region with many countries cloaked in political ambiguity, Syria may be one of the most enigmatic for anyone trying to make predictions about its future policies and activities.

G. Conclusions on RS Countries

Bottom line: Yemen, Jordan and the Palestinians supported Iraq. They got economically hammered. Jordan got a reprieve when it signed the peace deal with Israel. The Palestinians signed a peace deal with Israel, but that seems to be worth less than the paper it is on at the moment. The Palestinians economy is still in severe crisis in 1996. Yemen is still reeling from the return of 850,000 of its people. The civil war in 1994 did not help at all. No real major reprieve can be expected in the near future. Oil and agriculture are the only industries showing any real significant growth. The future does not look good for Yemen. Egypt and Syria supported the coalition. They first were harmed by the loss of remittances from the Gulf during the war and soon after. But debt write-offs grants, foreign aid increases, and increases in work permits for their people may have far outweighed the costs to these two countries of the war. The increase in oil prices during and just after the war also helped these small oil producers cope with the "New World Order." Economic reform and structural adjustment programs in these countries are yet to be fully worked through. Recent successes, especially in Egypt, make things look better in the future – with many costs attached, of course.[184]

Egypt and Syria have benefited from the warming of relations with the GCC. The Palestinians, Yemen and Jordan have been feeling cold political winds out of the Gulf. These cold winds toward the Palestinians were part of the reasons behind the GCC's support of a softening of the boycott of Israel, their tacit support of the Madrid, Oslo and Washington meetings on the "peace process," and the tacit support they gave to the Jordanian-Israeli Peace Treaty. The economic and political hammering the Palestinians received from the Gulf War and the fall of Iraq was one of the main reasons why they went to the negotiating tables with the Israelis – and why they signed such lopsided agreements. What choice did they have?

Netanyahu's behaviour and policies, since his election in May 1996, however, have brought the Palestinians increasing difficulties. The "peace process" is just about dead. Yet, the fall of the "peace process" and the anti-Arab and confrontational manner of the Netanyahu regime has also, oddly, given some political breathing space to the Palestinians - and some increasing support from the Arab world for their plight. As the Israeli government became more anti-peace, the more support the Palestinians began to get from the Arab world, even so, it still seems like less support than before the Gulf War.

Jordan also seemed to be pushed to the table by the fallout of the War and the fall of Iraq, though some Jordanians would deny this.[185] Yet, it is hard to believe that the economic difficulties Jordan faced had nothing to do with the decision to sign a peace treaty. Their aid from the GCC was cut back significantly, debts were mounting, trade with Iraq was considerably less than the pre-war days, and the chance for debt write-offs and western aid was presented as part of the peace package. The Israeli-Jordanian peace treaty is without a doubt partly a result of the effects of the Gulf War on Jordan.

Pivotal Effects on Oil Sensitive (OS) Countries:

A. The Oil Holiday ends with a Bang

The Gulf War cost the GCC countries plenty.[186] The payments made to the multinational coalition from the GCC States may have been over $100 billion. Saudi Arabia may have spent as much as $65 billion. Kuwait pledged $5 billion to Desert Shield and $14.8 billion for Desert Storm.[187] The U.A.E. may have spent as much as $6 billion.[188] Bahrain, Qatar, and Oman also contributed in cash. All of these countries also contributed in kind, such as allowing troops etc. to be prepositioned or stationed on their territories. Post war military build-ups and reconstruction[189] At the end of the Gulf War of 1991[190] it became tragically clear that the waste of oil money in the past may likely lead to unsustainable budget imbalances and debt also in the future. The costs of the war, and GCC profligacy, have added up to debt, deficits, and in the case of Saudi Arabia, seeming instability. It is not possible to go through the litany of the GCC's economic mistakes of the past. Let it be left that the Gulf War of 1991 showed the cracks in the system and the weaknesses of their internal economies even amongst seemingly massive wealth. On the other hand, the Gulf War brought more oil money as Saudi Arabia, Oman, and U.A.E.[191] took up the slack left by the exit of Kuwait and Iraqi oil in 1990, and Iraqi oil still. But the war had also begun to make clearer to these countries that they have to start to coming to terms with what oil has brought them- and what it has not.

The Gulf War was the signal that the oil-financed holiday that many of these countries started in 1973 – the party really got going in 1979 – had gone on too long.[192] The overindulgence and indiscipline during the holiday led to problems with digesting the economic changes that occurred during the oil price fall of 1985-86. Profligacy was the rule. Long term planning and wise economic and financial leadership were rare. The GCC States are hardly impoverished, but are now facing debt, chronic budget imbalances, and the acceptance of the fact that they cannot defend themselves alone, among other things.

Even with this long-term diminishing revenue base and the heavy expenditures by the GCC states toward the Gulf war there were enormous expenditures on the military after the Gulf war. This is strong evidence for the shock-value of the war on the GCC. From 1992-1994 Kuwait spent $25.6 billion on the military.[193] During 1900 and 1991 they spent close to

$30 billion.[194] Saudi Arabia had spent some $131 billion on the military from 1990-1994. Close to $73 billion had been spent from 1992-1994.[195] The U.A.E. has spent some $13.6 billion since 1990, almost $6.1 billion since 1992.[196] The largest arms importers in the Middle East from 1992-1994 were as follows:[197]

Country	Amount of Arms imported in billions of U.S. $	Percentage of Middle East Arms Imports
Saudi Arabia	20.5	60
Egypt	4.1	12
Israel	3.0	9
Kuwait	2.0	6
Iran	1.8	6
Others	2.8	8

B. Replacing the Iraqi Oil

> Iraq's invasion of Kuwait had positive and negative impacts on the GCC economies. The largest positive economic impact (Kuwait excepted) occurred in the oil sector. The shortfall of 4.5 million b/d of oil from world markets due to the loss of Iraqi and Kuwait output provided an opportunity for the remaining GCC members, except for Bahrain, to increase their oil output. In 1990, Saudi Arabia, the U.A.E, Oman and Qatar accounted for about 71% of the replacement oil...Oil prices also increased to the highest levels seen since the early 1980s.... These higher oil prices gave an additional boost to oil GDP in 1990 for all the GCC members except Kuwait.[198]

The following chart from William Watson gives some idea of the range of short-term benefits, as measured by real GDP growth rates that accrued to the GCC states in 1989-1990:[199]

Country	1989 over 1988	1990 over 1989
Saudi Arabia	6.2	15.9
Kuwait	12.4	(25.4)
U.A.E.	16.2	20.6
Oman	9.4	7.1
Qatar	15.3	2.1
Bahrain	1.5	1.7

The following chart gives some idea of the relative importance of Iraq and the GCC when it comes to oil reserves proven in billions of barrels in 1994-1995[200]:

Country	End – 1994	End – 1995	Regional Share	Reserve/Production Ratio
Algeria	9.2	9.2	1.30	20.5
Egypt	3.3	3.9	0.60	11.8
Iran	89.3	88.2	12.60	65.9
Iraq	100.0	100.0	14.20	>100.0
Kuwait	96.5	96.5	13.70	>100.0
Libya	22.8	29.5	4.20	57.5
Oman	4.8	5.1	0.70	16.2
Qatar	3.7	3.7	0.50	23.1
Saudi Arabia	261.2	261.2	37.20	83.8
Syria	2.5	2.5	0.40	11.2
Tunisia	0.4	0.4	0.06	12.7
U.A.E.	98.1	98.1	0.14	>100.0
Yemen	4.0	4.0	0.60	32.9
Total	696.0	702.5	100	80.9

We can see that Iraq is in a pivotal position with regard to oil. It may be that as the sanctions are kept on Iraq's importance in the regional oil picture will become more vital. That is, the other regional "giants," like Kuwait and Saudi Arabia, are lifting their oil out at high rates, much of Iraq's oil remains in the ground. The production/reserve ratio for Iraq must be the lowest in the world even after the oil-for-food deal. As we will see in the next section of the paper, Iraq has barely touched its potential reserves. It may have another 50 billion barrels of oil or more left to be commercialised.

Iraq's production has been minuscule since the war, 576,000 barrels[201] a day in 1995, compared to its available supplies.[202] Until December 1996 UN Resolution 661 still held, imposed following Iraq's invasion of Kuwait in 1990 and renewed every 60 days since them it continues to prevent Iraq from exporting oil, except for small amounts (around 50,000 b/d) to Jordan. Prior to the war, Iraq was producing over 3 million b/d and exporting 2.8 million b/d (1.6 million b/d via the Turkey pipeline, 800,000 b/d via the IPSA2 pipeline across Saudi Arabia, 300,000 b/d from Iraq's Mina Al-Bakr export terminal, and somewhat less than 100,000 b/d by truck through Turkey).[203]

Even with the "oil-for-food" deal started in late 1996, and its many oil production increase deals, Iraq's production is much less than before the war. Under UN Security Council Resolution (with amendments) Iraq could, starting the beginning of 1997, sell $1 billion every 90 days. This was revised to $2 billion in 1998. The $2 billion works out to about 1.46 mbd at $15 per barrel and 1.1 mbd at $20 per barrel. In June 1996 OPEC gave Iraq a 1.2 mbd quota in expectation of these moves.[204] In 1989 Iraq was producing 2.9 mbd. It is capable, with significant infrastructure improvements, foreign investment, and further exploration of its many as yet fully explored and developed fields, of producing over 6 mbd within a couple of years.

Repairing the oil industry to the state where Iraq could produce some 2-2.5 mbd, and export all but the Iraqi domestic needs, could cost as much as $5 billion. To get the production up to a rate of 3.5 mbd could cost $5-7 billion. (Arab Petroleum Research Center, 1995). Already Iraq has put some $6 billion into repairing the oil refineries damaged by the 1991 war. It may cost as much as $30-40 billion to get Iraq to its targeted production capacity of 6+ mbd by 2010. (Energy Information Agency, 1996) After the major repairs are finished, Iraq will likely have a relatively low cost for increasing production capacity, compared to most other oil producers.[205]

It is an oil rich country that is poor.[206] Poor because of the devastating effects of the war, the Iraqi "Intifada" and the strangulation of the country under draconian multilateral sanctions which have no historical precedent aside from the medieval sieges of cities. The physical and mental health and standard of living, even the culture of Iraq, have been severely damaged by these sanctions. Crime has increased dramatically. Families have broken up. Iraq has become a harsh desert of despair for most, and a corrupt oasis for a few.[207] When Iraq is freed from these sanctions it will still have heavy recovery, restitution and development costs to pay. Iraq, however, has the benefit of a history of successful industrialization, a good agricultural base, and was, frankly, the most developed Arab country in the 1970s. There is considerable hope even within all of the sadness for a complete economic recovery for Iraq.[208]

Of the 73 oil fields discovered in the country, only 15 have been brought into production up to now, but once the embargo is lifted Iraq is planning to develop 25 new fields and eight reservoirs that are only partially exploited. Those 33 structures have a combined production capacity of 4.5 million b/d, with the 10 biggest fields alone having a potential of 3 million b/d between them. They include 5 super-giant fields in the south of the country, whose development Iraq is planning to contract out to foreign companies under production sharing agreements.

The GCC gained from replacing Iraqi oil. Even so, GDP growth rates for the GCC already began to slow down to more normal levels in 1992 and 1993, dropping to a fairly slow 3% in nominal terms for the entire GCC in 1993. By 1994 GDP growth in real terms for the entire GCC was close to 0. The 1993 growth rate for the UAE was about 1%; for Saudi Arabia 1%; for Qatar -2.5%; and for Bahrain it was just 2%.[209] 1995 and especially 1996 proved to be much better years. Saudi Arabia can hardly complain about an increase in 3+ mbd in oil output increase from 1989 to 1992. When the price increases by $1 that is another $3 million dollars per day, or $1.1 billion per year, for the country.[210] As we will see, the Gulf War showed both how fragile and how strong these enormously wealthy countries were. I will focus on Saudi Arabia and Kuwait because they were the most affected in the medium run – and because of limitations in space and time.

C. Saudi Arabia

Saudi Arabia's dependence on oil has been profound.[211] In 1989 GDP was based 30% on oil the oil trade. In 1972 it was 80%. In 1979 it was 75%.[212] Recently it has been about 37%. From 1974 to 1992 oil has accounted for between 75% and 95% of government revenue.[213] For almost the entirety of the 1980s and 1990s so far oil has accounted for about 95% of export receipts.[214] During the glory days of 1973-1984 the country was blossoming economically. The oil shock of 1985-86 and the subsequent drop in the real price of oil, even in early 1998 hammered the country economically. It is still wealthy, but its macroeconomic data have mostly been on the downswing since 1984. Domestic debt may be as much as 86% of GDP – having grown from 52% of GDP in 1992. Domestic debt instruments have covered much of the budget shortfalls since the fall in the real price of oil. Foreign debt has been kept relatively low.[215] The syndicated loans of $7.6 billion taken out by Saudi Arabia in 1991-1992 are an indication of the cost of this war to even a wealthy country like this one. During 1990-91 Saudi Arabia had about SR111.4bn in emergency spending.[216] Nevertheless, Saudi Arabia's defence spending continued to grow for some time after the war was over.

These loans in 1991-1992 were unusual for Saudi Arabia. For the entire decade of the 1970s Saudi Arabia took out just $600 million in syndicated loans, mostly for financial trade reasons. For the entire decade of the 1980s they borrowed in international markets – commercial markets that is – about $4.3 billion.[217] As the price of oil went down, so also did the foreign commercial loans, but the Saudis were by the end of the decade more and more turning to domestic debt to pay off their chronic budget deficits. The higher oil prices, and changing policies on subsidies have helped somewhat to reduce the deficits in 1996 and 1997. The government deficits are, however, still mostly oil-price-determined.[218] This little tidbit from the Energy Information Agency, Department of Energy, U.S. Government[219] is something of a wake-up call:

> Terrorist bombings – in November 1996 and June 1996 – have highlighted concerns regarding the long-term stability of Saudi Arabia, by far and away the world's most important oil-exporting nation. These bombings are considered by many analysts to be a direct challenge to the Saudi ruling family, already preoccupied with the question of choosing a successor to King Fahd, who had been ailing for years and in November 1995 suffered a serious stroke. Fuelling opposition to the ruling Al-Saud family in recent years has been economic difficulties brought about by: 1) greatly reduced oil revenues compared to the late 1970s and early 1980s; 2) a rapidly growing population and a relative decline in the population's economic standing; 3) the 1990/1 war with Iraq, which cost Saudi Arabia approximately $50 billion in military expenditures; and 4) massive government debt, which makes it more difficult for the government to maintain expansive social spending considered critical to maintaining popular support.

Anthony Cordesman, one of the top experts on the region states:[220] The 1991 Persian Gulf War left the country with an estimated $55 billion debt. Saudi Arabia sustained large current account deficits in the early 1990s, and official reserves fell from $23 billion in 1987 to only $7.4 billion in December 1994.[221] The cabinet reshuffle in August 1995 was a sign that the persistent problems from the war and from the near continuous decline in the real oil price were being perceived as not being tackled properly. All of the ministers in the government, except for the Minister of Planning, were replaced.[222]

On the positive side, the war helped Saudi oil production increase significantly. It rose from 5.6 mbd in June 1990 to 8.2 mbd in September 1990. The Saudis took up most of the oil lost to the world markets due to the invasion of Kuwait and the shutting off of Iraqi oil by UN Resolution 661.[223] The Saudis have seen this as a chance to increase their share in the market and to get, possibly, back into the position as a major hegemonic player in OPEC.[224] Even though the oil revenues to Saudi Arabia were booming the Saudi economy was in trouble in 1991:

> 1991 was a year of large deficits. While the current account deficit was $4 billion in 1990, unofficial estimates are that this rose sharply to $24 billion in 1991. The deficit was equivalent to 23% of GDP. The commitments undertaken by Saudi Arabia in relation to the crisis (i.e., payments to the U.S. and others who had stationed forces in Saudi Arabia, and to those to be compensated for losses related to the war) needed to be paid, for the most part, in 1990 and 1991. The official estimates for total war costs in 1990 and 1991 were $49.6 billion, of which the U.S. received $12.8 billion in cash plus $4 billion in kind.[225]

Also:

> In May 1991, a consortium of twenty international banks signed an agreement with Saudi Arabia for a loan of $4.5 billion. In addition the government borrowed $2.5 billion from local banks. They were given no choice on the matter and each was assigned a minimum "contribution." These figures do not include loans made to public and semi-public companies. Between 1983 and 1988, the government financed its deficits by drawing down its financial reserves accumulated in the "years of plenty." Since 1988, and especially since the Kuwait crisis, the government has had to increasingly recourse to debt, external and domestic, to finance its deficits.[226]

The Saudi Arabian government has subsidized agriculture, industry and more for years. Everyday items like telephone service and gasoline, education and food were highly subsidized. Free medical treatment or paid overseas holidays were taken for granted by some Saudis. Over the years since the war many of these items have had their subsidies reduced or cut off. The possibilities for lucrative, and easy, employment of college graduates has been brought into question. Saudiization has begun in an attempt to get jobs to Saudi citizens that would otherwise go to guest workers.

Saudiization of the labour force has been a government goal since the early 1980s, but it is receiving more and more attention because of the coincidence of a number of demographic and economic factors. First, the number of Saudis entering the job markets for the first time is climbing, and, with more than half of the national population under the age of 15, the outlook is for a steady stream of new participants entering the labour force for the foreseeable future. (Saudi Arabia, at 3.5% has one of the fastest population growth rates in the world.) Second, many Saudi nationals are accustomed to finding employment in government service, but the government's goal of reducing its fiscal deficit means that jobs are not as plentiful as in the past. These two factors may be increasing unemployment for the first time job seekers, although the government does not publish unemployment figures. Third, the expatriate labour force is a major drain on Saudi Arabia's hard currency earnings. In 1994 expatriate workers remitted $15.3 bn. In the first nine months of 1995 remittances totalled $10.2 billion.[227]

It is possible that the Gulf crisis may have shocked this economy enough that the demand for outside labour will go down, not up, in the long run. The growth rate in the labour supply in Saudi Arabia is expected to be close to 3.5% per annum until 2025.[228] The population growth rate of Saudi citizens is expected to be one of the highest in the world, at close to 3% over the next decade. The government has made some progress in privatisation, structural change, and diversification in the economy since the war.[229] Taking a longer run view, the oil trade as a percentage of GDP had dropped from 90% in 1974 to 30% in 1993. Yet, oil still was responsible for 99% of Saudi Arabia's export revenues in 1993.[230]

The fact that Saudi Arabia has taken the place of Iraq in the production of about 2+/- mbd has helped. The following figures from the Economist Intelligence Unit show how this reliance on oil can be a blessing and a curse:

> The sharp rise in oil prices in 1973/74 and in 1980/81 contributed to an increase in GDP per head from $1,200 in 1972 to $16,650 in 1981. Reflecting the decline in production and price trends in the oil industry during the 1980s GDP per head fell back to $5,500 by the end of the 1980s. The 1990-91 Gulf War helped to increase the figure, and it has remained fairly steady since then reaching $7,420 in 1996.[231]

The current account at first boomed because of the oil windfall to Saudi Arabia. Then as imports increased, mostly military imports and military expenditures, the current account balance dropped from $22.7 billion in 1990 to $13 billion in 1994.[232] In 1991 some 79% of the massive current-account deficit the result of exceptional wartime expenditure was met by inflows of private capital. In 1992-1995 declining current account deficits led to corresponding reductions in the nominal value of private-sector inflows, but they were still a major means of funding current-account deficits. With the exception of 1993, when the authorities drew down $5.8 billion in official foreign assets, private capital inflows funded around 80% or more of the deficits. Despite the current-account surplus in 1996, private-sector inflows were around $7.6 billion and were used to build up the stock of net official assets.[233]

The oil price drop in 1993 did not help matters here. Imports were also especially high in 1992-1993, averaging about $30 billion.[234] Total reserves dropped from about $13 billion in 1989 to about $5 billion in 1994.[235] They dwindled from a 1981 high of close to $28 billion.[236] Foreign exchange reserves have dropped from $24 billion in 1981 to $8.5 billion in 1989 and on to $4 billion in 1994.[237] Non-gold reserves could cover about 16 weeks of imports in 1994. In 1992 they could only cover about 9 weeks. In 1989 they could cover 40 weeks.[238] However, if we look at net official foreign assets we see a different story:

> Reflecting the use in recent years of private capital inflows to finance imbalances in the current account, Saudi Arabia's net official foreign assets have not declined much as a result of the Gulf conflict. Official foreign assets at end-1995 dipped to $67.4bn before recovering to $72.9bn in 1996, but this latter figure was still below the end-1989 figure of $76.7bn. Most of the reduction took place in 1993, when $6bn of the foreign assets of the Saudi Arabian Monetary Agency (SAMA), the central bank, were tapped to fund the current-account deficit. Most of the drop in net foreign assets during 1989-94 can be attributed to the use of SAMA's overseas assets; those of the autonomous government institutions (AGI's) fell by only $1.2 billion between 1989 and 1994.[239]

The budget deficit for 1993 and 1994 were -28bn and -33bn rials respectively. For 1996 and 1997 they were -19bn and -17bn rials.[240] Oil revenues, an unstable source of income, still constitute about 75 to 80% of the government budget. That, in part, explains the wild swings in deficits over the years.

A year ago, the economy looked to be on the verge of collapse, burdened by more than 12 years of deficit financing and the heavy costs incurred by the Gulf war to liberate Kuwait. Bankers now estimate that the kingdom can call on no more than $5 to $10 billion of liquid assets out of a total foreign holdings estimated by the International Monetary Fund at about $45 billion. Oil revenues meantime continue to give cold comfort to the situation. Income from crude oil and refined products was expected to total $33 billion last year compared with $37 billion the year before. Such figures contrast sharply with the 1981 peak of $116 billion. Its ability to recover will depend on world demand for oil and whether Iraq will be allowed to return to the oil market.[241]

The Saudis were briefly stunned, economically and politically, by the war. They seem to be continuing stunned by how fragile their economics and politics really are. The Saudis seem to be slowly and cautiously moving toward change, but the country may need a more dynamic approach to fend off real political-economic problems in the future. Many of these problems are unrelated to the Gulf War and its effects. However, some of them were uncovered by the deep shock that Saudi Arabia felt from this war.

Saudi Arabia, however, has had some good news lately. One could hope that the good news will not be used as an excuse to postpone real needed change. This good news may also be a sign of the start of the full recovery from the oil holiday wastage, as well as the Gulf War? Saudi Arabia's economy, which accounts for over 40% of the ESCWA region's GDP and around 58% of the combined GDP of the GCC countries, performed very well in 1996. After being basically stagnant in 1995, Saudi Arabia's real GDP was conservatively estimated to have registered a 5% growth rate in 1996. In nominal terms, the Kingdoms GDP grew by 8.6% in 1996, according to official estimates. With oil production averaging 8 million b/d, the country's oil revenues were estimated to have increased by more than $8 billion, to a total of around $51 billion in 1996, a 19.3% increase over 1995. The growth of the oil sector, which accounts for over one third of the Kingdom's GDP and around 90% of its exports, was clearly the main factor in boosting the economy and reducing the country's internal and external imbalances. The increase in oil revenues was more than sufficient to wipe out the budget deficit. Instead, however, the Government apparently opted to repay its outstanding debts to private contractors, increase governmental expenditure above planned levels, and simultaneously narrow the budget deficit.

D. Kuwait

I will not go through the long list of damages, human, physical, financial or whatever. Let it be said that the Kuwait economy was shattered by the war. The following chart from a UN report by Abdulrahim A. Farah gives some idea of the damage to the infrastructure of the country due to the Gulf Wars of 1990-1991:[242]

Infrastructure	Cost (US$ bn)
Oil industry	5
Electrical System	1
Ports, airport, national airline	2
Road transport fleet	5
Telecommunications	1
Radio, TV, press	0.5
Housing	2.5
Hotels	1
Wholesale and retail	1
Other urban infrastructure	0.5
Total	19

Yahya Sadowski gives us another view of the problem:

> Even though it had rebuilt most of its damaged assets within two years of the 1990 Iraqi invasion, the emirate was left with massive bills. For almost two years in Kuwait, there was no "gross national product," no oil exports and no banking. To restart the economy, the government had to spend perhaps $65 billion, including $20 billion for rebuilding the oil industry and another $20 billion to stabilize the financial sector. After its liberation, Kuwait also acquired a new and ongoing drain on its resources: subventions to the Americans to ensure a continuation of their security umbrella against renewed threats from Iraq and Iran. In 1992 alone, Kuwait not only paid Washington $16 billion as a part of a deal to cover all the costs of Operation Desert Storm, it also authorized $11.7 billion in new arms imports largely from the US.[243]

The cost of the Gulf War of 1991 to Kuwait may have been more than $66 billion. This cut the "Fund for Future Generations" from $100 billion to around $35 billion.[244] The Kuwaiti government liquidated around $100 billion in assets and borrowed on international commercial markets (in 1991 $5.5 billion was borrowed in a syndicated loan) to fund the war.[245] Reconstruction costs from both wars, first estimated at $100 billion, were recalculated to be only in the range of $20-25 billion later on.[246] The

Kuwaitis planned to borrow as much as $34bn in these costs on international markets but chose to liquidate their assets instead. Rising oil revenues also helped to dodge such heavy debt. Kuwait's total foreign debt was about $10 billion in 1993. By 1996 this had dropped to $6bn. Kuwait has paid back its debts on time and has continued to take a very conservative approach to debt.[247]

Restoring oil operations was expensive. In January 1992, the oil minister announced Kuwait had already spent US$1.5 billion for putting out fires and planned to spend another US$8 to US$10 billion to repair further damage. A National bank of Kuwait report in mid-1992 estimated that reconstruction expenses in the oil sector for the 1992-1995 period would reach US$6.5 billion.[248] The focus on oil is hardly misplaced. Oil has for the last decade, 1990-1992 aside, accounted for 90-95% of Kuwait's export earnings and on average around 30-40% of its GDP. Trade in fuels accounted for about 40% of GDP in 1994 and 47% in 1984. Oil also has generally accounted for around 90+% of the Government budget since 1986.[249] Even the "non-oil" manufacturing sector is dominated by oil refining and petrochemicals.[250] Kuwait's economy is also subject to the whims of oil prices and the prices of its major imports, foodstuffs and manufactured goods.

Kuwait has also succeeded in rebuilding its electricity generation from 7.5 mkwh in 1991 to 20.9 mkwh in 1995. Its port was repaired. Roads and airports were repaired. The stock market increased from 116 KD million being traded in 1992 to 5.7 KD billion in 1996. Petrochemical productions has increased substantially. Area production increased from 257,000 tons in 1992 to 850,000 tons in 1995. Salt, chlorine gas, caustic soda, and hydrochloric acid production have all shown considerably and quick increases.[251] The re-export markets to Iraq have vaporized and those to Iran have considerably dropped.

One of the oddest facts of the Kuwaiti economy in the post-war era is the stability of its currency. Very few countries would have been able to boast being able to keep its currency stable with the US dollar after such enormous devastation in 1991. It's GDP fell from over $24 billion in 1989 to around $11 billion in 1991.[252] Yet, Kuwait's growth rate in real terms was 70% in 1992 and 25% in 1993.[253] In constant 1985 dollars Kuwait's GDP dropped from about $18 billion in 1990 to about $10 billion in 1991. By 1992 it was back up to almost $18 billion. By 1993 it was close to $22 billion.[254] In 1995 it was around $24 billion. In 1996 it had reached about $29 billion. The recovery was phenomenal after the liberation of the country. Even so, in 1987 dollars the real income per capita in Kuwait is a bit more than 1/2 what it was in 1970 and only a bit more than 2/3 what it was in 1979.[255] Also, the economic and physical violence of the war is likely to have changed the way Kuwaitis look at the world and at their own small and vulnerable country. It seems, however, that the Kuwaitis, with the help of their previous enormous wealth, were able to get their economy almost back to the way it was in economic flow, if not stock, terms. The government succeeded in spending the country out of its destruction. Kuwait's oil production increased from 460,000 b/d in 1991 to over 2 mbd by 1996. Oil exports increased from 370,000 b/d in 1991 to 1.9 mbd by 1996. Oil export receipts increased from $0.86 billion in 1991 to $13 billion in 1996. Total government revenues went up more than fourfold in the same period.[256]

Then again, they could draw down on some $100+ billion in overseas assets even after the debacle with the investment house in Spain. The "hard foreign assets" claimed by the Government in 1995 were about $65 billion.[257] There are other claims that Kuwait only had about $20-25 billion to draw on.[258] The budget deficit was, as would be expected, quite large in 1991-1992 during the rebuilding effort. In 1991 it was about $18 billion. In 1992 it was about $6 billion. In 1993 the budget deficit was about $4 billion.[259] It has been pared down even more so during 1996 and 1997. The expectation is for even lower budget deficits to the year 2000, according to the EIU.[260] Importantly, in 1995 the government launched a five-year plan, covering the period 1995-2000, aimed at reducing the budget deficit to zero by the end of the plan period. With both oil revenue and non-oil receipts projected to remain fairly stagnant, government spending is set to decline over the long term, although this may prove difficult in reality; the 1997.98 budget marked a 4% increase over the previous year's budget.[261]

Defence expenditures have been, understandably, booming even during these times of new "austerity." Defence spending before the Iraqi invasion typically accounted for less than 5% of GDP. Since the invasion the defence budget has increased every year, despite a climate of public-sector austerity. Spending on the armed forces (including internal security) accounted for 20% of total spending in the 1995.96 fiscal year the equivalent of 12% of GDP and defence spending absorbed 30% of total government spending in 1996.[262]

Cutting back on subsidies and sinecures too rapidly, without some form of democratic change, will likely lead to some problems in the future.

These problems may be more handleable for Kuwait than Saudi Arabia given its relative size. However, despite the economic problems Kuwait has faced since the war:

> [T]he government has felt politically obliged to sustain insofar as possible the pre-war standard of living. Some of the largest domestic post-war expenditures have gone directly to Kuwaiti households. The banking debt buyout [related to the failure of the Suq al Manakh stock market] was but one of a series of measures taken by the government to help nationals hurt by the invasion. The government decided to pay all government employees (the majority of the working nationals) their wages for the period of the occupation. In March 1992, the government raised state salaries. The government also agreed to write off about US$1.2 billion in consumer loans, a measure benefiting more than 120,000 Kuwaitis. It wrote off US$3.4 billion worth of property and housing loans made before the invasion. Each Kuwaiti family that stayed in Kuwait through the occupation received US$1,750. In July 1992, the government exempted Kuwaitis from charges for public services due as a result of the occupation, such as bills for electricity, utilities, and telephone services and for rents on housing.[263]

There has also been a post-war policy of reducing the number of foreigners in the country. This has harmed some of the banks and other private businesses that have found themselves short-handed or employing persons who did not have the proper skills to get the job done. The packing of the KIO with persons who are not particularly adept has also caused some problems. The stock market crash in the 1980s is still being paid for.[264] The changeover from long-term use of Palestinian labour to new Asian and other Arab labour has also not been as smooth as many hoped. There has been, however, some growth in the non-crude oil sector of the economy, especially refining. Construction and trade, after the boom of the post-war era, are looking at tough times.[265] Even so, it is clear that there is considerable denial of the country's problems. But the "denial factor" was much less than before the war.

The Gulf War succeeded where the Manakh crisis failed. Kuwait's economic problems are now clear for all to see. But had it not been for the strength engendered in years of work by the KPC, KIO, and KFTCIC, the wounds would have been much deeper. It cannot sacrifice economic growth for short-term political gains.[266] Kuwaiti banks came out of the war with some $21 billion in "uncollectible or non-performing debts on their balance sheets."[267] It was not until 1994 that they started to get this under control after a massive bailout of the banks, similar to the bailout of investors after the stock market crash in 1982. These bailouts have been costly.

On the macro-level, Kuwait's capital and financial account dropped from \$28 billion to -\$3.9 billion between 1991 and 1994.[268] Also, as the imports to help rebuild begin to slow down the imports of military equipment continued in a high range. Exports since the war, especially of oil, have increased dramatically and thankfully for Kuwait, from \$1 billion to well over \$15 billion. Official total reserves dropped by over \$1 billion from 1992-1994.[269] Foreign exchange reserves, even with a large return of Kuwait assets to Kuwait, had dropped from \$3.5 billion to \$2.2 billion between 1992 and 1994.[270] They increased to about \$3.4 billion by 1996.[271] Investment as a percentage of GDP was close to 40 in 1991 due to the inflow of Kuwait assets in the rebuilding effort. This has become quite a bit more moderate over the last few years as the economic situation became clearer - even with the recent increases in the price of oil.

Remember that the price of oil that counts is the real price of oil. The yearly average of the real price of oil in 1996 was about the same as it was in the doldrums of 1985-86. However, for Kuwait, GDP per capita has increased from \$5,230 in 1991 to \$14,700 in 1993, and on to \$13,476 in 1996.[272] With continuous cumulative government deficits, increasing internal and external debt, and a significant reduction in the income from its overseas investments, the continuation of subsidies toward the "dolce vita", and the large (and often wasteful) military expenditures, the sustainability of such growth seems questionable.

Kuwait has made some strides in downstream and upstream investments in the industry and toward diversification. It also seems to be getting its investment houses in order after the massive losses they made in the early 1990s. Kuwait is putting efforts into expanding oil production to 3-4 mbd "by the early 2000s."[273] On the other hand, its budget deficit and domestic and foreign debt situations are still not being realistically faced. For example, Kuwait has no direct taxation, and Kuwait's Finance Ministry has stated that the country spends about \$1.8 billion a year on utility subsidies and free health care alone. It was spending \$1 billion a year on subsidizing water and power, and \$600 million on subsidizing health care.[274]

It will take some time to recuperate fully and financially from the war. If Iraq comes back full-steam into the oil markets and into its past strategic position in the Gulf Kuwait's position could be even more tenuous. Yet, it has strong outside backing and a resilient and educated population, and the benefits of a considerable dose of "reality check" after the Gulf crisis.

There are considerable economic structural and political problems to be solved in Kuwait. Yet, there is some good news. The GDP in Kuwait was estimated to have increased by 3.9% in 1995 and by 5.2% in 1996. Economic conditions improved remarkably in Kuwait in 1996, owing mainly to an estimated 19.1% rise in Kuwait's oil revenues, which have increased the country's balance-of-trade surplus and simultaneously reduced its budget deficit. In addition, during the fourth quarter of 1996, Kuwait repaid its last instalment of the $5.5 billion loan that it borrowed at the end of the Gulf War. Moreover, Kuwaiti assets abroad, which was estimated by unofficial sources at $35 billion in 1995, must have increased considerably in 1996, owing to additional deposits by the Government and the significant appreciation of the overseas investments during that year.[275]

The recent severe declines in the price of oil to around $12 per barrel will likely reduce, if the oil price continues to be so low, economic growth in Kuwait in 1998.[276] The real price of oil is now less than it was in 1970. It is about 1/6 what it was in 1979-80. Nevertheless, Kuwait has returned, literally, from the political and economic dead with considerable hard work – and even more considerable assets that the country had been packing away for decades. The conservative nature of the Kuwait government when it comes to its massive oil revenues saved it for another day.

Conclusions

The Gulf War and the fall of Iraq had many strong impacts on the MENA region economies. The strongest impacts were to be felt on remittances and debt for countries like Egypt, Yemen, Jordan, Syria, and the West Bank and Gaza Strip. These remittance sensitive countries felt the "pivotal" nature of Iraq each in a very unique way according to whether they supported Saddam Hussein or not, how much they were reliant on remittance incomes, and how far along they were in the economic reform and structural adjustment programs. The oil sensitive states were also affected. The two we focused on where the most effected. Kuwait, because it was the country that Iraq brutally invaded and it has paid enormous costs for its liberation and for its reconstruction, and Saudi Arabia, because it footed much of the bill for the war and benefited most from the increase in its oil production.

With this increased production it can benefit more in oil revenues when the market is good. Most of these countries have recovered from the effects of the war. Jordan, Yemen and the West Bank and Gaza have recovered the least.

What complicates the analyses of the effects of the fall of Iraq and the Gulf War on these countries is that there are many other things going on in the MENA region and in the world that have significant impacts that may either subdue or magnify such war-related phenomenon. The "peace process" is falling apart and some consider it dead. The international price of oil is often determined by factors outside of the control of the producers of that oil. The financial effects of the price declines of the 1980s were far greater than the financial effects of the Gulf War and the fall of Iraq. This is true for both the oil producing states and the remittance sensitive states. The implementation of economic reforms in the MENA states could have vastly more important effects on their economies than the Gulf War. The inflow of private funds to offset the oil-determined government investments is a case in point.

Iraq's return to the regional economy may be vital for remittance income. It may also tend to reduce oil revenues to Kuwait, Saudi Arabia and the other GCC states. Trade between Iraq and the other MENA states was not a significant determining factor of the pivotal nature of Iraq and the war, except in the case of Jordan. Unemployment remains a problem, especially for the West Bank and Gaza Strip and Yemen, but also for most of the MENA countries excepting Syria. Even the GCC states suffer from unemployment and underemployment of their indigenous populations. These unemployment problems are mostly independent of the fall of Iraq and the Gulf War, excepting the continuing reluctance of the GCC states to hire Yemenis and, and less so but still significant, Palestinians.

Inflation and many other macrodata for most MENA countries are now almost totally independent of the Iraqi situation. Even (legal) trade, except for Turkey and Jordan, has become almost totally independent of Iraq. Opening up Iraq again will likely help trade for these two countries in the region the most. Iraq's former "major" trading partners in the region, such as Kuwait and Saudi Arabia, will likely have little trade with Iraq even when the sanctions are taken off.[277] The UAE might benefit significantly from re-exports to Iraq. The big winners will be those countries in the industrialized world that can supply Iraq with material and technology needed for a full rebuilding. Food exporters will also benefit. Many of the countries of the Middle East may also benefit from exports to Iraq as it rebuilds. Jordan and Turkey might be the largest beneficiaries from this. The GCC will likely continue to give Iraq the cold shoulder for as long as Saddam Hussein, or someone like him, remains in power.

Politically Iraq has proven to be a pivot in the public and private opinions of the Arab world. Economically it was a pivot for those persons and countries that were most tied to it. Militarily Iraq has been a regional pivot for many years. In the oil business the pivotal nature of Iraq is undeniable. Controlling 10%+ of the world's reserves makes one pivotal. On the other hand, over the last seven years Iraq has been almost completely shut off from most of the economies of the region. They have looked for new trading partners and new places to find work. Some have been successful, others not so successful. Possibly, the full pivotal nature of Iraq will become apparent when it is reopened to the region. This may be as much of an economic and political shock to the Arab region as the war itself.[278]

The Gulf War, and to a much less extent the fall of Iraq, led some of the Arab states to have more active participation in the "peace process" with Israel. The Palestinians went to the table and signed interim and other agreements partly because they were nearly bankrupted by the combination of the Intifada and the effects of the Gulf War. The Jordanians may also have considered going to the peace table as a way of extracting itself from the economic, and other, effects of the Gulf War. The Kuwaitis may have pushed for a slight warming of ties between Israel and the Arab world because of its anger at the Palestinians alleged support of Saddam Hussein. Other GCC states that were part of the multinational coalition may have also moved closer to Israel because of the loss of stature of the Palestinians in their eyes. The Gulf War may have succeeded in at least partially removing the link between the Palestinian issues from the rest of the problems the GCC has to face. It looks like Netanyahu brought back the linkage with his incendiary and counterproductive policies of confrontation.

Even with Netanyahu's antagonisms toward the Arab world the Arab world seems less concerned with the Palestinian issue after the Gulf War than it was before the war. Many countries in the Arab world, such as Egypt, Saudi Arabia, Kuwait, the UAE, and Syria seem more concerned with the own internal problems and their efforts toward economic development.

The breaking point for the GCC states seems to have been the Gulf War. The Palestinians backed the wrong person. The Palestinians were seen as a significant threat to the stability of the Gulf. They were seen as supporters of the biggest threat to the security and stability of the Gulf at the time, Iraq. During the Gulf War Israel seemed to have taken to the back burner of discussions and activities in the governments of the GCC. That was only logical. The invasion of Kuwait was a real shock to them. This invasion was not from Israel, but from an Arab state that was very well armed and had a massive, well-trained, and battle-hardened military. The Gulf War was a pivot in the peace process without a doubt. The policies toward the "peace process" of the GCC and many of the other Arab states that were part of the multinational coalition definitely switched after the war. It was not so much that they were now becoming best of friends with the Israelis. It was more that they were fed up with the Palestinian leadership, and in some cases the Palestinians as a group. It was also partly due to the support the GCC states, especially Kuwait and Saudi Arabia, received from the USA in particular during the Gulf War. After the Gulf War the USA was in a much better position to pressure, cajole and convince the leaders of the GCC to support the peace process with Israel and to abort the boycotts against Israel.

After the war there were trade delegations coming from Qatar and Oman to meet with their Israeli counterparts. This would have been unheard of before the war. On the other hand, after the war the USA became more open to the Palestinians. Why not? The peace game then seemed more one sided and more "doable." The USA helped broker a peace agreement that the Palestinians could hardly refuse considering their much-weakened position. If a peace deal were to be completed then the USA, and more so the EU, could then step in as the supporters of Palestinian development from the abyss. Yes, there were policy pivots through this war to be found in Washington, as well as Brussels, London, Paris and Bonn. Things were going well on the peace front and the pivots were fairly stable through the signing of the Interim Agreements and the Israeli-Jordanian Peace Treaty.

Soon after Netanyahu was elected it became clear that the warmth that the Arab states had shown toward Israel was a rather thin veneer and based more on the complexities of inter-Arab relations than the turning of a new leaf in Arab-Israeli relations. The "peace process" rather oddly benefited from the economic and political shocks of the Gulf War. The ground work and hard-won diplomatic (and other back room) deals that preceded the war also helped develop the proper initial conditions for the monumental meetings in Madrid, Oslo and Washington and the signing of treaties and agreements. The Gulf War shocked the parties into negotiation rooms. This can be seen as the culmination of a series of connected and unconnected events rather than the results of the sort of absurd conspiracies often theorized about why the Gulf War happened.

One could say that the Gulf War related economic shocks that harmed many of these Arab states have mostly dissipated. The Gulf war-related shocks to the peace process that culminated in the Israeli-Palestinian accords and agreements and the Israeli-Jordanian Peace Treaty have also dissipated – mostly due to false steps in the peace process after these documents were signed and the interventions of such groups as Hamas and Israel's own brand of fundamentalists. Above all, the pivotal effects of the Gulf War on the peace process have been dissipated by the actions of one man, Netanyahu, and his most ardent and inflexible supporters. For the peace process then one could say that the Gulf War was moderately pivotal. But the shock was not great enough, and the forces to keep the peace process not strong enough, to overcome the dangerous mix of Israeli and Palestinian internal and external politics.

This paper has focused on the economic "pivotalness" of the Gulf War and the fall of Iraq. It has been shown that such economic "pivotalness" was moderate over the range of the countries studied. Each country studied, however, was affected in different ways than the others. These differences in effects were mostly due the differences among these countries of their domestic and international economic structures, behaviours and performances. They were also due to the differences in policy responses by each country and each country's allies, the IMF, World Bank and others. Other explanations of the differences can be found in how well tied each country was to Iraq, either directly through trade and labour, or indirectly through being in different degrees part of the international oil and financial markets. Changing internal policies such as economic reform and structural adjustment also seemed to have reduced the impact of the war on those countries, such as Egypt, who have been the most successful in the region with these policies. The ability to bounce back from the war was also a function of how much savings and other assets were available to a country, with Kuwait being the obvious beneficiary of its own past financial conservativeness. Debt rescheduling and write-offs helped other countries, such as Egypt and Syria. The past squandering of remittance and aid money by some, such as Yemen and the Palestinians, was to magnify the effects of their disastrous political decisions prior to the Gulf War. On the other hand, increased aid after the war, especially from the GCC, also considerably helped Syria and Egypt. The Palestinians and the Yemenis saw their Arab-sponsored aid evaporate. International politics also played a large part in the "pivotalness" of these events to each country. Those who seemed to have supported Saddam Hussein were economically hammered and found aid, labour markets, assets, savings, etc. cut off from them. As the effects of the Gulf War began to play out another part of international politics took over, the "peace process." The GCC, Jordan and the Palestinians became more engaged with the peace process after the Gulf War. This led to some short-term positive political developments. It also led to some short to medium run positive economic developments to those most directly engaged in the process with Israel, the Palestinians and Jordan. The expected positive economic results to these two groups likely had much to do with their agreeing to sign agreements and treaties. The actual results proved much less than anticipated, particularly for the Palestinians. As the negligibility of the peace dividends to these two groups became more and more apparent, as the anti-peace aggressiveness of the Netanyahu regime became more ominous to them, the peace process collapsed. The Gulf War also showed more clearly the economic and political canyons that separate the haves from the have-nots in the Arab world. The Gulf War also seems to have fuelled further domestic and international political turmoil between the rulers of the Arab states and their fundamentalist detractors. The Gulf War stunned the Arab world economically, militarily, socially, politically, and, some would say, even culturally.

The economic story of the Gulf War and the fall of Iraq seems to be winding down for most of the Arab world, the Palestinians and Yemenis aside. The political, military, social and cultural stories may just be at their beginning.

Notes

* Data from and about Iraq are often contradictory or differ considerably according to the source. Although not to the degree that it could be said about Iraq a similar caveat should be mentioned about data about and from other countries in the region. Clearly the issues involved in each and every one of the countries and regions discussed here could have at least a series of books on them. However, I was asked to write a chapter on the overall economic impacts of the Gulf War and the collapse of Iraq on the MENA region. This has been a daunting task. I hope that those who read this chapter will consider this as a launching pad for further discussion, thought, and research on these very complex and important issues.

1 Paul Kennedy, "Pivotal States and U.S. Strategy," *Foreign Affairs*, (January/February, 1996), pp. 33-51.

2 *Ibid*, p. 33.

3 *Ibid*, p. 34

4 *Ibid*, p. 38

5 One could set up different shock wave maps: economic, political, geographic, military-strategic and so forth and construct measurements of the shocks and the distances traveled, as well as the time span covered to analyse a series of events such as the Gulf War, the invasion of Kuwait, the 1967 War and so on.

6 Some of the short term costs to countries outside of Iraq's region found by Nazem Abdullah (1991) are for Bangladesh $1.5 billion, India $2.9 billion, Pakistan $2.1 billion, Philippines $1 billion, Sri Lanka $200 million, Vietnam $377 million, Bulgaria $1.4 billion, Czechoslovakia $2.1 billion, Poland $1.5 billion, and Romania $4 billion. Russia's $10 billion in debt to Iraq was put in jeopardy. Yugoslavia may have lost $1.3 billion, and all of sub-Saharan Africa $2 billion.

7 I am currently working on a paper entitled "A theory of economic pivots," which I plan to finish early this year.

8 EIU, *Country Report, Iraq, 4th Quarter 1995*, p. 3.

9 United States, *Statistical Abstract of the United States, 1994*, p. 449.

10 Source: UN, UNCTAD, *World Investment Report 1997, Transnational Corporations, Market Structure, and Competition Policy.* These regions are defined as follows in this source: North Africa is Algeria, Egypt, Libya, Morocco, Sudan and Tunisia. West Asia is defined as Bahrain, Cyprus, Iran, Iraq, Jordan, Kuwait, Lebanon, Oman, Qatar, Saudi Arabia, Syria, Turkey, UAE, and Yemen. One of the problems with data on the regions analysed in this paper are that different sources use different definitions for the target areas.

11 *Ibid.*

12 *Ibid.*

13 UNCTAD, 1997.

14 *Petroleum Intelligence Weekly*, 12 February 1990.

15 IMF, *Direction of Trade Statistics, 1993.*

16 United States, *Statistical Abstract of the United State, 1994*, p. 820.

17 The market capitalization of Microsoft Corporation in July 1998 was around $246 billion. See *International Herald Tribune*, July 4-5, 1998, p. 11.

18 *Ibid.*

19 Iraq was also world class in historical importance, archaeology, strategic location (when geostrategy meant much more than it does now), and some other mineral resources, such as sulfur and natural gas.

20 If the sanctions continue for much longer and Iraq is able to explore its many undeveloped fields successfully, and if Saudi Arabia continues to produce oil at 8+ mbd, then Iraq might have the single largest reserves of any country. This may be one of the contradictory results of the sanctions.

21 The moderately pivotal nature of Iraq may have been part of the calculation of the multinational coalition to get into the war in the first place. Iraq was economically small enough to be "expendable" given the military and other threats it was presenting. There was also the knowledge that there was enough excess capacity in the oil industry to make up for the losses of Iraqi (and Kuwaiti) oil in the medium run. (See Sullivan, Paul, "Oil: Challenges and Prospects" (1997)) From September to November in 1990 oil output for Saudi Arabia, the UAE, Oman, and Qatar went up by 71%. Other OPEC production went up by 24%. The excess capacity was there. (See Watson, *Economic Prospects for the Gulf Cooperation Council*, p. 179).

22 Unites States, *Statistical Abstract of the United States, 1994*, pp. 851 and 856.

23 World Trade Organization, *Annual Report, 1996, Volume II*, p. 7.

24 *Ibid.*

25 Alonso-Gamo, Susan Fennel, etal, "Adjusting to New Realities: MENA, The Uruguay Round, and the EU-Mediterranean Initiative," p. 9.

26 *Ibid*, p. 3.

27 John Page, "Economic Prospects and the Role of Regional Development Financial Institutions," in *Regional Economic Development in the Middle East: Opportunities and Risks*, p. 14.

28 IMF, *Direction of Trade Statistics Yearbook, 1994*, p. 245.

29 IMF, *op. cit.*, p. 245.

30 IMF, *Direction of Trade Statistics*, various years

31 So much for the theory that strong trading relations will reduce the chances of war in this case.

32 The biggest losers of exports to Iraq in absolute terms were the USA, $704 million, France, $570 million, Germany, $876 million, Italy, $239 million, the UK, $553 million, Kuwait $274 million, Turkey, $236 million, and Japan $298 million, but for all of these finding alternative markets in the medium run turned out to be not a major issue. Although at the firm level it was surely very costly. Yugoslavia, a country that was starting to go through turmoil at the time, exported $129 million to Iraq. (IMF, *op. cit.*, 1997, pp. 432-433).

33 IMF, *Direction of Trade Statistics Yearbook, 1997.*

34 IMF, *Direction of Trade Statistics Yearbook*, various years.

35 This would certainly have to be adjusted upward with improved data on trade with Jordan, Iran, and Turkey.

36 IMF, *Direction of Trade Statistics Yearbook*, various years.

37 *Ibid.*

38 Iran and Iraq are special cases. Because of the revolution in Iran in 1979 and the Iran-Iraq War from 1980-1988 their oil production and oil revenues were severely disrupted by events well outside normal oil market behaviour. One could also say the same for Kuwait in 1990-1992. Another thing to mention here are that the costs of the Iran-Iraq

War to these two combatants was well over $1 trillion. This is far more expensive than the Gulf War of 1991 and the invasion of Kuwait in 1990. Part of this $1 trillion bill is due to lost oil revenues and the destruction of oil fields.

39 OPEC, *Annual Statistical Bulletin*, various years.

40 World Bank, *Claiming the Future: Choosing Prosperity in the Middle East and North Africa*, p. 17

41 Sullivan, Paul, "Oil: Challenges and Prospects," p. 79.

42 Atif Kubursi, "The Economics of Peace: The Arab Response," in *Regional Economic Development in the Middle East: Opportunities and Risks*, CFPAP, 1995.

43 ACDA, *World Military Expenditures and Arms Transfers, 1995*, p. 81.

44 ACDA, *World Military Expenditures and Arms Transfers, 1995*, p. 81.

45 ACDA, *World Military Expenditures and Arms Transfers, 1995*, p. 92.

46 ACDA, *World Military Expenditures and Arms Transfers, 1995*, p. 98.

47 F. Gregory Gause, III, "Arms Supplies and Military Spending in the Gulf," *Middle East Report*, (July-September, 1997), pp. 12-14.

48 F. Gregory Gause, III, *Ibid*, p. 13, states that the cost to the US for its defence of the Gulf is becoming controversial in the US. He mentions that Graham Fuller and Ian Lessor in a recent *Foreign Affairs* article claim that it might be $60 billion per year. This is 1/5 of the US Defence Budget. Others claim it is less. Still these massive expenditures may lend further proof that the GCC cannot defend itself alone.

49 Because of the decline in real oil revenues this factor has endogenously become less important, although it is still very important, since the early 1980s.

50 Amer Bisat, Mohammed Al-Erain, and Thomas Helbing, "Growth, Investment, and Saving in the Arab Eocnomies," IMF, Working Paper, WP/97/85, 1997, p. 6.

51 *Ibid*, p. 6.

52 *Ibid*, p. 7.

53 Dropping investment in developing countries is never a good idea, especially if those investments are going to useful projects. Certainly some of these projects were rather absurd. Others have made significant positive impacts on the MENA countries. Yes, to truly understand what these investment figures mean one has to get into the details of them. However, it is sufficient in this context to point out the major drop that occurred as an indication of the weakening of the economies as the oil revenues declined. Recently, private investment has been taking the place of some public investment. This is a positive change in many ways for the MENA region.

54 The highest performing developing countries seem to have the highest investment and savings as a percentage of GDP. (See John Page, "Economic Prospects and the Role of Regional Development Finance Institutions," in *Regional Economic Development in the Middle East: Opportunities and Risks*, p. 5-18.

55 Bisat, El-Erain et. al, p. 8.

56 John Page, *op. cit.*, p. 15, gives us a chart that shows that from 1960-1990 the MENA region has had an overall negative growth in total factor productivity.

57 *Ibid*, p. 17.

58 *Ibid*, p. 33.

59 IMF, *World Economic Survey, 1998*, p. 151.

60 UN, UNESCWA, ECSOC, Substantive Session, Geneva, 30 June-25 July 1997, "Summary of Survey of Economic and Social Developments in the ESCWA Region, 1996-1997," UN,E/1997/45, 28 April 1997, at internet gopher.un.org/00/esc/docs/1997.

---

61 *Ibid.*

62 *Ibid*, p. 3.

63 *Ibid*, p. 2.

64 *Ibid*, p. 3.

65 *Ibid.* p. 5.

66 Pierre Van Den Boogaerde, *Financial Assistance From Arab Countries and Arab Regional Institutions*, IMF, Occasional Paper 87, Washington, DC, 1991, pages 75 for net workers' remittance, p. 84 for remittances per GNP, p. 85 for remittances and imports.

67 Other countries in the Arab world were also damaged by the crisis: "The Gulf crisis has also adversely affected other labour sending Arab countries, particularly Djibouti, Somalia, Tunisia and Maraca. Djibouti and Somali are categorized as least developing countries. Djibouti's loss from the suspension and/or postponement of investment projects financed by Kuwait and Iraq and other Arab funds is estimated at $800 million. Moreover, the rise in oil prices have cost Djibouti $17 million, the loss of trade revenue is estimated at $68 million and import/transport costs are estimated at $30 million. Tunisia was recently strengthening its economic ties with Iraq and was hoping for trade cooperation and new outlets for its exports. The repercussions of the Gulf Crisis on Tunisia are serious, particularly on the country's balance of payments. Tunisia has estimated that losses caused by the Gulf Crisis amounted to [in the short run only] $209 million in 1990 and are expected to total $345 million in 1991. Morocco, already confronted with a large external debt burden, had to pay a sharply higher oil-import bill." (See Nazem Abdalla, 1991. There were huge losses due to trade being cut off, increases in oil prices, lost remittances, etc. to Asian countries. For lack of space in this article we cannot get into too much here, but country estimates include over $5 billion for India in 1990-1991, $2.1 billion to Pakistan, close to $500 million to the Philippines for 1990-1991, Vietnam $377.3 million, Sri Lanka $90 million per year in lost remittances. These are, of course, short-term phenomenon's that have been changing as the crisis proceeds to 1996 and beyond. There were also significant short-term losses to European countries, especially Eastern European countries. Eastern European countries were owed oil from Iraq to repay debts; they had project in the works in Iraq, and traded with Iraq. Bulgaria may have lost $1.39 billion, Czechoslovakia $2.1 billion, Poland $2.4 billion, Romania $2.9 billion, Turkey $5 billion, Yugoslavia $1.3 billion – most just in 1990 alone. Africa south of the Sahara may have lost $2 billion. Many Latin American countries, especially Uruguay, Brazil and Argentina lost much due to the increase in oil prices. (See Nazem Abdulla, *op. cit.*, pp. 28-33).

68 These charts are from Nazem Abdulla, "Report Prepared for the United Nations Development Programme's Gulf Task Force: Impact of the Gulf Crisis on Developing Countries," June 1991, p. 5a. He listed the source of these data as "Estimates of the International Labour Organization, Ministerial Meeting on Migrant Workers Affected by the Gulf Crisis, 19 November 1990."

69 Nazem Abdulla , *op. cit.*., p. 7b.

70 Nazem Abdalla, p. 11a, based on ILO, UN field office visits, and many Government Reports.

71 Numbers of returnees from Nazem Abdulla, *op. cit.*, p. 11a.

72 Nazem Abdulla, *op. cit.*, p. 11b.

73 Bishara A. BahBah, "The Economic Consequences on Palestinians," in The Center For Policy Analysis on Palestine, *The Palestinians and the War in the Gulf*, pp. 17-21.

74 The countries are also engaged in legal proceedings and diplomacy to get reparations for these returnees and others. Private citizens from these countries are also trying to get reparations, most of which will come through the UN. There have been some reparations payments made already, but they hardly measure up to the losses some of these persons had.

75 Sadek Wahba "The Israeli-Palestinian Peace Agreement: Consequences for Labour Migration," *Harvard Middle Eastern and Islamic Review*, (vol. 2, no. 1, Spring 1995), p. 42. [Presumably, these na's (not available) at the year 1991 are because he situation was so fluid it is hard still to figure out what exactly was going on].

76 Radwan Shaban, Ragui Assad and Sulayman S. Al-Qudsi, "The Challenge of Unemployment in the Arab Region," *International Labour Review*, (1995, vol. 134, no. 1), p. 74.

77 The Palestinians economy is not just in the West Bank and Gaza but stretches to wherever one finds large groups of Palestinians. Often remittances and other funds cross many borders and come from Palestinians from many regions before they get to the West Bank and Gaza. For example, a family in the West Bank may have a son who had travel documents from the Occupied Territories, or was simply ejected, another son who has Jordanian passport and, possibly another son who has Syrian or Lebanese travel documents. The West Bank and Gaza, especially before the Intifada and the Gulf War was very much tapped into various streams of international remittance flows.

78 The Occupied Territories and Jordan are intertwined through this diaspora population.

79 See Paul Sullivan, "Palestine: Vulnerable Economy, Vulnerable Peace," and "Arab Labour and Peace."

80 IMF, *Balance of Payments Statistics Yearbook, 1994*, p. 212. See sections on Egypt and Syria below for an explanation of some of the complications attached to these remittances data.

81 *Ibid*, p. 684.

82 *Ibid*, p. 684.

83 Ann Lesch, "The Palestinians in Kuwait", p. 49.

84 Some of the losses to the Palestinians and other Arab and Asian labour have been paid back through the UN via reparation payments from Iraq. These have not been on a dollar-for-dollar basis and have been the source of much tension in recent years. There are significant outstanding reparations claims even in 1998.

85 Nazem Abdalla, *op. cit.*, p 10.

86 Bishara A. Bahbah, "The Economic Consequences on Palestinians," p. 18.

87 *Ibid*, p. 17.

88 Nazem Abdalla, "Impact of the Gulf Crisis on Developing Countries," p. 5a.

89 Nazem Abdalla, *op. cit.*, p. 5a.

90 Cheryl Rutenburg, "The Gulf War, The Palestinians, and the New World Order," p. 324

91 Bishara Bahbah, "The Economic Consequences on the Palestinians," p. 18.

92 *Middle East Contemporary Survey*, (1991), p. 536.

93 *Middle East Contemporary Survey*, (1991), p. 536.

94 *Middle East Contemporary Survey*, (1991), p. 536.

95 Bishara Bahbah, *op. cit.*, p. 18.

96 Bishara Bahbah, *op. cit.*, pp. 18-19.

97 EIU, *Country Profile, Israel and the Occupied Territories, 1997-1998*, p. 73.

98 JMCC, *op. cit.*, (quoting George Abed, "The Gulf's toll in the Palestinians," *The Christian Science Monitor*, (29 November 1990), pp. 18, 121.

99 JMCC, *op. cit.*, p. 62-63.

100 JMCC, *op. cit.*, p. 63.

101 Samir Abdullah, "Middle East Regional Development: A Palestinian Perspective," p. 19.

102 "World Population Data Sheet." from the Population Reference Bureau, Inc., 1875 Connecticut Ave., Washington, DC.

103 Paul Sullivan, "Palestine: Vulnerable Economy, Vulnerable Peace," p. 6.

104 EIU, *Country Profile, Israel and the Occupied Territories, 1997-1998*, p. 73.

105 Gil Fieler, "Labour Migration in the Middle East Following the Iraqi Invasion of Kuwait," (IPCRI, vol. 2, no. 7, December 1993), p. 19.

106 IMF, *Balance of Payments Statistics*, various years p. 375.

107 Bishara Bahbah, *op. cit.*, p. 20.

108 Some of these increased remittances may also be part of reparations agreements and legal cases.

109 The World Bank, *Peace and the Jordanian Economy*, p. 36.

110 The World Bank, *Peace and the Jordanian Economy*, p. 6.

111 Nazem Abdalla, "Impact of the Gulf Crisis on Developing Countries," pp. 5a, 7a, and 7b.

112 *Ibid.*

113 *Middle East Contemporary Survey*, (1991), p. 487.

114 *Ibid*, p. 487.

115 Radwan A. Shaban, Ragui Assad and Sulayman S. Al-Qudsi, "The Challenge of Unemployment in the Arab Region," p. 73.

116 *Middle East Contemporary Survey*, (1991), p. 488.

117 *Middle East Contemporary Survey*, (1991), pp. 487-488.

118 www.undp-jordan.org/programmes.html#patterns, UN, "Advisory Note for Jordan."

119 *Ibid.*

120 *Star*, December 14, 1995.

121 *Star* is found at www.arabia.com/star.

122 *Middle East Contemporary Survey*, (1991), pp. 485-486.

123 The World Bank, "Will Arab Workers Prosper," p. 3.

124 *Ibid*, p. 5.

125 World Bank, *World Development Report, 1995*, p. 145.

126 See, for example, Amal Abdel-Fattah Kandeel, "Jordan's Peace Dividend: Effects of Peace on Labor and Water Resources," unpublished MA Thesis, American University in Cairo, May 1998.

127 IMF, *Ibid*, p. 73 and 65.

128 IMF, Staff Country Report no. 97/16, "Jordan Satistical Appendix," March 1997, p. 1.

129 *Ibid.*

130 *Ibid*, pp. 34-35.

131 *Ibid.*

132 EIU, *Country Profile, Kuwait, 1996-1997*, p. 15.

133 *Ibid.*

134 UNESCWA, "Summary of the Survey of the Economic and Social Developments in the UNESCWA Region, 1996-1997," p. 6.
135 King Hussein died on February 7, 1999 and was succeeded by his eldest son, Abdullah. King Abdullah has not departed from his father's foreign and domestic policies.
136 Even the degree and success of these reforms is under doubt. The World Bank and Jordan are in sharp disagreement about economic growth figures for 1996 and 1997. Jordan claims that they were.
137 Some have been getting reparations payments. Other reparations are still under consideration both at a Government-to-Government level (Kuwait and Egypt), Government-to-UN level, and at a personal level.
138 Nazem Abdalla, *op. cit.*, p. 5a.
139 Michael Bonine, "Population and Labor After the Gulf War: Trends for the 1990s," *Middle East Insight*, (January/February, 1996), pp. 37-40; p. 38.
140 See World Bank, "Will Arab Workers Prosper in the Twenty-First Century?"; and World Bank, "Arab Republic of Egypt: Agricultural Strategy for the 1990s," World Bank, 1993.
141 See Sullivan, Paul, "Dilemmas of Economic Reform in Egypt."
142 *Middle East Contemporary Survey*, (1991), p.344 and footnote 56, p. 372.
143 *Ibid*, p. 344.
144 *Middle East Contemporary Survey 1990*, p. 344.
145 *Ibid*, p. 345.
146 *Middle East Contemporary Survey 1990*, pp. 345-346.
147 EIU, *Country Profile, Egypt, 1997-1998*, p. 54.
148 *Ibid.*
149 *Ibid.*
150 *Ibid*, p. 74.
151 IMF, *Balance of Payments Statistics Yearbook, 1994.*
152 UNESCWA, *op. cit.*.
153 EIU, *Country Profile, Egypt, 1997-1998.*
154 EIU, *Country Profile, Egypt, 1997-1998*, p. 15.
155 Michael Bonine, *op. cit.*. p. 39.
156 IMF, *Balance of Payment Statistics, 1995.*
157 Michael Bonine, *op. cit.*, p. 39.
158 EIU, *World Outlook, 1997.*
159 UNESCWA, *op. cit.*, p. 24.
160 IMF, *International Financial Statistics Yearbook, 1995*, p. 147.
161 *Ibid.*
162 IMF, *Ibid*, p. 73.
163 IMF, *Ibid*, p. 65.
164 The World Bank, *World Development Report, 1995*, p. 145.
165 The World Bank, *Will Arab Workers Prosper of Be Left Out in the Twenty-First Century?*, p. 3.
166 *Ibid*, p. 8.
167 EIU, *World Outlook, 1997.*
168 World Bank, *World Development Report 1997*, tables at the end.
169 Yemen's economy has many problems not associated with the Gulf War that have been chronic and long term.

170 UNSCWA, "Summary of the Survey of Economic and Social Developments in the ESCWA region, 1996-1997," p. 7.

171 BBC News, WorldService, "Yemeni tribal conflict deepens," on internet news.bbc.co.uk/hi/english/world/middle_east/ on June 28, 1998.

172 Nazem Abdalla, *op. cit.*, p. 20.

173 EIU, *Country Profile, Syria, 1997-1998*, p. 31.

174 IMF, *Balance of Payments Statistics, 1995*, and UNESCWA (1997).

175 EIU, *Country Profile, Syria, 1997-1998*, p. 31.

176 EIU, *Country Profile, Kuwait, 1996-1997.*

177 World Bank, *World Development Report, 1995*, p. 145.

178 The World Bank, *Will Arab Workers Prosper?*, p. 13.

179 www.polrisk.com/syri000a.html, 11/10/96.

180 IMF, *International Financial Statistics Yearbook, 1995*, p. 131.

181 World Bank, *Will Arab Workers Prosper?*, p. 13.

182 Even many in Syria admit that Egypt is doing a much better job of it.

183 There is a succession issue here as well. What happens when Hafez Al-Asad is no longer in charge? Who will take over? Will the stresses and strains in Syrian politics lead toward further internal and international confrontation? How will the Alawi-Sunni tensions work out without such a powerful and ruthless leader? Will the economic stresses push more people into the fundamentalist camps in Syria? There are many unknowns here.

184 This, and the following survey of the OS states are broad brush survey. Each of these countries really needs a book to its own for an analysis of the effects of the Gulf War.

185 Interview of a former Foreign Minister of Jordan in Jordan by the author and his wife on October 6, 1996.

186 *Middle East Contemporary Survey*, Volume XV, 1991, p. 523.

187 *Middle East Contemporary Survey*, Volume XV, 1991, p. 523.

188 *Ibid*, p. 717.

189 For Kuwait, that is. There were some minor repairs in the other states.

190 Payments to the mulitanational coalition may have been much higher than reported, most particularly some off-budget items that may not have been politically sound to publicize.

191 From the *Petroleum Economist*, (May 1995), p. 60: Saudi Arabian oil production increased from 5.158 mbd in 1989 to 8.405 mbd in 1991. Abu Dhabi's production went up form 1.4 mbd in 1989 to 1.98 mbd in 1991. Libya's went form 1.1 mbd to 1.245 mbd. Iran increased from 2.892 mbd to 3.341 mbd in the same period. Countries such as Nigeria also seemed to have gained.

192 Vahan Zanoyan, "After the Oil Boom: The Holiday Ends in the Gulf," *Foreign Affairs*, (November/December, 1995).

193 ACDA, *World Military Expenditures and Arms Transfers, 1995*, p. 81.

194 *Ibid*, p. 81.

195 ACDA, *op. cit.*, p. 92.

196 ACDA, *op. cit.*, p. 98.

197 ACDA, 1995, various pages.

198 William Watson, "Economic Prospects for the Gulf Cooperation Council," p. 178.

199 *Ibid.*

200 *Middle East Economic Digest*, (19 July 1996), p. 16. Their source: *BP Statistical Revue of World Energy 1996.*

201 www.eia.doe/emeu/cabs/hot.html.

202 Under U.N. Resolution 986 Iraq may export $1 billion every 90 days for 180 days. (see eia.doe.gov/emeu/cabs/hot.html).

203 www.eia.gov/emeu/cabs/sanction.html.

204 See Paul Sullivan, "Oil: Challenges and Prospects," p. 73 and USDOE, EIA, web pages on Iraq.

205 *Ibid*, p. 75.

206 Arab Petroleum Research Institute, 1995.

207 I will get more into issues like these in my forthcoming paper, "The Development of Iraq: 1979-1996."

208 See Paul Sullivan, "Iraq The Phoenix: redevelopment and revitalization of a former pariah state?"

209 UNESCWA, *op. cit.*, p. 20.

210 A small proportion of the increase in the oil production of the GCC (especially in 1988-1990) was due also to the collapse of the oil production in the USSR. Most of the increase was due to the loss to the markets of much of the production of Kuwaiti crude from 1990-1992, and most of the production of Iraqi crude even to today, but certainly to January 1997 when UN Resolution 986 came into effect.

211 This reliance, of course, changes with the real revenues of oil relative to other sources of income for the country. These numbers change from year to year.

212 Cordesman, *Saudi Arabia*, p. 52.

213 *Ibid*, p. 53.

214 EIU, *Country Profile, Saudi Arabia, 1996-1997*, p. 13; and Cordesman, *op. cit.*, p. 55.

215 The EIU tells us, however, where this might be misleading. Many of the public sector firms are borrowing on international commercial markets, but the borrowing is not registered as central government debt. For example, Saudi Arabian Airlines borrowed $5bn in order to purchase planes from Boeing. (EIU, pp. 49).

216 *Ibid*, p. 14.

217 OECD, *International Capital Markets Statistics, 1950-1995*, (OECD, 1996), pp. 243-250.

218 EIU, *Country Profile, Saudi Arabia, 1996-1997*, p. 14.

219 www.eia.doe.gov/emeu/hot.html.

220 Cordesman, Anthony, *Saudi Arabia: Gaurdin the Dsert Kingdom*, p. 49.

221 But, as with many others in the GCC, if we look at foreign assets during the period 1980-1994 there is a steep decline after 1982. The Gulf War just picked up the pace of the trend of decline.

222 EIU, *Country Profile, Saudi Arabia, 1996-1997*, p. 19.

223 Eliyahu Kanovsky, "The Economic Consequences of the Persian Gulf War: Accelerating OPEC's Demise," p.12.

224 *Ibid*, p. 12.

225 Eliyahu Kanovsky, *Ibid*, p. 14 [Since these estimates were made the actual costs of the war to Saudi Arabia increased to about $65 billion.]

226 Eliyahu Kanovsky, *Ibid*, p. 16.

227 The Economist, *Country Report, Saudi Arabia, 3rd Quarter, 1996, p. 15The Economist, Country Report, Saudi Arabia, 3rd Quarter*, (1996), p. 15.

228 World Bank, *World Development Report, 1995*, p.145.
229 UNESCWA, *op. cit.*, p. 20-21.
230 The World Bank, *Claiming the Future*, p. 17.
231 EIU, *Country Profile, Saudi Arabia, 1996-1997*, p. 21.
232 *Middle East Economic Digest*, "Special Report: Saudi Arabia," (11 November 1994), p. 38.
233 EIU, *Ibid*, p. 49.
234 IMF, *International Financial Statistics Yearbook, 1995*, p. 131.
235 IMF, *Ibid*, p. 73.
236 IMF, *Ibid*, p. 73.
237 IMF, *Ibid*, p. 65.
238 IMF, *Ibid*, p. 53.
239 EIU, *op. cit.*, pp. 50.
240 EIU, *op. cit.*, pp. 54.
241 Kathy Evan, "Shifting Sands at the House of Saud," *The Middle East*, (February 1996), pp. 6-9.
242 As found in Gregory Quinn, *op. cit.*, p. 36.
243 "The end of the counterrevolution? The Politics of Economic Adjustment in Kuwait," *Middle East Report*, (July-September, 1997), p. 7.
244 Cordesman, Anthony, *Kuwait: Recovery and Security After the Gulf War*, p. 18.
245 OECD, *International Capital Market Statistics, 1950-1995*, p. 243 and EIU *op. cit.*, p. 9.
246 Metz, Helen Chapin, *Persian Gulf States, Federal Research Division*, Library of Congress, 1994, p. 99.
247 EIU, *op. cit.*, p. 32.
248 Metz, Helen Chapin, *op. cit.*, p. 97.
249 On budget data see UNESCWA (1997). For the other data see World Bank (1995). For GDP and trade percentages in the earlier years see Cordesman, Anthony, *Kuwait: Recovery and Security After the Gulf War*, chapter 3.
250 EIU, *op. cit.*, pp. 9.
251 EIU, *op. Cit,*. pp. 9.
252 Gregory Quinn, *op. cit.*, p. 35 quoting The Economist, *Country Report, Kuwait.*
253 UNESCWA, *op. cit.*, p. 20.
254 UNESCWA, *op. cit.*, p. 20.
255 Cordesman, Anthony, *Kuwait: Recovery and Security After the Gulf War*, chart one on p. 21.
256 Cordesman, Anthony, *Kuwait: Recovery and Security After the Gulf War*, p. 18; and EIU, *Country Profile, Kuwait, 1996-1997*, pp. 36 and 43.
257 Charles Hoots, "Facing a Testing Time," *The Middle East*, (Jul/August 1995), p. 15.
258 *Ibid*, p. 15.
259 UNESCWA, *op. cit.*, p. 73.
260 EIU, *op. cit.*, pp. 36.
261 EIU, *op. cit.*, p. 10. There are some quirks in the Kuwaiti budgets that tend to make analyses of them different from other national budgets. One of these is the investment for the Reserve Fund for Future Generations being registered as expenditures. (EIU, *op. cit.*, p. 11).
262 EIU, *op. cit.*, p. 8.

263 Metz, Helen Chapin, *op. cit.*, p. 100.

264 Charles Hoots, *op. cit.*, pp. 15-17.

265 UNESCWA, *op. cit.*, p. 19.

266 Charles Hoots, *Ibid*, p. 17.

267 *Middle East Economic Digest*, "Testing Times for Kuwait's Democracy," (26 May 1995), pp. 3-4.

268 IMF, *International Financial Statistics Yearbook*, 1995, p. 147.

269 IMF, *Ibid*, p. 73.

270 IMF, *Ibid*, p. 65.

271 EIU, *op. cit.*, pp. 33.

272 Cordesman, *op. cit.*, p. 19 has very different and more optimistic figures. These are from EIU, *World Outlook, 1997*, p. 208.

273 Cordesman, Anthony, *op. cit.*, p. 24.

274 Cordesman, Anthony, *Kuwait: Recovery and Security After the Gulf War*, p. 47.

275 UNSCWA, "Summary of the Survey of Economic and Social Developments in the ESCWA region, 1996-1997."

276 If the OPEC and non-OPEC oil producers are able to organize a "new market control mechanism" they may succeed in the short run to raise the price of oil a couple of dollars. Given no unexpected and significant shocks to oil markets during the rest of 1998 the Asian Crisis and the general glut in oil left over from last winter will keep the price of oil below $18, and possibly $16 for the rest of 1998.

277 Unless, of course, there is a new pro-GCC regime (pro-Saudi, pro-Kuwaiti, etc) established in Iraq, or at least a regime that is no longer a threat to Saudi Arabia and Kuwait. Some aid might flow in. Some has already trickled in from Saudi Arabia and Kuwait to Iraq for "humanitarian and Pan-Arab" reasons.

278 See Sullivan, Paul, "Iraq: The Phoenix," especially the section on the possible comparisons of Germany in the interwar period and Iraq in the post-sanctions era.

5 Balance of Power and Nuclear Deterrence: The Middle East after the Gulf War

ADEL SAFTY[1]

Introduction

The term balance of power was sometimes used to mean equilibrium as for instance in the sense used by A. J. P. Taylor in his book *The Struggle for Mastery in Europe 1848-1918*.[2] At other times, it was used to mean a general system viewed as essential for the preservation of a certain political system. This view was most clearly asserted by Fenelon, a one time spiritual advisor to Louis XIV, in his exposition of the duties of royalty.[3] Once a Power was allowed to rise to a position of predominance, Fenelon believed, you could not count on its good behaviour. Where a powerful state arose, Fenelon argued, neighbouring states had an obligation to form a kind of commonwealth; otherwise the most powerful country will eventually dominate the rest of them.

The Treaty of Utrecht (1713) incorporated the notion of balance of power as a principle of international society justifying the separation of the crowns of France and Spain so that "the Peace and Tranquillity of Christian Europe may be ordered and stabilized in a just Balance of Power (which is the best and most solid foundation of mutual friendship and a lasting general concord).[4]

Similarly the treaty of Vienna of 1735, incorporating the French guarantee of the Pragmatic Sanctions, stated that this too was designed to preserve the European balance. The alliance treaties of 1813 between Austria, Prussia, Russia and Britain likewise declared that their purpose in defeating France was to restore the balance of power. The First Treaty of Paris of 1814 echoed Utrecht in stating that it was designed to establish a system of "real and permanent Balance of Power in Europe."

Martin Wight observed that with the partition of Poland and Turkey at the end of the 18th century; of Turkey, Africa and China at the end of the 19th, "the balance of power, in effect, came to mean ... the principle of equal aggrandizement of the Great Powers at the expense of the weak."[5]

Thus, the term balance of power is in fact often used to describe a state of disequilibrium. As Nicholas J. Spykman put it: "The truth of the matter is that states are interested only in a balance which is in their favour. Not equilibrium, but a generous margin is their objective... The balance desired is the one which neutralizes other states, leaving the home state free to be the deciding force and the deciding voice."[6] Spykman cites a cogent illustration from the headlines in *The Times* newspaper in 1963: "Mr. McNamara says West now has Superiority: U.S. Forces nearing proper balance for Peace."[7]

This meaning of the term balance of power has consistently been the one applied to the Middle East in the post-World War II era. Ever since the Tripartite Declaration of 1950 by which the three Western Powers the U.S., UK and France sought to preserve the territorial status quo and maintain the prevailing balance of power, it was clearly understood that the term meant maintaining Israel's military superiority over all its neighbours combined.

In all of its various meanings and certainly underlying its meaning as a disequilibrium of power in favour of one given side, the term balance of powers relies on the conceptual notion that power is the ultimate aim of all international politics, as the realist thinker Hans Morgenthau described in his seminal book *Politics Among Nations: The Struggle for Power and Peace*.[8]

Even diplomacy is viewed within the context of struggle for power and as such becomes equated with war. Frederick L. Schuman observes that "the primary objective of foreign policy in peace and in war is neither war nor peace but something common to both: the enhancement of the power of your State to resist the will of others and impose your will upon them and the diminution of the power of others to resist your will and impose their will upon you. In "war" this goal is pursued by overt violence, and in "peace" by bargaining supported by threats of force."[9]

But power is a relative thing and the power of one country can only usefully be measured in relation to any other country engaged in the same struggle for power. Great powers or regional powers will engage in the balance of power game in pursuit of power. Small states cannot be full players in the game and the only viable option for them in order to preserve their independence is through a system of alliance with one or more of their powerful neighbours.

The physical application of power has been the ultimate arbiter of inter-state disputes. A. J. P. Taylor cites Bismarck: "When men dislike Bismarck for his realism, what they really dislike is reality. Take his most famous sentence: "The great questions of our time will not be settled by resolutions and majority votes – that was the mistake of the men of 1848 and 1849 – but by blood and iron. Who can deny that this is true as a statement of fact?"[10]

In the post – World War II era, the use of force has figured prominently in American foreign policy. One scholar calculated that during the Cold War "American presidents have used military force in support of U. S. Foreign policy over 200 times."[11] Since the arrival, literally *en force*, of the USA on the Middle East scene with the Eisenhower doctrine, and the landing of American Marines in Lebanon in 1957, Washington may be said to have followed a policy of realpolitik in the Middle East designed to preserve its interests and defend its allies. This policy culminated in the outright reliance on force announced by President Carter in 1980 with the creation of the Rapid Deployment Force. It was most dramatically put into practice during the Gulf War.

The establishment of Israel in 1948, and its expansionism, offer a cogent illustration of a successful use of power politics including the physical application of force to accomplish political goals defined in terms of struggle for power.[12] Calculations of regional balance of power, or regionalism and ideological illegitimacy, as Alan Taylor described it in his book *The Arab Balance of Power*[13] have prevented the Arabs from harnessing the enormous potentialities of their economic, human, and intellectual resources. In their confrontation with Israel, they were unable to redress a perennially unfavourable balance of power. Many of the current difficulties of achieving a just and enduring peace in the Middle East flow from the fact that the peace treaties signed between the Israelis and the Palestinians are more a reflection of the realities of the regional balance of power, understood as a disequilibrium of power, than of mutually shared values of justice and peace.

Globally and regionally, the nuclear balance of power and its concomitant non-proliferation regime reflect a conception of balance of power based on the principle of disequilibrium of power in favour of a given side. What are its characteristics globally and regionally? What are its implications? And can a critical assessment of the balance of nuclear deterrence offer the Arabs, and more specifically the Egyptians, the possibility of achieving a better balance of power in the region?

The Nuclear Powers and The Non-Proliferation Regime

Nuclear inequality is a prominent, if unpopular, feature of international relations today. It has its roots and finds justification in the "realism" of the post World War II era; it received legal codification in the Nuclear non-Proliferation Treaty, which came into effect in 1968, and has been indefinitely extended in May 1995.

Unlike the post World War I era which witnessed a multiplication of idealist theories and attempts to ban war and aggression forever, the post World War II era saw the confinement of the noble ideals of humanity to the debating chambers of the United Nations General Assembly, and the acknowledged return of the balance of power system in international relations. The UN Security Council reflected some of the power realities that emerged after the war such as the exclusion of the defeated powers from decision-making affecting the international community and the granting of the veto power to the so-called great powers. The realism of the era was given theoretical justification in Hans Morgenthau's seminal book *Politics Among Nations* in which he convincingly argued, "international politics, like all other politics, is a struggle for power. Whatever the ultimate aims of international politics, power is always the immediate aim."[14]

The realities of constant struggle of power overwhelmed many ideals, including that of a common approach to controlling the enormous potentialities of the destructive energies of the nuclear bomb - the greatest modern symbol of power. They also provided a basis for the principle of nuclear inequality. Thus, shortly after Truman showed the world, and the Russians, what the nuclear bomb could do in Hiroshima and Nagasaki in 1945, the United States tried to ban the bomb. The American plan (the Baruch plan) proposed, in 1946, a scheme for controlling and inspecting national atomic energy and punishing transgressors. The scheme would escape Soviet veto and would, therefore, be used to prevent the USSR from acquiring the bomb. In the meantime the U.S. would keep the bomb until it ensured that no country could possibly have it. President Truman's position was: "We should not under any circumstances throw away our gun until we are sure the rest of the world can't arm against us."[15]

The Soviet Union rejected the plan and presented its own plan, the Gromyko Plan. It required the elimination of American atomic weapons first, to be followed by the establishment of a control and inspection scheme. When, in 1949, the Soviet Union became a nuclear power, Washington and Moscow directed their efforts at preventing others from acquiring the bomb. President Eisenhower's proposal "Atom for Peace" was designed to codify the nuclear status quo and called for joint American-Soviet efforts to stop others from joining the exclusive club. In the 1950s the United Kingdom became a nuclear power; and as was to be expected, the new atomic club pursued the same goal: keep the club membership at its present status while striving to prevent others from joining it.

It was in that spirit that, in 1963, the three nuclear powers signed in Moscow, the Nuclear Test Ban Treaty, outlawing nuclear tests in the atmosphere, outer space, and under water, while permitting underground testing. Since they had the technology to carry on their nuclear tests underground but others did not, the three nuclear powers hoped that the treaty would make it both more difficult and more costly for other countries to try to acquire the bomb. These efforts culminated in the successful negotiation of The Nuclear Non-Proliferation Treaty (NPT), which came into force in 1968. The NPT legalized nuclear inequality. It committed the non-nuclear countries not to develop or acquire nuclear weapons, and in return, the nuclear powers undertook to negotiate in good faith towards nuclear disarmament, while in fact continuing to test and develop new nuclear weapons.

The NPT came up for renewal in April 1995 and as part of the U.S. strategy to neutralize criticisms from the non-nuclear weapon countries and help bring about the indefinite extension of the treaty, President Clinton announced in February, 1995, that he was extending indefinitely the U.S. moratorium on nuclear weapons testing; he also withdrew a plan to allow the easy resumption of such testing in the future. The White House said this was the centrepiece of an American strategy to achieve a comprehensive nuclear test ban (CTB) treaty by 1996. The American President said that Washington wanted a "comprehensive" test ban, which will not even allow the so-called "peaceful" nuclear explosions.

However, the decision did not stop the non-aligned nations' growing criticisms, up till and during the extension conference, about the inequality of the NPT, and about the great powers discriminatory enforcement of its provisions. Indian Ambassador to the United Nations Arundhati Ghose, who vigorously articulated the opposition to the CTB, told this writer that India was entitled to and had to insist on equality. The NPT obligates the nuclear weapon-states to "pursue negotiations in good faith on effective measures relating to cessation of the nuclear race and to nuclear disarmament." In reality, the nuclear powers have done everything to vertically proliferate their own arsenals. Thus, the strategic warheads of the five acknowledged nuclear powers increased, under the non-proliferation regime, from 5,610, in 1968, to 24,462, in 1990. It is true that the Strategic Arms Reduction Treaty (START), signed in Moscow in July 1991, will reduce U.S. and Strategic arms to about 6,000 "accountable" warheads for each nation by 1999. START II, signed in Moscow in January 1993, will further reduce each country strategic arsenal to fewer than 3,500 warheads. But this is still far from nuclear disarmament; by all objective criteria this is still "overkill."[16]

Nuclear-weapons states have often placed commercial and political considerations above their commitment to the NPT provisions. Consider the following examples: To compensate Pakistan for its co-operation in facilitating American military assistance to the anti-Soviet Afghan Mujahedeen, Washington acquiesced in Pakistan's nuclear weapons program. China provided Pakistan with hands-on assistance at the Kahuta enrichment plant; Beijing also provided a tested bomb design and enough highly enriched uranium for two bombs. This seems to have had no adverse effect on Sino-American relations; on the contrary, the U.S. negotiated an agreement with China for peaceful nuclear co-operation, which included the export of U.S. nuclear plants to China. Beijing also exported un-safeguarded heavy water to India and an un-safeguarded research reactor to Algeria.

In return for concessions on trade issues, Washington entered into a nuclear agreement with Tokyo in 1988, which paved the way for Japan to recover from U.S.-supplied nuclear fuel more plutonium than in all U.S. and Soviet nuclear weapons combined. The U.S. non-proliferation policy accepts the reality of the plutonium "haves" and "have-nots"; but in the face of the plutonium-hungry Japanese industrial powerhouse, some analysts have wondered for how long the Koreas can remain indifferent.[17] France sent to Israel the Dimona reactor, its processing plant, and, according to a senior French official, a tested bomb design.[18]

On the other hand, being a member of the Nuclear Non-Proliferation Treaty did not necessarily mean forswearing nuclear weapons forever. Both North Korea and Iraq are good examples. In fact, some people have argued that membership in the NPT facilitated the acquisition of research reactors, uranium fuel, and equipment for processing plutonium. In addition, the International Atomic Energy Agency (IAEA) safeguards proved ineffective in detecting Iraq's nuclear weapon program even when it was located within nuclear-safeguarded installations. At the same time, membership in the NPT did not afford Iraq any protection against Israel's policy of unilateral enforcement of its nuclear monopoly in the Middle East. In June 1981 Israel, which has refused to join the NPT, destroyed Iraq's Osirak Power reactor.

The criticisms were not confined to the nuclear powers' vertical proliferation and discriminate horizontal proliferation, or the lax safeguards of the NPT; they extended to the apparent contradiction inherent in the nuclear powers' treaty commitment to nuclear disarmament and their effective policies and statements of policies suggesting a continued commitment to and reliance upon nuclear weapons in their strategic planning. More worrisome for the non-nuclear weapon states, the nuclear powers seem not only to value nuclear weapons for their deterrence role but also for their military contributions to war fighting strategies. Officials and strategists of the nuclear powers have rarely suggested that nuclear weapons should be eliminated, or that their use should be banned. Dulles' massive retaliation, Kissinger's limited nuclear war, Wohlstetter's delicate balance of terror, McNamara's flexible response, and the Air-land battle doctrine, all accepted the use of nuclear weapons as important military weapons.

The governments of the nuclear powers have repeatedly reaffirmed that nuclear weapons have a crucial role to play in their defence strategies. For example, on July 6, 1990, the London Declaration by the Heads of state and government of NATO countries stated that nuclear weapons "will continue to fulfil an essential role in the overall strategy of the alliance to prevent war by ensuring that there are no circumstances in which nuclear retaliation in response to military action may be discounted."[19] The U.S., UK and France are committed to nuclear deterrence and war-fighting strategies, including the use of nuclear weapons in the Third World. Moreover, according to an internal U.S. document declassified and recently obtained by the Natural Resources Defence Council, a Washington-based arms control-monitoring group, the U.S. is engaged in secret new nuclear build-up, bigger than at the height of the cold war, growing by US$4 billion a year compared to $3.7 during the cold war.[20]

The nuclear inequality inherent in a policy which accepts the validity and indeed value the contributions of nuclear weapons to defence and military strategies for the nuclear haves but reject them for the nuclear have-nots has usually been explained away by reference to the danger of the bomb. For instance, former Special Assistant for National Security Affairs McGeorge Bundy, former Chairman of the Joint Chiefs of Staff William Crowe and professor Sidney Drell of Stanford presented the following argument in Reducing the Nuclear Danger: The bomb is so dangerous and "so destructive that in all the conflict and tumult of the Cold War no one chose to use it or to provoke its use by others."[21] Therefore, the authors concluded, the United States should lead a world-wide effort for the avoidance of further nuclear proliferation. Such efforts would be directed against the usual suspects: Iraq, Iran, North Korea and Libya. Friendly countries such as Israel are given the benefit of the doubt to compensate for their small population (a peculiar argument in itself since the small population of Israel has never acted as a hindrance in the consistent Israeli military superiority over her vastly more numerous but distinctly militarily inferior Arab opponents).

If nuclear weapons play an important role in preventing war, and if they are so dangerous that no one dared to use them or provoke their use, even during the tumult of the cold war, it follows that they were extremely effective at preventing war without being used? Why could this inexorable nuclear deterrence logic not apply between other regional nuclear powers? It may be because a credible nuclear arsenal makes its possessor less vulnerable to coercion, and there is no doubt that, as a group of scholars from MIT recently put it, "one-sided possession of nuclear weapons confers such a great military advantage that it has implicitly meant the coercion of the have-nots," a form of "nuclear imperialism."[22]

The issue of nuclear inequality and its implications has been raised with some urgency in the Middle East, where Iraq is being forcibly disarmed while Israel's nuclear arsenal remains unchecked, and the American commitment to banning weapons of mass destruction in the region is not taken seriously. Israel is not likely to allow any significant control over its proliferating nuclear arsenal; and internal pressure is growing in Egypt, the most important Arab country, to respond to Israel's monopoly of nuclear power. The pressure on Egypt is also coming from an obvious and alarming deterioration in the regional balance of power.

The Balance of Power after the Storm

By balance of power I mean the relative distribution of power between the competing regional parties. By power, I refer to what Raymond Aron illustrated in his classic work *Paix et Guerre*, namely capabilities, policies, and motivation. In the October 1973 war, the Arabs were able to translate their capabilities into a set of co-ordinated military, political and economic policies, supported by a common motivation to put an end to the Israeli occupation of Arab territories. Arab political assertiveness threatened to focus on the contradiction inherent in the dual objective of American foreign policy in the Middle East, namely: access to the strategic resources of the Arabs, and, at the same time, commitment to the military superiority of their enemy. But such a risk was removed by Sadat's eagerness to enter into a partnership with the United States, even though his American interlocutors made it clear to him, that such a partnership had to be subordinated to the United States special relationship with Israel.

Gradually, the separation of Egypt from the Arab camp after the separate peace with Israel following Camp David in 1978, and the emergence of revolutionary Iran as the principal enemy to both the petro-monarchies and the conservative Camp David order, made the conflict with Israel seem less urgent. By 1987 it was not even on the Arab agenda; the Amman Summit's final communiqué (December 1987) ignored the Palestine question altogether. Although the Palestinian uprising (December 1987) forced the Palestine issue back into the agenda, no common Arab front emerged. The Iraq-Kuwait crisis and the subsequent Iraqi confrontation with the United States, which ended in the Gulf War, accelerated the process of division and decline of Arab power.

Today, the picture of Arab power, however it may be defined, is rather discouraging: politically, the peace treaties signed with Israel reflect the realities of unequal power, accentuated by divisiveness in Arab ranks; economically, with some notable exceptions, the new economic order is eroding national sovereignty through the strictures of the IMF, the World Bank, and the exigencies of U.S. Aid and U.S. protection; intellectually, there is a woeful lack of any serious cultural or philosophical project reflecting a common Arab vision. Militarily, the Gulf War left Iraq with about 30% of its pre-war divisions, 25% of its total manpower, less than 50% of its tanks, and shattered its best armoured and mechanized units. The overall operational strength of the Syrian army cannot deter an Israeli attack, nor can it permit Damascus to engage in any protracted offensive operations against Israel. All of Jordan's major population and industrial and military centres are within two-minute flying time of Israeli air bases.

Iraq and Libya are under siege, Lebanon is still partly occupied, Jordan is neutralized, the PNA is caught between the rock and the hard place, and an Egyptian military option is practically ruled out; Syria is virtually alone and without allies; and Israel was, until the Likud came to power in May 1996 and began reneging on international peace agreements, enjoying growing international respectability, increasing economic and political cooperation with Europe, and even more privileged strategic cooperation with the United States; Thd Israeli nuclear arsenal continues to grow in sophistication and coercive power. Given a dramatically unfavourable regional balance of power, the Arabs, it need hardly be pointed out, may continue to ignore Fenelon's classic advice about the imperative necessity for the weaker parties of dealing collectively with the predominant power, at their own risk and peril.[23]

Egyptian-Israeli Balance of Military Power

A number of Western strategists have commented on Egyptian vulnerability to outside pressure and to coercive actions. They have remarked that the Israelis have never been as militarily strong and dominant as they are today. After the Six-Day War debacle,[24] Nasser set out to radically reform the Egyptian army and to obtain advanced military technology from the Soviet Union; he succeeded in the former, but largely failed in the latter. After his death, his successor Anwar El-Sadat followed the same path with the same result. In frustration at Moscow's refusal to provide Egypt with advanced military technology, Sadat expelled the Soviet military advisors from Egypt in 1972. Still, the improvements in training, organisation, application of new warfare doctrines, and the common front forged with the Arabs, paid off with the remarkable showing of the Egyptian army in crossing the Suez Canal and overwhelming Israeli fortifications in the October 1973 War.[25]

The Egyptian army was then rightly proud of its achievements, and Egypt of its military power. For a variety of reasons, President Sadat saw fit to reverse course and decided to abandon the political, economic and military front he helped forge in 1973; he also began to unilaterally disarm Egypt, advancing the naive argument that he was ushering in a new era in international relations. He credited his unique "science of diplomacy," as he told the Egyptian people, with: "overcoming the dangers of the Cold War, the easing of international tension ... the elimination of colonialism, furtherance of the war against racial discrimination, and the promotion of a democratic conception of international relations."[26] If Sadat's "science of diplomacy" could achieve all that, it could certainly resolve all outstanding problems with Washington and Tel-Aviv and usher in another new era in which balance of power calculations would become superfluous relics of the past. But it was not to be; for as Egypt disarmed and pursued the "science of diplomacy," Israel armed and pursued the levers of power.

Sadat responded to growing rumours about Israel's nuclear weapons by forging a diplomatic partnership with the Shah of Iran designed to ban the introduction of nuclear weapons to the Middle East. Thus, Egypt sponsored with Iran a UN resolution for the establishment of a Nuclear Weapon Free Zone (NWFZ) in the Middle East; the resolution was adopted by 128 votes to none, with two abstentions (Israel and Burma). After the fall of Shah, in 1979, Egypt began to sponsor the resolution alone, with no appreciable tangible results. On February 22, 1981, Egypt ratified the NPT in an effort to encourage Israel to join it, and thus move closer to the goal of establishing a NWFZ in the region. On June 7, 1981, only two days after his meeting with Sadat, Israeli Prime Minister Begin responded to Sadat's move: He sent his air force, guided by ultra-secret American satellite intelligence pictures, to destroy Iraqi nuclear plants, and establish a doctrine of Israeli nuclear monopoly in the region, enforced by pre-emptive strikes.

As Israel continued to expand and improve its military, conventional and nuclear, power, Sadat's heavy reliance on the "science of diplomacy" to improve Egypt's position in the regional balance of power, continued to produce the opposite result. Sadat's successor, Hosni Mubarak, inherited that difficult legacy. Today, Egypt will likely have difficulties defending itself against an Israeli attack.

Egypt's active army manpower dropped from 313,000 in 1984 to 290,000 in 1992; the number of trained Egyptian reserves also dropped from 176,000 in 1984 to less than 150,000 in 1992. The Arab Organisation for Industry which Sadat set up with the financial support of Saudi Arabia and Qatar and the United Arab Emirates in 1975 has faltered; it produced some helicopters, some trainer aircraft, and some spare parts but was unable to meet the severe shortages in spare parts for Western and Soviet weapons. It is estimated that up to a third of the Egyptian army, the air force, and the navy consist of low grade combat forces with aging equipment and little modern training. In addition, Egyptian conversion from Soviet-based arms and strategies to Western-based arms and strategies is slow and not expected to be completed before the year 2000. The Israelis believe and claim that Egypt is building north of Cairo major plants for chemical weapons feed stock and will soon have a substantial independent capability to produce nerve and mustard gases and may be able to produce biological weapons. There is no sign, however, of any serious nuclear weapons development.

The Egyptian air force is reported to have limited reconnaissance ability, and only modest offensive strike capability; its airlift capability is considered only adequate for supporting defensive missions on Egyptian territory, but it could not, for any sustained period of time, provide support for offensive operations in non-contiguous areas without strategic lift support from the U.S. or other Western allies. The mix of the Egyptian air force, Soviet, American, Chinese, and French aircraft is awkward and fraught with limitations. The Egyptian navy is very weak, with many obsolete or quasi-operable ships. It lacks an effective logistical support and maintenance system. Over 60% of Egyptian naval units are considered to have reached or to be near the end of their useful operational lives. Thus, with ageing ships suffering from lack of maintenance and absence of logistical support, the Egyptian navy is severely limited in the operations it can undertake and in the contributions it can make to an overall co-ordinated Egyptian military strategy.[27] Reportedly under pressure from Washington, Cairo terminated its collaboration with Iraq and Argentina in the development of the 500 mile range Al-Abbas missile. The joint American-Egyptian production of the American tank M1A1, commenced in Cairo in 1984 as part of the military inducements offered to Sadat to sign the Camp David accords, has not accomplished the advertised goal of Egyptian military self-sufficiency in this area. This is largely because the modern technology of the tank was withheld by the United States on the grounds of "security reasons." Egyptian self-sufficiency was limited to spare parts and to routine maintenance.

The Egyptian opposition party described revelations to that effect, made in a report to the American Congress, as proving "clearly and without need for analysis or interpretation, how the United States uses its relations with Egypt to maintain Egypt's militarily weakness ... as if all that was required of our army is to remain as an appendix to the American army without any choices to enable it to protect the country should Uncle Sam suddenly get upset with us or ally himself more closely with an enemy of ours."[28] American strategists predict that Egypt would require substantial arms imports from the U.S. for at least the next decade before Egypt can even hope to "play a strategic role in the Gulf." Egypt is said to be "currently tied to operations near its bases ... and lacks the logistic and service support capability and combat support mobility needed for effective power projection."[29] Indeed, the most recent joint Egypto-American military manoeuvres were described by the semi-official paper *Al-Ahram* as designed to facilitate strategic transport of troops and long distance projection of power.[30]

It is reasonable to assume that in the various contingencies of power projection beyond the contiguous areas of Egypt, Cairo will be the junior partner. All in all, a leading American military expert concluded, Egyptian operational military strength today is "far lower" than what it had been in 1973.[31] Egyptian officials have responded to the changing balance of power by emphasizing different strategic concerns, commensurate with their declining military power. Thus, shortly after the Gulf War, Egyptian officials pinned their hopes on a security role for the Egyptian forces in the Gulf region; this was the expectation engendered by the Damascus Declaration following the end of the Gulf War in 1991; but the Gulf countries frustrated Egyptian and Syrian hopes, and preferred to rely on American security guarantees, and secret arrangements with Washington.

Cairo focused on Libya and at least 40,000 troops and two heavy divisions are reportedly stationed in the Western border area to deal with the contingency of an armed conflict with Libya. Iran and Sudan were also emphasised as major Egyptian security concerns; they were presented as the source of Egypt's problems with local militant Islamic groups[32]; and, for a while, Egyptian officials focused on preparedness to engage Sudan militarily.[33] The preoccupation with the Nile, and its water resources, was also highlighted as a major security concern, particularly after Ethiopia. The origin of over 80% of the Nile water began receiving assistance from Israel for building a Blue Nile Dam. All this is helping keep Egyptian security concerns in Africa, away from the Arab-Israeli balance of power, which is where Israel wants it to be.

Israel, on the other hand, has never stopped improving its armed forces and adding to their diversity and strength. Israel's annual military expenditures grew from $644 million in 1967 to over $6,160 billion today in current dollars; its fully mobilized army shot up from 275,000 in 1967 to 750,000 in 1992. The number of tanks passed from 900 in 1967 to over 3200 today; the air force from 290 air-planes in 1967 to over 575. In addition, Israel has developed highly advanced night-vision and electro-optical targeting systems as well as battlefield surveillance and tactical intelligence systems that will enable her to fight the kind of war hardly any of her potential enemies is prepared for. In addition, Israel is developing an anti-tactical ballistic missile system called the Arrow, with the ability to intercept short-range ballistic missiles with ranges up to 500 kilometres. As part of its Strategic Defence Initiative, which has been scraped in the U.S., the American government is paying for 80% of the development cost of the Arrow.

The Israelis are now in a position to deploy intelligence satellites covering the entire Arab world; they also possess the necessary equipment and technical expertise to suppress the air defences of their Arab competitors in a matter of hours, before establishing air supremacy over their respective skies. The Israeli air force enjoys a huge qualitative edge over its Egyptian counterpart. It has about 2.5 trained pilots per combat aircraft versus less than 1 trained pilot per combat aircraft in the Arab world. The IAF has some of the most advanced combat aircraft in the world such as F-15 and F-16; pilots are given one of the most advanced training systems in the world, with access to U.S. training centres; and the air force itself is the only one in the Middle East organized for strategic air-attacks on its neighbours.[34]

Israel's more than 200 nuclear warheads can be delivered by an integrated triad: Land-based missiles, black squadron bombers, and possibly two cruise-missile carrying submarines. Israel has also developed nuclear-armed missiles on mobile launchers; the multistage Jericho III, reportedly tested in September 1989 across the Mediterranean, had a range of 1450 Kilometres, enough to cover the entire Arab world. Some 30 to 50 of these missiles have reportedly been deployed, thus affecting a radical leap forward in the qualitative edge Israel already enjoyed over all of its Arab competitors. The assessment of U.S. strategic analysts is consistent with the view that "Arab countries would be extremely vulnerable to strikes on key cities. A single high-yield weapon of 100 kilotons or more could effectively destroy a Syrian city like Damascus, Aleppo, or Homs; a Jordanian city like Amman, Irbid, or Zarqa; an Iraqi city like Baghdad, Basra, or Mosul; a Libyan city like Tripoli or Benghazi; or most of the larger Egyptian cities of Cairo, and Alexandria …"[35]

Israeli strategic reach is advertised to go from Pakistan to Morocco. Israel has already targeted between sixty and eighty industrial and urban centres, including the Persian Gulf oil fields, Damascus, Baghdad, Cairo, Teheran, and Tripoli and military facilities as far away as Ain Oussera in Algeria and Kahuta in Pakistan. In addition to access to U.S. Intelligence data, the Israelis have launched, starting in 1988, a series of Ofeq satellites – the latest of which is able to stay in space for up to two to three years instead of a few months; their new Amos satellite, whose booster, the Shavit, is said to cover virtually all of the Arab world, will provide military communications, and overall command and strike co-ordination for missiles, bombers and submarines against practically any target in the Arab world, substantially enhancing Israel's advantage in the regional balance of power.

It is worth noting that Israel's imposing nuclear arsenal was not acquired or developed through the pursuit of the "science of diplomacy." Much of the material for Israel's bombs has been covertly acquired. Thus, in 1968, Israeli agents hijacked a German flag freighter with a shipload of 200 tons of uranium[36]; between 1979 and 1983 Israeli agents covertly and illegally acquired 80 krytrons (fast triggers to start a nuclear fission detonation) from EG&G Inc. of Massachusetts. Israel has also tried to extend her doctrine of regional nuclear monopoly through pre-emptive strikes: in addition to the 1981 Israeli strike against Iraq, Tel-Aviv has reportedly proposed, in 1985, a strike against Pakistan's uranium enrichment plant at Kahuta. Israeli diplomats have reportedly approached India for collaboration and secret refuelling facilities at an Indian air force base to facilitate the Israeli strike against Pakistan, but India refused.[37]

Should Egypt withdraw from the NPT and pursue a Nuclear Option?

Given the obvious deterioration in the balance of power between Egypt and Israel, Cairo is naturally concerned about the huge qualitative edge the Israelis have achieved since Camp David, and about Egyptian inability to even consider competing with Israel in this field. But there is little Egypt could do in the area of conventional weaponry to try to reduce the huge qualitative gap between the two countries. There is something, however, that Egyptian officials could and did do: they protested, publicly and loudly for the first time, about the nuclear inequality between the two countries sanctioned by the United States and given a seal of legitimacy by the Nuclear non-Proliferation Treaty to which Egypt belongs and Israel refuses to adhere. In the months leading to the NPT conference, which was convened in April 1995 in New York, Egyptian officials, including President Mubarak himself, said that Egypt would not agree to an indefinite extension of the NPT unless Israel agreed to join it. Egyptian Foreign Minister Amr Moussa even said that Egypt was prepared to "deal with the consequences" that may result from its refusal to back an indefinite extension of the NPT.[38]

The Egyptians offered three options to Israel: (1) sign the treaty in May; (2) set a time frame for joining the treaty and Egypt will freeze her renewal of the treaty until that time; or (3) pledge in a letter that Israel will sign on a specific date with Israel automatically becoming bound by the treaty at that date. The Israeli government rejected all three options. When he came to Washington in April, President Mubarak was reminded of the $2.1 billion in American aid annually paid to Egypt. He raised but was unable to exploit the lopsided trade deficit between the two countries in which the U.S. exports to Egypt $4.3 billion worth of goods and imports from Egypt only $600 million worth of goods. By the end of his visit, the three Egyptian options offered to Israel were out. Mubarak only expressed "sincere hope that Israel will approach this issue in a positive and constructive spirit." The threat to withdraw from the treaty was out, Mubarak assured his American audience: "we will never withdraw from the Treaty." For his part Clinton said that he had been only "informed" of Egyptian concerns, but clearly was prepared to do little about them and reiterated the American position for "indefinite and unconditional" extension of the NPT.[39]

Many in the now anachronistically-named non-aligned nations denounced the inequality of the non-proliferation regime, and the nuclear powers selective enforcement of its provisions as was pointed out above. As one analyst put it: "Why should India and Pakistan fall in line with American demands when the United States has a tainted record of pursuing selective proliferation in relation to its friends - especially Israel - and selective non-proliferation in relation to the Third World."[40]

At their Bandung Conference in April 1995, the non-aligned nations pointed out that the issues raised by the NPT extension conference were not related solely to the question of the treaty's extension. They identified a number of other issues which they considered crucial for the success and universality of the treaty: they accordingly asked for the creation of nuclear-free zones, the extension of security guarantees to non-nuclear weapon states, and the stepping up of international cooperation in the peaceful usage of nuclear energy. But the nuclear weapon states were able to secure, in May 1995, the indefinite extension of the treaty without acceding to any of these requests.

The conference adopted by consensus the U.S.-backed proposal for an indefinite and unconditional extension of the treaty. The non-binding "declaration of principles and objectives" provided for annual conferences to review progress toward the objective of complete elimination of nuclear weapons. American diplomats deservedly congratulated themselves on their skills in neutralizing criticisms and opposition from countries such as Mexico, Indonesia and Egypt. The nuclear powers, however, made some symbolic concessions: they sponsored a resolution adopted by the Security Council in April, promising unspecified assistance (medical and humanitarian but no security guarantees) to the non-nuclear weapon-states that signed the NPT in case of threat or use of nuclear weapons against them. They also undertook to work for the complete elimination of nuclear weapons.

These "concessions", however, may have been primarily designed to secure the extension of the treaty without affecting in any substantial way the nuclear powers' pursuit of their military interests as they see fit. The American ambassador to the NPT conference Thomas Graham said that serious negotiations for the complete elimination of nuclear weapons were "not possible under any foreseeable circumstance." China has just conducted an underground nuclear test and France announced that it intended to resume nuclear testing. In addition, Pentagon officials have recently begun to urge that Washington's pledge to the United Nations in May to support a comprehensive test ban treaty not be at the expense of America's ability to conduct nuclear tests. Some senior members of the American Department of Defence have in fact proposed that the United States resume underground nuclear testing at a level equivalent to hundreds of tons of TNT. They pointed out that President Clinton's decision to endorse the speedy completion of a test ban treaty also specifically provided that "the CTB treaty must not prohibit activities required to maintain the safety and reliability of our nuclear stockpile."[41]

Meanwhile, Egyptian military officials staged in the Sinai a military exercise designed to reassure Egyptians that despite the now public nuclear inequality between Egypt and Israel, Egypt was still in a position to defend herself against an enemy using weapons of "mass destruction." Major General Saad Abu Rida, the second army commander told Al-Ahram, that in the two exercises Bassel 1 and Badr 2 "every participating unit is required to deal with a situation in which the enemy has used weapons of mass destruction." The Egyptian forces, it was reported, crossed the canal successfully and managed to defeat the forces of the "blue state" which used weapons of mass destruction. Egyptian Defence Minister Field Marshal Mohamad Hussein Tantawi "was so pleased with the performance of the participating forces that he ordered the payment of LE22,000 as a reward for them."[42]

In reality, though, there is no need for Israel to resort to the use of chemical or biological weapons since its unmatched conventional superiority can easily assure the achievement of its military goals in any confrontation with Egypt; this is all the more obvious that the military gap between the two countries has been growing steadily. The possibility that the exercises' reference to "weapons of mass destruction" could be understood to mean nuclear weapons would be preposterous; this is because a claim by the nuclear powers themselves, let alone a third world nation, that they can successfully defend themselves or their troops against an enemy using nuclear weapons would be viewed with suspicion and disbelief. In addition, here again, Israel does not need to use nuclear weapons against Egypt since its conventional superiority can, today more than ever before, achieve victory over Egypt or any combination of Arab armies.

In fact, the political objective of the Egyptian exercises is more compelling than their military logic. The fact that the exercises coincided with the first open and public discussion in Egypt about Israel's nuclear arsenal and Egypt's obvious inability to do much about it were serious causes for security concerns which needed to be allayed. Egyptian inability to do much about Israel's nuclear monopoly and American acquiescence is increasingly publicly discussed by critics and opposition parties. A growing segment of Egyptian public opinion find it hard to accept nuclear discrimination in the region and do not understand how it can be reconciled with peace and normalization of relations. The deputy leader of the opposition Labour Party, Helmi Murad, called for Egyptian withdrawal from the NPT even at the cost of losing American aid.[43]

Other Egyptian observers have argued against withdrawing from the NPT.[44] They maintain that withdrawing from the NPT would weaken Egyptian negotiating position vis-à-vis Israel because as a member "Egypt can urge the international community to put pressure on Israel to join the NPT." But this argument ignores that Israeli policies have seldom been actuated by regard to international public opinion. The opinion which carries some weight in Israel is that of the American government but the historical record shows that Israeli governments have not been invariably responsive to American pressure; if anything, the reverse may have happened more often, or at least more openly and more dramatically; there are many instances where American presidents, most notably Jimmy Carter, were sensitive to Israeli pressure (as for instance when Carter, under pressure from Moshe Dayan, was forced to retreat from the Soviet-American communiqué of October 1977).[45]

In addition, in the rare instances when American governments attempted to exert pressure on Israel, as for instance during the horrific Israeli siege of Beirut in August 1982, the Israeli government ignored those pressures. Now, if Israeli governments are generally too independent in the course of policies they pursue even when subjected to pressure from their staunchest ally and supporter, why would they be willing to change their commitment to nuclear weapons when Washington has not only refrained from pressuring Israel but has in fact been an indirect supporter of the development of Israeli nuclear weapons?

In fact, the various American administrations, starting with President Kennedy, played a major role in helping Israel develop her nuclear arsenal. As William E. Burrows and Robert Windrem noted in their recent book *Critical Mass*: "Although Washington denied Israel off-the-shelf nuclear weapons, it did almost everything else possible to ensure that the Israelis developed exactly what they needed. This was particularly true during the Johnson and Reagan administrations. Naiveté was never a factor."[46] Given these realities why should Israeli governments be more responsive to pressure to put an end to their nuclear programs? And who is going to exercise that pressure when the only superpower left not only does not exert pressure but also in fact is steadily increasing its strategic co-operation and intelligence sharing with Israel?

The second argument put forward by those who say Egypt should not withdraw from the NPT relates to Egypt's traditional commitment to abide by international regulations. But this argument is based upon the assumption that Egyptian withdrawal would be tantamount to a violation of Egyptian international obligations and would therefore harm its international image of a responsible member of the international society. But withdrawal from the NPT need not involve the violations of international commitments since the treaty itself provides that member states have the right to withdraw from the NPT "if certain exceptional circumstances related to the NPT proved to be detrimental to their national security." Egyptian officials could make an argument that Israel's refusal to join the NPT and American acquiescence in this nuclear inequality in the region, and refusal to provide security guarantees to Egypt against Israel's use or threat of use of her nuclear weapons against Egypt, represent such "exceptional circumstances" which make belonging to the NPT detrimental to Egyptian security. An argument could be made that there is more security in a nuclear option for Egypt than in a treaty, which does not control Israeli nuclear monopoly in the region. A growing imbalance of power in favour of Israel could make coercion tempting for Israel, and defence impossible for Egypt.

The third argument against Egyptian withdrawal from the NPT suggests that if Egypt withdraws from the NPT this will reduce its chances of acquiring nuclear technology for peaceful purposes, as stipulated in Article 4 of the agreement. Although this argument has some merits, particularly if we think of the example of Iraq whose membership in the NPT facilitated the acquisition of nuclear technology, its applicability to Egypt is debatable given the historical record. For instance, Egypt has been a member of the NPT for over 15 years with little to show for in terms of peaceful nuclear technology acquired under the NPT. Further, Egyptian officials reminded their American counterparts during the April 1995 visit, which paved the way for President Mubarak's visit to Washington on the eve of the NPT conference, of the American offer to finance a peaceful Egyptian nuclear program that was made to encourage Egypt to join the NPT in 1981. Shortly after Egypt joined the NPT, the offer was withdrawn. Neither Egyptian officials' entreaties nor the non-aligned nations' pleas for stepping up international co-operation for the sharing of nuclear technology for peaceful purposes elicited any firm commitment on the part of the nuclear powers. In addition, the competition between the suppliers of nuclear technology is such, that a determined nation can without difficulties acquire the necessary nuclear technology it needs on the open market. The case of Iranian purchase of Russian nuclear technology and Russian refusal to give in to American pressure to completely cancel the contract is illustrative in this regard.

The call for Egyptian withdrawal from the NPT is accompanied by an implicit, or an explicit call for Egypt to pursue a nuclear option. This is because Egypt cannot hope to redress the present gross and dangerous imbalance of power through the pursuit of conventional military parity with Israel. Conventional military parity with Israel is impossible because of Egypt's total reliance on the U.S. for military aid and American commitment to maintaining Israel's military superiority over her Arab neighbours.

Because of its relatively inexpensive production cost, and the absence of linkage between deterrence ability and the size of nuclear arsenal, nuclear weapons may represent the most efficacious, and most cost effective means available to a country like Egypt to improve its intrinsic strength and relative power. The knowledge to build an atomic bomb has been easily obtainable in the United States since 1964. The November 1979 issue of *The Progressive* contained an article explaining how to construct a hydrogen bomb. Furthermore, if the necessary technologies could not be obtained in the open market, building the facilities for processing uranium are not beyond the capabilities of a country like Egypt. While Egypt may not be as industrialised as South Korea or India, she is certainly not far behind Pakistan, which seems to have developed its own nuclear bombs.

A study conducted for the United States Arms Control and Disarmament Agency (ACDA) in 1976 found that the cost of designing, building and testing a plutonium-based nuclear device would be $51 million, and if the country in question already possessed the fissile materials, the cost would be a mere $1 million. The formidable American nuclear arsenal accounts for less than 25% of total U.S. military expenditures. The imposing Israeli nuclear arsenal cost only $5 billion. This is the most cost-effective deterrence-based security money can buy, especially compared to how much a country like Egypt spends on conventional weapons, with no dramatic effect on the Egyptian-Israeli military balance.

Because of the cost effectiveness of a nuclear deterrence strategy, the nuclear option could in fact alleviate the defence burden on the Egyptian economy, and free resources for economic and industrial development projects. In addition, the modern technologies and the infrastructures which go with scientific nuclear research and development, could have a spin-off effect on the woefully deficient area of industrial scientific research and development in Egypt; and this could help revive the Egyptian industrialisation project to go beyond making shirts, producing military spare parts, and assembling GM trucks and European and Japanese cars. Egypt possesses a surplus of highly skilled Egyptian engineers, physicists, and scientists, who leave the country and seek employment abroad because of lack of opportunities at home. In short, the industrialisation project in Egypt does not need skilled technicians to take off; it needs a political design.

The development of nuclear weapons by Egypt need not lock Egypt and Israel into a nuclear arms race; first because Egypt is unlikely to have the resources or the desire to aim for nuclear parity with Israel; secondly, and most significantly, nuclear parity is not necessary. Unlike conventional arms-based strategies, a nuclear deterrence strategy does not need parity to be effective; it needs credibility, but not parity. Nuclear weapons confer some form of deterrence equality even between nuclear countries not possessing equal strength, as measured in conventional terms. As Michael Waltz pointed out: "[A] country with well less than half of the economic capability of the leading producer can easily compete militarily if it adopts a status-quo policy and a deterrent strategy."[47] This is one of what, over thirty years ago, Pierre Gallois called *les paradoxes de la paix*.

Nuclear Deterrence

Nuclear deterrence is fundamentally a function of credibility: military credibility and political credibility. Militarily, it is not enough to have nuclear bombs and missiles to deliver them; a country relying on deterrence must have a survivable nuclear force: that is, a force capable of surviving a pre-emptive attack, and thus capable of posing the threat of unacceptable retaliatory devastation. Politically, it is not enough to communicate commitment to the use of nuclear weapons; it is important that the stake for which such a commitment is made be credible; the most credible stake is national existence; the political credibility is therefore highest when it commits nuclear weapons to the defence, through deterrence, of national existence, and conversely it is lowest when it purports to commit the use of nuclear weapons to the pursuit of political goals not affecting the country's national existence.[48]

When the Soviet Union developed the missile technology to enable it to threaten the national territories of the United States in the late 1950s, the standing American strategic doctrine of massive retaliation lost credibility. It was not politically credible that the United States would use nuclear weapons against the USSR, and thus risk direct nuclear retaliation upon its own territories, for the sake of a third party in Asia, or even in Europe. And so the doctrine of massive retaliation was replaced by a commitment to a doctrine of flexible response, giving the U.S. the right not to choose national suicide.

The logic of nuclear deterrence based on mutual assured destruction makes it possible for the weak to deter the strong. One analyst calculated in 1974 that China could mount a nuclear attack against the Soviet Union and destroy 25% of its industries and 25% of its population. China need not demonstrate an actual capacity to inflict such damage for deterrence to work; the mere probability that Beijing could mount such an attack was enough for deterrence to work between China and the Soviet Union.[49] Saddam Hussein may have credibly advertised his political will to launch his missiles against Tel Aviv in order to drag Israel into the Gulf War, but because he lacked military credibility to inflict substantial damage without incurring unacceptable devastation, his threats did not deter the American-led coalition forces from unleashing their storm on Iraq. There was no military credibility and therefore there was no deterrence.

Similarly, although Egyptians and Syrians may have known that Israel possessed a militarily credible nuclear arsenal, this knowledge did not stop them from trying to recover, in 1973, their national territories occupied by Israel since 1967. This because it was not politically credible that Israeli leaders would use nuclear weapons for the purpose of defending, not their country's national existence, but territories conquered from countries unwilling to accept their losses and enjoying the support of the international community in condemning the illegality of the Israeli territorial conquests.

Some have argued that Israel's nuclear weapons did not deter an Arab attack on Israel in 1973. But they did. They deterred even the thought of an attack on Israel's national existence, and forced the Arabs to limit their war aims to liberating some of the Arab territories captured by Israel in 1967; the Egyptians specifically refrained from advancing in the Sinai when the way was open to them to do so in the first days of the war; there was no question of liberating Arab territories captured in the

1948-49 war, much less of liberating all of Palestine, and putting an end to Israeli national existence. And that was precisely because the Arab leaders knew that such an aim was impossible to achieve militarily; and even if it were, it could not be done without putting at risk the very national existence of their own countries. Nuclear weapons protected Israel's national existence; but they could not protect Israel's military conquests. The former was a credible stake the latter was not.

In short, nuclear weapons have rendered the national territories of their possessor's sanctuaries that could not be violated, and as such they are the ultimate guarantors of national defence. As Pierre Gallois repeated in his recent work *Geopolitique: les voies de la puissance*, nuclear weapons have transformed the age-old equation of political power based on military power; they severed the old relationship between politics and war, the latter no longer being the continuation of politics by other means. Nuclear weapons can only be assurance against the most extreme calamities; they draw their virtue from their "power of intimidation."[50]

Thus, nuclear weapons may be said to be the ultimate weapons of defence because they can achieve their goal without being used, as former Secretary of Defence Robert McNamara would later recognise.[51] It may not be a flattering observation about humanity that peace is best preserved through blackmail, but in any context dominated by the realities of balance of power, the ability to affect the will of the enemy without going to war is certainly preferable to the use of force to try to achieve the same end.

Clausewitz' famous thought about war being the continuation of politics by other means may be adapted to the nuclear era to convey a pertinent thought: possession of a credible nuclear deterrence is the continuation of politics by other means. In providing an effective and credible deterrent, nuclear weapons make war not only unthinkable, since it could not possibly achieve political goals, but also unnecessary, while at the same time affecting the political will and calculations of others.

Israel may have successfully blackmailed even her staunchest ally, the United States when Israeli leaders reportedly threatened to use nuclear weapons in the early stages of the October 1973 war to compel the United States to provide massive shipments of conventional weapons. Seymour Hersh reported in his book *The Samson Option*[52] that Israel also threatened to use nuclear weapons against Iraq during the Gulf War, and thus managed to compel the United States to include in its prosecution of the war, Israeli war aims against Iraq.

Egyptian Nuclear Deterrence

The Nuclear non-Proliferation Treaty regime has codified nuclear inequality but has stopped neither vertical proliferation nor discriminate horizontal proliferation of nuclear weapons. It has not brought nuclear disarmament any closer to reality and nuclear powers continue to prize the value of nuclear weapons in preventing wars and even in war fighting strategies. There is no reason why the nuclear deterrence logic, which worked successfully between nuclear powers, cannot apply between regional nuclear powers. The deteriorating balance of power in the Middle East is creating a situation where the national defence of Egypt, the most important Arab country, may be inadequate. Conventional military parity with Israel is out of the question; nuclear parity is not necessary. A credible nuclear deterrence strategy, we would like to suggest, offers Egypt the most effective means of assuring her national defence against growing Israeli conventional and nuclear power.

Raymond Aron claimed that successful nuclear deterrence in a geographical cultural context could not be exported; some have argued that nuclear deterrence therefore would not work in the Middle East because of cultural reasons; deterrence is based on the notion of rationality, and rationality has not been a strong feature of Middle East conflicts. Similarly, others have referred to supposed unique cultural and geo-strategic circumstances lacking in the Middle East and the Third World to justify their rejection of the notion that more nuclear states may be better because new nuclear-states will feel the constraints experienced by the present nuclear powers. They claim that the Middle East, and other third world regions, lack a tradition of just war doctrines and are not sensitive to the pressure that a massive public opposition to destructive warfare brings to bear upon decision-makers and governments in the West; and this presumably makes it difficult for Middle Eastern leaders to "to think of nuclear and other high-leverage weapons as usable only in last resort."[53]

These objections are untenable. The historical record shows that in the anarchical order of international society of power struggle and self-help, cultural characteristics and geo-strategic idiosyncrasies were not primary factors in the major conflicts of the post World War II era. Further, neither the Western tradition of just war doctrine (the claim that the Middle East does not have a tradition of just war is rather peculiar) nor the tradition of public opposition to massive warfare prevented Hiroshima or Vietnam. Colonial wars as in Algeria in the 1950s, imperial invasions as in the Soviet invasion of Czechoslovakia in 1968 and the Soviet invasion of Afghanistan in 1979, and the American war in Vietnam, were all justified by the traditional raison d'état and its corollaries and did not particularly exhibit a brand of rationality absent from the Middle East or anywhere else in the world.

Neither the doctrine of just war nor the tradition of popular opposition to destructive warfare seem to have prevented the nuclear escalation of the Cuban missile crisis, Nixon's attempt to make the Vietnamese believe in the "mad man" theory about his supposed willingness to use nuclear weapons, or the secret American bombing of Cambodia, or in the nuclear alert advertised during the Arab-Israeli war of 1973.

Moreover, other powers with distinctly different cultural traditions from those of the West have understood the imperatives, and have reacted in conformity with the logic of nuclear deterrence. This is the case for instance between China and the Soviet Union. Their respective access to nuclear power status modified their international perspectives, more gradually so in the case of China than in the case of the Soviet Union;[54] it moderated their ideological zeal and made them reject the inevitability of war and acknowledge that of peaceful co-existence. Although both powers continued to support wars of liberation, their own relationship with the world and their mutual relations with one another exhibited the logic of nuclear deterrence.

There is nothing in the Middle Eastern wars of the post World War II era, from the Palestine war in 1948, the Suez invasion in 1956, the Six-Day War of 1967, the October War of 1973, the Iran-Iraq war in the 1980s and the Israeli invasion of Lebanon in 1982 which can not be explained by reference to the notions of struggle for power, nationalism, expansionism and legitimate self-defence. With the possible exception of the Israeli invasion of Lebanon where the Begin government sought nothing less than the total destruction of its enemy, the Palestine Liberation Organisation (mistakenly assuming that total military destruction would mean total extinction of Palestinian nationalism), none of the other wars involved the risk of total annihilation of the enemy's national existence, not even the 1948 Palestine war. The threat of nuclear war, on the other hand, involves the contemplation of total national annihilation and this is bound to figure prominently, much more significantly than nationalism, expansionism or raison d'état, in the calculation of the parties involved regardless of their culture, religion or the ideological nature of their conflict.

There is no reason why nuclear deterrence, which worked between nuclear powers, cannot work between Israel and Egypt. Both countries are clearly committed to their respective national existence; nuclear deterrence effectively protects national existence by making the cost of its violation uselessly and unacceptably high. In pursuing a nuclear option, Egypt will not be motivated by ambitions of territorial expansions or imperial domination; it will be moved by the imperious necessity of providing for Egyptian national defence, and stopping the Egyptian-Israeli imbalance of power from reaching a point where coercion becomes tempting for Israel and defence impossible for Egypt.

The successful development of a credible nuclear deterrence strategy by Egypt will reduce the risk of future wars between Egypt and Israel. First, because it will sever the link between politics and war, thus ensuring that no political or ideological difference could lead to a military confrontation; none would be worth a confrontation between nuclear powers. Secondly, because it will place serious restrictions on the strategy of escalation, which were skilfully exploited by the Israelis in the 1956 and the 1967 wars. The Blair House Treaty of 1979 brought the first line of Egyptian defence closer to the Suez Canal, and the Egyptian heartland. Under nuclear deterrence, this and other Egyptian national defence vulnerabilities will be neutralized. And that is because a credible nuclear deterrence strategy makes traditional strategic considerations such as territorial depth, supply lines, and mobility of armed forces, less important.

A credible nuclear deterrence strategy will thus provide an unassailable shield for the defence of Egyptian national existence, where conventional military power seems inadequate for the task. It will ensure, for instance, that Israel's punitive and unchallenged air raids deep inside the Egyptian heartland during the 1969 war of attrition could never happen again. In 1969, Nasser was able to persuade the Soviet Union to provide Egypt with modern anti-aircraft missile batteries. The Soviet Union is no longer there, and Egypt cannot, and should not, expect to be able to persuade Washington to come to the rescue against Israel. One might argue that the Egyptian-Israeli peace treaty should guard against the nightmare scenario of Egyptian loneliness in the face of Israeli might. In a rational world it should; but we live in this world.

In assuming the primary responsibility of defence of national existence, Egyptian nuclear deterrence strategy will free the declining Egyptian conventional military forces for other security tasks, commensurate with their strength and nature. They can thus be more effectively organized: Their size made smaller, their mobility greater, their ranks and training more professional. This will add credibility to conventional forces, and rationality to their contributions to a coherent overall modern Egyptian security strategy.

At the Egyptian-Israeli balance of power level, a credible Egyptian nuclear deterrence strategy will obviate any dangerous temptation for Israel to make coercive use of her preponderance of military and nuclear power. It will thus remove the risk inherent in the humiliating alternative of either backing down or giving in to Israeli demands in any future dispute. Differences between the two countries will simply have to be resolved bilaterally or through arbitration. This can only serve the interests of peaceful relationships between the two countries.

Balance of power calculations are dynamics of constant direct and indirect bargaining to enhance one's power and neutralize the opponent's. In the current balance of power dynamics, Israel and the United States are the only powers which can afford to say with credibility to any Arab interlocutor on practically any issue: take it or leave it.

A strong Egypt will no longer be on the receiving end of such an injunction. An Egypt that has no option but to take it or leave will find it difficult to play a leadership role in the regional balance of power. A weak Egypt unable to lead or stop the decline of its own power will inevitably mean that the region will gravitate towards and around Israel, the increasingly dominant military, and industrial power. The subordination to Israel of Arab economic and political destinies will translate into cultural subordination, and all the attendant identity crises that accompany such traumatic transformations for a people with a long history and important contributions to civilisation. The opposition from within to regimes acquiescing in such transformations will intensify and likely engulf the region in turmoil and upheavals.[55]

A strong Egypt, which is not seen as subordinate to Israeli power and easily coerced by it, will provide an alternative pole to the one offered by Israeli might. It will thus provide some equilibrium to the regional balance of power. This will help provide stability to a region where balance of power calculations are a permanent feature of the political landscape. Finally, by ending military vulnerability, credible Egyptian nuclear deterrence will rehabilitate Egypt as a strong and independent Arab country. This will revitalize Cairo's political and cultural leadership role in the region. It will also help disseminate a moderating and democratizing Arab vision. This can only serve the interests of peace and stability in the region.

Israel's doctrine of pre-emptive strikes to enforce its nuclear monopoly, however, and American support for it, make the Egyptian nuclear option problematic. Should Egypt seriously consider the nuclear option, the following pertinent question will have to be considered: is the Egyptian-Israeli peace strong enough to accommodate Egyptian nuclear sovereignty, or is it contingent upon Egyptian acquiescence in Israel's doctrine of nuclear monopoly? If it is the former, this is all the more reason to strengthen it by making Egypt stronger and more independent; if it is the latter, this is all the more reason not to rely on it to protect Egyptian vital interests. In the absence of a just and enduring peace in the region, and an Israel largely integrated within it, the requirements of a more balanced distribution of power, and the logic of nuclear deterrence, may, one day, make such an answer more compelling than it seems today.

Notes

1. Adel Safty wrote this chapter while he was Director of the Centre for International Studies, International Affairs Commentator for UTelevision, and professor at the University of British Columbia. The views expressed herein are his personal views and are not those of any institution hey may have represented or may be representing today. Professor Safty is the Author of *From Camp David to the Gulf: Negotiations, Language and Propaganda, and War*. (Black Rose Books, New York & Montreal, 1993) which was selected Publisher's Choice in 1993 and a second addition of which was published in 1996.
2. A.J.P. Taylor, *The Struggle for Mastery in Europe 1848-1918*. (Oxford: Clarendon Press, 1954), p. 528.
3. See Francois de Selignac Fenelon, *L'Examen de conscience sur les devoirs de la royaut* (c.1700).
4. See Sir Geoffrey Butler and Simon Maccoby, The Development of International Law, Longmans, 1928, p. 65.
5. See Herbert Butterfield and Martin Wight (eds.). Diplomatic Investigations, (London: George Allen & Unwin, 1966), pp. 149-175 . p. 156.
6. See Nicholas J. Spykman, America's Strategy in World Politics (New York: Harcourt, 1942), pp. 21-22; cited p. 15.
7. *The Times* (November 19, 1963), (Spykman, p. 158).
8. *Politics Among Nations: The Struggle for Power and Peace* (New York: Knopf, 1949).
9. See *International Politics: Anarchy and Order in the World Society*, (New York: McGraw-Hill, Seventh Edition, 1969), p. 277.
10. See A. J. P. Taylor, *Rumours of War*, (London: Hamish Hamilton, 1952), p. 44.
11. Cited by James Meernik, "Presidential Decision Making and the Political Use of Military Force," *International Studies Quarterly*, Vol. 38, No. 1, (March 1994), p. 121.
12. This historical reality was candidly recognized by former Israeli Prime Minister Moshe Sharette in his memoirs.
13. Alan Taylor, *The Arab Balance of Power*, (Syracuse University Press, 1982).
14. H. J. Morgenthau, *Politics Among Nations: The Struggle for Power and Peace*, (New York: Knopf, 1949), p. 13.
15. See Walter Lafeber, *America, Russia, and the Cold War 1945-1984*, 5th edition, (New York: Alfred A. Knopf, 1985), p. 42.
16. See Roy Jerome B. Weisener, Phillip Morrison and Kosta Tsipis, "Ending Overkill," *Bulletin of the Atomic Scientists*, (March 1993), pp. 12-23, p. 16.
17. Paul L. Leventhal, "Plugging the Leaks in Nuclear Export Controls: Why Bother?" *Orbis: A Journal of World Affairs*, Vol. 36, No. 2, (Spring 1992), pp. 167-180.
18. See *The Sunday Times*, (October 12, 1986); and Steven Weissman and Herbert Krosney, *The Islamic Bomb*, (New York: Times Book, 1981).
19. See the "London Declaration," *Survival*, (September/October, 1990 IISS), pp. 469-472.
20. *The Guardian Weekly*, (August 24, 1997).
21. McGeorge Bundy, William J. Crowe Jr., and Sidney Drell, "Reducing Nuclear Danger," *Foreign Affairs*, Vol. 72, No. 2, (Spring 1993), pp. 140-155, p. 141.
22. "Ending Overkill," opt, cit., p. 14.

23 See Adel Safty, "The Arab-Israeli Balance of Power After the Storm," *International Relations (London)*, Vol. 12, No. 3, (December 1994), pp. 51-74.

24 See Mohammad Hassanein Heikal, *1967: The Explosion: The Thirty-Year War*, in Arabic, (Cairo: Al-Ahram Centre for Translation and Publishing, 1990).

25 See Mohammad Hassanein Heikal, *October 1973: War and Politics*, in Arabic, (Cairo: Al-Ahram Centre for Translation and Publishing, 1994).

26 See Adel Safty, *From Camp David to the Gulf*, (Montreal & New York: Black Rose Books, 1993).

27 See Anthony H. Cordesman, *After the Storm: The Changing Military Balance in the Middle East*, (Boulder & San Francisco: Westview Press, 1993), p. 349.

28 See *Al Shaab*, in Arabic, (Cairo: November 16, 1993).

29 See Anthony H. Cordesman, *After the Storm: The Changing Military Balance in the Middle East*, (Boulder & San Francisco: Westview Press, 1993), p. 349.

30 *Al-Ahram*, in Arabic, (Cairo: June 10, 1995).

31 *After the Storm*, *op. cit.*, p. 349.

32 See Adel Hussein's article in the opposition newspaper *Al-Shaab*, in Arabic, (April 16, 1993).

33 Shortly after surviving an assassination attempt on his life, while in Ethiopia in June 1995, President Mubarak remarked on Egyptian capabilities to overthrow the government of Sudan, which was suspected of involvement in the assassination plot, in less than ten days.

34 *After the Storm*, *op. cit.*, p. 224.

35 *Ibid.*, p. 244.

36 See the *New York Times*, "reporting the CIA as saying ..." *New York Times*, (April 29, 1977); see also the *Los Angeles Times*, (April 29, 1979).

37 "The Nuclear Nineties," *New Statesman and Society*, (April 6, 1990), pp. 22-23.

38 *Al-Ahram Weekly*, (Cairo: April 6-12, 1995).

39 *Ibid.*

40 Ashok Kapur, "Western Biases," *The Bulletin of the Atomic Scientists*, (January/February 1995), pp. 38-43, p. 43.

41 *The Washington Post*, reproduced in *The Guardian Weekly*, (June 25, 1995).

42 *Al-Ahram Weekly*, (Cairo: May 11-17, 1995).

43 *Al-Ahram Weekly*, (Cairo: April 27-May 3, 1995).

44 *Al-Ahram Weekly*, (Cairo: April 6-12, 1995).

45 *From Camp David to the Gulf*, *op. cit.*.

46 William E. Burrows and Robert Windrem, *Critical Mass*, (New York: Simon & Schuster, 1994), p. 309.

47 Kenneth N. Waltz, "The Emerging Structure of International Politics," *International Security*, Vol. 18, No. 2, (Fall 1993), pp. 44-79, p. 53.

48 See Pierre M. Gallois, *Paradoxes de la Paix*, (Paris: Presses Du Temps Present, 1967).

49 See Geoffrey Kemp, "Nuclear Forces for Medium Powers," *Adelphi Papers*, No.'s 106 and 107, (London: IISS, 1974).

50 Pierre M. Gallois, *Geopolitique: les voies de la puissance*, (Paris: Plon, 1990), p. 19.

51 Robert S. McNamara, "The Military Role of Nuclear Weapons: Perceptions and Misperceptions," *Foreign Affairs*, Vol. 62, No. 1, (Fall 1983), p. 79.

52 Seymour M. Hersh, *Israel's Nuclear Arsenal and American Foreign Policy: The Samson Option*, (New York: Random House, 1991).

53 Brad Roberts, "From Nonproliferation to Antiproliferation," *International Security*, Vol. 18, No. 1, (Summer 1993), pp. 139-173, p. 159.

54 See for instance O. Edmund Glubb, *China & Russia: The Great Game*, (New York: Columbia University Press, 1971); see also Andre Fontaine, *Histoire de la guerre froide*, (Paris: Fayard, 1971); see also Walter LeFeber, *America, Russia and the Cold War: 1945-1984*, (New York: Alfred Knopf, 1985).

55 See "The Arab-Israeli Balance of Power after the Storm," *International Relations*, *op. cit.*.

6 Some International Law Implications of the Oslo/Cairo Framework for the PLO/Israeli Peace Process

RICHARD FALK[1]

The New Context

After the Likud victory in the Israeli elections of May 29, 1996, there was widespread concern about the future of the Palestine/Israel peace process. Can such a process survive at all, given the evident resolve of the Netanyahu leadership to insist on a better bargain for Israel as a precondition for going forward? And can going forward in this atmosphere ever be reconciled with the core Palestinian claims of national self-determination, essentially sovereign rights and status in relation to West Bank, Gaza, and, eventually, Jerusalem? These questions are inevitable at this stage.

At the same time, too much can be made of the Israeli change of domestic government. From many Palestinian perspectives, the agreements and their implementation had never been satisfactory, and had always been flawed by the Israeli insistence on solving their security problems (including extensive mechanisms of protection for the settlements) at the expense of basic Palestinian rights. In this other sense, then, the Israeli elections merely reinforced the one-sidedness of the earlier negotiating relationship, and did not change prospects as much as generally assumed.

It should be recalled that it was the Labor Government of Shimon Peres that launched Operation Grapes of Wrath, an onslaught of 17 days (April 10-27, 1996), a show of force in Lebanon that revealed the continued reliance on an Israeli military approach to security concerns, without regard to international law or world public opinion. Of course, commentators tended to view such a display of force mainly as a move in Israeli domestic politics, an effort that turned out to be futile, to demonstrate Labor's adherence to a tough security line in dealing with hostile elements in the Arab world. The Israeli attack on Lebanon had been justified initially as retaliation for Hizbollah rockets that were launched against Galilee targets. The character of the attack was unable to inflict damage on Hizbollah directly, but was clearly intended to impose heavy costs on Lebanese civilians living in the southern part of Lebanon. As many as 400,000 civilians were forced to abandon their homes and villages, and many died. The most serious incident being the attack on a place of refuge maintained by the United Nations at Qana.[2]

Anticipating the next phase of Palestinian/Israeli diplomacy is difficult at this time. The Likud campaign commitments on such issues as expansion of the settlements, retention of Jerusalem, avoidance of Palestinian statehood, and retention of the Golan Heights do not bode well. Such a pessimistic reading is reinforced by Netanyahu's rejection of a so-called unity government with Labor, choice of an ideological coalition with several small religious parties that would tend to be even more extremist than Likud, and the inclusion of arch-hawk, Ariel Sharon, in the cabinet.

Despite these factors that would indicate blockage, there are other considerations that point in an opposite direction. There is, first of all, the Israeli Government's desire to sustain the flow of investment capital that had increased as a result of peace prospects, and the high economic growth that followed. Furthermore, there is the prospect of some real pressure on Israel from Washington to move forward on the course set at Oslo, especially after the November 1996 presidential elections, reflecting concerns with Islamic militancy threatening other American interests in the region.[3] There is also a deeply divided Israeli citizenry, a portion of which would offer considerable resistance to governmental policies that aroused broad currents of Palestinian militancy and induced a new cycle of Arab efforts to isolate Israel in the region. And finally, there is the Likud memory of Menachim Begin's embrace of the Camp David framework, a precursor of land for peace, returning the Sinai in exchange for peace with Egypt.

It is difficult, then, to interpret the Prospect for a continuation of Palestinian/Israeli diplomatic efforts to resolve their conflict through negotiations. Will it slow down the pace set by Labor? Will it reverse the process in some respects? Will the Arab world remain passive in the face of Israeli aggressiveness? How will Hamas relate to the new situation? Such questions yield no answers at this stage. What we know is that Israeli tactics and objectives will be reformulated, as will those of their Palestinian counterparts.

In the background of inquiry are further questions about what it means to describe Palestinian/Israeli negotiations as "a peace process." Is it merely a matter of a renunciation of violent tactics by the two sides? Or is the reference to a peace process a series of steps that by its end has resolved the conflict to the degree that the two states can live side-by-side in a condition of amity? Or more elaborately, is the reference to an outcome that brings "security" to Israel and "self-determination" in the form of a sovereign state to Palestine? This latter level of concern suggests a normative result that associates "peace" with a set of substantive conditions.

Against such a background of conjecture and complexity, the problematic dimensions of the early stages of the Palestinian/Israeli diplomacy emanating from the Oslo Declaration of Principles will be examined.

What Sort of Peace Process

Every peace process is distinctive, acquiring its own characteristics based upon the overall mix of circumstances that led parties to a prior armed conflict to move, often unexpectedly and even abruptly, in the direction of "peace." Nothing is assured. Even the genuineness of the presumed quest for peace itself cannot be taken for granted. Parties may pursue negotiations and a peace settlement for purely tactical reasons, to provide a lull in actual combat, to strike a sympathetic pose for the sake of world public opinion, and to create new conditions that would be more favourable upon the resumption of active hostilities, and to impose humiliating conditions on the weaker side. At the core of most diplomatic efforts to achieve peace is a negotiating process the product of which will be an international agreement, or a series of agreements, that provides a framework for future adjustments and relations among the parties, establishing the modalities for the momentous shift from war to peace, and, in this instance, from occupation to self-rule and political independence. Depending on its form, such a process of agreement may be to varying degrees obligatory for the parties, providing common ground in the event of further controversy about respective rights and duties. Often, also, outsiders are invited to play special roles, including the provision of military and civilian presences to ensure compliance and the avoidance of dangerous frictions.

The Oslo/Cairo framework for the Israel/PLO peace process is definitely illustrative of such an effort to impart structure and give guidance to the transition to peace after a long, anguishing period of intense warfare. It was dutifully negotiated in secret by mutually acknowledged official representatives of each side, and was ritualised in a dramatic ceremony on the White House lawn in September of 1993. By outward appearances, the agreements negotiated provided a solid foundation for a cumulative movement toward peace. But there were many treacherous difficulties that have confronted the parties from the outset. It is the contention of this chapter that if this peace process is ever to eventuate in "peace," then it will need strong reinforcement from time to time by external actors, especially by the United States, but also by European states, as well as by Arab countries in the region, by the European Union and possibly by the United Nations.[4] More than this, at the level of implementation, NGOs, transnational citizens associations, and private diplomacy will turn out to be indispensable.[5] Somehow, the early assessments of the peace process did not give any serious consideration to the volatility of domestic politics on the Israeli side. To the extent these concerns existed, it was in relation to the Palestinians, centering upon the fear that if the PLO were to be displaced by Hamas then the process would come to a halt. In many Israeli eyes, the peace process could only unfold if Arafat held onto control on behalf of the Palestinian Liberation Organization, recast as the moderate Palestinian alternative after years of repudiation as terrorist.

First of all, the disparity in power, wealth, influence, information and negotiating skill between Israel and the PLO has pervaded all phases of negotiation, and subsequent implementation; this multi-layered disparity has tilted the process from the outset very much in Israel's favour, especially on matters of interpretation and with respect to the political willingness of the parties at each stage as to whether to go ahead to the next stage in the process. Of course, it is characteristic of such conflicts that a negotiated settlement exhibits a disparity between the parties, as was the case in Algeria in the negotiations between France and the FLN or in Vietnam in the negotiations between the United States and North Vietnam/National Liberation Front. However, in those instances, the "weaker" side at the negotiating table from a diplomatic standpoint had essentially prevailed on the battlefield, and the "stronger" side had an urgent political need for a rapid exit. Here, the PLO was at the brink of defeat, if not collapse, and Israel had plenty of incentives, but no urgent pressure to leave the occupied territories in the wake of defeat, and no intention to do so altogether, insisting always on retaining an extensive security role within whatever Palestinian entity eventually emerged. In such circumstances, the disparity inevitably expresses itself in the bargaining process, leading to a bad bargain for the weaker side, and absent wisdom and concessions on the stronger side, a non-sustainable arrangement that will in time be denounced as illegitimate engendering opposition and resistance.

Secondly, each side in the process contained important divisions, minority factions deeply opposed to allowing the Oslo/Cairo framework to become the effective basis of an Israel/Palestine peace. On the Palestinian side the Islamic Jihad and Islamic Resistance Movement (Hamas) committed their organizations to a disruptive posture that included resort to terrorism against Israeli targets of all variety, including civilians. On the Israeli side, extremists among the settlers and the Likud opposition all along opposed the whole idea of Palestinian self-rule, especially on the West Bank; the extremist and violent settler fringe resorted to terror tactics, most spectacularly the February 25, 1994 mass killing of Muslims while at prayer in a mosque by a single Israeli militant, Baruch Goldstein, at Hebron's Tomb of the Patriarchs.[6] Terrorist incidents from suicide bombers caused heavy Israeli casualties and generated strong demands by Israeli leaders for more effective PLO control of extremists among the Palestinians. During the phases of the peace process the Government of Israel repeatedly imposed several types of collective punishments, including the periodic sealing of Israel's borders, thereby denying Palestinians access to their Israeli jobs, imposing severe burdens on the entire Palestinian population, diminishing the efforts in Gaza and the West Bank to trade agricultural products across borders, and causing added hardship for a Palestinian society that has been experiencing a steady and dramatic process of economic deterioration since the start of the arrangements brought into being by the Oslo/Cairo framework. Israeli officials have periodically threatened that the peace process will be halted indefinitely unless the Palestinian Authority manages to suppress anti-Israeli violence, even if the perpetrators were never within Palestinian-controlled areas, and not withstanding the Israeli failure to achieve such control during the long period of unconditional occupation.

Thirdly, the Palestinians living as refugees outside the West Bank and Gaza Strip were essentially unrepresented by the PLO during the negotiations. It remains to be seen whether any sort of "right of return" is incorporated into the peace process at some subsequent stage, and whether Palestinians in exile become a factor in the negotiations.

The interplay of these factors is complex and controversial, often being manipulated by various actors to demonstrate either that the peace process is failing due to its intrinsic weakness or that its essential integrity needs to be preserved in opposition to extremists on both sides. This dynamic suggests a precarious situation that is dominated by political factors, continuing to remain uncertain as to overall impact even as the Gaza arrangements are extended to cover most of the remaining occupied Palestinian territory. Such a dynamic is in sharp contrast with other dimensions of the wider peace process, especially the Israel/Jordan agreements. In this latter interaction the element of disparity, although present to a degree, seemed much less evident with respect both to the resolution of substantive issues and the relationship between the parties; furthermore, the outcome of these inter-governmental negotiations didn't arouse extremist opposition of serious consequence on either side, and especially not on the Israeli side. This state-to-state relationship, barring truly fundamental changes in the underlying circumstances, seems likely to proceed in rough approximation to the terms agreed upon, although it may, over time, be linked once more to mutually acceptable arrangements on such unresolved regional issues as the future of Jerusalem, the sharing of water rights, the establishment of a Palestinian homeland, Israeli renunciation and abandonment of nuclear weaponry, and reactions to Israeli recourse to force against Arab countries as occurred in April 1996 when Israel attacked Lebanon. For the present, however, negotiated arrangements between Israel and its neighbours are much more likely to be respected as feasible and mutually beneficial than are comparable Israel/PLO arrangements. Of course, the intense mutual entanglement of Israel and occupied Palestine makes this negotiation by far the most ambitious and difficult of the various negotiating tracks that together comprise the Middle East peace process, although the Likud stance in Golan makes problematic the Israel/Syria negotiating track. However, the limits of the state-to-state and regional peace process have surfaced both in relation to the U.S./Israeli backed proposal for a Middle East Development Bank, with Gulf countries disclosing their reluctance in the mid-1990s to establish close ties with Israel until more overall progress toward normalcy has occurred and with respect to Egypt/Israel tensions over Arab adherence to an extended version of the Non-Proliferation Treaty despite Israeli non-adherence.[7]

An optimistic assessment could never have been responsibly made with respect to the Israel/PLO arrangements embodied in the Oslo/Cairo agreements: partly, the terms of agreement, reflecting the disparities, were too one-sidedly in Israel's favour, and partly, the attacks on Israeli vital interests prompted by the peace process has generated a political crisis in Israel that placed the Rabin government on the defensive, leading it to suspend agreed upon timetables for implementation of removal of troops and elections on the West Bank and to consider seriously such radical solutions to the security challenge as the complete "separation" of the two peoples.[8] Then, of course, the assassination of Rabin in November 1996 followed by Grapes of Wrath and the Likud victory have shattered the earlier international mood, which was never truly justified in the first place.

In retrospect, it now seems absurdly premature for leaders on either side of the negotiations to have been awarded a Nobel Peace Prize in 1994, although it is by no means the first time that the prize committee in Oslo has used its prestige to express support for unresolved moves that seem to move in the direction of peace and reconciliation. Even earlier, when the prizes were initially announced, such recognition seemed like a mixture of forgetfulness about the past and wishful thinking about the future, while at the same time reflecting the then real acknowledgement that world public opinion was prepared to hope against hope, giving tangible expression to the view that what was started in Oslo required the courage to break with the violent past and needed as much symbolic moral support as possible to sustain the process until it reached a desired outcome. A similar acknowledgement a year earlier by way of Nobel Peace Prizes to Nelson Mandela and F.W. de Klerk seems to have fared much better with the passage of time, reflecting both the quality of the individuals honoured, particularly in Mandela's case, and even more so the degree to which the peace process in South Africa tangibly and heroically scaled back the injustices of apartheid. No relinquishment of control comparable to the adjustments in South Africa has been evident on the Israeli side in relation to Palestinian territories, not even as regards the initial transfers of authority. Instead, Israel has sought to push its advantageous position as fully as possible, thereby restructuring the disparities while only pretending to transform them. Not only is this reflected by the persistence of extensive Israeli security claims even in relation to Gaza, but by the provocative moves to expand Israeli settlements in West Bank areas slated for self-rule, and by obstacles placed in the way of Palestinian investment, trade relations, and employment. The extensions of Oslo/Cairo to the West Bank exhibited similar characteristics.

In effect, the Oslo/Cairo framework to support an ongoing peace process depended upon several kinds of action by the parties, especially by

Israel. To undercut extremism it was in Israel's interest to improve the lot of the Palestinians living under the Palestinian Authority at a street level as quickly as possible. Similarly, it was important for the PLO leadership to expand its political base in areas under its control by creating employment opportunities and improving life circumstances for Palestinians, especially for those living in refugee camps. Further, when the Hebron massacre occurred, it provided a moment for the Israeli Government to rein in the settlements as part of any serious strategy to make the peace process a success for both sides.[9] Similarly, it seems destructive for Israel to blame Hamas terrorism on the enforcement laxity of the Palestinian Authority and to justify delays in negotiations or punitive countermeasures. These are precisely the results being sought by Hamas. The stance adopted by the Government of Israel thereby ironically provides ample incentives for the continuation of their activities. It would have been more useful for the Israeli Government and media to focus Palestinian responsibility narrowly, thereby undercutting popular support for Hamas's terrorist action as a way to neutralize Israeli use of coercive tactics to punish innocent Palestinians. What was allowed to develop was a tacit conspiracy on both sides to ensure a substantial discrediting of the Oslo/Cairo framework, which has predictably produced the unwelcome outcome of strengthening the political leverage of extremist elements in both Israel and among Palestinians. Unfortunately, there is no way to test the consequence of a more balanced Israeli approach. If a Likud victory had occurred, as happened in any event, then it would certainly have been attributed to the soft policies of Rabin and Peres. Even with the actuality of a tough-minded, pragmatic Israeli approach to the negotiations, Rabin was assassinated and Peres reviled because of their alleged softness.

Against this background of uncertainty and deteriorating confidence it remains useful to evaluate the Oslo/Cairo framework from the perspective of the international legal order. Despite the difficulties described, both sides continue to express their grievances and disappointments by reference to the Oslo/Cairo agreements, and have, at this point, substantially agreed upon elaborate arrangements of a similar character for much of the West Bank. Even the Likud, which would have avoided negotiations with the PLO in the first instance, has indicated its willingness to abide by the agreements and not to question such implementation as has occurred. Even without the contextual difficulties that have been discussed, a negotiated peace process and its international legal implications need to be understood as possessing several special attributes.

The phrase "international legal implications" refers both to the rights and duties of the parties to the autonomy agreements so far negotiated between the PLO and Israel since the September 1993 Declaration of Principles on Interim Self-Government Arrangements and to the relationship of this process to legal claims on a global level by representatives of the peoples involved, as well as by third-party governments, international institutions, and nongovernmental organizations. It touches on the extent to which the texts negotiated and to be negotiated are authoritative and binding with respect to such matters as sovereignty, statehood, self-determination, refugees, boundaries, resources, Jerusalem and protection of human rights.

Formally, these crucial issues remain contested and unresolved as between Israel and the PLO, pending the conclusion of the permanent status negotiations that are unlikely to occur soon, despite the commitment in the Declaration of Principles to commence this phase no later than two years after the start of the interim period.[10] A legal, political uncertainty affecting the whole process is the extent to which these parties have and will be treated as having the representational capacity to resolve issues that concern either Palestinians living outside the occupied territories or governments in the region with an interest in the process, particularly, arrangements for Jerusalem, water rights, and a Palestinian right of return. Even for Palestinians living under Israeli rule the representation issue is real. The PLO's authority and legitimacy has been under siege, not only from Islamic elements, but also from progressive secular social forces, and these misgivings were not removed by the first series of elections held under Palestinian authority. Some aspects of this present and future will be examined from the perspective of international law.

Deference

There is a strong tendency in international law to respect whatever framework parties to a conflict can agree upon to resolve their differences, especially if their accord is undertaken against a background of prolonged warfare, and with the encouragement of influential members of the international community. Disparities of power, negotiating competence, and knowledge between the parties are not treated as legally relevant; peace treaties imposed by battlefield outcomes in war are generally respected in international law, although acquisitions of new territory by force of arms have been legally problematic within the domain of the United Nations, regardless of what the parties may decide.

Also, if the disparities seem too great, or political conditions change, then legal deference to an earlier "peace process" may be dissipated by subsequent developments. Indeed, there is an important distinction between "legality" and "legitimacy" that may turn out to be relevant to the evolving PLO/Israeli relationship. This process, which has so far enjoyed widespread deference on an inter-governmental level and within the United Nations during its early stages, is increasingly subject to attack and widespread criticism by Palestinians and by governments and international organizations as "illegitimate." This is so both because the terms imposed on the Palestinian people fall far short of their rights of self-determination and, contrariwise, because the PLO has failed to follow through in relation either to the Palestinian people or to Israeli expectations arising from the agreed texts.

The Israeli leadership has already revealed its unwillingness to implement aspects of the early empowerment phases of the self-government provisions unless the PLO abides by its commitments (as interpreted by Israeli officialdom), especially its obligation to deny extremists safe haven and manage successfully to sustain the security of Israelis living within the jurisdiction of its authority, as well as follow through on its commitment to revise the Palestinian Covenant by removing challenges to Israel's right to exist as a state on its present territory. Various Palestinian leaders, representing facets of Palestinian public opinion, have also challenged the capacity of Chairman Arafat to negotiate in secret and act unilaterally on behalf of the PLO and have also complained about alleged PLO failures to implement in territory under its control the democratising provisions in the agreements.

So far the organized global community treats as authoritative the PLO/Israeli peace process as negotiated by the parties. Paragraph 3 of UNGA Res. 48/58, adopted 14 December 1993, "Expresses its full support for the achievements of the peace process thus far," singling out the Declaration of Principles (DOP) as especially notable, and ends by urging "all parties to implement the agreements reached." This resolution was adopted in the General Assembly by a vote of 155 to 3 (Iran, Lebanon, Syria), with one abstention (Libya), and was drafted by the key third-party states (Norway, Russia, the United States), with the active participation of both the PLO and Israel. From an international law perspective, such an expression of consensus, reinforcing as it does the normal pattern of deference in the setting of a peace process, is until repudiated or withdrawn quite definitive in relation to states and the United Nations, with the possible exception of the four states that refused to support the UN resolution.

This prospect of deference is also reinforced by geopolitical considerations. First of all, continuing Israeli peace negotiations with Arab neighbours had been leading toward a condition of regional normalization, although as yet incomplete and subject to shifts of attitude or even reversals. Grapes of Wrath represented a setback for normalization, as did the Likud electoral victory. Secondly, the agreements so far negotiated facilitate the accommodation of the two overriding interests of the United States in the region, favourable access to oil and support of Israel; in this regard, a one-sided peace process is more likely to engender U.S. deference than one that was more balanced in its disposition of controversial issues. This geopolitical context is not favourable to the most fundamental Palestinian concerns, and arguably, never has been, although during the cold war and in the course of belligerent relations between Israel and the Arab World, "the Palestinian card" was played by Arab governments and the Soviet Union as a dimension of opposition to Israeli statehood and expansion. At present, there are no strong incentives to play this card, except possibly on Syria's part, but even Assad's diplomacy was seemingly moving inexorably in the direction of a negotiated reconciliation with Israel until the April 1996 attack on Lebanon and the May 1996 elections in Israel. For several years the peace momentum has proved resilient, withstanding the psycho-political impact of the Hamas tactics, settler violence, Likud opposition, Israeli punitive responses, and PLO ineptitude and oppressive tactics. Whether this resilience can withstand the reorientation of policy under Likud leadership remains to be seen, but the outlook at this point is quite bleak.

Given this background, Palestinian prospects for the protection of both their broader claims to self-determination, statehood, and sovereignty, and their narrower claims to full implementation of the agreements, including provisions on democratisation of the Palestinian governance process, will be more dependent than ever, and to an unusual degree, on continuing, and rapidly expanding, grassroots activism by Palestinians, reinforced by the transnational support of citizens' associations dedicated to peace, democracy, and human rights. The more extreme cases of East Timor and West New Guinea (Irian Jaya) are suggestive, the circumstances of abuse being deliberately overlooked by most of the international community because of the absence of geopolitical incentives to challenge Indonesia; without grassroots resistance and the efforts of transnational political forces, these issues would have disappeared from the international political agenda and fallen into the black hole of geopolitics. The Palestinian plight is somewhat similarly situated, although the Islamic interest in the status of Jerusalem and concern about Israel's nuclear weapons and regional economic ambitions makes it unlikely that Palestinian concerns will be indefinitely neglected within wider regional and global political circles.

Sui Generis

The point here is a simple one. There is little relevant precedent. The PLO role in the Gaza Strip, Jericho, as well as elsewhere on the West Bank and in relation to Jerusalem is embedded in a unique set of circumstances, shaped by the interactions of the past several decades of occupation, which have influenced the conditions imposed on the transfer of authority to the PLO in a variety of fundamental respects. The persistence, and even expansion, of Israeli settlements and security zones give these interim arrangements a particularly unresolved, precarious character. The structures and circumstances of dual authority is quite an anomaly in the post-colonial era where the exercise of rights of self-determination normally extinguish enclaves of foreign privilege at an early stage, and imply an unconditional transfer of sovereign rights as a matter of right in relation to territory within national boundaries. The arrangements for Hong Kong after 1997 or in the various parts of the United Kingdom (Scotland, Ulster, Isle of Mann) are illustrative of self-rule, dual or incomplete sovereignty. Yet, the anomalies here are, for the time being at least and from the perspective of the agreements themselves, subordinate to the deference accorded whatever texts are negotiated, especially as argued above, since the agreements reached are the essence of a diplomatic process instituted to supersede a condition of prolonged and bitterly resisted belligerent occupation, a diplomacy that the world is determined to regard, with the U.S. Government in the forefront, as "a peace process."[11]

In the end, the acceptability of the process will depend, of course, on the success of the status negotiations that were supposed to begin within two years after the inception of the interim arrangements and end within five years of this date. The substantial postponement, or even cancellation, of these negotiations is likely to be one of the first indications of Likud resistance to further implementation of the Oslo/Cairo process. If somehow the peace process still manages to go forward, even if more slowly than agreed upon and the supportive consensus of 48/58 in the UN holds firm and the PLO remains sufficiently credible among Palestinians and on the international level as the sole legitimate representative of the Palestinian people, then the prospects are reasonably good that the agreements as negotiated will remain generally authoritative from the perspectives of international law, at least for some more years. But if any of these conditions weakens, then the agreements seem vulnerable to a variety of lines of stress, and outside attack, including repudiation, and are not insulated by any earlier persuasive precedent or wider doctrine. The Likud electoral victory has cast severe doubt on further implement of the arrangements already agreed upon, and may set in motion a process that radicalised Palestinian leadership and reengages the Arab governments on behalf of the Palestinian struggle.

With respect to international law, the disparity between the two sides being reflected in the one-sidedness of the arrangements is both the strength and weakness of the peace process. It is strength because, to date, essentially one side, according to its priorities, has guided the process. This same side enjoys superior access to the media and to the geopolitical forces in control of world order. It is the main weakness of the process that this one-sidedness, if effectively exposed, undermines the legitimacy of whatever has been agreed upon, especially if the Palestinians themselves, either by way of the PLO or in opposition to its leadership, regard the agreements as not satisfying, in a reasonable time interval, their basic aspirations for sovereignty, statehood, and improving material conditions. Despite their one-sidedness in Israel's favour, the agreements are also vulnerable to varying degrees of repudiation or non-implementation on the Israeli side, possibly either through the return to control of the Likud or by escalating violence against the Israelis. The Likud contention, as related to the analysis presented here, is to say, in effect, that the agreements comprising the Oslo/Cairo process are not one-sided enough! This vulnerability has recently become much more manifest, especially with respect to Israel's refusal to abide by the agreed timetable on Palestinian elections and empowerment and its insistence on taking unilaterally whatever security measures it deems necessary even if their enactment imposes unwarranted collective punishment on the Palestinians as a people.

Status

On a textual level, the Palestinians arguably have actually lost ground in their basic quest for statehood and sovereignty, while the PLO has gained in its external contention of representing the Palestinian people, as epitomized by the signing ceremony on the White House lawn and by the abrupt transformation of Yasser Arafat from "terrorist" to normal, even indispensable political leader entitled to treatment equivalent to that accorded a head of state of an important country. With some irony, this external acceptance of the PLO, as represented by Arafat, has been coupled with an internal erosion of the PLO's claim to be the authoritative representative of the Palestinian people and with widespread Palestinian dissatisfaction about the results and style of Arafat's leadership, which now ironically includes serious abuses of democratic elements and rights of Palestinians living under the jurisdiction of the Palestinian Authority. Even verbal criticism of the PLO's role and Arafat's adequacy as a leader can lead a Palestinian to be subject to imprisonment and abuse.

The negotiating framework and the agreements issuing forth reflect this underlying ambiguity on matters of status. As never before, the state of Israel operationally accepted the PLO and Arafat as diplomatic equals, as "parties." Yet formally and textually, as well as in substantive arrangements, inequality of status was enshrined throughout the process. The Preamble of the DOP identifies the Palestinian party as "the PLO team (in the Jordanian-Palestinian delegation to the Middle East Peace Conference)," while the Israeli party is described simply as "[t]he Government of the State of Israel," a status confirmed by the September 9, 1993 exchange of correspondence. In later documents the PLO is simply described as such, given an authoritative relationship to the negotiations to establish a Palestinian Interim Self-Government Authority, and Arafat in the September 9, 1993 exchange of letters with Rabin undertakes, without deadline, to submit to the Palestinian National Council proposals to make "the necessary changes" in the Palestinian Covenant in accordance with the PLO acceptance of Israel's right to exist as a sovereign state, a step that was finally taken by the Palestinian National Council in April 1996.[12]

Throughout the agreements, there is no acknowledgement whatsoever of Palestinian sovereignty over West Bank, Gaza, and Jerusalem areas, and no implication that the Palestinian Authority is a vehicle for emerging Palestinian statehood. Numbered paragraph 4 in the

May 4, 1994 exchange of letters specifies that Arafat will "use the title 'Chairman (Ra'ees in Arabic) of the Palestinian Authority' or 'Chairman of the PLO', and will not use the title 'President of Palestine'." This attempt to circumscribe the Palestinian status is further confirmed in Article VI of the Gaza-Jericho Agreement by denying the Palestinian Authority "powers and responsibilities in the sphere of foreign relations" and throughout the interim arrangements by severely restricting the Palestinian role even in internal security to the extent that Israeli interests are directly involved. At the same time, Israel acknowledges the PLO right to negotiate with foreign governments and international organizations on matters pertaining to economic development, aid, cultural, scientific, and educational matters. (Gaza-Jericho, Article VI(2)(b)).

Prior to the peace process, the PLO was recognized as the government of the State of Palestine by more than a hundred countries, and had many diplomatic representatives and facilities at different levels abroad. In the interim arrangements, despite the PLO having a territorial base of governmental control for the first time, the legal competence to engage in foreign relations is narrowly circumscribed, including either the establishment of Palestinian diplomatic facilities abroad or foreign facilities in Gaza or Jericho (Article VI(2)(a) and (c)). Additionally, Israel claims an informal authority to regulate entry, including that of foreign heads of state, as was early seen in the incident over Benazir Bhutto's proposed visit to Gaza in the fall of 1994. Rabin rebuffed Bhutto at the time by attacking her lack of "manners," evidently because of her failure to obtain Israel's approval of the visit before announcing her intention. The fact that the visit did not take place lends credence to the perception that Israel insists upon and retains many of the operative rights of occupation even after it has redeployed its troops.

It is uncertain how practice will evolve. Will there be a tacit tolerance by both sides of gaps between the textual denials of emerging Palestinian statehood and the behavioural expressions of it, or will Israel press the issue that the Palestinian Authority is without the formal or substantive attributes of sovereignty? How will third parties, whether states or international organizations, treat the issue? How will the PLO? Such questions assume an added dimension of significance given the shift of Israeli leadership from Rabin/Peres to Netanyahu.

The issue of status casts a shadow over the nature of the agreements. Because the Palestinian side is so far definitively not treated as a state in the negotiating process, and the PLO has accepted this diminished status, the agreements reached are not treaties in a technical sense under international law. Yet, the White House signing and endorsement, the diplomatic rituals emphasizing the equality of the parties, the Norwegian role in encouraging the negotiations, the tendency in recent customary international law to give respect to the outcome of self-determination negotiations conducted with a non-state actor, and the UN expressions of formal support have internationalised the process in a definitive way, at least for the present. This gives the PLO a state-like de facto role in the process and makes the resultant arrangements treaty-like for most purposes. Of course, the PLO and the Palestinian Authority would not currently have full access to any arena that relies on formal criteria to specify rights of access, as limited to states (e.g. the International Court of Justice).

In these regards, some language in Article XXIII(5) of the May 4, 1994 Cairo agreement has a potential relevance for the Palestinian side:

> Nothing in this Agreement shall prejudice or preempt the outcome of the negotiations in the interim agreement or on the permanent status to be conducted pursuant to the Declaration of Principles. Neither Party shall be deemed, by virtue of having entered into this Agreement, to have renounced or waived any of its existing rights, claims or positions.

Such an "escape" clause seems inconsistent with the substance, tone, and language of the agreements so far negotiated, but it gives a legal basis in the future to the reassertion of claims relating to Palestinian sovereignty and self-determination that have been so far not explicitly acknowledged. This clause also gives Israel the possibility of reasserting territorial claims to the West Bank, as might happen now that the Likud has acquired control of the negotiating process.

The early disputes under the agreements have confirmed that Israel holds the main cards, and intends to play them aggressively, suggesting that the rate and quality of implementation of the agreements will depend almost exclusively on the will of the Israeli government. This Israeli advantage is accentuated by the failure of the PLO to challenge significantly Israeli unilateralism or to move swiftly toward a more democratic relationship with the Palestinians under the jurisdiction of the Palestinian Authority. Such a development raises to prominence a neglected and generally unanticipated dimension of the peace process, namely, the legal and political vulnerability under the agreements of the Palestinians who are seeking to uphold human rights and achieve democratic governance. Unlike rejectionist elements (e.g. Hamas), Israel seems to view democratically inclined Palestinians as matters for the PLO to handle as it sees fit. Israel, despite its claim of support for a democratic Palestinian entity, does not appear distressed by the suppression of these Palestinians, possibly because Israel may prefer to deal with autocratic and corrupt rule by the PLO that seems content with a minimalist conception of self-determination, and is more easily held accountable, than to confront the fuller demands of Palestinians who insist on a much fuller exercise of the Palestinian right of self-determination. This relationship could change if the Palestinian leadership is radicalised by provocative Likud policies.

Among the legal issues posed here is the extent of Israeli responsibility for violations of human rights of Palestinians as a result of the activities of the Palestinian Authority, recalling that Article XIV of the Gaza/Jericho agreement pledges both sides to proceed separately to carry out its respective responsibilities on the basis of international human rights standards and the rule of law. Events, to date, involving arbitrary arrests, allegations of torture and intimidation, interference with freedom of the press, and with rights of free expression make it evident that such Palestinian concerns with protecting themselves against the new Palestinian rulers are not fanciful, but also that the Article XIV legal commitment is being ignored, at least by the two negotiating parties. If the Israeli Government does not press such claims on behalf of the Palestinians, then it would seem that the UN would still be in a position to do so to the extent that Israeli occupation has not yet been terminated in the sense decreed by Security Council Resolution 242 and 338, and sovereignty has not been transferred to an emergent Palestinian state. Israel retains, at least during the interim period, extensive security and economic prerogatives, as well as plenary control over foreign relations and in relation to the settlements and to Israelis, including further responsibilities and duties that arise from this evolving set of circumstances. These issues are also subject to action taken by transnational human rights groups.

Self-determination

Not only is the issue of eventual Palestinian statehood and sovereignty suppressed (along with Palestinian claims in relation to Jerusalem), but more remarkably, the right of self-determination for the Palestinian people is never explicitly and unconditionally affirmed in the arrangements negotiated to date. Instead, the DOP unsatisfactorily refers in Article I under the heading "Aim of Negotiations," to "a permanent settlement" after the five year transitional period "based on Security Council Resolutions 242 and 338." It will be recalled that 242 was adopted in the aftermath of the 1967 war, having as its central tenet Israeli withdrawal from the territory occupied in exchange for being accorded security by other states in the region, yet without ever specifying what precisely is meant by withdrawal or territory. Palestinian claims were at the time dealt with in the resolution as a peripheral matter, not even by direct reference, but within the supposed ambit of clause 2(b) of the resolution, which refers to the "necessity for achieving a just settlement of the refugee problem."

It is plausible in the present climate of expectations to assume that such a just settlement would be only possible of achievement if it involved the creation of a secure and viable Palestinian homeland enjoying comprehensive sovereign rights, including some participation in the administration of Jerusalem. Whether such a just settlement also implies that all refugees claiming a Palestinian national identity would enjoy a right to return, and whether the exercise of this right would be eventually regulated by the Palestinian governance process that will be established is less assured. There are also complex issues arising from Israel-Jordan negotiations, carried on in June 1994 without Palestinian participation, yet addressing issues that bear on self-determination for the Palestinian people, such as economic control over West Bank resources and responsibility for controlling access to Islamic holy places in East Jerusalem.

Resolution 338, adopted in 1973, merely reiterates the imperative of implementing 242 by way of negotiations, and sheds no further light on the status or extent of legitimate Palestinian claims. If the textual language of these resolutions were to be treated as authoritative, it would be quite consistent with a transfer of sovereign control over the occupied territories to Jordan (or any other entity), provided only that Israel withdrew its military forces and that some agreed arrangement of "the refugee problem" was achieved. It is somewhat astonishing that the PLO negotiators have accepted this outmoded textual framework as the agreed basis for a permanent settlement of the conflict, presumably obliged to accept a minimalist version of the land for peace formula enshrined in 242 and 338 without any assurance on broader claims. The informal assurances provided by the Labor government have now, of course, vanished. It is conceivable that in the new setting the Likud will move toward a more literal interpretation of the underlying mandate established at Oslo. Up until the May Israeli elections, the dynamics of the actual negotiating and implementing process had been far more favourable to the satisfaction of

Palestinian claims to achieve substantial sovereignty by way of a Palestinian state of some sort located within the occupied territories, but this has yet to be reflected adequately in the language of the formal texts that have emerged from the negotiations. The surmise of a Palestinian state had been based on the consequences over time of *de facto* self-rule, as well as the private musings of Israeli leaders, especially Shimon Peres. Yet such a surmise was always suspect until the status of Israeli settlements and security rights are clarified in relation to the final outcome of the peace process, which is currently subject to Likud control. As has always been the case, what sort of Palestinian entity would emerge from negotiations was in doubt. Pre-Likud critics of PLO diplomacy always attacked Oslo for its acceptance of a humiliating Palestinian bantustan after so many years of struggle and sacrifice. Other Palestinians saw the Oslo/Cairo process as of uncertain destination, and were hence prepared to suspend disbelief. As of mid-1996 this willingness has virtually disappeared on the Palestinian side, despite their formal control over much of the territory previously occupied, although far less than is conveyed by media accounts of Israeli withdrawal from all parts of the West Bank except Hebron.

As has been pointed out from the outset by Palestinian critics of negotiations, Gaza and the West Bank have been shifted from "occupied territory" to "disputed territory."[13] Such a change gives the contemplated Israeli "withdrawal" a more problematic character, making Israeli retention of extensive residual rights and privileges an expected feature, especially with respect to security and economic development, and allowing the settlements to remain exempt from territorial law. The requirements of 242 are thereby reduced to the outcome of negotiations in a context of gross asymmetry and deference, reinforced by an Israeli tendency to seek as favourable a bargain as possible, allegedly, in part, so as "to sell" the process and arrangements at home, and in the face of stiff domestic opposition.[14] With the Likud coalition now in control, this prior justification for one-sidedness no longer applies, although arguably, the Likud might have repudiated the results of Oslo/Cairo altogether had it been based on greater mutuality. Article V of the DOP does leave open the shape of the permanent disposition of issues, including in V(3) "Jerusalem, refugees, settlements, security arrangements, borders, relations and cooperation with other neighbours, and other issues of common interest." V(4) also confirms that the "permanent status negotiations should not be prejudiced or pre-empted by agreements reached for the interim period." Such a mandate allows for the possibility that the permanent status negotiations will move toward a more comprehensive understanding of Israeli withdrawal that would be alone compatible with the exercise of Palestinian self-determination (unless self-determination is understood formalistically as whatever designated leaders of a people agree to even in circumstances of virtual compulsion). The new government in Israel has not yet shown its hand on these crucial matters, but it is not expected to be as forthcoming as the Rabin/Peres leadership, except possibly on matters of more open borders between Gaza/West Bank and Israel.

Implementation

Many fundamental issues with respect to the peace process are unresolved at this stage, including the degree to which a successor government in Israel or a different Palestinian (or PLO) leadership would be bound by agreements negotiated and partially implemented, especially if important obligations were breached by either side. On this matter, the diplomatic and military disparities between the two sides constrain the Palestinians while giving the Israelis virtually unrestricted discretion to reinterpret their obligations. Since the DOP, and other arrangements, is not technically a treaty, its international character can always be denied, although the involvement of other governments, the formalization derived from the White House signing, and the UNGA endorsement create a strong presumption that both sides have good faith legal obligations to carry out the agreed arrangements without retaining any option to repudiate. Even Netanyahu has indicated his acceptance of this line of reasoning. Of course, the test of the political viability of the process has now been brought to the fore by the drastic change of government in Israel. If Arafat were to lose control of the PLO another challenge to the process would be posed. If, and when, permanent status negotiations get underway such fundamental long-term issues as statehood, sovereignty, Jerusalem, settlements and external refugees will provide the substantive test of political viability.

During the interim period, with the leadership on the two sides stable and unconditionally committed to the negotiated process, inter-governmental disputes of even a serious character were resolved by diplomacy. On this basis the Palestinian Authority gradually acquired a *de facto* statist character and considerable international legitimacy even if Israel continued to deny the *de jure* implications of statehood and maintained a huge security presence in relation to the settlements that amounted to seriously encroaching upon the sort of territorial supremacy normally associated with statehood. The longer the interim process drags on and the more extremist opposition on both sides gains control of subsequent stages of diplomacy, the less likely it is that the process can be maintained in its present form.

The provision for Palestinian elections (DOP, Article III) and the constitutional arrangements proposed for the Palestinian Authority in the Agreement on the Gaza Strip and the West Bank have been carried out after considerable delay. Whether the transfers of political authority that has so far taken place will remain acceptable without further progress toward self-determination is in doubt. How long will Palestinians be subject to autocratic and inept rule deprived of political participation, of human rights, and of basic material necessities abide by the constraints on their struggle? Suppose further, as seems likely, that neither Israel, the United States, the UN, nor even other Arab Governments lend support to Palestinian allegations of non-implementation, especially if other aspects of the process are going forward relatively smoothly. How, then, can the rights of the Palestinian people be upheld? It is here that the informal roles of NGOs in reinforcing governmental and inter-governmental procedures are likely to be crucial. It would be of great legal relevance to have reliable monitoring procedures in place that identify, expose, and evaluate accusations of non-implementation of the democracy and constitutionalism portions of the peace process, and issue periodic reports; similarly, with respect to human rights for the Palestinian people, regardless of who is in charge. The UN retains a special responsibility toward the Palestinian people living in the occupied territories, at least until 242 is fully implemented, and this includes the protection of human rights. The challenge is to activate this latent legal responsibility by mobilizing effective political pressure through exposing violations, giving the prospect of exposure some possible deterrent effects on the governance approach adopted by the PLO and the Palestinian Authority. With the focus shifted to what can be expected from the new Likud-led Israeli government, it is more difficult than ever to get any strong response to Palestinian abases directed at Palestinians.

The other confusing context, with respect to implementation, is the degree to which Israel/PLO negotiations can extinguish or supersede the legal claims of unrepresented parties. Because of the overall interest in peace, reinforced by regional and global geopolitical factors, there is a tendency to disregard third party interests, especially if not effectively voiced in the form of objections. UN resolutions of support for the existing framework of negotiations and arrangements give a legal colouring to this disregard. It might be appropriate at this point to urge the General Assembly to request an Advisory Opinion from the International Court of Justice on such outstanding matters as the status of Jerusalem, the rights of Palestinians living outside the Gaza Strip and the West Bank, and the distribution of water rights. Such a reference would be especially appropriate if Netanyahu restrictively interprets aspects of the Oslo/Cairo framework that have yet to be implemented.

Conclusion

At this stage, from the perspective of international law, it is difficult to provide any clear guidelines as to the likely reception of the Palestinian/Israeli peace process under international law, especially as it pertains to the protection of human rights of Palestinians subject to the authority of the Palestinian Authority and with respect to final status arrangements. The fluidity of the situation makes it critical for all concerned parties, especially associated with the rights of citizens and associated with the Palestinian Diaspora, to posit their legal claims and grievances at an early stage in as effective a form as possible. This is particularly true with respect to those claims not likely to be protected by the perceived self-interest of the two negotiating sides and of no distinct interest to the U.S. Government.

It is in relation to human rights, democratisation and constitutional governance that grassroots Palestinian initiatives, reinforced by transnational citizens' associations, may yet have their greatest contributions to make, especially if substantiated by independent academic analysis and by respected media accounts. In other words, the human rights dimensions of the peace process, if implemented, will likely depend upon further activating the capabilities and imagination of an emergent and genuine, even if yet still weak and uneven, global civil society.[15]

Such dependence is likely to diminish to the extent that the authority structures of emergent Palestinian statehood are effectively democratised, but this is not likely to be brought about by the peace process itself, but by activism within Gaza and the West Bank, reinforced by a more mobilized external public opinion. In the end, the role of international law is likely to relate to the mobilization of world public opinion in support of Palestinian nongovernmental efforts to achieve constitutional democracy, including human rights, especially the core struggle for statehood and the full exercise of self-determination. No matter how one-sided the agreed texts, Palestinian rights of self-determination are intrinsic and inalienable. Their application may be ignored, or even repudiated, for a time, but never truly lost.

The test of this process of establishing normalcy has been somewhat widened by Israeli loosening of control over a substantial portion of the West Bank. Despite Israel's retention of security rights and settlements, the Palestinian reality has been strengthened, at least temporarily, by these developments to the point where the operational situation is increasingly one of a Palestinian state, although qualified as to the exercise of sovereign rights, vulnerable to intervention, and not able yet to assert itself formally in many international arenas including the United Nations. If such arrangements turn out to be the end-point of "the peace process" it is not to be confused with the realization of Palestinian rights of self-determination. Such concerns were always contained, if concealed, in the Israeli peace offerings to the Palestinians, but now become evident under the new Israeli leadership generated by the Likud control of the negotiating process. Arguably, such a shift in Israeli leadership changes little, while exposing the pre-existing inadequacies of the Oslo/Cairo framework from the Palestinian viewpoint. As such, it may have the positive effect of clarifying the work that remains to be done if the Palestinian struggle is to be carried eventually to a successful end.

Notes

1 I would like to thank Raji Sourani and the Gaza Centre for Law and Rights for providing the occasion for the presentation of an initial version of this paper at the "International Colloquium on Human Rights: Protection Mechanisms and Political Change," 10-12 September 1994, my colleague at Princeton, John Waterbury, for perceptive comments and a close reading, and John V. Whitbeck, a specialist on Palestinian/Israeli relations, for help in overcoming inaccuracies present in an earlier draft.

2 For argument along these lines see Patrick Cockburn, "The End of a terrible, dangerous peace," *The Independent*, (19 May 1996), p. 14.

3 See Robert Fisk, "Seventeen Minutes at Qana," *The Independent*, (19 May 1996), pp. 12-14; see also "Death in Lebanon," *The Economist*, (June 13 1996), pp. 41-42.

4 For loss of U.S. credibility as intermediary see Steven Erlanger, "U.S. Mideast Policy: Losing Its Balance?" *Int'l Herald Tribune*, (May 6, 1996), pp. 1, 10.

5 Illustrative of this role for external political actors was the high-profile United States Government initiative to induce Israel and the PLO to do more on behalf of both the negotiating progress and on the implementation of what had been previously negotiated (including arrangements for elections and Israeli troop withdrawals). Steven Greenhouse, "Clinton Intervenes to Help Revive Stalled Mideast Peace Talks," *NY Times*, (Feb. 13, 1995); see also George Graham, "Clinton Pledge in Mideast," *Financial Times*, (Feb. 13, 1995).

6 Such initiatives seem peculiarly relevant at this stage with respect to human rights as neither negotiating party appears motivated to support compliance in self-rule areas. See "The Gaza Strip and Jericho: Human Rights under Palestinian Partial Self-Rule," Human Rights Watch: *Middle East*, (Feb. 1995).

7 The contention is not that there was a settler conspiracy, but that settler attitudes generate and ratify terrorist acts against Palestinians. For perspective see Edward Said, "Hebron Was Inevitable," *The Progressive*, (May 1994), pp. 25-27.

8 See Youssef M. Ibrahim, "Gulf Nations Balk at Proposal for Mideast Development Bank," *New York Times*, (Feb. 17, 1995).

9 Elaine Fletcher, "Israel's Great Wall? Critics Belittle a Barrier Against Palestinians," *Christian Science Monitor*, (Jan. 27, 1995); see also Thomas L. Friedman, "It's Time to Separate," *New York Times*, (Jan. 29, 1995).

10 Indeed, the Rabin government has been reluctant to challenge directly efforts to memorialise the memory of Baruch Goldstein at the Kiryat Arba settlement. See Barton Gellman, "Palestinian Killed in Clash on Massacre Anniversary," *Washington Post*, (February 15, 1995).

11 Article V(2) commits the parties to begin negotiations "as soon as possible ... but no later than the beginning of the third year of the interim period;" that is, after two years; [my emphasis].

12 For background see Falk and Burns H. Weston, "The Relevance of International Law to Palestinian Rights in the West Bank and Gaza: In Legal Defense of the Intifada," 32 *Harvard International Law Journal*, Vol. 129(1991); see also Michael Curtis, "International Law and the Territories," 32 *Harvard International Law Journal*, Vol. 457(1991); and Falk and Weston, "The Israeli-Occupied Territories, International Law,

and the Boundaries of Scholarly Discourse: A Reply to Michael Curtis," 33 *Harvard International Law Journal*, Vol. 191(1992).

13 In addition to the absence of deadlines (contrasting with the specified date for holding election), there is no assurance in the Arafat letter that, in fact, the PNC will accept the proposed changes, and no indication that their failure to do so is a violation of Palestinian obligations or gives Israel a legal pretext for not fulfilling its commitments.

14 See Burhan Dajani, "The September 1993 Israel-PLO Documents: A Textual Analysis," *Journal of Palestine Studies*, Vol. XXIII:5-23(1994); Raja Shehadeh, "Questions of Jurisdiction: A legal Analysis of the Gaza-Jericho Agreement," *Journal of Palestine Studies*, Vol. XXIII:18-25(1994).

15 I have elsewhere drawn a distinction between "a bargain" struck on the basis of inequality, and "a solution" that meets the reciprocal needs of both sides, and is likely to be politically viable over time; a peace treaty that embodies the results of victory and defeat is likely to be an unstable bargain if the stronger side exacts maximum advantage and the weaker side is denied basic rights. The Versailles Agreements after World War I are an exemplary instance of the vulnerability of one-sided arrangements to subsequent repudiation, as well as to links between one-sidedness and political extremism as a reaction to such perceived weakness and humiliation. See Falk, "Can U.S. Policy Toward the Middle East Change Course?" *Middle East Journal*, XLVII:11-20 (1993). For a more general advocacy of this line of thinking see Falk, *On Humane Governance: Toward a New Global Politics*, (Cambridge, UK: Polity, 1995).

Part Three:

The Global Context

7 Britain's Shadows: Post-Colonialism and Palestine

JOHN STRAWSON[1]

Britain casts a long post-colonial shadow over the Middle East and this essay will visit one cultural site of its colonial occupation, legal narratives in Palestine. The vantage point for viewing some critical moments of this legal occupation is the Palestinian-Israeli Accords, which encode much of this history. British heritage originates from the Mandate period and indicates that current political, cultural and legal discourse of the late 20th century remains entangled within the colonial experience. The inequalities brought about by European imperial powers have stamped themselves, not merely upon the map but upon the mind.

It is difficult to see Tony Blair's new Labour government as the successor to the British Mandate. Since its election in May 1997, Blair's government has in rhetoric, at least, attempted to distance itself from the imperialist past. Blair and his ministers pepper their speeches with the word "new", describe Britain as a "young country" while journalists celebrate "cool Britannia." While it is possible that Blair could be initiating a post-post-colonial phase, its policies on the Middle East are more complex. Two images appear to confront each other. In the first Foreign Secretary Robin Cooks stands on Jabel Abu Ghenien (the site of the planed Israeli settlement Har Homa) and in rain and wind pointedly shaking the hand of a member of the Palestinian Legislative Council, an event that sparks the ire of Israeli Prime Minister Binyamin Netanyahu. In the second Tony Blair visiting Israel on its fiftieth anniversary holding smiling meetings with Netanyahu and indeed Arafat believing that he can rescue the faltering peace process by inviting them to London. In the first there is an element of the beginnings of solidaristic foreign policy. In the second there is the imperial edge. Britain's enthusiastic support for the U.S. policy on Iraq and for the August 1998 raids against "terrorist" installations in Sudan and Afghanistan underlines this. None the less Robin Cook's protest at the Jerusalem settlement draws attention to the post-colonial contradictions of modern Britain. Balfour's successor stands on land stolen from the Palestinians by Israel and effectively protests the legitimacy of the British colonial law used as means of appropriating it.

Until recently law has escaped the interest of those engaged in post-colonial studies,[2] which represents the success of colonial powers in inserting law as a somehow neutral element in the construction of power. Yet it is in legal cultures that a society creates an official view of itself, as Raja Shehadeh puts it, "a legal narrative is how a people tell the story of their right to a land using the symbolic language of law."[3] The British Mandate period[4] laid the basis which deprived the Palestinians of their own legal narrative, in particular in the way in which it alienated title of their own land.[5] The Palestinian-Israeli Accords have been constructed on the dubious legitimacy of this heritage. As the Middle East prepares to enter the 21st century it is necessary to address this post-colonial presence in order to overcome it.

The Palestinian-Israeli Accords

The Palestinian-Israeli Accords comprise a series of legal texts which began with the Declaration of Principles (1993, often called the "Oslo Agreement") and encompass, the Cairo Agreement (1994), the Interim Agreement (1995, sometimes referred to as "Oslo 2"), and the Hebron Agreement 1997.[6] These documents which have been signed by the parties in a fanfare of publicity with much talk of the historic reconciliation of two peoples it should be underlined have been negotiated in the English language and the only official versions are in English. This symbolizes a level of alienation between a people and their legal narrative as the idea that a people can articulate interests to their own territory in the legal language of another (former colonial) power draws both Israelis and Palestinians on to the terrain of English legal culture. It is stunning that documents dealing with the "legitimate rights" of two peoples only appear only in the authoritative English (translations into Arabic and Hebrew are unofficial). The English is also the legal English, which attaches to the common law system and to the history of the occupation of law in Palestine.[7] The idea that English and English officials provide an impartial medium between Arabs and Jews is rooted in the colonial project, "in Palestine" writes Norman Bentwich, "on account of the tense feelings between Jews and Arabs, it is frequently necessary to place a neutral Englishman in a responsible post which is touch with the general public."[8] This is the historical perspective in which we should see English legal idioms and values enter the texts and imprint themselves upon the current peace process.

In reflecting on the character of British rule[9] in Mandatory Palestine in the 1930s, Norman Bentwich, who was the Legal Advisor to the government, explains how British power and a perceived veto by the Jewish community then in Palestine forced the British to limit legislative jurisdiction. "It was recognized by Great Britain and by the Council of the League [of Nations],"he says, that, on account of the special purpose of facilitating the establishment of the Jewish National Home, there could not at once be a democratic government, but the process must be developed in stages. The mandatory therefore directed to secure the development of self-governing institutions and to encourage local autonomy. But the Arab majority could not be allowed uncontrolled legislative power to prevent the fulfilment of the Mandate in relation to the minority Jewish population."[10]

In reading this passage the formulas of the Palestinian-Israeli Accords come to mind in the way in which they have carefully crafted stages through which the Palestinian people are able to gain self-government, in limited spheres and over small plots of land, integrated into a specified time frame. The Declaration of Principles (Oslo 1) provides for the election of the Palestinian Council and the transfer responsibilities from the Israeli Military government and Civil Administration in stages. This is given effect in the Cairo Agreement and in the interim agreement (Oslo 2), but rather like the approach of Bentwich we have notice the careful stages. The Palestinians will be able gain a measure of control over, "education and culture, health, social welfare, direct taxation and tourism.[11] These powers are extended with in the election of the Legislative Council (which took place in January 1996) as provided for in Oslo 2.[12] This incremental approach, which denies the Palestinian people even full powers within tiny geographical areas, is a striking illustration of the post-colonial character of the Accords. Through these stages of "autonomy" the Palestinian people are being treated as not yet ready to exercise their rights and these stages have been exercises, which if successfully passed through could lead to other things. The other matters of are course spelt out as subjects for discussion in the permanent status negotiations where it is stated that these will "cover the remaining issues, including: Jerusalem, refugees, settlements, security arrangements, borders relations and cooperation with other neighbors, and other issues of common interest."[13] As can be seen from the formulations these issues remain matters for negotiations indicating that many more stages may yet await. Bentwich's comments are appropriate here too:

> The Government of Palestine, as of most countries, is divided between central and local authorities. In its central aspect it is a benevolent autocracy. In its local aspect it includes representative and self-governing bodies subject to a certain control and supervision by agents of the central authority.[14]

Perhaps only the word "benevolent" now appears out of place.

Legal Occupations

The Accords are also framed in the legal methods of the English common law. This methodology is particularly flexible and is rooted in the development of principles through conflicts, rather than an attempt to use principles as a way of solving conflicts. The Israeli legal system has inherited this methodology and it is marked in the text through open-ended formulas, circular references (where phrases such as "within the terms of this agreement" are common) and general imprecision. As Shehadeh points out the Palestinian legal community had been largely educated within another European legal culture prevalent in the Middle East; that of the French influenced civil law system. This system begins rather with principles and abstract formulations, codes and the like through which issues of conflict are seen and reconstructed.[15] The interpretation of the Declaration of Principles by the Israeli Legal Advisor, Joel Singer, in which he explains how the ambiguities of the text provide the Israeli side with huge discretion, illustrates this tradition as well as giving rise to concern within Palestinian legal circles.[16] An example of the ambiguity is seen in the way in which the definite article disappears in the Declaration of Principles on the question of the jurisdiction of the Council, "Jurisdiction of the Council will cover West Bank and Gaza Strip territory" it reads indicating the indeterminate character of its jurisdictions and accurately following the English legal method. This leaves entirely open in how much territory the Council (now the Palestinian Authority and its Legislative Council) might expect to exercise over in the interim period. According to Oslo 2 the West Bank is divided into three categories of territory, "A" under the control of the Palestinian Authority, "B" under Palestinian self-government but still under Israeli overall control and "C" under exclusive Israeli control. The Agreement stipulates that six months after the elections there will be three stages of Israeli further redeployments. However, as neither Oslo 1 nor Oslo 2 stipulates any specified amount and as it can be argued that Palestinian Jurisdiction was not intended to extend to the West Bank and the Gaza Strip a great deal of discretion has been left in the hands of the Israelis. An English draftsperson would applaud the skill of this slight of grammar.[17]

The influence of English law bites deep into one of the central questions of the permanent status negotiations, that of Israeli settlements. The question of settlements remains perhaps the most important issue in the ability of the Palestinians to gain their right to self-determination. By 1998 it had become clear that the Netanyahu government had set on a course of stealing as much West Bank and East Jerusalem land as possible in order to frustrate Palestinian attempts to create a viable state.[18] British colonial conquest has, however, played an important role in elaborating the Israeli discourse on the question of Palestinian land occupied in 1967.

The conquest of territory was at the heart of colonialism. From the legal perspectives of the late 20th century such conquests we can argue are contrary to *jus cogens* in that the principle of self-determination has become a pillar of international law. In the case of Palestine the issue of identity, as linked to land and people has taken on the features of one of the most intractable problems of modern times.[19] The attachment of a people to a territory is not the same as the type of legal relations, which exist between individuals or families to plots of land, but there is a close relationship. Occupation disrupts the relations of a people and individuals to land. Land, which has been seen as "home," which signifies security and confers identity becomes contested. Possession, ownership and use of land are wrestled out of the hands of the inhabitants and turned into servants of imperial interests. The colonial officials use their "own" legal system as the medium through which this is achieved. The British Mandate authorities, replaced the occupation of the Ottomans and so British colonial gaze fell, not on Palestinian, so much as Ottoman legal culture. It is through this colonial engagement with the Ottoman Land Code 1858 and the Mejelle that land narratives take shape.

Orientalism

These arguments rely on a reading of Said's *Orientalist* methodology[20] and its elaboration in relation to legal texts in colonialism.[21] The development of legal orientalism has had a deep impact on Western legal theory although it often appears superficially to be marginal. As the mists of the Cold War clear we are confronted not by a *new* world order, so much as a *post-colonial* world order. The post-colonialism of world order takes the form not so much of power manipulation, but of continued intellectual conquest by the West. In this way the West has become the constructed norm, the reference point.[22] This post-coloniality of knowledge has the effect of undermining attempts at engagement between the two sides of the colonial divide as engagement has become victim of a predetermined Western superiority achieved in Said's words by a "strategic location". In this scheme of things the West's methodology has become the arbiter and thus the non-Western contribution in their artistic and governmental culture appears somehow incomplete, defective or backward.

Mitchell in his work[23] addresses this strategic location, which is carefully analysed as he explains the detailed processes through which colonialism conquered not merely land but also the mind. In his account of the colonization of Egypt Mitchell used the concept of an exhibitionary order in which Egyptian life becomes enframed just as artefacts stolen from Egypt become removed from their context and placed under glass in the exhibition hall. This idea of enframement has important consequences for the analysis of what happens to legal cultures during colonialism. Within this perspective legal texts assume a particular significance in that they record the manoeuvres of colonial occupation. At times the texts may constitute manoeuvres themselves. The purpose of these manoeuvres is to isolate aspects of legal culture from their current setting and to reposition them within the colonial project. In the legal exhibition hall, the occupied legal culture is classified and categorized in terms of the dominant system, and like any exhibit in a good museum there will be copious explanations and historical references as to its origins.

Legal Orientalism in Palestine

Legal orientalism constitutes an enduring element of the post-colonial. It posits a particular history of legitimisation of power from the vantage point of the occupier. "It is not necessary here," Goadby and Doukhan[24] inform us:

> ... to enquire to what extent, if at all, the Moslem conquerors permitted the survival of pre-existing Byzantine land laws and customs. Traces of Byzantine institutions may be still discoverable in the present land system, but for practical purposes we make the Arab and Ottoman law our starting point.[25]

For the lawyers of the British Mandate period in Palestine legal sources are not merely recognized but approved. This text constitutes a form of legislative narrative. This is made quite clear in the preface, where the authors explain:

> In 1927 the Palestine Government commissioned us to prepare a Statement on the Land Law then in force in Palestine for the use of Officers engaged in the work of Land Settlement. This Statement then prepared has been given wider circulation than was, perhaps, at first intended and, copies having been made for sale; it has proved useful both to practitioners and students. Circumstances appear to call for a republication of the Statement in a more convenient form and this has been made possible with the consent of the Government.[26]

This book, *The Land Law of Palestine*, possesses not merely an indicative title so much as an authoritative one. For the purposes of the British occupiers it *is* the land law of Palestine. The content becomes not merely a description of land law but a construction of it, which secretes its authority amongst both the colonizer and the colonized. Raja Shehadeh draws upon Goadby and Doukhan for some his arguments on the illegal use of land by the Israeli occupation of the West Bank for building Israeli settlements. In discussing the character of a legal narrative he says, "It is by necessity a constructed narrative. For it to stand it must have consistency and internal logic. It must relate to reference point outside of it, which others can relate to and understand. It must be communicable."[27]

Yet the legal narrative with which he engages is that which has been constructed by the British Mandate authorities and most explicitly by Goadby and Doukhan. Shehadeh argues that the Israeli authorities, after 1967, acted illegally by interpreting that portion of land designated as *miri* under the Ottoman Land Code, 1858, as state land.[28] Legal orientalism thus succeeds in drawing a contemporary legal confrontation on to its own terrain.[29]

Much of the process of colonization of occupied legal cultures took place through a series of manoeuvres conducted, not only on the grand scale of colonial edicts and acts of Governors, as through the scholarly and administrative output of judicial officials. Edicts did play their part, in the case of the Palestine Mandate; the British issued the Palestine Order-in-Council 1922, which created the framework for legal regulation. However, it is the way in which these instruments were mediated by a series of translations and expository works that the process is carried into the life of the occupied legal community. Textbooks play a particular role in the development of legal knowledge and most systems acknowledge them as serving as reference points if not actually authorities. In the common law system they posses a particular significance as their commentaries often create the only systematic form of the law and they are frequently referred to by the courts. For the occupying power the exact legal norm was secondary to the power to make the choice of norm. The exposition of the new legal order through textbooks and in introductions to translations of legal works became necessary for both the colonial administrators and for the "local" lawyers. In the case of land law one of the first publications was Tute's, *The Ottoman Land Laws*.[30]

Tute's work comprises of a translation of the Ottoman Land Code (1858) and a commentary, "this book" he says, "is intended to furnish an explanation of the Law of *Mirie* and other State lands in Palestine, for the benefit of English speaking judges and lawyers."[31] He warns his readers that, "it differs from the ordinary legal textbook in that it does not contain references to decided cases." What he means by this is that the structure of his work will be different to those used to English law, but assures that:

> ...pains have been taken to show the policy underlying matters which are likely to be unfamiliar to the English lawyer, such as the devolution of land by right of Tapou, and the manner in which the strange tenure known as Quasi Mulk came into existence.[32]

To these comments he adds the caveat that, "the author is keenly conscious of the inadequacy of the equipment of an English lawyer for the task undertaken.[33] It is strange modesty from the President the Land Court in Jerusalem.

The British decision to apply the Ottoman Land Code was part of the colonial policy of the adoption a legal regime. As has been mentioned this was contained in the Palestine Order-in-Council, 1922. This regulation which was akin to many others applied to colonial situations and was only modified by the incorporation of the terms of the Mandate drawn up under the auspices of the League of Nations. The Mandate was a thin disguise for the reassignment of a colonial power from the Ottoman to the British.[34] The British legal policy was born of experience of Empire and as a consequence, Palestine, could be based on other models. The British administration both adopted local laws and added their own discretion to modify them.

From India to Palestine

Hooper's work, *The Civil Law of Palestine and Trans-Jordan*,[35] illustrates the subtle ways in which the colonization of law takes place. His book contains a translation of the *Mejelle* (Volume I) and the expository discussion if it (volume II). In a revealing chapter entitled, "The Nature of the Civil Code", Hooper is quite explicit about the enframement of the *Mejelle*, by the British Mandate authorities. He comments, "A knowledge of the sources of the *Mejelle* is of definite practical value in deciding cases questions upon which the *Mejelle* is silent, ambiguous or leaves room for more than one opinion." The sources of the *Mejelle*, drawn from the *Hanafi*-school of jurisprudence, were well known to the British from their experiences in India. From the late 18th century the British had attempted to harness Islamic law for colonial purposes. The *Hedaya* had been translated in 1791 and a large number of expository works written by British, and later Indian, scholars and officials. Thus in discussing the resolution of conflicts of opinion within Islamic jurisprudence, Hooper can rely on nearly a century and half of British jurisprudence, and thus on contrasting the influence of Abu Hanifa, Abu Yusuf and Imam Muhammad can write:

> The relative weight of these authorities in Anglo-Muhammadan law is unsettled, except that the opinion of Muhammad will in general be outweighed by that of the other two - Abu Hanifa because he was the founder of the School, and Abu Yussef because of the very important judicial office which he held. But the scale may be turned in favour of any one of them by proof that his opinion was preferred by the compiler of some standard Digest, such as the Hedaya of the Fatawa Alamgiri, or the Court may adopt the view, which in its opinion is most in accordance with justice in the particular case before it.[36]

Hooper then explains that the court must take in account the sources of Islamic law, "(1) some text of the Koran directly on the point, or (2) some duly authenticated tradition as to what the Prophet said or did, or (3) some evidence as to the unanimous opinion of the companions of the Prophet, or (4) some inference by way of analogy or otherwise." However he continues:

> But again, these secondary sources are of less weight (for the purpose aforesaid) than the practice of the Courts of British India. In other words, a judge is not at liberty to decide a point of law according to his own

> reading of a Muhammadan treatise (The Hedaya, for instance) in opposition to a single decision of the Privy Council, or in opposition to the a series of decision of the High Court which he represents or to which he is subordinate.[37]

Thus while the niceties of Islamic law are to be referred to the real authority for interpretation has been passed into the hands of the British Courts and maintained through the application of the doctrine of binding precedent. The individual judge looks to the decision of the hierarchy of the English courts. In this way the colonial regime supervises the application of legal norms. As a consequence Islamic law is subject to a meta-jurisprudence, which is in the hands of the occupying power. Hooper in drawing attention to the lessons of British India for Palestine and Trans-Jordan demonstrates that colonial power built an international juridical cadre that was able to assimilate the lessons of more than one area of occupation. As such we can begin to see that occupied legal cultures are subordinate not to merely to a local caste of administrators, but to an international system. This colonial system becomes the basis for engagement between legal cultures and provides the narrative of this process.[38] Thus the colonization of the *Mejelle* is made easier for the occupiers because their experience in British India. Indeed a whole jurisprudence exists into which the *Mejelle* can be drawn.

Moments of Legal Occupation

The character of the survival of "Ottoman law" in Palestine and Trans-Jordan after the British Mandate in 1920 is thus not straightforward. Ottoman law becomes entangled within a new jurisprudence. Indeed Article 46 of the Palestine Order-in-Council, 1922, makes clear that its incorporation is essentially contingent on the operation of the new occupier's regime. The Article, as Hooper writes, specifies four sources of law: (1) Ottoman Law; (2) Orders-in-Council affecting Palestine and Palestine Ordinances and Regulations; (3) The substance of the common law and doctrines of equity in force in England; (4) The Powers, Procedure and Practice of the English Courts.[39] Within this cacophony of the legal, the Ottoman law is subject of modification and transformation merely through the choice of law. The terms of the Article make clear the strategic location within the new legal regime:

> The jurisdiction of the Civil Courts shall be exercised in conformity with the Ottoman Law in force in Palestine on November 1st, 1914, and such

> Ottoman Laws as have been made or declared to be in force by Public Notice, and such Orders-in-Council, Ordinances and Regulations as are in force in Palestine at the date of the commencement of this Order, or may hereafter be applied or enacted; and subject thereto and so far as the same shall not extend or apply, shall be in conformity with the substance of the common law, and doctrines of equity in force in England, and with the powers vested in and according to the procedure and practice observed by or before Courts of Justice and Justices of the Peace in England.... Provided always that the said common law and doctrines of equity shall be in force in Palestine so far only as the circumstances of Palestine and its inhabitants and the limits of His Majesty's jurisdiction permit and subject to such qualifications as local circumstances render necessary.[40]

In this instrument the contours of occupation of a legal culture emerge. The Order-in-Council hands to the British administration and its judicial arm the power to define the scope and purpose of Palestinian laws. The ambiguity of the Order should not obscure the way in which the legal authority and methodology of the occupier becomes dominant. It is the British Mandate authorities that will decide the criteria and circumstances where one legal source will be used as opposed to another.

In discussing the Palestine Order-in-Council, Hooper turns to the references to the common law and doctrines of Equity in force in England.

> It is submitted that the meaning and intention here is the introduction and incorporation into in the corpus of Ottoman law and jurisprudence, of certain portions of the Common Law and Law of Equity of England. It is a matter of local ascertainment as to what this law is....[41]

Hooper attempts to assist his reader with an explanation of the term, "the substance of the common law." He begins with the masterly understatement "the term 'common law' is an elusive expression."[42] He then somewhat daringly suggests that the common law is "based on custom and precedent, it was what the people and the Courts found to be acceptable and right."[43] This interesting democratic twist to English common law is possibly aimed at bolstering his earlier argument that:

> ... it appears to have been thought that the corpus of Ottoman Law supplemented by Palestine legislation was not enough to meet the rapidly changing conditions brought about by the institution of the new government and it was, therefore, thought desirable and convenient to place at the disposal of the Courts ready-made English law when they found Ottoman Law and Palestinian Legislation insufficient or defective.[44]

Colonial occupation thus has as one its advantages convenience, in a ready made and yet democratic legal order possessing a better range of remedies. This ready-made law is however, elusive and defies the attempt of a straightforward explanation of what it is and indeed where it can be seen as a corpus.

When Hooper approaches a definition of Equity, the situation becomes even more confusing, as he says; "equity in its ordinary sense means nothing more than that which is proper and just. But it acquired a special legal sense when invoked to temper the vigour of the rules of the common law which had become fixed and inflexible.[45] In explaining its origins in English legal history, Hooper tells us that it was introduced to restrain the "harsh rules and doctrines of the common law."[46] Thus on the one hand the common law is supposed to be based on what was thought to be "acceptable and just" for both the people and courts and yet on the other as "rigid" and possibly "harsh". The vagueness of the concept of common law and equity is nothing new to the English lawyer, but for the Palestinian seeking redress in the courts open many questions as to the exact sources of law. In particular the new methodology, common law has been incorporated into the Ottoman law (both the Land Code and the *Mejelle*) conceived under the influence of the French civil law system. The entry of the common law into the Palestinian legal system brings not only a new approach, but as Hooper has explained, legal norms developed over the course of English history. Without wishing to give credit to his democratic account of the development of the common law, it is certainly true that the principles have been seen by English Courts to be "acceptable and right". This formula is quite close to the answer, which a subsequent Master of the Rolls gave in answer to the question "What is the law?" He said, "the law was that which beats in the heart of the judge."[47] It is this apparent discretionary system which the British introduced with the Palestine Order-in-Council.

Colonial Rule and the Law of the Ruled

The common law system is evidence of the impossibility of law in the sense that the European enlightenment spoke of the rule of law. Its particular features hand to the judiciary a series of constructionary and deconstructionary methods that invite endless arguments over the interpretation of common law (reported) principles, doctrines and Statutes. This system has many advantages for the colonial occupier, who can at once be seen to be administering the law of the occupied population, whilst subtly changing it "as conditions demand." The pedigree of this approach is deep within legal orientalizm and eloquently advanced by Hamilton:

> The permanency of any foreign dominion (and indeed, the justification of holding such a dominion) requires that a strict attention be paid to the ease and advantages, not only of the governors, but of the governed; and to this great end nothing can so effectively contribute as preserving to the latter their established practices, civil and religious, and protecting them in the exercise of their own institutes; for however defective and absurd these may appear, still they must be infinitely more acceptable than any we could offer; since they supported by the accumulated prejudice of ages, and in the opinion of their followers, derive their origin from the Divinity himself.[48]

In the division of legal orders into that of the governors and that of the governed we see the concept of "local" or "indigenous" law take shape. The latter's underdeveloped features are to be distinguished from the formers complete and superior legal system. In the case of land law in Palestine there is rapid development contained in the Palestine Order-in-Council (article 2) which creates the new category of Public lands: Government of Palestine by virtues of Treaty, conventions, agreement "All Lands in Palestine which are subject to the control of the or succession, and all lands which are or shall be acquired for the public service."[49]

According to Tute article 12 vests this land and their accompanying rights in the High Commission. As he comments, "it is difficult to assign the limits to the application of the very wide terms of the definition of public lands."[50] Tute suggests that *mahlul* lands that were left vacant by heirs or by failure of cultivation would become Public lands.[51]

The provisions of the Ottoman Land Code and those relevant sections of the *Mejelle*, which apply to land, are thus at once put to work for the colonial power but on a new basis and within a new framework. The development of a class of public land modifies the principles of land holding and by placing them at the discretion of the High Commissioner extends his powers. This is particularly the case due to the fact that he would have to exercise them under the framework of the Palestine Order-in-Council and in accordance with English common law and equity, which have been a notoriously weak restraint on power of British governments themselves.

In commenting on these provisions, Goadby and Doukhan say; “A used in the Order-in-Council the term public land appears therefore, t include only such and as the State exploits or is free to exploit in any wa it pleases, uncontrolled by any law or custom determining the method o exploitation.”[52] This gloss is indicative of the care with which they develo the narrative carefully weaving wide discretionary powers into th substance of their view of the Ottoman law. Significantly they seem to tak a more limited view of the effect of the creation of public land than Tute This could lead the reader to conclude that which appears potentiall draconian, could in fact been subject to reasoned legal limitations. Indee that is precisely their case, as they develop their argument by explainin that the Palestine provisions of the British are less extensive than the Frenc Mandatory in Syria.

Goadby and Doukhan then turn to detailed considerations of th effects of this Article in relation to the land code. A discussion ensues o whether or not *miri* is *per se* state or public land. Their case is that onl when *miri* land becomes vacant, that is *mahlul*, will it become public lanc Their next target is *jiftlik* (or *mudawara*) land which of the most pa comprises of land, which although in origin private, became part of th State domain under the Ottoman Empire. In Palestine they argue this wa sometime in order to protect the status of the land from the encroachmen of Bedouins. “This was thought” they write, “would make them mor secure as the Bedouins would refrain from interfering with the Sultan’s ow property, and the event proved this surmise correct.”[53] As a consequence o this added protection the tenants were forced to pay double the tithe a fift as opposed to a tenth. This fascinating piece of Ottoman legal history serve the British well as having become within the State domain; this class of lan becomes public land.

Mines and minerals are the next class that they address, althoug as they comment, “Mines and Minerals” are distinguished from “Publi Land” in Articles twelve and thirteen of the Order-in-Council, but this i merely for the convenience of phraseology.[54] They continue this enigmati line by saying, “strictly speaking minerals in land are part of the land an minerals under Public lands became vested in the High Commission in trus by effect of Art. 12.”[55] A footnote to this records that, “a mine is by Moslen law regarded as a constituent part of the land in which it lies. This i *Hanafite* doctrine. *Hedaya*, at p. 15 (Hamilton’s Translation).”[56] However “the terms of art. 12 (1) appear wide enough to vest in the Higl Commissioner in trust all State rights to minerals under *Mewat*, *Metruki* *Miri* and State domain proper.[57] The authors do not accept that th consequence of this article is to place all minerals, even those under the *mulk* class of land, in the hands of the High Commissioner. They do record that some interpretations take the alternative view.

In dealing with forestland, Goadby and Doukhan explain that these can become public lands in two ways, either by proclamation of the High Commissioner in the case land not being private or if they are private they can be deemed to be forest reserves. In explaining these positions they cite the Forests Ordinance, 1926, sections 3 and 20. Thus the passing of forests into public land, it seems, is presented an issue of public policy. It has to be said that this phrase is, however, never used.

Goadby and Doukhan conclude their arguments about public land by turning to three more issues, land and buildings the property of the state by purchase, *mewat* land and land and water of the *metruki* class. In the first case they introduce the concept of expropriation as being a legitimate way of acquiring land by the State. This policy is surrounded by many caveats so it appears perhaps exceptional, but never the less they do says that this includes, "any land which *mulk* in the hands of the state by purchase, escheat or other form of appropriation."[58] As far as *mewat* land is concerned, our authors allow for this falling into public land by virtue of the Treaty of Lasuanne. They comment: "a very large part of the area of Palestine is *mewat*.[59] In the last instance they are clear that land and water in the *metruki* class are also public land:

> It is, however, better to place these in a class apart since they are "public" in the sense of being open to common use, and the ownership of them must (semble) be regarded as vested in the State. But Public Domain proper is not by law open to common use, but possessed and controlled by the State and representing the community.[60]

Making Authenticity

These "nice" legal arguments are indicative of the way in which the legal norms and methodology of the occupied legal culture are subject to a radical transformation as they are subject to colonial judgment. In these legal arguments we are witness to the construction of a colonial discourse, legal orientalism. The discourse it should be noted is not a crude frontal assault on the pre-occupation Palestine law. Instead at the centre of the discussion are nuanced analysis of the Ottoman Land Code and the relevant sections of the *Mejelle*. The narrative gently draws the concepts of Ottoman law within the discourse of English law. These are referenced throughout; indeed the five classes of land are extensively investigated and indeed explained. In many places the historical context is outlined so that the reader can better understand the point that is being made.

Frederic Goadby had a good grasp of the historical experience of Empire in dealing with law. He reflected on these issues in an earlier work in a text prepared for law students in Egypt. In turning to lessons of training a judiciary British India with a view to Islamic law, he explained:

> Steps were taken to enable the British judges to form their own opinions upon points of Mohammaden law. The *Hedaya* and other Arabic treatise were translated into English, and many Englishmen became accomplished students of the original Arabic authorities and published works in English upon the law. Moreover, collections of decisions given by the judges in accordance with the "*fetwas*" of the muftis were made. As time went on a trained and mature Bar came into existence, and many members were appointed to the Bench and have reached the highest offices. Consequently, by 1864, the Government abandoned the rule requiring the judges to consult the mufties, and since that time the Mohammadan law applied in British India has been administered entirely by the State Courts, the judges of which inform themselves of the provisions of the law with the assistance of the arguments of counsel.[61]

In this passage he is outlining the culmination of a process that had begun in the 18th century and was carefully approached at the outset by Sir William Jones and Charles Hamilton. As a result of their sensibilities to the conquered peoples they were able to found a genre of legal writings, which was able to form the basis for the creation of a "mature Bar".[62] Beginning in the 18th century the British were careful to craft a history of pre-British India with all its attendant implications for legal cultures.[63] Goadby is well placed to turn his attention to Palestine.

The historical account and the sensitivity to the pre-occupation legal sources are, it should be stressed, moments in the occupation of a legal culture. They take command of the narrative and enframe it within the dominant colonial perception. For example, as we have seen through a careful manoeuvre the class of public land arises engages with the pre-occupation categories and establishes its legitimacy.

In Hooper we see there is the grand historical perspective as he charts the development of the Ottoman legal system from its Turkish origins in central Asia. This historical narrative transmits an authenticity about contemporary developments to the reader. There is something significant about rooting the present in a secure past. In a few paragraphs[64] Hooper takes us from the "a system of law ... a purely Turkish designation; that of *yarghouji*."[65] through the adoption of Islam and thus of *shari'a* to the adoption of the *Mejelle* and the French legal influence. Added authenticity is gained by reference to Ibn Batuta's 15th century observations of Anatolia. In this way Hooper "centres" his reader as we are led into the history of the Ottomans. These passages can be compared to Hamilton's account of the origin and early development of Islam in his preliminary discourse to his translation of the *Hedaya*.[66] The reader is thus manoeuvred into a particular appreciation of history which must necessarily be a result of fact selection and analysis of the writer. In Goadby and Doukhan the historical context is also a strong element of their narrative. The English administrator or judicial official is in this way supplied with the historical context for the work. Despite a distance of nearly one and half centuries, that separates Hamilton from Hooper, Goadby and Doukhan all possess that special skill of the translator, as penetrates to the heart of the conquered culture, its language. All therefore are able to provide confident history for those who rely upon their translations.

The discourse of legal orientalizm subjects the non-Western legal system to its judgement and can become legislative. The studied ambiguities of the English common law and equity lend themselves particularly well to this process. They secrete themselves into the pores of the new legal order and so establish the power of the British authorities through a deftness that can attract a generation of Palestinian lawyers to it. The Jerusalem Law Classes and training at the Council of Legal Education at the Bar in England will further draw Palestinians into the discourse.[67] In such a manner the Ottoman Land Code, amongst others is thus turned into local law.

Conclusions

This visit to a site of colonial occupation has highlighted the depth of English penetration into the legal culture of Palestine. It demonstrates that it is not only land but they way in which title to land is conceived is brought within the perspectives of colonial power. The Israeli occupation since 1967 has exposed the post-colonial character of the land law narratives through the appropriation of land for settlements. Much of the legal argumentation advanced to justify these appropriations is drawn from the British Mandate attitude to public land and to *miri* land as discussed above. This British period of rule provided a pivotal moment for the construction of this legal narrative. One, which provided for the advantage the occupier, at the expense of the population in elegant and academic tones. In this way individual rights to land holding give way to a claimed public right which is inevitably determined by the occupying power.

Raja Shehadeh explains the layering of this process; "Some of this legislation that was in force when the Israeli occupation began, had its origin in Ottoman or British Mandate times. Every legislative period is built on the period preceding it.[68] In turning to the way in which the Israeli authorities have utilized Military Orders to interpret these sources so as to implement their projects, he continues:

> Examples of this are the interpretations of certain sections of the Ottoman Land Code. The Israeli authorities have claimed that when the Palestinian claimant is unable to establish continuous use of his land for ten consecutive years, then according to the Ottoman Land Code, which remains in force, his land is deemed to have become public land. Military Order 59 enables the Custodian of Public Land to take control of this land which is then, in the majority of the cases, handed over for the exclusive use of the settlers.[69]

British Influence in Palestine thus sustains itself long after Britain's exit from the territory. The flexibility of the English law continues to provide a neat way of depriving the Palestinians of their right to self-determination. It forces all in Palestinian society, in particular researches, policy makes and legislators to deal with a legal discourse foisted on Palestine some seventy years ago in the age of the Great Powers. British influence in Palestine and the rest of the Middle East is not only reliant of current economic relations, but is carefully reinforced through the promotion of British cultural values through its diplomatic representatives, the British Council and British universities. This is the nurturing of the British elements left within the region.

New Labour may be at odds with this colonial and post-colonial legacy. Whereas the Conservative Thatcher-Major years consciously integrated the images of claimed tradition and nostalgia for Empire, the Blair administration may offer a new course. The Foreign Office's ethical foreign policy that places respect for human rights at the centre of Britain's international relations and some actions like the banning of land mines sales appear to support this. The mission statement has a glitzy video, which represents Britain as a progressive multi-cultural player in the world. Gone is the desire for gunboats and naked power and in its place a view of an international democratic world order. As far as Palestine is concerned, Prime Minister Blair met President Arafat within two months of taking office and the International Development Secretary, Claire Short, made such a solidaristic speech to the charity, Medical Aid for Palestine, as to solicit a rebuke from the Israeli Embassy. These may be just surface impressions, but a government that is strangely new has produced them.

Blair appears to have grasped that the time has come to reinvent Britain and in the process to discard the imperial past. His administration has dealt with aspects of the post-colonial within Britain. The government is inclusive, women who in significant numbers have been shifted to the centre of power, immigration and asylum laws have been liberalized and devolution has been granted to the peoples of Scotland and Wales. This post-post-coloniality at home may bode well for international policy. Overcoming the past will mean a systematic challenge to the attitudes that permeate the entire British establishment. The British government of the Mandate period vetoed democracy in Palestine, the challenge will be see if the Blair government can banish British shadows over Palestine through an active intervention on the side of Palestinian rights. Britain's legal system has, however, surprised itself in allowing legal proceedings to go ahead against the former Chilean dictator Augusto Pinochet for major human rights abuses. Perhaps the Israeli foreign minister Ariel Sharon, who advised Israelis to "grab as many hills as possible" in the Palestinian West Bank in the Fall of 1998 should think carefully about future visits to Britain. The new Labour government could be the instrument to rupture Britain's post-colonial romance, but the Palestinians should not rely on it.

Notes

1. Much of this essay is based on a paper presented to the International Association of Middle Eastern Studies, Sixth Congress, at Al al-Bayt University, Jordan, April 10-14, 1996. I would also like to thank the students on the Masters in Law program of the Birzeit University Institute of Law for their challenging engagement with it while teaching there in the Falls of 1996, 1997 and 1998.
2. The growing literature on post-colonial discourse is instructive in general see: Nicholas B. Dirks (ed.), *Colonialism and Culture* (Ann Arbor: University of Michigan Press, 1992), on England see: Bill Schwarz (ed.), *The Expansion of England* (London: Routledge, 1996). There is growing number of scholarly journals concerned with the area, the latest of which is *Interventions - International Journal of Post-colonial Studies*, see Volume 1, No 1 (1998-9).
3. Raja Shehadeh, "The Weight of Legal History: Constraints and Hopes in the Search for a Sovereign Legal Language," in Eugene Cotran and Chibli Mallat (eds.) *The Arab-Israeli Accords: Legal Perspectives*, (London, The Hague, Boston: Kluwer International Law, 1996) 3-20, at 18.
4. The British occupied Palestine in 1917 and the Mandate ran from 1922 to 1948. For a critical account of British colonialism in the region from the beginning of this period see: David Fromkin, *A Peace to End all Peace: Creating the Modern Middle East 1914-1922*, (London: Andre Deutsch, 1989).
5. For an analysis of British policy see: Kenneth W. Stein, *The Land Question in Palestine 1917-1939*, (Chapel Hill and London: The University of North Carolina Press, 1984).
6. The formal names of these texts are: Israel-Palestine Liberation Organization: Declaration of Principles on Interim Self-Government Arrangements, September 13, 1993; Agreement on The Gaza Strip and the Jericho Area, May 4, 1994 [and signed in Cairo, thus its name]; Israeli-Palestinian Interim Agreement on the West Bank and the Gaza Strip, September 28, 1995; the Agreement on Hebron and the accompanying Note for the Record, January 1997. The Wye River Agreement of October 1998 implemented further redeployments provided for in the Interim Agreement. For an early Palestinian commentary on the first Accord see: Ibrahim Abu-Lughod, Ziad Abu-Amr & Roger Heacock (eds.), *The Palestinian-Israeli Declaration of Principles*, (Birzeit: Birzeit University Publications, 1995). See also: Edward W. Said, *Peace and its Discontents* (London: Vintage, 1995).
7. For an account of this process see: Assaf Likhovski, "In Our Image: Colonial Discourse and the Anglicization of the Law in Mandatory Palestine," *Israel Law Review*, Vol. 29 No. 3 (1995), pp. 292 - 359.
8. Norman Bentwich, *England in Palestine*, (London: Kegan Paul, Trench, Tubner, 1932), p. 267.
9. It should be stressed that British rule meant the application of English law. The idea of 'British law' does not exist within Britain, which has three legal systems: in England and Wales, Scotland and Northern Ireland.
10. Norman Bentwich, *England in Palestine*, 88. This book is consciously evocative of Milliner's book on Egypt [see: Alfred Milner, *England in Egypt* (London: Edward Arnold, 1892)]and indicates Bentwich s approach.
11. Article VI (2) of the Declaration of Principles, 1993.
12. See: Articles IX and XVIII of the Interim Agreement ,1995.
13. See: Article V (3) of the Declaration of Principles, 1993.
14. Bentwich, *England in Palestine*, 239.

15 Raja Shehadeh, The Weight of Legal History, 17. It is interesting that Shehadeh does not elaborate the character of the choice that is presented to Palestinians between the legal systems of one imperial power over another. This is a matter of some importance in discussing the nature of legal narratives in the way that he does.

16 Joel Singer, "The Declaration of Principles on Interim Self-Government Arrangements: Some Legal Aspects," *Justice* No. 1 (1994), pp. 4 - 13. For a Palestinian legal commentary see Eugene Cotran, "Some Legal Aspects of the Declaration of Principles: A Palestinian View," in Eugene Cotran and Chibli Mallat (eds.) *The Arab-Israeli Accords 67-77.*

17 It was of course another English draftsperson Lord Caradon whose omission of the definite article before the word territories in Security Council Resolution 242 (1967) has always left ambiguous the extent of withdrawal by Israel the international community demanded after the 1967 War. The relevant section of the resolution talks about "withdrawal of Israeli armed forces from territories occupied in the recent conflict." This is relevant to the current discussion as we are told that the purpose of the Accords is the implementation of Resolution 242, thus meaning that by the time of the end of the interim period, the Palestinian Authority will have jurisdiction over some territory and that the Israelis have to withdraw from some territory. It is already clear that the Israelis will argue that they will have fulfilled their obligations under both the Declaration of Principles and resolution 242, all because of the omission of the definite article.

18 See John Strawson, "Netanyahu's Oslo: Peace in the Slow Lane," *Soundings*, Issue 8 (1998), pp. 40-60.

19 See Glenn Bowman, "A Country of Words: Conceiving the Palestine Nation from a position of exile," in Ernesto Laclau (ed.), *The Making of Political Identities*, (London and New York: Verso, 1994), pp. 138-170.

20 Edward Said, *Orientalism*, (Harmmodsworth: Penguin Books, 1978).

21 I am well aware that some jurists with interests in Islam and the Middle East have argued either that Said's methodology is not applicable to law or that it is not always applicable. An example of arguing both positions is Anne Elizabeth Mayer, *Islam and Human Rights*, (Boulder Co., Westview Press, 1991), where she argues that Said is irrelevant to law and the second edition: Anne Elizabeth Mayer, *Islam and Human Rights*, (Boulder and San Francisco: Westview Press, 1995), where she argues the latter opinion. However, these arguments are based on positivist methodology which finds its answer in the work of critical legal school, see for example: Costas Douzinas and Ronnie Warrington with Shaun McViegh, *PostModern Jurisprudence: The Law of the Text in the Texts of the Law*, (London: Routledge, 1991) and Peter Fitzpartrick, *The Mythology of Modern Law*, (London: Routledge 1992). For the elaboration of some these positions in the colonial/post-colonial context see Eve Darian-Smith and Peter Fitzpatrick (ed.) *Law and Critique* Vol. VI. No 1 (1995), Law and Colonialism special issue.

22 For a stimulating review of the debates on this issue see: Bill Schwarz, "Conquerors of Truth: Reflections on Post-colonial Theory," in Bill Schwarz (ed.), *The Expansion of England*, (London: Routledge, 1996), pp. 9-31.

23 Timothy Mitchell, *Colonising Egypt*, (Cairo: American University in Cairo Press, 1989).

24 Frederic M. Goadby and Moses J. Doukhan, *The Land Law of Palestine*, (Tel Aviv: Shoshany's Printing Co., 1935).

25 Goadby and Doukhan, 2.

26 Goadby and Doukhan, iii..

27 Raja Shehadeh, *The Weight of Legal History*, 18.

28 Raja Shehadeh, *The Law of the Land*, (Jerusalem: Palestinian Academic Society for the Study of International Affairs, 1993) 11 - 30. *Miri* is one of five categories of land holding referred to in the Code. The other four are *mulk* (full-ownership), *mewat* (dead land) *metrouki* (land left over) and *waqf* (land held under a religious endowment). The *miri* class was land originally held by the Emir, but had passed into a form of state land.

29 Shehadeh attempts to work within this framework as a tactic to defend the rights of Palestinians, see Raja Shehadeh, *The Third Way: A Journal of Life in the West Bank* (London, Melbourne, New York: Quartet Books, 1982).

30 R.C. Tute, *The Ottoman Land Laws*, (Jerusalem: Greek Orthodox Press, 1927).

31 *Ibid.*, p. 13.

32 *Ibid.*

33 *Ibid*, p. 14.

34 Some jurists have of course argued otherwise, arguing that the Mandate system created international obligations of a different type, for a recent example see: Pail J.I. M. de Waart. *The Dynamics of Self-Determination in Palestine*, (Leiden, New York and Koln: E.J. Brill, 1994), pp. 98--114.

35 C.A. Hooper, *The Civil Law of Palestine and Trans-Jordan* (Jerusalem: Azriel Printing Works, 1933) Volume I and Volume II (1936).

36 Hooper, Volume II, 22. The British used the terms Mohammedan Law and Anglo-Mohammedan law to refer to Islamic law. Fyzee, referring to India, comments that this is an "ugly term," but it has meaning in that, "not the whole of the *Fiqh*, but only a certain part is applied to Muslims." Asaf A. A. Fyzee, *An Introduction to the Study of Mohamedan Law* (Calcutta: Oxford University Press, 1931), p. 8.

37 *Ibid.*

38 The speed within which this international system acts can be seen in Goadby's works. The third edition of his introductory study to law, written originally for Egyptians is adapted to include Palestine even before the enactment of the Palestine Order in Council, 1922. In his preface Goadby comments, "Lack of time has prevented me doing much to adapt the text to the special needs of the new class of students now coming into existence through the establishment of law classes at Jerusalem under British auspices. The law of Palestine is not by any means so dominantly French in character as that of Egypt. The *Mejelle* is still applied, and new legislation follows English or Indian models. Thus, the Palestinian student will value less my numerous references to French and Egyptian cases and codes. In deference to his requirements I have introduced some references to and remarks upon Palestinian law. But in spite of its Egyptian character, I believe that this book is likely to prove more comprehensible to the English-speaking Palestinian than the standard English text book written for students whose earlier course of studies has been so widely different." See: Frederic M. Goadby, *Introduction to the Study of Law - A Handbook for Use of Law Students in Egypt and Palestine*, (London: Butterworth & Co., 1921), v-vi.

39 See: Hooper, Volume II, 28-29.

40 *Ibid.*

41 Hooper, Volume II, 64.

42 Hooper, Vol. II, 65.

43 *Ibid.*

44 Hooper, Volume II, 64.
45 Hooper, Volume II, 67.
46 *Ibid.*
47 Lord Denning, "The Dimbleby Lecture," (London: BBC, 1976). The Master of the Rolls is the President of the Court of Appeal in England, this is the second most important Court in the internal legal hierarchy: the first is the House of Lords.
48 Charles Hamilton, *The Hedaya*, (London: T. Bensley, 1791), iv.
49 Tute, 17.
50 *Ibid.*
51 *Ibid.*
52 Goadby and Doukhan, 61.
53 Goadby and Doukhan, 62.
54 Goadby and Doukhan, 64.
55 Goadby and Doukhan, 65.
56 *Ibid.* In fact Hamilton's *Hedaya*, records that Goadby and Doukhan are correct if the mine is within a house, but that if it is on the land outside the house, there is a dispute as to whether it is free of *zakat* or whether a fifth is due. (Charles Hamilton, *The Hedaya, A Commentary on the Mussulman Law,* with a preface and Index by Standish Grove Grady, (London: Wm. H. Allen, 1870). From the page references it is clear that this is the edition referred to.
57 *Ibid.*
58 Goadby and Doukhan, 67.
59 *Ibid.*
60 *Ibid.*
61 Frederic M. Goadby, *Introduction to the Study of the Law: A Handbook for the Use of Egyptian Students*, (London: Butterworth, 1910), p. 192.
62 The Council of Legal Education which is the body responsible for the education and training of the English Bar, established classes in "Mahommedan Law", leading to an examination in 1869. The classes stopped in 1874, but were resumed in 1907 and continued until 1977.
63 See for example: Alexander Dow, *The History of Hindustan*, (London: T. Becket and P.A. De Hondt, 1772), 3 Volumes.
64 Hooper, Vol. II, 29-34.
65 *Ibid*, p.30.
66 Charles Hamilton, *The Hedaya* , iii-lxii.
67 In drafting the Basic Law, Palestinian lawmakers have begun to reverse this process, see: John Strawson, "Palestine's Basic Law: Constituting New Identities Through Liberating Legal Culture," *Loyola of Los Angeles International and Comparative Law Journal*, Vol. 20, No. 3 (1998), pp. 411-432.
68 Raja Shehadeh, *The Declaration of Principles and The Legal System in the West Bank*, (Jerusalem: Palestinian Academic Society for the Study of International Affairs: 1994), p. 25.
69 *Ibid*, p. 27.

8 Post-Communist Eastern Europe and the Middle East: The Burden of History and New Political Realities

ANDREJ KREUTZ

The collapse of the Communist system in Eastern Europe and the emergence of a completely new geopolitical and social reality that is strikingly different from its forerunner, probably represented the most important breakthrough in modern world history, by far exceeding the limitations of their regional boundaries and the relatively brief period of time. However, the results for almost all Third World nations were unfortunately, predominantly negative.[1] Even though they're direct impact on and the importance for those nations varied greatly, depending on the strength and character of their links with the post-Communist region and the available option(s) of other alliances and directions of development. For a number of reasons to be discussed later, the impact of the historic events in Eastern Europe on the situation in the Middle East – particularly in the Arab World and Israel – has been especially dramatic and important, and some of the future consequences are still difficult to predict. In discussing the relations of post-Communist Eastern Europe with the Middle East, I would like to focus on three different and yet strictly interwoven issues:

I. The role of the Soviet bloc countries in the Middle East and the importance of its collapse for the region.

II. Russia and its former Eastern European allies, and the Middle East – the burden of the past and the search for new prospects in the region.

III. The present Russian Middle Eastern Policy: Its basic features and directions

At the very end of my chapter I would like to take a look at Eastern European-Middle Eastern relations from the general historical and geopolitical points of view and to indicate some repeated patterns of the mutual relations between various parts of both regions which, despite all their great differences and frequent mutual hostilities, also seem to have quite a few similarities in their cultures and political history.

The Role of the Soviet Bloc Countries in the Middle East and the Importance of its Collapse for the Region

The collapse of the Soviet bloc might be seen as one of the greatest blows to the interests and aspirations of all Third World countries. The collapse first of all caused the disappearance of the bipolar international structures which, in spite of all their inherent risks and inadequacies, nevertheless secured a global balance of power and provided smaller and/or weaker states with a freedom to manoeuvre and the opportunity to defend their own interests. The more radical regimes in the developing countries have now lost their mighty protector and source of military and economic aid and assistance. In the new situation nothing now seems to be able to restrain the power of the only remaining superpower, the U.S.A. and the economic forces of the global market and the international financial institutions that are supported by it.

Because of the special geographical proximities and well-established historical links between Eastern Europe and the Middle East, the impact of the changes was particularly important and noticeable in the Middle Eastern region at large from North Africa to the Transcaucasus and Central Asia. It is useful to be reminded here that the southern tier of the former Soviet bloc countries such as Bulgaria, Romania, Moldavia and even parts of Hungary and Ukraine had for centuries been part of the Ottoman Empire, just as the Arab World had been. The historical Ottoman, and at least the partly Muslim background of countries such as Yugoslavia and Albania which were not Soviet allies but still socialist and anti-Western, was even stronger. The northern tier of the former Soviet bloc countries such as Poland, Hungary, Czechoslovakia and the G.D.R. had far fewer historical connections with the Middle East, but as a part of the socialist camp did not deviate greatly in their policies from those of the other members and basically followed the Soviet leadership without any challenge. Russian links with the Middle East and the Islamic World at large have been unusually deep-rooted and long lasting. Located on the Eurasian lowland, Russia has always been a territory having a “natural coexistence, mutual influence and interaction between the Eastern Slavic and Turkish, Caucasian and Persian peoples" which, as many Russian scholars argue, "created the foundation for a positive relationship between Russians and Muslims."[2]

Russia's relations with the Arab World have always been particularly friendly. The origins of the Russian diplomatic, religious and commercial presence can be traced back as far as the early medieval period of Kiev Rus when numerous Russian pilgrims, merchants and soldiers had already found their way into the region. One of them, Father Superior Daniel, made a pilgrimage to the Holy Land in 1104-1107 and wrote an original and very interesting account of it.[3] Also, in the 19th century and at the beginning of the 20th, the Russian Empire was not involved in the colonial carve-up of the area and its "moral credentials among the Arabs, both on the official and popular level were considerably higher than the West's."[4] As early as 1901, the Emir of Kuwait applied for Moscow's protection, and some other Arab rulers also looked for communication, trade and cultural links with the Russian Empire.[5] Tsarist Russia had generally supported the renaissance of the local Christian Orthodox communities, always siding with the indigenous Arab elements against both the Turkish authorities and the high clergy, who were often of Greek origin and inclined to disregard the vital interests of their faithful.[6]

The Imperial Orthodox Palestinian Society established in the second part of the 19th century founded schools, hospitals and hostels there and provided substantial material aid to the indigenous population, thus earning their gratitude and general sympathy.[7] After the October 1917 Revolution, the victorious Bolsheviks inherited a strong base to build on and were able to add a new ideological dimension to it. The Communist revolutionary appeal was at that time enthusiastically greeted by many Muslim and non-Muslim peoples of the Middle East and Asia who saw in it a historic chance for the fulfilment of their social and national aspirations which had long been suppressed by the Western Powers' domination. The Bolsheviks condemned their underhand diplomacy toward the Muslim countries and published a number of secret agreements from the archives of Imperial Russia's Foreign Ministry, including the famous Sykes-Picot Agreement, which particularly compromised France and Britain among the Arab population of the Middle East. Going even further, the Soviet government's appeal of December 20, 1917 to "All the Working Muslims of Russia and the East", which was signed by Lenin himself, officially declared that "the Arabs as well as all Muslims had the right to be masters of their countries and to decide their own destinies as they wished."[8] In

1920 the Bolshevik government consequently refused to acknowledge the legitimacy of the British-mandated rule in Iraq, Palestine and Transjordan, and of France in Syria and Lebanon. The very concept of the mandate system was also repudiated by the egalitarian Treaties of Friendship and Brotherhood concluded in 1921 by Soviet Russia and the Muslim countries of Turkey, Afghanistan and Iran. The USSR was the first country to establish full diplomatic relations with Hejaz (after 1932 the name was changed to Saudi Arabia) and in 1926 recognized an independent Yemen.[9] Although during the Stalinist period, political problems and wars in Europe and the Far East, and Stalin's own denial of the progressive values of the national liberation movements had put a long freeze on further Soviet Middle Eastern involvement, by the mid 1950s, Khrushchev's rise to power and the Egyptian President, Gamel Abdul Nasser's political turnabout opened a new period of the USSR's political and military presence in the region.[10]

During the following decades up to the second half of the 1980s, the USSR and her Eastern European allies supported the Arab people's cause, and in practice, all fronts of their national liberation struggle towards economic and social development. Algeria, Iraq, Syria, Libya, South Yemen and, last but not least, the most difficult clients to protect – the Palestinians – had all in their own time received generous diplomatic, economic and even military help from the Soviet bloc countries which, in addition, often protected them in the international arena against threats of direct Western intervention and annihilation. The relations between the Soviet-led Eastern European counties and the Arabs consequently had multifaceted political, military, economic and cultural dimensions and the Soviet leaders did not have economic benefits in mind, but rather the goal of winning Arab support for their regional and global policy.

In the period 1955-1973 only, the USSR provided Egypt with military aid, to the tune of over three billion dollars,[11] and the volume of its trade with the Arab World rose from $50 million in 1956 to 4.48 billion in 1981.[12] Soviet specialists built the Aswan Dam in Egypt and the Eufrat Dam in Syria, and helped in the construction of numerous other projects at a time when many thousands of Arab students completed their cost-free university education in Eastern Europe.[13] However, even at the peak of Soviet Middle Eastern involvement and that of their allies, there were some serious limitations to the scale of their engagement and the effectiveness of their influence. Despite its apparent increase, the economic exchange of the

Soviet bloc countries with the Arab world was still, in global terms, relatively negligible and much less attractive to the mainly Western-oriented Arab elites. In 1973 at the height of their influence the USSR and its Eastern European allies accounted for only 3.7% of the Arab countries' exports, compared with 47.9% for the European Union, 12% for Japan, and 5.2% for the United States, and only 7.7% of Arab imports compared with 42.3% in the case of the European Union, 10.4% for the U.S. and 7.3% for Japan.[14]

The class structure of Arab societies and the Western cultural influences which were still predominant among their elites, prevented the Soviets from getting a firm foothold there and, as the history of Egyptian-Soviet relations under Sadat would abundantly prove, made them susceptible to the vagaries of local Arab politics. However, the most important limitation was probably the fact that the Soviet's Middle Eastern policy had always been subordinated to their global outlook and requirements. The USSR had never withdrawn its recognition of Israel and had never provided its Arab protégées with its most sophisticated weapons, which they had desired.[15] The perestroika period, which started after Gorbachev's rise to power in 1985, brought to Soviet politics a completely new outlook and new directions. Following the so-called "new political thinking", and trying both to bring to an end the Cold War with the American superpower and alleviate Soviet economic problems, Gorbachev and his advisors looked for better Soviet-Israeli relations and limited the previous Soviet support for the more radical Arab regimes – especially Syria, Iraq and Libya. In 1990 they also accepted the final end of the Marxist Revolutionary Regime in South Yemen and its merger with the non-socialist North Yemen. Further victims of the new political line were the Palestinians, even though Soviet relations with the P.L.O. who represented the Palestinians, had in the past always been complex and not free from a certain noticeable ambiguity. During the Iraqi-Kuwaiti crisis in 1990-91 and the Second War in the Persian Gulf, the Soviet Union basically supported the U.S., even though at a later stage of the drama, Gorbachev's envoy, Y. Primakov, tried to conclude some form of agreement between the Iraqi government and the U.S.-sponsored coalition, and to prevent its ground military attack. However, his efforts were apparently spurned by the Americans and the collapsing Soviet Union was in fact both too weak and too internally divided to take a stronger position.[16]

The political attitude of the former Soviet Eastern European allies, especially that of Poland, Czechoslovakia and Hungary, was much more pro-American and anti-Arab. When, in the fall of 1989 both the Socialist system and Soviet influence collapsed, all those countries which were now led by staunchly anti-Communist politicians of a very pro-American and neo-liberal orientation moved swiftly to the Western and pro-Israeli camp. They did not only participate in the economic sanctions against Iraq, but according to some sources their intelligence services made use of their previous knowledge of the area to provide the U.S. and Israel with valuable political and strategic help and information.[17]

At the time when in the fall of 1991 the Americans chose Moscow as their partner in the Middle Eastern peace process conceived by them, the Soviet Union was on the verge of total collapse. It was giving ground on strategic negotiating points and was ready to normalize its diplomatic links with Israel without asking in return for any Israeli concessions.[18] According to an American analyst[19] Moscow might have been motivated either simply by a desire to appease the U.S. or by a wish to cut its own costs by reducing arms supplies to Syria. It might also have been persuaded by the U.S. argument that reassuring Israel would provide a chance for her to have a more positive political attitude toward the Palestinians and its Arab neighbours in general. Whatever the causes, and probably due to all of them, as early as mid 1989 the Soviet authorities had reopened Jewish immigration to Israel, thus greatly contributing to the further transformation of the domestic Israeli and regional balance of power.[20] In October 1991 the USSR helped the U.S. to revoke the anti-Zionist U.N. Resolution,[21] and one week before the Madrid talks started, it finally re-established its full diplomatic links with Israel.[22] The USSR thus came to the Middle Eastern peace talks table significantly weakened, both by its domestic turmoil and its waning position as a global and Middle Eastern superpower.[23]

The well known Russian journalist Stanislav Kondrashov then described the Soviet role in Madrid as "the last tango".[24] Another Soviet commentator, Yurii Glukhov, went even further, arguing that it would be better for the USSR to refuse to participate in the Middle East Peace Conference than to be present in a purely ceremonial role, fully submitting to American wishes.[25]

The Middle Eastern developments demonstrated once again that the very nature of Soviet-American relations had changed dramatically and the collapsing Soviet Union was desperately looking for the patronage of the only remaining true superpower.[26] But even then, Moscow did not completely forget its Middle Eastern interests and its presence there was widely supported by many otherwise openly pro-American regimes in the region.

In the fall of 1990, in return for Moscow's opposition to Iraq's seizure of Kuwait, Saudi Arabia re-established its diplomatic relations with the Soviet Union, which had been suspended since 1937, and two weeks later Bahrain followed the Saudi example.[27] Just before its end, the USSR had thus achieved an open access to all the Gulf countries – the long-term goal of Russian and Soviet Policy. In the spring of 1991 a prominent Russian scholar even argued that: "The USSR's position in the Middle East is unique today; not having fired a single shot, Moscow has in general retained its influence in the region. The Middle East is the only region of the globe where our country can prove that it has still remained a great power."[28] In September 1991 Gorbachev sent Primakov to the Middle East again in order both to express his personal gratitude to the leaders of Egypt, Saudi Arabia, the United Arab Emirates, Kuwait, Iran and Turkey for their support during the failed coup and to ask them for economic assistance for the Soviet economy. His later evaluation of the trip was quite revealing for an understanding of the political role and importance of the Soviet Union in the region. According to him, all the countries he visited "clearly did not want the disintegration of the USSR" and saw the need to preserve it as a united economic and strategic area in order to secure its power and influence. As he said to the press on September 20, 1991, "the leaders I have met want the USSR's presence in the Near and Middle East because this would preserve the balance of power. Nobody wants one superpower to maintain a monopoly position there."[29]

Moscow's role as co-chairman of the Madrid Peace Conference was welcomed by virtually all regional actors,[30] even though its real importance would only be negligible. Two months after it was convened, the Soviet Union finally disintegrated and its successor state, Russia, inherited both its close links with the region and most of its political and economic assets, which were by then, however, greatly diminished. The vacuum of power in the region had thus increased even more and was subsequently quickly filled by further growth of the apparently unlimited American domination. The roles and importance of Russia and its former Eastern European allies did not, however, completely come to an end there. In fact they were going to be resumed soon even though in different directions and dimensions.

Russia and its Former Eastern European Allies and the Middle East – the Burden of the Past and the Search for New Prospects in the Region

From the Middle Eastern perspective, the former Soviet Eastern European allies are now somewhat internally differentiated, but overall are of little political importance. The northern tier, countries such as Poland, the Czech Republic, Slovakia and Hungary, are in the process of joining NATO and the European Union, and the ruling elites there are greatly committed to Israeli interests and American leadership. It is particularly true in the case of Poland, which wants to distance itself as much as possible from some of its previous anti-Semitic traditions and where previous hostility against the Jews is often directed against the Arabs, Muslims, or brown-skinned people in general.[31] However, the possible problem there might be, how to combine American, Israeli and other Western interests, which are sometimes different or even contrasting.[32] Although after 1993/94 the political role of the European Union started to become more noticeable, its real impact is still secondary to the enormous American, or even direct Israeli influences. The more independent Middle Eastern policy of France is in Poland often publicly criticized and disliked,[33] and yet during the tenure of the left of centre government from 1993 to 1997, Polish-Palestinian relations have nevertheless improved considerably. In the fall of 1996 Hanah Ashrawi came to Poland and was received by Polish officials, including the Polish President, Aleksander Kwasniewski, and in January 1997 Polish Prime Minister Cimochowicz visited Gaza and met Yasser Arafat.[34] However, the return to power of the right wing government after the September 1997 elections was tending to bring some new changes again.[35] In February 1998 the Polish Foreign Minister, Bronislaw Geremek even declared Poland's readiness to send its armed forces in order to take part in the then-debated American action against Iraq.[36] The main reason for that, however, was the Polish government's ardent desire to get American approval for admission to NATO, and there was little social support for any eventual military involvement in the Middle East.[37] It is also necessary to remember that some Polish right wing politicians are by no means anti-Arab.[38]

The Czech Republic's policy towards the Middle East seems more open and nuanced, probably mainly because of the Czechs' well-established economic links with the region. The Czech President, V. Havel, who is personally quite balanced and free from anti-Arab prejudices, might also play some role here.[39] Slovakia is still internally too weak and internationally too inexperienced to demonstrate any real Middle Eastern interests and the same is true about almost all the post-Soviet republics including even those whose populations are mainly Muslim in background. Some exceptions might eventually be Ukraine, which is the strongest post-Soviet state after Russia and which demonstrates marked ambitions for an independent foreign policy, and Belarus, whose current pariah state-status makes her naturally closer to the Middle Eastern states, producing a similar situation to that of Iran and Syria.[40] Ukraine has already tried several times to develop close economic cooperation with Iran, but due to American pressures these efforts have not been successful. However, it is still a possibility that due to its geopolitical location close to the Middle Eastern region and certain apparent cultural similarities, Ukraine might play a much more important role there in the future. In marked contrast to the majority of the other post-Communist Eastern European states which, during the December 1998 Anglo-American bombing of Iraq expressed their "support", or at least "understanding of the strikes."[41] Ukraine opposed them outright.[42] On December 17, 1998, Ukraine's Foreign Ministry stated that "Ukraine, which has consistently pronounced for resolving any conflict situations by peaceful political means, cannot agree with force methods of tackling this issue" and warned against "unpredictable consequences [of the strikes] for the region and whole world.[43] Byelorussian President Aleksander Lukashenko and his anti-American and populist-socialist regime look for an alliance with Iran, Syria and perhaps some other states in the Middle East, offering them arms supplies and expecting in return energy resources and political cooperation. In March 1998 President Lukashenko visited both Iran and Syria and stressed that his country "favour[ed] a multi-polar world" because "only then can [an] international system be stable."[44] President Lukashenko also condemned the December 1998 U.S. and British air strikes against Iraq, calling them "bandit actions" that would never have happened had the Soviet Union existed.[45]

Hungary follows a course, which is broadly similar to that of Poland, but it has relatively more economic and political links with the region.[46] As already mentioned, the southern tier of the former Soviet-bloc countries such as Romania, Bulgaria, Moldavia, and the independently socialist former Yugoslavia and Albania, are from a cultural point of view much closer to the Middle East, and their economies are also oriented more to the East. There difficult domestic problems and their subsequent general weakness have, however, now made them virtually unable to assume any meaningful international role whatsoever.[47]

Among all the post-Communist countries of Eurasia, Russia is now in fact the only country that is still willing and able to be an independent and meaningful player in the Middle Eastern arena. In addition to historical traditions, there are numerous other reasons why Russia, as such, independent of its actual political regime, has always been and is also now interested in the broadly understood Middle Eastern region as a whole, including Turkey, Iran, the Arab World and Israel, without even mentioning its previous dependencies (now the "Near Abroad") – the states of Transcaucasia and Central Asia.

The first and probably most important reason is the geographical proximity of the region to Russia's borders in the south, which many Russian scholars and politicians, including Primakov himself, consider to be her "soft under-belly."[48] Any military threat from the region and the presence there of powerful foreign armies equipped with the most modern arms are apt to cause fears and anxiety in Russia, especially in view of the fact that the Russian Federation is not now guarded by the defence perimeter installations which had been built on the former Soviet borders and that to recreate similar installations around her present borders would be virtually impossible for economic reasons.[49] According to some authors, the Russian military, who are particularly well informed about both the new strategic needs and the costs of fortifying the country's new borders, are thus claiming that it is "Moscow's historic duty to protect the outer borders of the former Soviet Union."[50] Russians are particularly concerned about the possibilities of Western control over Iraq and Iran. According to them, if such a situation happened, it would be very harmful for Russia's interests and threatening to its security.[51]

A second reason and one of growing importance, is economic. In the 1970s and 1980s the USSR was undoubtedly a major arms supplier to the Arab states of the region – Syria, Yemen, Iraq and Libya especially – exceeding Western powers from that point of view. As late as 1988 the USSR supplied the Middle East with arms worth over $14.5 billion, against $12.2 billion delivered by the U.S.[52] The commercial value of that trade, however, was questionable. For instance, according to data from 1995, Syria owed Russia $11 billion for arms, and the total debt of the Arab World was calculated at $32 billion.[53] Post-Communist Russia is looking instead for profits and for that purpose wants to preserve as much as possible its control over Caspian Sea oil and its transportation to the West.[54] In that area, just as in the Middle East as a whole, "although the Cold War has ended, geopolitical competition has not,"[55] and Russia has to face the growing impact of the Western Powers, especially the U.S., which now have concrete interests in the development there of the natural gas and petroleum industry. Because of the rise in America's oil imports, from 31% of consumption in 1983 to 52% in 1996, and the political need to find an alternative "prospect of oil supplies from a region that is not Arab or Iranian,"[56] the U.S. government is now showing a marked interest in the Caspian region. Russian fears and anxiety are consequently only to be expected and in order to find a better accommodation with the new realities of the global oil market and international pressures, many Russian politicians want to look for cooperation with the Arab oil-producing countries which are geographically close to the area and which in addition have already acquired considerable experience in dealing with similar economic and political problems.[57]

Another goal of such cooperation is to find customers for Russian industry among those countries that are relatively rich but still poorly developed. Efforts in this direction are presently seen as being more urgent since previous hopes for integration into the Western-developed economy are generally now considered as largely unsuccessful and most Russian commentators are calling for a search for alternative customers and economic partners.[58] With apparent exaggeration and yet not without some reason, Israeli researchers from the Begin-Sadat Center for Strategic Studies at Bar Ilan University have said that: "Unlike the past ... economic benefit, not geopolitical strategy, is the driving force behind Russia's Middle East policy."[59] According to them, a clear indication of this was the fact that in 1997 the Russian government concluded a deal worth several hundred million dollars with Israeli Aircraft Industries to equip Russia's Ilijushin aircraft for electronic surveillance operations. The deal was finalized during Israeli Prime Minister Netanyahu's first state visit to Moscow in March 1997. A no less valid example of the new Russian pragmatic attitude is its renewal of trade and economic cooperation with Egypt, including the important fields of electricity and energy.[60]

The third reason for Russia's Middle East involvement is cultural and religious links which, in Russia's case, are much stronger than is the case for other parts of Europe.[61] Those links might be seen as a reflection of the fact that Russia, at least in its cultural traditions, is predominantly Eastern Orthodox, but is also a Muslim country, and its Jewish community has been one of the most numerous, and in cultural terms, most active in the world. At present about 15% of the Russian population (about 20 million people) are of Muslim cultural background.[62] Although after the long period of Communist persecution, relatively few of them still practise their inherited religious traditions, they are nevertheless differentiated from the rest of society by their special social culture and from the political point of view they are both anti-Western and anti-Israeli.[63] In the view of the Deputy Director of the Department of the Middle East and North Africa at the Russian Foreign Ministry, Alexei Tchistiakov:

> The Muslims living in Russia are more numerous than in some Muslim countries. The impact of "Middle East Islam" has already made itself felt. The existence of a large Jewish community in Russia and numerous emigrants from [there] in Israel draws the situation in the Middle East and Russia closer together, strengthening their interconnection. There is also reason to forecast a stronger role for Orthodoxy in relations between Russia and the Middle East.[64]

Since the early 1990s Israel is not only Russia's major trading partner, second after Turkey in the Middle East, but over 800,000 Israeli citizens who came from the former USSR have developed an unusually strong cultural bond between the two nations.[65] Israel is in fact the place of the biggest Russian Diaspora outside the former Soviet Union and the new Israeli political party made up primarily of Russian immigrants (Yisrael B'Alyah) wants to promote further development of Russian-Israeli relations. This party, which is led by the famous former Soviet dissident, Nathan Sharansky, is now a part of the ruling coalition.

In addition to all these traditional ethnic and religious connections, Russia's cultural links with the region might also be seen as an outcome of its Eurasian character – acceptance of which is increasingly popular in Russian society, and since 1993 has found repercussion even in President Yeltsin's official pronouncements.[66] In fact a major shift in the direction of the Eurasian orientation which has been noticeable since 1993 has coincided in time with changes in Russia's new policy toward the Middle East. Although in view of some observers Russia's geopolitical position "has prompted the formulation of Eurasianism as an ideology of interaction and integration between the cultures,"[67] Eurasian ideas "may subsequently serve as an ideological basis for its future foreign policy."[68] However, the final shape and international role of that policy, just like its Middle Eastern implications, are still far from certain and subject to volatile changes and intrinsic development. Although Eurasianists want to stress Russia's distinctive national interests based on "its unique geographical and historical position straddling Europe and Asia,"[69] they are nevertheless not necessarily anti-Western. Their real goal is rather to preserve the country's freedom of action and to defend its interests "even when this produces some discomfort in the United States or other Western countries."[70]

Since its very beginning in December 1991, up to the first months of 1999, post-Soviet Russian foreign policy has nevertheless undergone substantial transformations and some of its goals and directions might now be discerned and analysed. Compared with the Soviet period, its first and most striking feature is its weakness. Despite its still enormous territory, in 1992 Russia's population numbered only about 50% of the previous Soviet population, and its economic potential has also been reduced by more than 30%.[71] The political and military implications of this were even stronger because of the total loss of influence over its former Eastern European allies and the Baltic States, and the continuing economic and social decline. For instance, in 1995, in comparison with the 1990 figure, the GNP of Russia itself amounted to only 62%, and similar figures for many of the other former Soviet republics were even lower.[72] As a result of the collapse of the USSR and the ensuing unprecedented economic crisis in 1995, Russia's GNP was more than ten times smaller than that of the U.S.A., and in 1996 it dropped 7% more.[73] As a Russian scholar then admitted: "now it is getting clear that the Cold War ended by a victory of one side – the U.S.A. – and the total collapse of the other, the USSR."[74] Since the new economic crisis in August 1998, the Russian average per capita income has decreased again from $160 U.S. to $50 U.S. per month and the cost of imported goods has risen 3.5 times compared with July 1998.[75] The present-day economic crisis in Russia and the population's misery are shocking and staggering, even in view of the long and tragic history of this great country.

What was also important in the 1992-94 period was that the people who surrounded Yeltsin were mainly of neo-liberal and occidentalist orientation. They wanted to reject the Soviet heritage as much as possible and as the first Russian Foreign Minister Andrei Kozyrev put it, to join the "civilized world."[76] Behind this pro-Western orientation also lay widely shared expectations for generous economic help from the U.S. and its allies, and their recognition of Russian interests in the former Soviet bloc area.[7] Due to both the weakness of the country and the political attitude of its leadership, the Russian foreign policy of the first two-year period, with the partial exception of Bosnia and Iran, was in general quite pro-American and avoided any confrontational approach or even following an original direction. It participated fully in the sanctions against Iraq and Libya and enthusiastically supported the Arab-Israeli peace process which was sponsored by the Americans.[78] At that time some voices were even heard saying that the Middle East as a whole is outside the range of Russia's national security interests and overall, "Russian mass consciousness ... has tended to pay less attention to the region."[79] The disappointment of their excessive hopes for Western assistance was nevertheless soon destined to cause a reaction, which was simultaneous with a new growth of nationalist and communist influences. In the fall of 1992 the acting head of Moscow's Institute of African and Arab Studies and a prominent Russian Orientalist, Alexei Vassiliev, spoke on the country's increasing disillusionment with "putting all its foreign policy eggs in one Western basket."[80] He also characterized Russian Middle Eastern policy as being in "a state of limbo."[81] By December 1992 the opposition to the pro-Atlantist foreign policy, which was symbolized by Andrei Kozyrev, started to be voiced more by the supporters of the Eurasian orientation, nationalists and communists in the Russian parliament the Duma. In early 1993, even President Yeltsin, addressing a session of the Foreign Ministry Collegium, criticized the Ministry for: "many errors and blunders ... excessive timidity towards the West whilst allowing relations with the Third World to weaken."[82] When on June 27, 1993, the U.S. Air Force bombarded Baghdad, despite the Russian government's official approval, the Russian press was unanimous in its condemnation of the operation. "The most deplorable thing is that American piracy was justified by Russian leaders" wrote the Communist *Pravda*.[83] The Liberal *Izvestia* described it as "an act of retribution which looked more like muscle-flexing" and expressed an opinion that "our multi-polar and interdependent world" should not give any state "the unlimited right to act as supreme judge and bearer of the ultimate truth."[84] In a similar vein, *Komsomalskaya Pravda* suggested that "the White House needs an enemy" and indicated that "had Saddam Hussein been killed, the U.S. would have had to find a new villain."[85]

In an expression of a growing mood of renewed self-assertion and defiance towards U.S. hegemony, by the summer of 1994 Russian officials had begun to call for the lifting of sanctions against Iraq. On July 18, 1994 a Russian representative told the U.N. Security Council that it should look into "the swiftest possible establishment of a restricted control period at the end of which ... it should be prepared to examine the question of lifting the oil embargo."[86]

In the period between August to December 1994, the Iraqi Foreign Minister, Tariq Aziz, was received three times in the Russian capital. In

October and November of the same year, the Russian Foreign Minister himself, Andrei Kozyrev, visited Baghdad twice and addressed a session of the Iraqi Parliament. As an official outcome of his visits the Iraqi government declared its readiness to recognize Kuwait as a sovereign state and to accept its present boundaries in return for the prospect of the sanctions being lifted. Although Minister Kozyrev was very proud of his achievements,[87] some Russian journalists immediately indicated that his diplomacy "enabled Saddam to drive a wedge between Moscow and the West.[88] The reactions of the United States and Britain to this modest success of Russian diplomacy were predictably quite negative.[89] As the Russian press then indicated, in addition to the unwanted Russian presence in the region, the Russian initiative also exposed American intentions to continue sanctions until the total collapse of the present regime took place, independently of its political concessions.[90]

Despite negative American reactions, the Russians continued their contacts with Iraq and still supported its goal of weakening or even ending the sanctions. In February 1995, the Russian Deputy Foreign Minister, Victor Posuvaliuk, went as far as to suggest that if the U.N. Security Council did not take into account the positive actions of Iraq, the situation in the Middle East would deteriorate further.[91] Even earlier, another example of Russia's newfound self-assertiveness in the region was its reaction to the tragic Hebron massacre of Palestinians by an Israeli settler in February 1994. The Russian government, then acting for the first time independently of the Americans in the matter of the Arab-Israeli conflict, called for a second plenary meeting of Madrid's Middle East Peace Conference and asked the U.N. Security Council to give "serious attention" to the idea of international protection for the Palestinian population in the Israeli-occupied territories.[92]

During the whole period in question following the end of the Soviet Union in December 1991, the Russian arms trade and friendly relations with Iran have never been disrupted, even though because of U.S. pressures, they have sometimes been submitted to serious limitations. Although in the immediate aftermath of the collapse of the Soviet Union many people in Russia considered Islamic fundamentalism as one of the major political threats to the country,[93] even at the peak of the Russian-American "honeymoon" in 1992, Yeltsin was ready to endanger U.S.-Russian relations by the sale of arms to Iran.[94] Although, due to American pressure in May 1995 during his summit with U.S. President Clinton he had to back down on some equipment which allegedly might have contributed to Iran's acquiring nuclear weapons, the promise to sell her other nuclear installations was still to be respected.[95] As one Russian commentator indicated then, "Russian society is arriving at a consensus on the question of national interest. The political elite will not allow the President to yield to pressure from the West."[96]

In the period from 1994-95, despite all the political and economic weaknesses of the country, and even partly because of these, Russian foreign policy, both Middle Eastern and global, was apparently turning away from its initial Euro-Atlanticist direction toward an avowedly more independent and balanced orientation. Though not socialist or revolutionary any more, Russian leaders are nevertheless now calling for a multi-polar world which would not be based on U.S. hegemony[97] and they perceive similarities between Russia's international interests and those of the many Third World countries of Asia and the Middle East.[98] The main features of their new foreign policy have thus slowly emerged and crystallized, even though its definite shape and stability are still far from being certain. In January 1996 the replacement of Andrei Kozyrev by Yevgeny Primakov, a prominent Arabist and former head of the Russian Foreign Intelligence Agency, as the new Foreign Minister of the country, had both real and symbolic importance and inaugurated its far more articulated and independent period of international involvement.

The Present Russian Middle Eastern Policy: Its Basic Features and Directions

Since he assumed his post as the new Russian Foreign Minister, Y. Primakov has adopted the motto, "Russia was and remains a great power. Its foreign policy should correspond to that status."[99] The policy he then introduced and reasserted again after becoming Russian Prime Minister in September 1998 still has broad social support in the country and should be analysed as a further stage in the development of post-communist Russia's global and regional role and importance. What are its basic features and present directions?

Expressing a wide consensus among the Russian political elite and following trends which were already noticeable during the last two years before his coming to office,[100] Primakov wants to stress both the greatness and global political interests of Russia. As he stated during his first press conference as Russian Foreign Minister, Russian foreign policy should correspond to its great power status and be active "in all azimuths."[101] He has already repeatedly indicated that his policy is not intended to be anti-American and even less anti-Israeli, but rather one in which Russia will seek to "diversify" its perceptions, and that the Arab World will have a "considerable place" in it.[102] He certainly does not want, and in fact he is simply even unable to look for, a confrontation with American power. However, he also does not want to continue the mainly pro-Atlantist policy of his predecessor in its previous form and meaning. Instead he wants his country to be more assertive politically in regions where the Russians think their interest's lie and where they can use the remnants of their power. According to the prominent Russian political analyst Aleksei Pushkov, the policy which can be defined as the Primakov doctrine wants to "promote and advance relations with the West, while playing an independent game in other fields ... and is essentially about interacting with the main world players without joining anyone too closely."[103] This obviously needs to include the Middle East[104] where, as in October 1997 one senior Israeli official said, after his meeting with Primakov, he "made [it] clear that he wants Russia to demonstrate its sense of being a power in the region."[105]

Between 1992 and 1997 Russia had already moved from a period of virtual submission to the U.S. on almost all Middle Eastern issues (its arms sales to Iran were here the only meaningful exception), to a position of an active and independent protagonist in the area. By the middle of 1996 there were already several pieces of proof that Russia had again started an active and independent policy toward the region.[106] They included, among other things, its renewed and increased diplomatic effort to limit or even lift the sanctions against Iraq, to independently mediate in the Israeli-Hezbollah confrontation in southern Lebanon and its reinforced links with Iran.[107] This trend was later to continue and develop much further, culminating in Russian efforts to mediate in the two new stages of the Iraqi crisis in November 1997 and January and February 1998. Primakov visited the region even before the first stage had developed in the last week of October 1997. His efforts then were directed mainly toward Arab-Israeli relations and the assertion of the Russian presence in the region. He blamed the Israeli Prime Minister, B. Netanyahu for the stagnation of the peace process and promised Yasser Arafat that Russia would recognize a Palestinian state as soon as it was proclaimed.[108] He has also suggested Russian mediation to the Israelis and Syrians and in an example of shuttle diplomacy he himself tried to narrow the gap between Damascus and Jerusalem. By the very end of his Middle Eastern visit in Cairo, in a 12-point proposal for adopting a Code of Conduct in the Security Sphere for the region, he once more stressed that: "There can be no forward movement towards a Middle East peace settlement unless each country complies with the agreements it has concluded with its neighbours," and that "negotiations on the Palestinian, Syrian and Lebanese tracks should proceed in parallel."[109] The same open and friendly attitude towards the Arab people characterized Russian diplomacy in its subsequent dealings with Iraq. In November 1997 it was exactly Iraq's acceptance of Russia's proposal that allowed the return of U.N. weapons inspectors in exchange for the Russians' promise "to do their best to get the sanctions lifted"[110] which then prevented new U.S. military intervention. At the next stage of the confrontation in early 1998, the Russian Minister of Defence, Igor Sergejev indicated to his American counterpart, W. Cohen during his visit to Moscow that the Iraqi crisis represented a threat to vital Russian national interests and it could not be approached only in the context of American-Iraqi relations.[111] President Yeltsin himself went even further, publicly stating that American President Clinton's threats of military action against Iraq might lead to a new world war.[112] President Yeltsin's pro-Iraqi stand was then strongly supported by the Russian parliament, the Duma, which called for the use by Russia of her veto against the acceptance of American military intervention by the U.N. Security Council.[113] In addition, the Duma then authorized the government to repudiate the sanctions against Iraq if the U.S. really attacked.[114] During the December 1998 American and British bombing of Iraq, Russian politicians of all orientations expressed their harsh condemnation and protests. Both President B. Yeltsin and Prime Minister Y. Primakov called for an "immediate end to military action"[115] and the Duma's draft statement, which was approved by all the factions, condemned the bombing of Iraq as "an act of international terrorism"[116] and indicating that the recent actions of the U.S. and Britain "have once again demonstrated the danger that eastward NATO expansion poses for Russia"[117] recommended that the government review Russia's current and future relations with the U.S., Britain and NATO, as well as ending Russian compliance with U.N. sanctions against Iraq.[118] Communist party leader Gennodii Zyuganov called the strikes "an act of terror" and "an extreme manifestation of international gangsterism"[119] while one of his political arch foes, a powerful businessman, Boris Berezovskii told the media that "a new page was opened in a world order in which the dominant role of the U.S. in the world is absolute,"[120] and that "Russia joined a number of countries that don't have to be reckoned with."[121] The strongest statement, however, came from the head of the Russian Defence Ministry's Chief Administration for International Military

Cooperation, Col. Gen. Leonid Ivashov, who, elaborating on the position of top Defence Ministry officials, said that "if Russia's opinion continues to be ignored, Moscow will be forced to alter its military and political vectors and could become the leader of the segment of the world community that objects to diktat."[122]

And yet on all of those occasions there were some clear limits to the level of Russia's independent involvement and to its denial of American pressures. Despite all its efforts toward the lifting of sanctions against Iraq, Russia did not, however, abolish them unilaterally and while trying to protect Iraq against new American bombardments, at the same time stressed that Iraq should comply fully with all relevant U.N. resolutions and submit to further UNSCOM disarmament inspection.[123] In February 1998 it was none other than Primakov who, at Kofi Annan's request had persuaded Saddam Hussein to back down from insisting on a time limit for inspections of his "presidential sites,"[124] and in December of the same year, in spite of all the harsh protests against the U.S. and the U.K. air strikes against Iraq, an "informed source in Russian diplomatic circles" told the press on December 19, 1998 that "a return to confrontation [with the U.S.] is not worth it for the very reason that it is not in our interests."[125] Even earlier, on December 18, President Yeltsin's spokesman Dmitry Yakushkin stated to the media that: "There can be no talks of a rift between Russia and the U.S. and Britain ... we mustn't slip into the rhetoric of confrontation,"[126] and Boris Berezovskii called for separation of "our emotions from a rational assessment of events."[127]

Concerning the Arab-Israeli peace process, Primakov stressed that "it is possible at the current time to obtain real success only based on the principle of 'territory in exchange for peace', the Resolutions of the U.N. Security Council 242 and 338, and for Lebanon Resolution 425" and that "for no reason should one state attempt to monopolize the organizational-mediator mission in the Middle East settlement."[128] During Yasser Arafat's visit to Moscow in February 1997 Primakov subsequently assured him of "full support for the Palestinian leadership's policy on developing the negotiating process with Israel" and called for the "immediate and consistent implementation of all the provisions of the Palestinian-Israeli agreements" and the need to hold "constructive talks on the final status of the Palestinian territories as scheduled."[129] In a similar vein President Yeltsin promised Arafat that Russia "will continue to make vigorous efforts to help resolve disputes and secure peace in the region" and suggested that Moscow and Bethlehem become sister cities.[130] At the same time, however, the Russians wanted to accommodate Israeli fears and interests as much as possible. A joint statement issued at the end of Arafat's visit in February 1997 aimed to assure them that: "The Palestinians' aspirations, supported by the Russian co-sponsor [of the Middle East Peace Conference], to achieve realization of their national rights ... including their right to self-determination, does not harm Israel's legitimate interests."[131] One month later in March 1997 the Israeli Prime Minister B. Netanyahu was solemnly welcomed in Moscow and President Yeltsin accepted his invitation to officially visit the State of Israel as the first Russian leader in history to do so.[132] During his own visit to Israel in October 1997, Primakov also sought to calm Israeli concern about alleged Iranian armaments and told the Israeli Industry and Trade Minister Nathan Sharansky that Russia was ready to join ongoing cooperative anti-terrorist efforts in the region involving Israel, the U.S. and the Palestinian Authority.[133] Arafat's more recent visit to Moscow in October 1998 seemed to be far less promising than the one of February 1997. He lobbied for Russia's more active involvement in the Middle East peace process and asked Moscow to take part in the trilateral American-Palestinian-Israeli meeting which was then set for October 15, 1998 in Washington, D.C.[134] Yeltsin was not, however, in a position to give him a positive answer and promised only to reappoint a permanent representative to deal with Middle Eastern problems and visit the countries of the region.[135]

Strongly criticized in the U.S. and Israel, Russia's uninterrupted links with Iran are perhaps a partial exception to the general character of Russian foreign policy, which aims to manifest its independence but still has to remain accommodating and conciliatory. Even in this case, however, Moscow vigorously denies repeated Israeli allegations that it is "helping Iran build nuclear weapons and long-range missiles."[136] At the press conference on September 15, 1997, Primakov strongly indicated that "Not a single project of this sort is being carried out between Russia and Iran at state level" and that, according to his information, "there has not been any leak through non-state channels that could help Iran make nuclear weapons and long-range missiles."[137]

According to the pro-Western Russian daily, *Komersant Daily*, other "military contracts between Moscow and Teheran are worth about $1 billion and are due to be completed before 1999" and "the Russian government pledged several years ago not to conclude any new contracts."[138] Political and economic cooperation notwithstanding, Primakov nevertheless assured his Western partners that "Russia's relations with Iran or Iraq are not now, and will not become in the future, a function of NATO expansion" and they will not form a kind of "counter-measure" by Moscow.[139]

Russia's Middle Eastern politics, like its foreign policy in general, is thus now characterized both by an effort toward self-assertiveness, a continuity of its old traditions, and by considerable self-restraint caused by the present weakness and general crisis of the country. Its first and most important goal is to defend Russian national interests and to find for the country "a thought-out role ... in a difficult, zig-zag transition to a multi-polar world."[140] In the new geopolitical situation, after the collapse of the USSR, Russia is physically isolated from the traditionally understood Middle East region by the presently independent republics, its former dependencies of Transcaucasia and Central Asia. According to Primakov himself, those new states have now become one of the main strategic focuses of Russia's attention, which largely determines its policy toward the states of the Middle East itself.[141] Russian leaders are acutely aware of the power vacuum on the southern borders of the country and the possible threat of penetration of "alien forces" such as Pan-Turkism, Islamic fundamentalism and, most of all, Western influences.[142] In fact the American infiltration there in particular is now not just potential but quite real and is being watched with dismay by Russia.[143]

Iran has started to be considered as a strategic ally by Russia, both because of the commonly felt American threat and because of its apparently cautious and compromising policy toward the post-Soviet Muslim republics.[144] Despite its official Islamic revolutionary ideology, "Teheran's policy towards the Central Asian states and the Caucasus since the end of the Cold War has been constructive and non-ideological"[145] and even contributed positively to the shaky peace in Tajikistan.[146]

During the Iraqi-UNSCOM crisis on February 25, 1998, the Iranian Foreign Minister Kamal Khazzam arrived in Moscow and both parties expressed their willingness to fight a one-country hegemony in the region.[147] In spite of the still somewhat unclear language, their joint communiqué indicated their political orientation rather clearly: directed against the present-day U.S. domination of the Middle East. The Iranian Foreign Minister, praising the successful peace-making mission by U.N. Secretary-General Kafi Annan, also stated that this had clearly shown that "the era of domination by a single superpower that can dictate its terms to others is gone forever."[148] In addition to the new geopolitical requirements and a common stand against U.S. hegemony in the region, post-Communist Russia's policy toward Iran is also generated by its search for economic profit and money. In marked contrast to Iraq and Libya, which had already greatly suffered from U.N. sanctions, and Syria which cannot repay even its old debts to Russia, Iran for a long time was able to pay in hard currency (and is still able to do so, even though to a lesser extent) and thus provides the Russian economy with a much-needed market for its arms and atomic industries.[149]

At the very peak of the Iraqi-UNSCOM crisis on February 22, 1998, Russian Atomic Energy Minister Victor Mikhailov confirmed his country's readiness to comply with the $700 million contract to build a 1,000 MW light-water reactor at Bushehr on Iran's Arab Persian Gulf coast despite U.S. and Israeli misgivings that Iran might use the power station in order to produce nuclear weapons.[150] In November 1998 the new Russian Atomic Energy Minister Yevgeny Adamov went to Iran himself, accompanied by several State Duma Deputies and specialists in construction and operation of nuclear power plants.[151]

Because of the limited appeal of political Islam in most post-Soviet countries, with the single possible exception of Tadjikistan,[152] Iran had always been in a relatively weaker position there than Turkey in its struggle for political influence and the markets in the region. Most of the population there has traditionally belonged to the Sunni Islam of the Hanafite school and especially the urban population, which is playing a crucial role in the current changes, still remains under the strong influence of the Soviet schooling and inherited Soviet atheism.[153] Russia's friendly relations with Iran might thus also be perceived as a normal outcome of the regional balance of power and the common interests of both countries have also been demonstrated by their complete agreement on dividing and transporting Caspian oil and natural gas resources.[154]

In contrast to Iran, Turkey has never been seen by Russia as a strategic partner. In the past, Russian-Turkish relations had often been marked by bloody wars and territorial conflicts, and Turkey is now a long-standing NATO member and the ally of the U.S. Since 1991-92 Turkey has provided loans and assistance to the post-Soviet republics of Central Asia and Transcaucasia, and what was no less important, Turkey represented an example of modernization and moderate secularisation to many people in those areas.[155] Turkey is also involved in the "shadowy war" for control of the Caspian oil and natural gas of the region.[156]

Although, in contrast to Iran, Turkey does not have direct access to the Caspian Sea and its natural resources, it can nevertheless offer an alternative route to transport the resources by pipelines to the Mediterranean and Europe with the exclusion of a Russian intermediary.[157] In spite of its geopolitical location, but due to persisting U.S. pressure, Iran cannot bid successfully and control the direction of those pipelines through its territory.

However, the most important reason for the persisting Russian mistrust of Turkey remains the fact that the Russian political elite still views Turkey not just as one more autonomous and self-interested player in the area, but also, and perhaps even primarily, as a tool of Western penetration, especially American.[158]

In fact Russian leaders do not consider Turkey itself to be a serious threat and Russian-Turkish economic relations are quickly developing.[159] The Turkish Prime Minister Tansu Ciller's visit to Moscow in September 1993 and Russian Prime Minister Chernomyrdin's visit to Turkey in October 1997 were both quite friendly and indicated a growing political understanding among the parties involved.[160] Among other issues, both countries took a similar stand against the anti-Iraqi sanctions and agreed to cooperate to lift the anti-Iraqi embargo.[161] Apparent demonstrations of that were Russian and Turkish diplomatic efforts during the new stage of the Iraqi crisis in February 1998 and the Turkish negative attitude towards the air strikes against Iraq in December 1998.[162]

Compared with the Soviet period, Russian involvement in the Arab World, and especially in the Arab-Israeli conflict, is certainly much more modest. In the Gulf Region, Russia is trying to get loans and to sell arms to the rich Gulf Cooperation Council, (GCC), the Arab monarchies.[163] Despite some still-persisting problems in Russian-Israeli relations – especially concerning the above-mentioned deals with Iran – cooperation between the two countries is not only close, but is indeed and constantly expanding. During his first state visit to Russia in March 1997, Israeli Prime Minister B. Netanyahu went as far as to declare that his country "will henceforth consider Russia a friendly state and will strive to establish with Russia relations that are as close as Israel's ties with its No. 1 partner, the U.S."[164] In the view of many experts, the Russians are also likely to continue to be welcomed among the Arabs.[165] Russia offers them a chance to balance, or at least somewhat diminish, U.S. domination and in cooperation with some other states, such as France or even the European Union as a whole, might even force the Americans to reconsider their policy towards the region. This strategic goal was clearly expressed, even by the staunchly pro-American Egyptian President Hosni Mubarak during his state visit to Russia in September 1997. As he then said:

> There are two cosponsors of the Mideast settlement process, the US and Russia. The Americans came [to Egypt and the Middle East], they come all the time. But Russia ... it completely ignores us ... we are very interested in developing and maintaining good – the very best – relations

> with Russia. Especially since we remember very well the enormous assistance given to us by the Soviet Union. We will never forget that.[166]

A similar appeal to the Russian leadership for a more active role in the region was also brought to Moscow by the Lebanese Prime Minister Rafik Harari on his visit there in April 1997.[167] Although his meeting with Yeltsin was held behind closed doors, "to all appearances [nevertheless] … the sides were satisfied with each other."[168] But despite all those appeals and longstanding traditions, present-day Russia cannot afford to make a truly strong stand in the area. Its economic decay and domestic social crisis have recently caused the U.N. experts to reclassify and move Russia from the category of developed down to the category of developing countries, so it is in a similar state to some countries in Asia and Africa.[169] According to a very meticulous analysis by a German scholar:

> Russia can only move beyond its 1990 production level by the year 2005 under the assumption of the extremely optimistic forecast of an average economic growth of 5 per cent, without, admittedly, moving anywhere near to the level of income and production of the further expanding Western European countries.[170]

As he indicates: "An economic potential of this scale cannot provide a proper basis for an ambitious and self-confident foreign policy."[171] But although, with its GNP probably less than one-tenth of that of the U.S., Yeltsin's Russia cannot afford to stand up to the American superpower, its role in the region, as the Iraqi-UNSCOM confrontation of February 1998, and even the relative lack of success in bombing Iraq in December 1998 once more demonstrated, is not without its own special meanings and importance. A "Tiersmondization" process of the country and its society[172] and, connected with it, the Eurasian ideology which is very popular there, may even contribute to an increasing feeling of Russian solidarity with the other developing nations, and further involvement in the Middle Eastern dilemmas.[173]

Eastern Europe and the Middle East: A General Summary

Both Eastern Europe and the Middle East are regions with a long history and a highly complex present-day geopolitical environment. As we have seen above, from the point of view of the area's relations with the Middle

East, Eastern Europe may be divided into three parts, each of which has a different history and a different current political orientation. Nations of the southern part of East-Central and Eastern Europe, especially the Balkan Peninsula, have for centuries been submitted to Ottoman rule, and their cultural links with and understanding of the Middle Eastern peoples are consequently strong and often articulated. Due to the weakness of these nations, however, their political, economic and international importance is currently quite negligible.[174] The north western part of the region has traditionally been integrated with and/or submitted to the West and the nations there are now also following Western leadership, sometimes even showing a particular lack of sympathy and understanding toward the dark-skinned Middle Easterners and their painful political and social problems. Russia, and in the future perhaps also an independent Ukraine, have a marked interest in the Middle East which is based on their entire history as Eastern Orthodox and even partly Muslim countries, their geographical proximity to the region, and the subsequent numerous political and economic links with its peoples. Although after the collapse of the USSR and the ensuing internal crisis, Russia, and even less Ukraine, cannot be truly effective in their Middle Eastern policies, their links with the region and involvement in its problems are not going to disappear. The role of Russia there is, even now, by no means negligible and few can imagine a politically stable Middle East without Russian cooperation and acceptance.[175]

Despite all their differences, the people of Eastern Europe and the Middle East have some common features: when compared with the West's relative backwardness in industrial development, the still largely traditional character of their societies, the lack of stable legal and political institutions and the consequent importance of religious beliefs and religious institutions, and a marked proneness toward populist demagogy and authoritarian regimes. Coping with the difficult tasks of modernization and development, the peoples of both regions can learn much from each other and thus create a firm basis for better and closer relations in the future. The way to this end is certainly a long and difficult one, but some effort in this direction would be possible even now and probably quite beneficial for all the nations involved.[176]

Notes

1 For further discussion on that point see: Mohammed El-Doufani, "Futile interventions: Russia's disengagement from the Third World," *International Journal*, Vol. XLIX, (Autumn 1984), pp. 846-873. For the impact of the earlier stages of Gorbachev's new foreign policy on the Third World interests, see also: Zafar Iman, "The implications of perestroika for the Third World, particularly Asia," in R. Kanet, D. Nutter, & T. Resler, *Soviet Foreign Policy in Transition* (Cambridge: Cambridge University Press, 1992), pp. 217-235.

2 G. M. Yemelianova, "Russia and Islam: The history and prospects of a relationship," *Asian Affairs*, Vol. XXVI, part III (Oct. 1995), p. 278.

3 Alexei Chistyakov, "The Middle East in the light of geopolitical changes," *International Affairs* (Moscow), 1995, No. 8, p. 52.

4 Yemelianova, p. 284. At the same time, however, the Russian policy toward the southern states directly adjacent to its borders such as Turkey, Iran, and Afghanistan was in many ways similar to the one then employed by Western Europe. Hugh Seton-Watson, *The Russian Empire, 1801-1917* (Oxford: Oxford University Press, 1967), pp. 41-51, 57-62, 289-311, and 430-435.

5 *Asia i Afrika segodnia*, (1991), No. 4, p. 50.

6 Derek Hopwood, *The Russian Presence in Syria and Palestine 1843-1913: Church and Politics in the Near East*, (Oxford: Clarendon Press, 1969).

7 The author came across many examples of this in the region as late as the 1960s.

8 Alexei Vassiliev, *Russian Policy in the Middle East From Messianism to Pragmatism* (Reading: Ithaca Press, 1993), p. 2.

9 Yemelianova, p. 287.

10 Nicolai N. Petro and Alvin Z. Rubinstein, *Russian Foreign Policy From Empire to Nation-State*, (New York: Longman, 1996), p. 248; See also A. Potserebov, "On Russian-Egyptian Relations," *International Affairs* (Moscow), Vol. 43, No. 3 (1997), p. 107.

11 A. Sela, *Soviet Political and Military Conduct in the Middle East*,(London: MacMillan Press, 1981), p. 105.

12 Tareq Y. Ismael, *International Relations of the Middle East*, (Syracuse University Press, 1986), p. 194.

13 A. I. Vavilov, "Rossia-Syria i Liban: Polveka druzby i plodotvornovo sotrudnitzestva," *Asia i Africa segodnia*, No. 1, (1995), p. 29.

14 Ismael, p. 198.

15 The Egyptian President Sadat's decision to expel the majority of Soviet military advisors from Egypt in the summer of 1972 was, to a large extent, caused by Soviet refusal to provide him with the most sophisticated weaponry he had demanded. Galia Golan, *Soviet Policies in the Middle East from World War II to Gorbachev*, (Cambridge: Cambridge University Press, 1990), p. 215.

16 Soviet efforts during the Iraqi-Kuwait crisis are thoroughly presented in an investigative article by Alexei Vasiliev in *Komsomolskaya Pravda*, (Feb. 16, 1991) and a series of firsthand reports by Y. Primakov, "Vaina, kotoroi moglo nie byt," ("The war which was to be avoided"), *Pravda*, (Feb. 27, 1991), pp. 1, 7; (Feb. 28, 1991), p. 5; (March 1, 1991), p. 5; and (March 2, 1991), p. 7. For an example of American hostilities towards

Soviet peace efforts, see Suzanna Crow, "Primakov and the Soviet Peace Initiative," *RFE/RL Research Report on the USSR*, 3/9 (March 1, 1991), pp. 14-17. For a comprehensive account, see also A. Vasiliev, *Russian Policy in the Middle East*, pp. 335-345.

17 Several personal interviews with the author in Poland in the summer and fall of 1996. In the early 1990s there were also some leaks about it in the Polish press. According to Rex Brynen the former Soviet allies then terminated "most of their military and intelligence cooperation with the PLO and reduced the number of scholarships provided to Palestinian students." In at least some cases, "East European intelligence files were handed over to Israel, or otherwise acquired by the Mossad." (Rex Brynen, "Adjusting to a New World Order: the PLO," D. H. Goldberg and Paul Marantz, *The decline of the Soviet Union and the Transformation of the Middle East*, (Boulder, CO: Westview, 1994) p. 177, f 19. Even as recently as on February 4, 1999, Czech President V. Havel asserted that Czech intelligence services have enjoyed considerable prestige in the West because, as he put it, "they have a position in areas where the secret services of large democracies do not have access." According to him this recognition has resulted in political benefits for the Czech Republic and was a factor in its being invited to join NATO in the first wave of expansion (*RFE/RL Newsline*, Vol. 3, No. 24, Part II, 4 Feb. 1999.

18 Robert K. Herrmann, "Russian Policy in the Middle East: Strategic change and tactical contradiction," *Middle East Journal*, Vol. 48, No. 3 (Summer, 1994), p. 463.

19 *Ibid.*

20 Between 1989 and 1993 over 450,000 Jews from the former USSR emigrated to Israel. *New York Times*, (Oct. 5, 1993), p. A6.

21 See *New York Times*, (Sept. 25, 1991), p. A12.

22 "Israeli Embassy reopened after 24 years," *TASS*, (Oct. 24, 1991), in *FBIS-SOV*, 91-206, p. 7.

23 Irina Zviagelskaya and V. Naumkin, "Russia and the Middle East: Continuity and Change," in M. Mesbahi (ed.), *Russia and the Third World in the Post-Soviet Era*, (Gainesville: University of Florida Press, 1994), p. 334.

24 *Izvestia*, (Oct. 30, 1991).

25 *Pravda*, (Sept. 10, 1991). For the American commentary on the Soviet discussion, see Fred Wehling, "Three scenarios for Russia's Middle East policy," *Communist and Post Communist Studies*, Vol. 26, No. 2, (June 1993), pp. 188-189.

26 Zviagelskaya and Naumkin, p. 334.

27 Nicolai N. Petro and Alvin Z. Rubinstein, *Russian Foreign Policy: From Empire to Nation-State*, (New York: Longman, 1996), p. 258.

28 Alexei Vasiliev, *Moscow News*, No. 12 (March 24-31, 1991).

29 *Tass*, (September 20, 1991), (FBIS-USSR, Sept. 23, 1991), p. 10.

30 Zviagelskaya and Naumkin, p. 335.

31 Many personal interviews during my work in Poland from February 1996 to May 1998 and reading of the Polish press. About the attitudes of young Poles, see sociological research by the Polish scholar R. Holly, "The Chinese portrait of Poland's neighbours," *Politics and Individual*, Vol. 3, No. 1 (1993). Some other surveys are giving an even more negative picture of prevalent Polish attitudes towards the Arabs.

32 One of the most recent examples of that was the long and acrimonious dispute among Polish politicians on conflicting proposals concerning the technological equipment of the Polish military helicopter, Huzar. Under American pressure, which supported the

Boeing Company, the new right wing Polish government abrogated the contract with the Israeli Consortium Rafael-Elbit, which had been signed by the previous left-of-centre ruling coalition. For more information, see for instance: "Polowanie na Huzara: Polski rzad szuka sposobow, by zerwac miedzynaroda umowe," *Przeglad Tygodniowy*, No. 7 (18II, 1998), p. 4.

33 Many personal interviews during my work over a period of two years in Poland and reading of the Polish press.

34 The Polish press and two personal interviews in the Polish Ministry of Foreign Affairs in Sept. 1996 and March 1997.

35 Discussions with a senior Palestinian diplomat in Warsaw, Poland, Oct. 1, 1997 and April 30, 1998.

36 For the discussion of his statement, see for instance: "Gieremek wysyla na wojne," (Gieremek is sending for war), *Przeglad Tygodniowy* No. 7 (18 February, 1998), p. 5.

37 *Ibid.*, p. 15. On the other hand, however, on February 19, 1998 the Polish parliament in Warsaw passed a bill by 237 votes to 16, with 134 abstentions, which enabled the government to send to the Gulf 216 army specialists in chemical weapons detection. (*Guardian International*, February 23, 1998, p. 6).

38 Discussion with senior Palestinian diplomat in Warsaw, Oct. 1, 1997 and April 30, 1998. For instance, the former Prime Minister, now Minister of Justice, Hanka Suichocka was one of the international observers during the Palestinian elections in 1996 and later made surprisingly strong pro-Palestinian statements, *Tygodnik Powszechny* (18 February, 1996), p. 6.

39 See f. 35. See also Brynen, p. 182, f. 80. However, in February 1998 the Czech Republic, just as in Poland and Hungary, was ready to commit its forces and facilities to the then planned new American intervention against Iraq. *Guardian International*, (February 23, 1998), p. 6.

40 *Ibid.*

41 *Nezavisimaya Gazeta*, (March 11, 1998), p. 5.

42 For instance, Lithuanian President Valdas Adamkus and Slovak Foreign Minister Eduard Kukan "resolutely supported the strikes," while Polish President Aleksander Kwasniewski stated only that "serious circumstances had compelled the U.S. and Britain to take action." Czech President Vaclev Havel "understands the reasons" for the strikes and a similar statement was issued by the Hungarian Foreign Ministry. Among the other post-Communist East-Central European nations, only Bulgarian Foreign Minister Nadezhda Mihailova took a more critical position, saying that her country was waiting for a "speedy solution" to the crisis and the "suspension of military operations" (*RFE/RL Newsline*, Vol. 2, No. 243, Part II, Dec. 18, 1998).

43 *RFE/RL Newsline*, Vol. 2, No. 242, part II, Dec. 17, 1998.

44 *Ibid.*

45 Several personal interviews with journalists and politicians in Budapest in June 1996. See also f. 34. For instance, in February 1999 Nabil Ali Saat, Minister of Planning and Cooperation of the Palestinian Authority visited Hungary and held talks with high-ranking officials including Foreign Minister Janos Martonji and Economic Minister Attila Chican. Minister Martonji later said that his country wanted to become one of the Palestinian Authority's donor countries and the Palestinian envoy expressed the hope

that the two countries would represent a bridge between the European Union and the Arab World (*RFE/RL Newsline*, Vol. 3, No. 23, Part II, Feb. 3, 1999).

46 *RFE/RL Newsline*, Vol. 2, No. 243, Part II, Dec. 18, 1998.

47 See f. 34.

48 R. Goetz, "Political spheres of interest in the Southern Caucasus and in Central Asia," *Aussenpolitik*, III (1997), p. 266; See also N. N. Petro and Z. Rubinstein, *Russian Foreign Polich: From Empire to Nation-State*, (New York: Longman, 1996), p. 237.

49 Robert O. Freedman, "Russia and the Middle East under Yeltsin," Part I, *DOMES: Digest of Middle Studies*, Vol. VI, No. 2 (Spring 1997), p. 20.

50 Carol R. Saivetz, "Post-Soviet Russian Foreign Policy," William E. Ferry and R. E. Kanet (eds.), *Post Communist States in the World Community*, (London: Macmillan Press, 1998), p. 28.

51 A. Gusher and A. Slabohotov, "Strategiya nacionolnoy Besopanosti Rossii na Juge," (Strategy of Russia's national security in the South), *Afrika i Asia segodnia*, No. 1, 1997, p. 35.

52 Alexei Chistyakov, "The Middle East in the light of geopolitical changes," *International Affairs* (Moscow), No. 8, (1995), p. 51.

53 Stockholm International Peace Research Institute, SIPRI Yearbook 1995. *Armaments, Disarmament and International Security*, (Oxford University Press, 1995), p. 506; See also Alexei Tschistiakov, "Changes in the Middle East and the Outside World," *International Affairs* (Moscow), No. 5, (1994), p. 111. According to him the debts of Syria, Iraq and Libya amount to $28.5 billion.

54 Gusher and Slabohotov, p. 33.

55 Robert V. Barylski, "Russia, the West, and the Caspian Energy Hub," *Middle East Journal*, Vol. 49, No. 2 (Spring 1995), p. 217.

56 *Ibid.* On U.S. policy towards oil in the region, see also Dilip Hiro, "Why is the US inflating Caspian oil prices?," *Middle East International*, (Sept. 12, 1997), pp. 18-19.

57 See for instance V. Isaev, "Rozmyslenija ob arabskoi i rossijskoi neftu," (Meditation on Arab and Russian oil), *Asia i Afrika segodnia*, No. 5, 1994, pp. 5-10.

58 See for instance V. Isaev, "Reanimatsija interesov Rossiji" (Resuscitation of the Russian interests), *Asia i Afrika segodnia*, No. 4, (1997), p. 31.

59 *MERIA*, 12/11/1997, p. 2 (http://www).biu.ac.il/SOC/besa/meria/news.html#A.

60 Roger E. Kanet, A. V. Kozhemiakin, and Susanne M. Birgerson, "The Third World in Russian Foreign Policy," in R. E. Kanet and A. V. Kozhemiakin, *The Foreign Policy of the Russian Federation*, (London: Macmillan, 1997), pp. 171-72.

61 Yemelianova, "Russia and Islam...," p. 289. As in 1997, speaking at a briefing in the Russian Ministry of Foreign Affairs, Deputy Minister V. Posuvaliuk said: Russia "is tied to the Arab world with thousands and thousands of threats: humanitarian, economic and others." (A. Potserebow, "On Russian-Egyptian relations," *International Affairs* (Moscow), Vol. 43, No. 3 (1997), p. 112.

62 V. Polasin, "Kto w Boga wierzy?" (Who believes in God?), *Forum* [Warsaw], (22 March, 1998), p. 7.

63 *Ibid.*

64 A. Tchistiakov, "The Middle East Peace Process: Its new dynamics and new quality," *International Affairs*, (Moscow), No. 11, (1994), p. 50.

65 R. O. Friedmann, "Russia and the Middle East under Yeltsin," part II, *Digest of the Middle East* (DOMES), Vol. 6, No. III, (1997), p. 25.

66 As early as January 15, 1993, Yeltsin turned against the U.S. tendency "to dictate its own terms" concerning policies toward Iraq and Yugoslavia, and stated that Russian foreign policy toward the West "had to be balanced. After all, we are a Eurasian state." Fred Kaplan, "Yeltsin Hits U.S. Policy on Iraq, Yugoslavia," *Boston Globe*, (26 January 1993). For more background information see Suzanne Crow, "Yeltsin Wants Partnership with Asia," *RFE/RL Daily Report*, No. 20 (1 Feb. 1993).

67 Leszek Buszynski, *Russian Foreign Policy After the Cold War*, (Westport, Connecticut: Praeger, 1996), p. 229. For an early presentation of the problem, see Peter Ferdinand, "Russia and Russians after Communism: Western or Eurasian?" *World Today*, (Dec. 1992).

68 Buszynski, p. 229.

69 Paul J. Marantz, "Neither Adversaries nor Partners: Russia and the West Search for a New Relationship," in Roger E. Kanet and A. V. Kozhemiakin, *The Foreign Policy of the Russian Federation*, (London: Macmillan Press Ltd., 1997), p. 82.

70 *Ibid.*

71 For a detailed analysis of the unprecedented Soviet-Russian collapse, see V. Pogodin, "Rossiya i SSZA na poroge XXI veka," (Russia and the USA at the threshold of the XXI century), *Svobodnaya Mysl*, (April 1997), pp. 30-34.

72 *Delovoy Mir*, (March 1, 1996), (FBIS:FSU, April 8, 1996 [Supplement], p. 1).

73 Pogodin, p. 31.

74 *op. cit.*, p. 30.

75 *Vechernaya Moskve*, (28 Jan., 1998).

76 *Middle East International*, (Oct. 9, 1992), p. 8.

77 For an informative summary of American-Russian developments in the 1992-1997 period, see Raymond L. Garthoff, "The United States and the New Russia: The First Five Years," *Current History*, (Oct. 1997), pp. 305-312.

78 Friedmann, "Russia and the Middle East under Yeltsin," p. I, p. 13.

79 Anatoly Kasatkin, "Will the Middle East become a Russian priority?" *International Affairs* (Moscow), No. 7, (1994), p. 58.

80 *Middle East International*, (Oct. 9, 1992), p. 8.

81 *Ibid.*

82 Mohammed M. El Doufani, "Yeltsin's foreign policy – a third world critique," *The World Today*, (June 1993, p. 106).

83 *Middle East International*, (July 9, 1993), p. 5.

84 *Ibid.*

85 *Ibid.*

86 BBC, Summary of World Broadcasts, SV/2052, 20 (July, 1994), B3.

87 *Interfax*, (14 Oct. 1994), *FBIS - Central Eurasia*, (17 Oct. 1994), p. 3; *Interfax*, (24 Oct. 1994), *FBIS - Central Eurasia*, (25 Oct. 1994), p. 3.

88 *FBIS - Central Eurasia*, (19 Oct. 1994), pp. 6-8.

89 For a sample of the American reaction, see Friedmann, part II, pp. 4-5.

90 See for instance *Izvestia*, (10 Oct. 1994), p. 44.

91 *Interfax*, (Feb. 2, 1995), cited in *Commonwealth of Independent States and the Middle East*, (Jerusalem: The Marjorie Mayrock Center for Soviet and East European Research), Vol. 20, Nos. 2-3 (1995), p. 37.

[92] *Itar/Tass*, (February 25), 1994/FBIS-FSU, (April 26, 1994), p. 12. For some revealing comments on the issue, see also M. M. El Doufani, "Futile intervention: Russia's disengagement from the Third World," *International Journal*, 49, (Autumn 1994), p. 869.

[93] For a relatively balanced presentation of the problem from the Russian perspective, see: "Ugrazhaet li Rossiji Panislamism i Islamskij Fundamentalism," (Are Panislamism and Islamic Fundamentalism threatening Russia?) *Asia i Afrika segodnia*, No. 2, (1996), pp. 2-6. According to some researchers, Russia was using the fear of Islamic fundamentalism in the West in order to assert its predominance in post-Soviet Central Asia and the Transcaucasian regions. Lovell Bazanis, "Exploiting the fears of Militant Islam," *Transition*, (Dec. 29, 1995), pp. 6-10.

[94] Friedmann, p. I, p. 27.

[95] *op. cit.*, p. 28.

[96] Pavel Felgengauer, in Segodnija, May 26, 1995 in the *Current Digest of the Post-Soviet Press*, Vol. 47, No. 21 (June 1995), p. 3.

[97] See for instance the joint declaration of President Yeltsin and the Chinese President Jiang Zemin during his visit to Moscow in April 1997, in *The Current Digest of the Post Soviet Press*, Vol. 49, No. 17 (May 28, 1997), pp. 2-4.

[98] Olga Aleksandrova, "The 'Third World' in Russian Foreign Policy," *Aussenpolitik*, III/1996, pp. 244-253.

[99] David Makovsky, "Primakov makes clear Russia cannot be ignored in the Middle East," *Haaretz*, (31 Oct., 1997) <http://www3.haaretz...10/31/97>.

[100] Primakov's predecessor, A. Kozyrev had already, in January 1993, called Russia a Eurasian power whose sphere of influence extends in equal degrees to the West and to the East (*ITAR-TASS*, 26I, 1993 – as quoted by Aleksandrova, p. 250, f. 14. In December 1994 he was even more explicit, expressing his wish that Russia exert its future influence on a global scale, from Yugoslavia to Angola and from Haiti to Tadhikistan (BBC – Summary of World Broadcasts, SV/2189,30/12/1994, p. B10.

[101] Aleksandrova, p. 249.

[102] "Russia's New Middle East Policy," by Middle East Briefing, *MERIA* (12/11/1997). <http;/www.biu.ac:il/SOC/besa/meria/news6.html#A>.

[103] Aleksei Pushkov, "The 'Primakov Doctrine' and a New European Order," *International Affairs*, (Moscow), Vol. 44, No. 2, (1998), p. 12.

[104] According to the well-known Russian Middle Eastern and Third World expert, Georgi Mirsky, "the Middle East is now the only place in the world where Russia can still play a world role. Other areas are practically out of reach." A. Tchistiakov, "Changes in the Middle East and the outside world," *International Affairs*, (Moscow), No. 5 (May 1994), p. 111.

[105] Makovsky.

[106] Friedmann, part I, p. 22.

[107] *Ibid.*

[108] *Middle East International*, (Nov. 7, 1997), p. 6.

[109] *Ibid.* For further discussion of Primakov's 12 point proposal, see: A. Baklanov, "The Iraqi Dossier is not closed," *International Affairs*, (Moscow), Vol. 44, No. 2, (1998), pp. 19-20.

[110] *Globe and Mail*, (Canada), (Nov. 21, 1997), p. A11.

[111] *Rzeczypospolita*, (Warsaw), (13/2/1998), p. 4.

[112] *Nezavisimaya Gazeta*, (February 5, 1998), p. 1.

113 *op. cit.*, p. 3.
114 *Ibid.*
115 *RFE/RL Newsline*, Vol. 2, No. 243, Part I, (Dec. 18, 1998).
116 *Nezavisimaya Gazeta*, (Dec. 18, 1998).
117 *Ibid.*
118 *RFE/RL Newsline*, Vol. 2, No. 243, Part I, (Dec. 18, 1998).
119 *Ibid.*
120 *Nezavisimaya Gazeta*, (Dec. 18, 1998).
121 *RFE/RL Newsline*, Vol. 2, No. 243, Part I, (Dec. 18, 1998).
122 *The Current Digest of the Post-Soviet Press*, Vol. 50, No. 51, (Jan. 20, 1999), p. 5.
123 During the Iraqi Deputy Prime Minister Tariq Aziz's visit to Moscow on November 18, 1997, the Russian spokesman Tarasov stated: "Russia's position remains unchanged ... that the Iraqi authorities must annul their illegal step to impose conditions on UNSCOM. After that, and only after that, should other issues be discussed." *Christian Science Monitor*, (Nov. 21-27, 1997), p. 18.
124 *Guardian International*, (23 February, 1998). According to the U.N. official, the breakthrough came when Primakov told the Iraqis that they could not count on Russian support for a 60-day limit (*Ibid*). For a commentary on the event, see *Guardian* (25 February), p. 6.
125 *RFE/RL Newsline*, Vol. 2, No. 244, Part 1, (21 Dec. 1998).
126 *Middle East International*, (25 Dec., 1998), p. 10.
127 *Nezavisimaya Gazeta*, (Dec. 18, 1998).
128 Y. Primakov, "The world on the eve of the 21st century," *International Affairs*, (Moscow), No. 5/6, Vol. 42 (1996), p. 6.
129 *Kommersant Daily*, (Moscow), (February 20, 1997), p. 2 in *The Current Digest of the Post-Soviet Press*, Vol. 49, No. 8, (March 26, 1997), p. 20.
130 *Ibid.*
131 *op. cit.*, p. 21.
132 *Kommersant Daily*, (March 13, 1997), p. 4 in *The Current Digest of the Post- Soviet Press*, Vol. 49, No. 11 (April 16, 1997), pp. 25-26.
133 Makovsky, *Haaretz*, (31 October, 1997).
134 *Nezavisimaya Gazeta*, (Oct. 9, 1998), p. 6.
135 *Ibid.*
136 *Kommersant Daily*, (August 27, 1997) in *The Current Digest of the Post-Soviet Press*, Vol. 49, No. 34 (Sept. 24, 1997), p. 19.
137 *Nezavisimaya Gazeta*, (September 16, 1997), p. 2 in *The Current Digest of the Post-Soviet Press*, Vol. 49, No. 37 (Oct. 15, 1997), p. 21.
138 *Nezavisimaya Gazeta*, (Feb. 5, 1998), p. 20.
139 *Ibid.*
140 Y. Primakov, speaking to the new intake of young Russian diplomats, stressed that they should consider their country a world player in a world arena, but added: "The role of a world power is not an aim in itself, but a thought-out role for Russia in a difficult, zigzag transition to a multipolar world," *Guardian International*, (March 10, 1998), p. 7.
141 Interview by Primakov in the Italian journal *Limes*, (June-September 1996), pp. 53-56; see also *FBIS - Central Eurasia*, (June 13, 1996), p. 25.

142 R. Goetz, "Political spheres of interest in the Southern Caucasus and in Central Asia," *Aussenpolitik* III, (1997), p. 266.

143 See for instance Geoffrey York, "US vies for influence in Central Asia ...," *Globe and Mail*, (Canada), (November 21, 1997), p. A1 and A10.

144 Adam Tarock, "Iran and Russian 'strategic alliance'," *Third World Quarterly*, Vol. 18, No. 2, (1997), pp. 212-214.

145 *op. cit.*, p. 214.

146 *op. cit.*\., p. 213.

147 *Guardian International*, (March 25, 1998), p. 6, and *BBC World Service*, (February 26, 1998), broadcast at 8 o'clock GST.

148 *Izvestia*, (February 27, 1998), p. 3.

149 Freedman, part I, pp. 27-28.

150 *Guardian International*, (February 25, 1998), p. 6.

151 *Nezavisimaya Gazeta*, (Nov. 24, 1998), p. 6.

152 O. Rezinkova, "Rossija, Turcija i Iran v Centralnoy Asji," *Mirovaya Ekonomika i Mezdunarodnyje Otnoshenija*, No. 1, (1997), p. 57.

153 *Ibid.*

154 Segodnija, (February 27, 1998), p. 3 in *The Current Digest*, Vol. 50, No. 9 (April 1, 1998), p. 23.

155 Rezinkova, p. 57.

156 *op. cit.*, p. 63.

157 One of the recent examples of these efforts was organized at Turkey's initiative – a two-day meeting of the foreign ministers of Turkey, Azerbaijan, Georgia, Kazakstan, and Turkmenistan in Istanbul on March 1-2, 1998. The ministers discussed the problems of transport routes for Caspian oil and gas to the West, and neither Russia nor Iran had been invited. See *Komersant Daily*, (March 4, 1998), p. 5 in *The Current Digest*, Vol. 50, No. 9 (April 1, 1998), pp. 23-24. For some background information see also Marshall Ingwerson, "At your local gas pump soon: Caspian Sea Oil," *Christian Science Monitor*, (Oct. 11, 1995).

158 Roland Goetz, p. 262 and 263.

159 Freedman, p. II, p. 21.

160 An optimistic outlook for the future of Turkish-Russian relations was strongly expressed by the speaker of the Turkish Parliament, Mustapha Kalemly during his visit to Moscow in January 1997. *Asia i Afrika*, (1/1997), pp. 7-8.

161 *Washington Times*, (September 10, 1993).

162 *Middle East International*, (25 Dec.,1998).

163 A. Chistyakov, "The Middle East in the light of the geopolitical changes," *International Affairs*, (Moscow) No. 8 (1995), pp. 48 and 51.

164 *Izvestia*, (March 13, 1997), p. 31 in the *Current Digest of the Post-Soviet Press*, Vol. 49, No. 11 (1997), pp. 25-26.

165 "Russia's New Middle East Policy," *MERIA*, (11/12/1997).

166 *Nezavisimaya Gazeta*, (September 23, 1997), pp. 1, 5, in the *Current Digest of the Post-Soviet Press*, Vol. 49, No. 38 (1997), p. 20.

167 *Kommersant Daily*, (April 9, 1997), p. 3 in the *Current Digest*, Vol. 49, No. 14 (1997), p. 23.

168 *Ibid.*

169 *Nezavisimaya Gazeta*, (February 12, 1998), p. 2.

170 Roland Goetz, "Russia's Economic Potential as a basis for its foreign policy," *Aussenpolitik*, (11/1996), p. 145.

171 *Ibid.*

172 Olga Alexandrova, "The 'Third World' in Russian Foreign Policy," *Aussenpolitik*, (III/1996), pp. 246-247.

173 *Op. cit.*, p. 253.

174 The author wants, however, to mention here the important role of Romania during the Ceausescu period in the 1970s and 1980s when the country played the role of an intermediary in setting up contacts between Arabs and Israelis.

175 It is particularly well understood by many Israeli observers and politicians, including some leading members of the right wing parties, and often articulated in the Israeli press.

176 The well-known Russian scholar A. Vasiliev is even apt to argue "Russia's destiny will coincide in some respects with the destinies of the Middle East countries and will serve as an example for them." (*Russian Policy in the Middle East*, p. 370).

9 A New Orientalism: Europe Confronts the Middle East

PHILIP MARFLEET

During the 1990s, relations between the Middle East and its European neighbours officially entered a new era. States in the two regions pledged mutual commitment to "peace, security and stability", to be achieved "by all means."[1] Formal statements noted the two regions' common challenges and the need for exchange and co-operation, tolerance and shared prosperity:[2] such was the tone of amity that Euro-Mediterranean liaisons were dubbed "Club Med". Europe appeared to want a long-term relationship which put regional ties on a new footing: what the European Union (EU) called "a quiet but effective dialogue"[3] to establish a new partnership for the 21st century. By the end of the decade, however, the relationship was already under strain: according to one analysis, "lack of will" meant that even in it's the earliest phases the collaboration was in difficulty.[4]

How should these developments be assessed? An effective, long-term co-operation across the Mediterranean would raise serious questions about recent analyses of political, social and cultural relationships between the two regions. Since the collapse of the Communist bloc, it has been argued, the Middle East has become the focus for Western anxiety and political hostility. Islam – and by extension the Middle East – has become the preferred global antagonist. Esposito observes that in place of the "Red Menace" has come fear of "the Green Menace".[5] In a similar vein Delanty comments that for European states "the East" remains a focus of hostility, "the only difference being that it has been pushed further southward."[6] The formal aims of the Euro-Mediterranean Partnership suggest a different perspective and hold an implication that such analyses are inappropriate.

The new agreements also raise questions about historic relations between the two regions. Although European society has often shown a particular fascination with the Middle East, its concern has been above all an aspect of Western domination.[7] Said has argued that centuries of unequal relations have been a decisive element in the very *making* of Europe – that a subordinate Middle East has been "an integral part of European material civilization."[8] If recent changes offer different – and equal – relations between the regions they suggest that the legacy of colonialism is finally being addressed, to the benefit of the Middle East region. Evidence of an insubstantial or false relationship, however, might be seen as confirmation that old inequalities are being reasserted.

From Dialogue to Partnership: Club Med

In November 1995, foreign ministers of 27 European and Middle East states met in Barcelona to establish the Euro-Mediterranean Partnership. Their aim was to agree to principles for close collaboration: according to the EU's strategy document, "to promote a relationship of good neighbourliness.[9]

Fifteen participants represented states of the EU; the others being Turkey, Israel, Malta, Cyprus, and eight Arab countries: Algeria, Egypt, Jordan, Lebanon, Morocco, Syria, Tunisia, and the Palestinian National Authority (PNA). The conference was in effect a Euro-Middle East forum; more significantly, a Euro-Arab engagement, for not only did Arab states dominate the "Mediterranean" delegation but their specific development needs were prioritised on the summit's main agenda. The ambitious program finally agreed in a Barcelona Declaration pledged rapid movement towards a Mediterranean free-trade zone, together with agreements on security, energy, water, migration, and enhanced cultural relationships between peoples of the two regions.

The Partnership has since been constructed as a series of cross-cutting ties between governments of the two regions, the EU's supra-national bodies, and large numbers of public and private institutions in Europe and the Middle East. It has been directed by an annual meeting of foreign ministers of participant states and a "permanent follow-up mechanism" to track progress on strategic decisions.[10] Such a structure is a complex, closely monitored network of activities which is without parallel in the history of the EU. The financial commitment is also unprecedented: during the first five years over $6 billion was to be provided in grant aid to Mediterranean states, with an equivalent sum made available in loans through the European Investment Bank (EIB). The European Commission anticipated that a further $12 billion would be forthcoming from individual EU states.[11] These sums dwarf those made available by the EU to other regions of the Third World, even those with which the Union has well-established economic links.[12]

Of equal significance was the warm, almost fraternal character of EU observations about its new partners. According to EU officials, the new initiative was to be understood in the context of European convictions that "the Mediterranean and Middle East are vital interests."[13] The tone was one of high enthusiasm, with the relationship described as "a dialogue for peace and security" and "a unique forum."[14] It was also presented as a means to project European influence to the heart of Middle Eastern and especially Arab affairs. The EU had a high profile at Middle East and North Africa economic conferences held in Casablanca in 1994, Amman in 1995 and Cairo in 1996. Speaking at the Cairo meeting, the then President of the EU Council of Ministers, Irish Foreign Minister Dick Spring, identified strong ties between Europe and its partners "determined by links of history, the facts of geography and the thick network of relationships with the Middle East."[15]

Subsequently the EU appeared to intervene more directly in regional politics, notably in the Arab-Israeli peace process. In November 1996 its special representative to the process, Migel Angel Moratinos, seemed to suggest that Europe would take the initiative, asserting that, "We [European states] have a space to fill. We could play a role of confidence building between the parties [and] contribute to an atmosphere of trust."[16] Such comments led to suggestions that the Partnership had been conceived as a means of offering competition to the United States as the main Western player in Middle East politics. EU officials were indeed eager to assert that their involvement embraced "security" issues as well as economic matters[17] and Arab analysts suggested that this might have reflected European states' greater sense of freedom in regional policy-making since the end of the Cold War.[18]

Contrasts with earlier European ventures in the Middle East could hardly be more marked. The European Commission itself has argued that the new arrangement has in part been a response to criticism that "previous forms of co-operation had produced disappointing results.[19] Such comments invite a specific comparison between the terms of the Partnership and those of the abortive Euro-Arab Dialogue of the 1970s. They also raise questions over whether the outcome of today's experiment can be different, avoiding the allegations of cynicism and bad faith against Europe which followed collapse of the earlier initiative.

"Sop to the Arabs"

The Dialogue of the 1970s marked an important moment in Euro-Arab relations. Although it was conceived as a bridge across an old divide – and in this sense began by formalizing East-West difference – it nonetheless promised to revise a tradition of mutual hostilities which had been strongly emphasized during the anti-colonial struggles of the 1950s and 1960s. In initiating new links European states seemed at first to recognize the realities of a post-colonial world and to promise a new approach. But failure re-emphasized European distance from the Middle East, not only at the level of politics but also at that of socio-cultural relations, where European assurances of advance soon proved meaningless.

The Dialogue had begun as an initiative by European states attempting to deal with the energy crisis that followed the 1973 Arab-Israeli war. The oil boycott associated with the conflict had exposed the then nine members of the European Economic Community (EEC), all of which were dependent upon Middle East energy resources. In November 1973 the nine therefore embarked upon their first collective Middle East policy, emphasizing the need for a peace in which Arab rights would be recognized. British political analyst Edward Mortimer commented that the climate was "hardly an ideal one in which to embark on a Euro-Arab dialogue, but it least it made Western Europeans aware that the Arab world was an area of some importance, with which they were obliged to have relations."[20]

Arab states responded enthusiastically. The Europeans seemed to be suggesting a bi-regional arrangement, which went far beyond existing diplomatic links and would supersede the state-by-state relationships of the EEC's Global Mediterranean Policy – a highly restrictive trade program.[21] Within days of the EEC declaration an Arab summit appealed to Europe to recall that it was "linked to the Arab countries across the Mediterranean by deep affinities of civilization and by vital interests which could not be developed except in a situation of trusting and mutually beneficial co-operation."[22]

The Europeans could not respond in such positive terms, however. Despite the EEC's anxiety over oil, progress on implementing the Dialogue was fitful, especially as European states came under American pressure to exclude matters concerning energy and Israel. By 1975 a joint memorandum had nonetheless been agreed which proposed active links between the two regions. In a statement of intent which was to find an echo in the Barcelona Declaration of 1995, participants undertook to reduce the technological gap between Europe and the Arab world and to establish joint committees on agricultural and rural development, finance, science, technological and cultural collaboration.

The Europeans were never more than lukewarm. Even formal statements drafted ostensibly to indicate concern for Middle East peace revealed a modest enthusiasm. The Venice Declaration of 1980, for example, recognized that relations with the Middle East were shaped by factors beyond EEC control: these would "oblige [EEC members] to play a special role" and "require them to work in a more concrete way towards peace."[23] It went on to call for a just Middle East peace and even hinted at recognition of the PLO. But Venice proved the high point of the Dialogue. For a few more years the Europeans continued to make diplomatic gestures until in the early 1980s the Dialogue petered out.

In a post-mortem, Palestinian economist Yusif Sayigh observed that the Dialogue had been a specific, highly instrumental initiative, intimately associated with movements in the oil market:

> If I am allowed to be brutally frank, I will suggest that the Europeans encouraged a Euro-Arab dialogue in the 1970s mostly as a sop to the Arabs. The Europeans entered the dialogue in the 1970s mostly to humour the Arabs and to satisfy their *amour-propre* and newfound power, and also to get as much of their oil money as possible in orders for a wide range of goods and services. I wonder therefore if there is at all scope for a serious dialogue in the second half of the 1980s, given the eclipse of the oil power of the Arabs...[24]

There was in fact a series of issues affecting the Middle East which might have engaged European attention throughout the 1980s: the Iranian revolution of 1979; war between Iran and Iraq; Israel's invasion of Lebanon; American military offensives against "radical" states; and the Palestinian *intifada.* The EEC kept its distance, however; released from the specific pressures exerted by the oil crisis of the 1970s, it focused increasingly upon events in the Soviet Union and Eastern Europe. The Dialogue expired, revealing its shortcomings as van Nieuwenhuize called a "deception ... about short-term goals unachieved because misconceived."

Politics of Difference

Some Western observers saw the EEC's style of engagement with the Arab world as proof of the shallowness of European interest in the Middle East as a whole. As Mortimer observed wearily of official European attitudes in the mid-1980s: "Too many of us [Europeans] seem to take a purely mercenary attitude to the Arab world: we want your oil and your money but we are bored by your political grievances and show no more than a polite and condescending interest in your culture.[25]

But on the Arab side there was something firmer: a renewed conviction that even in the post-colonial era, Europe remained committed *against* effective collaboration with the Middle East. On this view, rather than exhibiting boredom or condescension in relation to the Middle East, Europe's leaders were demonstrating a familiar and deeply rooted hostility towards the region. Content to maintain bilateral relations with local states, notably the oil-producers, they remained reluctant to develop a positive approach to the region as a whole and were hostile to the notion of any collaborative venture.

Mansour argued that events proved there could be no organic link between European and Arab states. Despite their aspirations, states of the Maghreb, for example, would never be permitted to enter the EEC:

> It is a groundless hope, not only because of the enormous differences in levels of economic development between Europe and the Maghreb but perhaps more importantly, because of the cultural differences which Europe is not likely to forgive or forget in any near future, since its whole modern civilization, and not only its capitalism, is impregnated with a pronounced sense of exclusion of other cultures – especially the Arab-Muslim culture which for a number of centuries stood geographically too close, as its mentor and rival."[26]

On this account, the politics of engagement with the Middle East have remained inseparable from what Said calls Europe's "irreducible opposition to a region of the world ... considered alien to its own."[27] Here, European states are unable to articulate with the Orient by means other than assertion of an imagined superiority.

When the failed decade of Euro-Arab Dialogue was followed, paradoxically, by a far more assertive European engagement such views seemed to gain significance. In 1990 the key European states joined or endorsed the United States' Desert Storm coalition. Oil was again the centre of attention as the disinterest of the Dialogue was replaced by vigorous efforts directed against Iraq. The extreme violence used against a former ally which had violated regional power relations constituted, in Hentsch's words, "execution of sentence ... consummation of the sacrifice."[28] It seemed that European states were indeed deeply concerned with the Middle East, but only to the extent that direct economic and political interests were at stake and only to confirm a "deadly frontier" between East and West.[29] It is against this background that the sudden turn of the EU, with its new visions of amity, needs to be assessed.

Neighbours: Barcelona

The Barcelona Declaration provided for three levels of collaboration. The first was in the form of multilateral efforts at political, economic and social dialogue. The second turned around establishment of a series of Euro-Mediterranean Association agreements. Urgent early work before the Barcelona summit produced agreements with Tunisia and Morocco and by 1995 talks were under way with Egypt, Jordan, Lebanon and the PNA. According to the EU, by 2020 a comprehensive set of agreements would allow creation of a Mediterranean free-trade area. The third level of collaboration brought into being what the EU called "a raft of decentralized cooperation programs with key players in civil society."[30] These were to link hundreds of institutions across Europe and the Mediterranean: universities (through Med Campus); media organizations (Med Media); local authorities (Med Urbs); and agencies in specific fields such as technology transfer (Med Techno), investment (Med Invest) and migration (Med Migration).

There was some puzzlement when the scale and scope of the project became apparent. For decades concern for oil interests and sensitivity to oil prices had been the key factors shaping Europe's Middle East policies. Following the Gulf crisis of 1990-91 the oilfields had been judged secure, while oil prices fell steadily, and a further period of cautious European diplomacy might have been anticipated. In some Middle East states there was therefore unease at the ambitious character of the project. In Egypt, for example, diplomats involved in pre-Barcelona negotiations were called upon to provide assurances that the country would not be locked into arrangements it might later find unacceptable.[31]

It was difficult to discern an economic rationale of the type that had often prompted European intervention in the region. The EU already enjoyed a huge advantage vis-à-vis the Mediterranean region. According to Khader, by the mid-1990s, combined GNP of non-EU Mediterranean countries was less than 5 per cent of the GNP of Mediterranean European states and a fraction of the total for the EU as a whole.[32] Despite the proximity of the regions, the Mediterranean hardly featured in EU direct investment: only about 1% of global private European investment went to southern Mediterranean countries.[33]

In trade, Europe had more obvious concerns. By 1994 Mediterranean states received some 29% of all EU exports to developing countries.[34] This figure had not increased dramatically, however, and with more and more of world trade taking place between the "Triad" regions (Europe, Japan and North America), the Mediterranean share in EU world totals was not especially significant. On the other hand, the EU had long dominated Mediterranean states' global trade. According to Lister, by 1992 countries of the Maghreb were directing some 70% of their exports to the Union, making them "economically dependent" upon Europe.[35]

In the late 1980s the EU had noted the need for enhanced trade relations with the Middle East, which it viewed as a region in which Europe should compete more effectively with global rivals, notably the US and Japan.[36] But this was not prioritised as a strategic task for the Union. In fact, narrowly defined economic interests could not account for the change in approach formalized at Barcelona. Some European critics of the Partnership believed that they had an explanation, one that focused less upon the EU's economic concerns than upon its politicians' perception of new political threats posed by the Middle East. At an "alternative conference" held in Barcelona during the 1995 summit they alleged that the EU was not inspired by the wish for closer relations with its southern neighbours but by the desire for greater *isolation* from them. The main aim of the EU, it was argued, was to formalize agreements which would inhibit migration from the Middle East, especially the movement of people perceived by European governments and the EU as bearing malign political and cultural influences, notably those associated with Islam.[37]

This analysis maintained that Barcelona was a key structural component of "Fortress Europe", the attempt to seal the EU against penetration from without, especially against movement of people into Europe from countries of the South. In exchange for unprecedented sums of development aid, Arab governments were being induced to intensify efforts against domestic opposition movements and to restrict the movement of migrants who were judged unsuitable for settlement in Europe.

Well-briefed analysts in the European media had started to reach similar conclusions. In Britain *The Guardian* commented that processes set in train by the summit would soon become wrapped in the "elusive jargon which envelopes EU initiatives.[38] It was therefore important to spell out the real agenda at Barcelona, commented the newspaper. This was dominated by European states' concern that unfulfilled expectations among the youthful and growing populations of North Africa would lead to increased migratory pressures and to the spread of Islamic "fundamentalism".[39] The initiative was, therefore, an attempt to cope with the frustrated hopes of "the youngsters in Tetouan [Morocco]," the program of radical religious activism, and the attempt to manage crises likely to reassert old Muslim-Christian rivalries.[40]

Here, the Partnership did not mark a co-operation of European and Middle Eastern peoples but celebrated their perceived *differences* – those defined on the basis of an old religio-cultural dichotomy. New relations were not to be established; rather, earlier hostilities were being recognized and formalized. If there was indeed a "deadly frontier" between East and West, this was being given a physical manifestation that of the Mediterranean, now officially depicted as the barrier separating Europe from a historic adversary.

Urgent action

There were also strong criticisms of the Partnership from within structures of the EU. Members of the European Parliament alleged that Meda had been established hastily and without consideration for Europe's relations with other regions of the Third World. They criticized a "clearly political" shift in EU development policy. According to Glenys Kinnock, then leader of the Socialist group in the Parliament, by 1996 re-direction of aid to the Middle East had already subverted development work in regions such as Sub-Saharan Africa, leaving the latter "a lost cause."[41] The comments were endorsed by Solidar, an association of welfare agencies in Europe, which argued that aid policy had been reshaped to the benefit of Arab states and at great cost to needy areas elsewhere.[42] Oxfam declared that it was "disturbed by the trend … we think that aid should be used for the relief of poverty, distress and suffering. Instead it seems to be being used as an extension of EU foreign policy."[43]

According to Kinnock, the Meda budget itself was accessed with indecent haste. When ECU254 million was drawn down during its first month of operation in 1996, she declared: "God knows how they've done it. I cannot believe it represents good quality programs. To deliver that kind of money so quickly seems quite extraordinary."[44] The EU's own Court of Auditors reported "significant irregularities" in implementing Meda projects in Arab states, noting conflicts of interest, missing evidence and breaches of rules in 30 public contracts.[45]

Academic observers also noted a very rapid shift in EU aid strategy. Only two years after Barcelona, Parfitt noted that support to the African, Caribbean and Pacific (ACP) countries under the terms of the Lome Convention – which had shaped aid strategy for 20 years – no longer stood at the centre of the EU's development policy. In its place was "an enhanced relationship with the NMMS [Non-Member Mediterranean States]."[46] One casualty of this rapid redirection of aid was the long-term development program, earlier a feature of EU policy of "aid to the poorest". Detailed long-term plans did not feature among the Barcelona provisions.

Meda programs as a whole appear to have been devised with unusual haste. This is consistent with EU strategists' concern to develop *urgently* new policies towards a region they depicted as increasingly threatening and dangerous. From the late 1980s, EU analyses had begun to identify linked problems of population growth, unemployment, migration and radical Islamism. In 1992 they suggested that Maghrebi society as a whole had been seriously affected, arguing that "huge numbers of people – particularly young people – without work are easily seduced by intolerant and anti-democratic ideologies that find fertile ground in these countries with their young and sometimes fragile democratic institutions."[47] By 1994 threats from the region were depicted in even more sinister terms: conditions in North African states made for "instability leading to mass migration, fundamentalist extremism, terrorism, misuse of drugs and organized crime."[48] EU officials concluded: "These have a harmful effect both upon the region itself and on the Union.[49]

During preparatory meetings for the Barcelona summit, Spanish Foreign Minister Javier Solana warned of "a kind of paranoia" across Europe about threats emanating from the Middle East. This situation demanded action, he maintained, for unless radical measures were taken, old conflicts might resume:

> Look at the disparity in incomes between north and south, combine that with population growth and you have the ingredients for conflict between Islam and Europe that has made up so much of the unhappy history of the Mediterranean.[50]

In the face of such a prospect – real or imagined – EU leaders were to launch a pre-emptive strike. In the words of leading Spanish politician Manuel Marin, "The only way to quell extremism is to offer people [in North Africa] real hope of prosperity."[51] For the EU's senior political strategists the Partnership was, therefore, conceived as a means of killing the North African "threat" with kindness – with the prospect of rapid economic change, social advance and political stability. In this context the Partnership amounted to an emergency package of measures, which the EU hoped would induce passivity among the populations of the Arab world.

Green Menace

"Paranoia" among European politicians about an insurgent Islam can indeed be interpreted as the stimulus for the whole EU initiative. In a review of relations between Islam and the West during the early 1990s *The Economist* had identified a pervasive European fear of the Middle East associated with widespread expectation of conflict. The rise of religious activism had prompted both anxiety and anticipation, the magazine argued:

> This is what sets scalps tingling ... among Europeans. They see the Last Ideology on the march. A Muslim Crescent cuts threateningly around the southern and eastern edges of Europe. A new cold war could be on the way. And it may not stop at being a cold war.[52]

Islam had become Europe's "fundamental fear", *The Economist* concluded: "The future war that many people are now talking about [is] a general war between Islam and the West.[53]

There was a vast range of historical references around which the idea of such confrontation could be developed. As a series of critics of the Orientalist perspective have argued, from the earliest colonial times European states sought means to assert national ideologies, which were simultaneously rationales for domination in the wider world. The "Orient" which was thus imagined and integrated into ideologies that served European rulers, what Hentsch calls the "deadly frontier", was a borderline constructed *within* cultures of the West. Here perceptions of the East became aspects of differentiation internal to European society, providing rationales for local national loyalties that were consistent with the idea of violation by Europe of "alien" cultures. This process left indelible marks on European society itself.[54] A repertoire of images of difference has since been available to assert European identity in relation to an alien East always requiring subordination.

But to identify a new "Green Menace" is still far from an adequate explanation for the seriousness of the EU's initiative. There have been many recent anti-Muslim panics: the Iranian upheaval of 1979, for example, was greeted in the West as what Esposito terms "a revolution which had made the unthinkable a reality," generating a mood of "hysteria" towards Islam.[55]

On this occasion European states did not modify their collective approach towards the Middle East; indeed, this was the moment of *collapse* of the Euro-Arab Dialogue.

Persistent currents within European thought do indeed view Islam as a violent, vengeful and irrational ideology that the West is obliged to confront. It is unwise, however, to see such attitudes alone as shaping major political developments. Even strategists of the North Atlantic Treaty Organization (NATO) have felt obliged to warn of the dangers of such spasms. In a document on Islamic radicalism in the 1990s, they caution that the reaction of Western public opinion to Islamic movements "often borders on panic ... a confusion [stemming] partly from the extreme prominence given to Islamic terrorism [sic] in the media."[56] Other factors have been at work in consolidating Europe's approach to the Middle East. These are associated with conflict and change *within* Europe and with the attempt to construct a new European coherence – an effective economic union, a political "harmonization", and a new pan-European cultural identity.

Towards a 'New Europe': Crisis of identity

From the mid-1980s most states of Western Europe were deeply engaged in efforts to integrate within a supra-national entity. Their efforts had begun in the 1940s, when in the wake of war and in the face of perceived threats from the Communist East; the United States had encouraged formation of a European Common Market (EEC). As Milward and others have made clear, this strategy was consistent with the interests of specific national states: indeed, co-operation among the dominant European capitalisms was regarded as essential if they were to survive post-war instabilities and compete effectively within a much-changed world economic system.[57] As Harman has observed, such co-operation could be a basis for development of European states, which might allow positive integration of rival capitalist classes towards "the state structure of a European super-power" while avoiding the traumatic conflicts of earlier eras.[58]

Greatly assisted by the "long boom" in the world economy which lasted until the early 1970s, the EEC emerged as both a customs union and as an embryonic trans-nationalism. There were many conflicts, especially rivalries between the dominant founding states, France and Germany, later involving Britain, which joined the EEC in 1973. Governments engaged in intense disputes over allocation of EEC resources and power sharing, but their leaders continued to accept the requirement for a collaboration, which could assert European interests within an increasingly competitive world system. They were also affected by the rise of neo-liberal economic theory as a new global orthodoxy and by complementary notions of globalisation, which depicted an unstoppable process of world integration. The overall impact was to intensify efforts to place Western Europe advantageously vis-à-vis its main economic rivals.

Hirst and Thompson describe the EU that emerged by the early 1990s as "the most ambitious project of multinational economic governance in the modern world."[59] The Union had a continuing problem, however, in reconciling its multi*national* character with the agenda of increased integration. This difficulty intensified in the early 1990s as economic crisis affected each of the member states, prompting governments to compete more energetically for EU resources. Each also used the EU as an arena for political contests in which they hoped to gain attention from a domestic audience. Callinicos describes the structure which emerged from these struggles through the Maastricht Treaty of 1991 as a "bizarre European amalgam of supranational institutions and inter-governmental co-operation."[60]

By the early 1990s continental economic recession had also created circumstances under which local nationalisms could assert themselves with new vigour. In some countries there was increased resistance from below to unemployment and state welfare cuts, prompting establishment parties to reassert nationalist themes. The conjuncture of official "Europhilia" with an efflorescence of nationalism expressed all the contradictions of the European project: an attempt to integrate states with distinct national histories, institutions and nationalisms. These traditions were integral to ideologies of each state and at times of crisis were reasserted strongly. One outcome was rapid growth of the extreme right. Jenkins and Sofos comment on its "startling success" in France at this period, and on the "disturbing historical echoes in the reunified Germany and in Italy."[61] Fascist movements such as the National Front (FN) in France and the Republican Party (REP) in Germany found a wide audience, especially for populist "solutions" to unemployment and welfare cuts which targeted foreigners and various internal enemies. Thus in Germany, Mitchell and Russell identify the crisis of the early 1990s associated with recession and with reunification as the key factor in producing "a dramatic change in the nature and intensity of racist hostility and violence towards 'foreigners'."[62]

Increased influence of the extreme right heightened state racism, especially in immigration policy. In Germany, notes Knischewski, anxieties about migrants and asylum-seekers were "demagogically instrumentalized" in party-political campaigns for federal state elections.[63] In France de Wenden recorded "a shift of emphasis in migration policies." Such policies were no longer placed in the context of economic objectives, or "clothed in technocratic discourse":

> Immigration policies are now formed in response to the collective insecurities and imaginings governing public opinion; the clampdown on illegal immigrants, the need for tighter border controls, the threat of delinquency and of religious fundamentalism, the perceived loss of French identity, and fears of demographic invasion are characteristic reactions.[64]

Central to the generalized "clampdown" on immigration was a focus upon migrants from the Middle East. The notion of an intrusive, alien Islam was common to the extreme right across the EU. It depicted the Middle East, as the site of a demographic explosion from which human debris was being deposited in Europe, despoiling the latter's cultural integrity. Evans notes that in France:

> What Le Pen constantly reiterates is the demographic explosion taking place in the Third World. At the moment the population of North Africa is 50 million; by the year 2000 it will have reached over 100 million. The image Le Pen conjures up is one of this population literally spilling over to submerge France in what he calls "a wave of Third world misery."[65]

For the right, summary removal of migrants from the region was required in order to avoid contamination of national society by "a religion which is intolerant and intransigent", an Islam "whose aim is the eventual dominance of France."[66] Similarly in Germany the REP and DVU (German People's Union) called for the repatriation of all Turks, part of a program which mobilized explicitly Nazi notions such as that of national "living space".[67] A "paranoia" about the Middle East identified by Javier Solana at the Barcelona Summit reflected the extent to which some of these ideas had been absorbed by mainstream politicians and were affecting the agenda of national governments and of the EU itself.

'A gilded cage'

By the late 1980s the EU was widely viewed as a key player in global affairs, even as a superpower.[68] Increased expectations of the Union were not matched by increased coherence, however, and by the end of the decade it was in a state of permanent internal crisis, soon worsened by recession and by increasingly strident demands from local nationalists. In 1989 the President of the European Commission, Jacques Delors, attempted to bring problems to a head, calling for a move towards fuller integration in the key area of economic policy. He proposed "a transfer of decision-making power from member states to the Community as a whole ... in the fields of monetary policy and macro-economic management."[69] Delors immediately faced opposition from the German government, however, which viewed the prospect as a threat to its own financial regime and to the Deutschmark. There were similar difficulties in foreign policy, security and legal matters, where the Maastricht Treaty eventually provided only for political co-operation between governments, rather than for trans-national decision-making.

Cohen and Joly commented on the level of internal conflict in the EU during this period: "They [member states] find it difficult to decide whether to belong to a common political or economic association – and bicker endlessly about lamb imports, agricultural subsidies, monetary policy and the potential shape of a possible political union.[70] They also noted, however, that in one area – that of immigration – EU members were collaborating to great effect. Here, policy had quietly emerged from a series of ministerial meetings. Unprecedented close co-operation was producing a "Fortress Europe" – a genuine transnational collaboration, which aimed to seal the EU against penetration by migrants and refugees.

Among a cluster of secretive treaties, the Schengen Agreement was the most far-reaching. Signed initially by France, Germany and the Benelux countries in 1985, Schengen had been joined by a series of other states. It provided for passport-free movement within the territories of signatory states – so-called "Schengenland". "Free" movement, however, was to be accompanied by a strict policy of exclusion of persons deemed "ineligible" for entry. Cohen and Joly observed that the Europe that had emerged from this co-operation, "looks more and more like a gilded cage with Ministers of the Interior bracing and painting the bars."[71] By the 1990s, this structure represented the highest level of European collaboration.

Consistent with their role as guardians of the Fortress, EU officials now depicted Europe as a region under threat from vast numbers of unwanted migrants, especially those advancing from Eastern Europe and North Africa. Collapse of the Stalinist regimes had already produced warnings within the EU of a migratory assault from Eastern Europe. Castles and Miller observe that, "by 1990, a new spectre haunted Europe: that of an influx from the East ... mass migration on a scale not seen since the collapse of the Roman Empire.[72] "Buffer" states such as Poland received financial support from Western European neighbours, notably Germany, to contain the expected "hordes".[73] Some migrants were indeed detained and deported[74] but no sooner had the idea of a mass assault been conjured than it proved illusory. Burgess later noted: "There has been no mass influx ... yet few have highlighted this fact – even to draw a public sigh of relief that these peoples did not arrive on our [sic] doorsteps."[75] He suggested that the sense of demographic threat was not based on "real analysis or experience" but on continued prejudice towards a perceived "unstable East": "fear of foreign numbers is an expression of Western anxieties, not Eastern realities."[76]

Burgess concluded that the Western European focus "has now shifted to keeping out immigrants from North Africa."[77] In fact, the perceived Middle Eastern threat had long been central within EU thinking; by 1990 it was dominant, not only because the vision of Eastern European invasion could not be sustained but because the EU was already engaged in redrawing its eastern borders. With German unification accomplished all Cold War borders were being reassessed - in the territorial, political and cultural senses. A Western Europe that had been defined for 40 years against the Communist East was now ready to admit selected eastern neighbours in a "common European home". The European borderline required redefinition, especially for the purposes of bringing minimal unity to a fractured, conflict-ridden Union. It is in this sense that Delanty viewed the Middle East as the location of "a new post-Communist bogey", Europe's old historical frontiers being restored as "the East" is pushed southwards.[78]

EU officials now argued more aggressively that population pressures in the Maghreb were producing a "demographic gradient", along which hordes of migrants could be expected to advance, violating Europe's borders in both the physical and cultural senses. In 1991 a report for the Western European Union warned that emigration from the region was likely to affect Europe's internal stability and the conduct of its economic affairs.[79] At the same time, the EU produced a study focusing on the implications for migration of the "population explosion in the Maghreb."[80] Collinson comments on the growing importance at this period of "apocalyptic images of a Europe under siege."[81]

Some of the arguments invoked by EU officials were particularly crude. Lister notes that the prospect of increased migration from the southern to the northern shore of the Mediterranean was "frequently referred to by Commission officials, politicians and academics as a 'threat', a 'population bomb' or 'time bomb'."[82] Media quickly took up this neo-Malthusianism across Europe, becoming part of the international scenario within which Europe's wider relations were defined.[83] By the time of the Barcelona Summit in 1995, the European states' agenda was described as one intended to slow "huge migratory flows to the old [sic] Continent."[84]

The official EU scenario reproduced much of the analysis favoured by the extreme right. Little attention was given to analyses of migration, which reached less alarmist conclusions. On population growth, UNICEF found that rates of increase across the Third World were declining sharply; in the Maghreb, fertility fell by an average of more than one child per women between 1980 and 1991.[85] Investigating migratory pressures on Europe, *The Guardian* concluded that the idea of a threat from the Middle East was "certainly a fantasy."[86] The idea had nonetheless been central in consolidating exclusionary policies, for as Buzan and Roberson observe, "when viewed through the lens of societal security...a potentially more plausible vision of the threat comes into focus."[87]

'Europeanity': Choosing citizens

Construction of Fortress Europe was inseparable from attempts within the EU to define "Europeanity" – the quality of "Europeanness" said to reside in people of the Union. As migration controls tightened it became more important to define who possessed rights of residence and movement within the new Europe. Equally, absence of "Europeanity" and of such rights was to be a basis for denial of citizenship and of rights of entry to territories of the Union. Who is a "European"? Citizenship of European states had long been associated with specific *national* definitions. It had therefore varied according to the complex of traditions mobilized by such states and included various references to place of birth, language, ethnic status, cultural heritage, ancestry, and "blood". The quality of "belonging" to France, Italy, Germany or other states was itself constructed on the basis of *difference*, especially differences associated with intra-European national rivalries and with the European colonial venture.

Smith has commented on the difficulty this presented to ideologues of a new Europe. The EU, he observes, is a recent construction, which rests upon a specific strategy for economic and political integration. Unable to mobilize the traditions associated with national states, its ideologues are left merely with the outline of a European "culture". He observes:

> Here lies the new Europe's true dilemma, a choice between [national] historical myths and memories on the one hand, and on the other a patchwork, memoryless scientific 'culture', held together solely by the political will and economic interest that are so often subject to change.[88]

Eurocrats have also expressed their anxiety that a "memoryless" culture is inadequate as the basis for consolidation of the EU, even for popular consent to existing centralized decision-making. Waever and Kelstrup have noted that, "worried Eurocrats ... fear that there are limits as to how far one can push integration in the political and economic spheres unless people feel sufficiently European."[89] They have become increasingly concerned about the absence of effective symbols of European identity, using "Eurobarometer" surveys to test the popular sense of "belonging" to the EU.[90] The Union's "headline" agenda of economic integration has been judged inadequate: even the leading Eurocrat Jacques Delors queried its capacity to invoke among European populations the sentiments associated with national loyalty, asking: "Who falls in love with an Inner Market?"[91]

A European "tradition" had in effect to be invented to provide a basis for legal and administrative measures, which went beyond basic economic co-operation, and to prompt some popular identification with the bodies that supervised such integration. In the various attempts to discover this tradition the key factor has been that of cultural difference. Shore comments on the process of affirmation of Europe, which is being defined "with increasing precision and thus, as if by default, an 'official' definition of Europe is being constructed."[92] He concludes that, "the new European order ... is coming to mean a sharper boundary between 'European' and 'non-European'."[93]

Such definitions have been most precise in describing citizenship and rights of entry to the EU. Investigating the basis on which the EU has "chosen" its citizens, Martiniello observes they have been granted rights on the basis of "belonging" to one of the European Union nations and "on the basis of belonging to the European culture in construction."[94] He comments that: "The idea seems to be progressing that one should be a true European Citizen – above all 'culturally' European" – to be given access to the EU.[95] The outcome could be "a sort of ethno-racial conception of European society."[96]

Other Within

The alarmist vision of a Europe besieged from without cannot be dissociated from that of Europeanness challenged from within. Some ideologues of Europeanity have turned equally to "interior" racisms – to frontiers within the imagined continental identity and to what they regard as an irruption of alien cultural formations. Martiniello notes that official EU discussions on citizenship examine "exclusion from ... 'Europeanity' of those citizens living in Europe which [sic] come from a non-Christian civilization, for example the immigrant populations which come from countries where Islam is the main religion."[97] Here the official EU discourse meets that of the extreme right, with its "xenophobic spectre of not only a Muslim-dominated world but an 'Islamization of Europe'."[98] Islam becomes an "intensified" definition of authentic Europe by virtue of its new presence in continental society. An internal "non-Europe" – the Other Within – becomes a bridgehead for perceived external threats to European identity.

Such ideas are consistent with a long history of attempts to identify the culpability of ethnic/religious minorities – a practice intimately linked to the emergence of capitalism in Europe and to the rise of the nation-state. This has been most starkly expressed in the 20th century by the attribution to such communities of responsibility for economic crisis and social breakdown during periods of national and regional upheaval. Sixty years after the partisans of a "European culture" defined their project against an internal Semitic enemy a new politics of difference has been elaborated. That the ideologues of the EU can be distinguished from those of National Socialism does not make less significant the depiction of an "Oriental" threat to the imagined homogeneity of European culture. The image of a malign Islam which emerges from official EU analyses has obvious precedents: for Azmeh this amounts to "representation of a repellent exoticism by mass psychological mechanisms very like those involved in anti-semitism."[99]

The EU's preoccupation with exclusion has strengthened in proportion to the perceived advance of Islamist movements in the Middle East. Here the "Green Menace" syndrome is indeed at work, with a strong tendency to homogenize Islam, presenting Muslims in general as radical activists and identifying the Muslims of Europe as a sinister fifth column. In a survey of migrations and minorities across Europe, Castles notes the relationship between "external" and "internal" factors that has made Islam the main target within racist discourses: "Muslim minorities appear threatening partly because they are linked to strong external forces, which appear to question the hegemony of the north, and partly because they have a visible and self-confident cultural presence [in Europe]."[100] In a statement that reveals how far such views have penetrated the European political establishment, Danish minister Ellen Margrethe Loy observes:

> The challenges that the [Euro-Mediterranean] Partnership seeks to answer are multiple. From a European perspective one of the most visible challenges is that of Islamic radicalism. The perceived threats of Islamic radicals to Europe as well of the Middle East are sometimes only too real. Acts of terror, internal instability within Muslim countries, a possible increase in migration and export of radical ideas to migrant communities outside the Muslim world [sic].[101]

As problems of economic and political consolidation *within* the EU intensified in the early 1990s, assertions of "external" difference became more insistent. In a prescient analysis written in 1991, *The Guardian* suggested that EU anxieties about migration from the Middle East were intimately linked to concerns over an "alien" internal presence:

> Of course, what links concern over asylum, illegal emigration and even family reunion is the desire to halt the growth of non-Western, and particularly Islamic, communities in Europe.[102]

The "solutions" to European leaders' anxieties, the newspaper observed, were "trade-offs" with countries perceived to be the source of unwanted demographic pressures and threatening cultural influences. These would offer such countries "aid on a bigger scale than might otherwise have been the case, perhaps depriving more distant parts of the Third World of some of the aid they presently receive."[103] Three years later the EU initiated its move to Euro-Mediterranean Partnership.

Fault Lines: Civilizational difference

Attempts to define new cultural identities on a continental scale are not unique. Among other efforts to redefine "the West" in a post-Communist world are those of Samuel Huntington and his co-thinkers. Their notion of a world patterned by cultural or "civilizational" blocs has found a resonance among the ideologues of a new Europe. Although the EU quest for "Europeanity" predates Huntington's "clash of civilizations" theory, the latter has been drawn on readily by those who elaborate rationales for

European integration/exclusion. His theory of world affairs depicts the future as a series of confrontations in which cultural blocs defined by their religio-cultural heritage will shape world politics. Assuming a "kin-country" loyalty cemented by awareness of religious heritage, Huntington argues that world events will turn on the conflicts between such blocs. "Civilization-consciousness" will emphasize ancient "fault lines" marking the boundaries of the principal blocs, the most significant of which will be those based upon the "Judaeo-Christian" West, the "Confuscianism/ Buddhism" of East Asia, and Islam, centred on the Middle East.[104] The Islamic bloc, defined by its "bloody borders" and still asserting itself as an "ancient rival" of the West, will constitute the key threat to world order, one to which the West must be ready to respond.

The analysis repeats well-worn themes. In a post-Cold War world, Islam becomes the preferred antagonist – a "civilizational" Other. The novel feature of Huntington's design is the depiction of a *global* system of blocs. Its implications for Europe are not fully drawn out by Huntington and his co-thinkers but Mortimer, among others, has pointed to the way in which for several decades Cold War rivalries directed eastwards European concerns about continental coherence.[105] "Western" identity in general was defined predominantly against the Soviet bloc. Since the collapse of Communism it has been necessary to construct a new Europe. Theories of cultural conflict have been seized on by some of those engaged in defining Euro-Mediterranean relations. European academics and leading politicians within the EU have embraced notions of "civilizational" difference; during the Barcelona summit in 1995, official briefings led European media to describe the event as focused upon the Mediterranean as "the 'new fault line' that has replaced the old iron curtain."[106]

Similar ideas have also surfaced during discussions over applications for membership of the EU made by Turkey. As part of his world of civilizational blocs, Huntington depicts "torn countries", of which "the most obvious and prototypical" is Turkey.[107] A predominantly Islamic state but one on the "edge" of the European bloc, Turkey should be firmly excluded from the EU, he maintains. Endorsing the EU's embrace of selected states from the old Communist bloc (such as those of the Baltic region), Huntington has remained vehemently opposed to incorporation of cultures marked by perceived civilizational difference. He maintains that the EU "rests on the shared foundation of European culture and Western Christianity,"[108] a basis for successful economic regionalism that must not be violated by alien intrusion. Holmes sums up Huntington's view: "the

European Union is, and should be, a Christian club ... to bolster the West's inward coherence, we need to slam the door in Turkey's face.[109]

Despite European leaders' repeated assurances of goodwill to Turkey,[110] the EU has rebuffed every effort by the Turkish government to gain membership. Debate has centered upon whether Turkey could indeed be considered a member of "the European club"; when Turkey was included among Mediterranean participants at the Barcelona Summit, its status as a "non-European" state seemed to have been confirmed. An application to the EU was again rejected at a European summit in 1997, European newspapers commenting on "another slap in the face from the EU," likely to heighten suspicions that "Europe will never allow such a large Muslim country to become a full member.[111]

After Barcelona: Squabbles

By the time of the Barcelona conference the EU had developed a formal, public stance towards its Middle East partners, together with an informal approach that emphasized fear, hostility and exclusion. Its Middle East partners nonetheless largely accepted the Euro-Mediterranean agreement at face value. Government officials and local media in the region treated the Partnership primarily as a set of economic arrangements likely to be of benefit and there were few critical comments. At a conference in Egypt some academic participants expressed anxiety about the relative weight of the EU in relation to Middle East states and the capacity of the latter to benefit from the Partnership. A report noted that delegates feared that "Europe is calling the tune" and that to benefit fully from EU trading arrangements, Arab states themselves should develop a more meaningful integration.[112] But with Meda budgets soon being accessed readily even these modest reservations seemed unimportant.

Within a few years anxieties were growing. In 1997 Andre Azoulay, economic adviser to King Hassan of Morocco expressed his government's dissatisfaction with the EU, alleging that the Europeans had failed to keep their part of the deal. He commented that EU officials had "embarked us on a promising process" but had later entered into discussions on trade in the spirit of "grocers' squabbles."[113] By mid-1998 negotiations on association agreements with five Arab states had stalled: Sobh suggested that problems could be located in "lack of a strong political will to carry out the partnership process."[114]

Meanwhile public dissatisfaction was increasing. In May 1997 Moroccan trade unions denounced the Barcelona agreement, declaring that it had been signed without serious preparations and was "tantamount to mortgaging Morocco's economic sovereignty and imposing unequal conditions."[115] Jolly observed that by 1998 any optimism about the Partnership had been limited by the shortcomings of a project "which has not yet succeeded in establishing the notion of a shared space or in curbing the growing imbalance between North and South.[116]

There was also disappointment about EU failures on the political front. Since 1997 European leaders have adopted a lower profile on key Middle East issues, especially on that of Palestine. Following discussions between EU ministers and PNA officials in October 1996, Arafat was said to have received only "meagre offerings" from the Union: "nothing of substance ... other than the familiar incantations of support for the peace process."[117] As the peace process collapsed, Palestinian President Arafat urged that Europe as well as the US should be a broker in negotiations. The EU, however, continued to keep a respectful distance while pursuing negotiations on a trade agreement with Israel.

There has been less concern in the Middle East about matters on which the EU *has* acted decisively, notably in the area of migration. The Barcelona Declaration contained forceful statements on population movement. It noted that "current population trends represent a priority challenge which must be counterbalanced by appropriate policies," specifying that signatories agree "to strengthen co-operation to reduce migratory pressures."[118] Most important, it committed all participant states to halt "illegal" migration and "to readmit their nationals who are in an illegal situation."[119] At this level, the Declaration was in effect a statement by the EU that exclusionary policies were to be enacted with increased vigour.

In practice, the level of migration permitted by the EU is likely to vary. "Fortress Europe" *will* be accessible in order to accommodate the needs of European capital, with varying inflows to satisfy demands for cheap labour.[120] Here there is what Miles calls a predominant "class logic" to immigration controls imposed by the EU:[121] those with capital, influence and political connections will continue to move across continental frontiers relatively freely, while the majority of potential migrants – those with only their labour to sell, or those seeking asylum – will confront a regime of close control.

For the EU the first concern is not the number of potential migrants but the *principle* of control, which has been a key aspect of its own attempt at political self-assertion. This is reflected in the drive for harmonization of immigration and asylum policies across the Union, which accelerated sharply following the Barcelona summit. In 1996 the European police agency declared that control of immigration had become its top priority.[122] Germany dismantled asylum provisions in its constitution and the British government introduced legislation designed to exclude the vast majority of asylum-seekers. In Southern Europe attention was focused overwhelming upon North Africa. In Spain, a deadline for those wishing to legalize status was set for mid-1996; immigrants' organizations accused the authorities of treating Arab migrants "like common delinquents."[123] By 1998, Spain had erected extensive fences around its North African enclave cities of Melilla and Ceuta (in Morocco) to meet obligations under the Schengen Agreement. Refugees from Algeria held in a detention centre in Ceuta complained that they were "victims of the Schengen pan-European frontier treaty."[124]

In Greece, regarded as a "loophole" state in Fortress Europe, new laws bringing the country into line with EU requirements left hundreds of thousands facing deportation. Critics in Greece argued that the measures had been drafted "to please Brussels," condemning them as "xenophobic"[125] (an observation which suggests that, in certain contexts, the EU is generating an image more often associated with that of the nation-state).

Throughout the mid-1990s the EU increased pressure on Italy, described as "lax" in policy, to close its borders to prospective migrants. Before Italy joined the Schengen area in 1997 the Rome government was induced to introduce new laws providing for forcible repatriation of migrants, EU officials having expressed alarm that "illegals" entering Italy would be free to cross borders across a series of member states.[126] One outcome of the arrest and imprisonment of hundreds of Tunisian and Moroccan migrants during 1998 was rioting among migrants held in camps in Sicily.[127]

Frustrated expectations

The Partnership's Mediterranean participants are under a requirement to take complementary measures, reducing alleged migratory pressure at the Middle Eastern end of the "demographic gradient." Notwithstanding that, European anxieties about a migratory assault are imagined and highly prejudicial, they have been legitimised by Middle East governments. As part of the "trade off" in which they have accepted promises of aid and investment, the Mediterranean partners – in effect, the North African states

– are expected to co-operate in a regional effort that will curb population movements the EU judges unacceptable. They may be ill equipped to do so. Structures of regional collaboration are weak: the long-term crisis of Arab nationalism, the destabilizing influences of some Islamist currents, and the failure of numerous attempts at local unification have left a legacy of minimal local co-operation, often of deep mistrust. Recent attempts at economic integration may bring an advance but Europe expects more – control of movements across the Mediterranean "fault line."

These demands raise an awkward prospect for Arab governments. Already under pressure from opposition movements which have mobilized around the theme of regional subordination to the West, they find themselves responsible for policing a particularly aggressive EU policy associated with policies which offer meagre economic benefits to most people of the region. EU rhetoric has strongly emphasized the developmental outcomes of the Partnership for its Arab partners, and some evidence of advance is required. Khader has commented that development through Meda programs is certain to be "a long and slow process, facing many obstacles."[128] Parfitt points out that such programs may well have the effect of placing Middle East states in a more unfavourable trading position vis-à-vis the EU and that to this extent they incorporate "some major contradictions."[129] Lister goes further, commenting that the Partnership agreement as a whole is antithetical to development because its organizing principles have an entirely different purpose. She observes:

> At present the northern shore is preoccupied with crisis prevention in the southern Mediterranean and sees development as an instrument of that objective. For the longer term, perhaps the North would be wiser to concentrate on development in the Mediterranean and reap crisis prevention as a spin-off.[130]

The EU continues to speak of economic and social advance on a grand scale. There is no suggestion that its strategists have considered other outcomes: in particular, the possibility that the rhetoric of Partnership, with its promises of aid, increased employment and improved welfare, raises expectations which continue to go unmet. Further public commitments by the EU to "shared prosperity" and "good neighbourliness" are likely to be received less credulously, as evidenced by the frustration expressed in Morocco. In fact, with a new southern border in place, a unitary immigration policy and effective control of population movements from the south, the EU may feel less need to follow through on promises of aid and development. By 1999 there were already signs that the promised assistance might not be delivered.[131] Deepening social crisis in North Africa will no doubt be greeted by EU officials, media analysts and partisan academics as confirmation that "civilizational" differences are becoming more pronounced and that "fault lines" should be recognized and further fortified. Such an outcome could have serious consequences, especially for communities of Middle East and North African origin within Europe. Under such circumstances it will be appropriate to recall van Nieuwenhuize's observation on the last attempt at regional co-operation – "unachieved because misconceived."

Conclusion: 'Dream world'

Does the experience of the 1990s suggest that societies of Europe and the Middle East are indeed irreconcilable? Are these regions different in ways that must stimulate continued hostility? To suggest that this is the case would be to confirm the essentialist thesis of some European politicians and of those academics such as Huntington who wish to depict a world in which immutable difference makes for continued conflict.

Such arguments are unsustainable. They depend upon the depiction of what Axford calls a "dream world"[132] – a construction of history in which centuries of complex interactions between social and cultural groups are denied. This is what Sakamoto describes as "civilizational determinism",[133] a vulgar ideological construction that denies the mass of evidence for economic, political and cultural coherences that cut across "blocs" said to shape the contemporary world. Here, the pre-capitalist circuits of commerce described by Abu Lughod,[134] or the Mediterranean cultures described by Braudel,[135] which had a critical influence upon developments in Western Europe, are inconvenient and are simply ignored. In the case of Huntington this allows projection into the past of scenarios congenial to the US State Department in the 1990s. It is these views that have been absorbed by European politicians who wish to use the spectre of cultural "clash" in their efforts to establish a Fortress Europe.

What is striking about the EU move to such ideas is its *instrumental* character. During the 1950s, 1960s and the early 1970s, migration from North Africa to Western Europe was viewed as an important factor sustaining the latter's economic growth. Collinson notes that during this period Maghrebi emigration could be seen as "progressive transformation of labour into a structural component of the political economy of [Western

Europe]."[136] It was change *within* Europe, she notes, that later prompted a radical revision of such approaches, until the Maghreb could be viewed as a source of threat "to the very foundations and identities of the nation-states concerned."[137]

A similar situation obtains in the area of EU expansion, especially as it relates to countries of the East, notably Turkey. European states have long engaged directly with the Turkish government, notably through NATO. Turkey has been a key member of Western military alliances and of the Council of Europe. Western European societies have also received millions of Turkish migrants who, during the phase of economic expansion from the 1950s to the 1970s, and even well into the 1980s, moved routinely across national borders. In Germany – the main destination for Turkish workers – the "guest worker" policy meant that, like other foreigners, Turks were denied citizenship. Nonetheless they enjoyed what Mitchell and Russell describe as "a reasonable degree of tolerance"[138] within the wider society. Hostility towards Turks and the politics of *exclusion*, which from the 1980s affected mainstream German politics, have been associated with recession and with deepening problems faced by the German state. Leading politicians have since been prepared to engage in what Knischewski calls "demagogic instrumentalisation," identifying the "non-European" character of Turks and Turkey as the basis for exclusion of the latter from the EU.[139]

Redefinition of Europe has taken place within a specific context. Under different circumstances alternative constructions can take place, for as Delanty notes, national (or supra-national) ideologies are elastic: "Europe can mean whatever one intends it to mean."[140] It is true that in conjuring a "Green Menace", European politicians have turned to traditions of difference closely associated with the nation-state, within which "the East" has been viewed as alien and inferior. But such traditions can be emphasized or largely ignored. There is no intrinsic reason why Turkey or countries of the Maghreb should not be courted or even embraced by the European states. Contrary to the approach of Mansour and others who see North Africa and Europe as irreconcilable, Yachir suggests under conditions of a new expansion, European states might endeavour "to bind the Maghreb to their side."[141] Similarly, new requirements for labour in European economies can quickly produce modifications in immigration policy: indeed, the EU's tolerance of "illegal"/ "clandestine" migration at a certain level suggests that it wishes for flexibility in this area.

For the present, however, Euro-Mediterranean collaboration is deeply compromised by the cynicism of EU leaders. Debates about regional relations have revealed how rapidly new rationales are developed that can secure the latter's specific interests. The EU's Barcelona rhetoric of neighbourliness and peaceful co-operation has barely concealed an agenda focused upon prejudice and hostility towards people of Middle Eastern origin within Europe. Fortunately not all citizens of European states will respond to such promptings. As Nielsen concludes, they have an interest in rejecting an agenda that presents "the simplistic enemy image."[142] Like the nation building that dominated Europe in an earlier era, "Europeanization" is a "top-down" process dominated by states and bureaucracies. As in the past, when *internationalism* contested ideas of national difference and national hostility, friendship and solidarity will be built from below.

Notes

1 European Commission, *Euro-Mediterranean Conference, Barcelona, Final Declaration*, Info-Note 52/95, Brussels, November 1995, p. 4.

2 *Ibid* pp. 2 and 3.

3 "The Euro-Mediterranean Partnership", progress report sponsored by the European Commission, *International Herald Tribune*, 27 November 1996, p. 11.

4 Samir Sohb, "Euro-Mediterranean Partnership: A long and winding road", in *Arabies Trends*, July-August 1998, p. 38.

5 J. Esposito, *The Islamic Threat: Myth or Reality?* Oxford University Press (New York 1992) p. 5.

6 G. Delanty, *Inventing Europe*, Macmillan (Basingstoke 1995) p. 150.

7 See E. Said, *Orientalism*, Penguin (London 1978), and for a commentary on Said's thesis, A. Hussain, R. Olson & J. Qureshi (eds.), *Orientalism, Islam and Islamists*, Amana (Brattleboro, 1984).

8 Said, o*p. cit*, pp. 1 and 2.

9 *Bulletin of the European Union*, 2/95 (1995) p. 10.

10 For details of structures of the Euro-Mediterranean Partnership, see the report of European Commission in the *International Herald Tribune*, o*p. cit*, p. 2.

11 Figures quoted by European Commission General Director Jean Prat in A. Jerichow A. & J. B. Simonsen (eds.), *Islam in a Changing World: Europe and the MIddle East*, Curzon (London 1997) p. 160.

12 Countries of the Latin American Mercado de Sur (*Mercosur)*, for example, now Europe's fastest-growing export market, receive modest sums in comparision. See M. Lister, *The European Union and the South*, Routledge (London 1997), p. 33.

13 *International Herald Tribune*, *op. cit.*, p. 11.

14 *Ibid*, p. 11.

15 *Ibid*, p. 12.

16 *Ibid*, p. 12.

17 See interview with Jean Klarus, head of Mediterranean policy in the European Parliament. *Ahram Weekly*, 30 November 1995.

18 See the analysis by Egyptian foreign policy analyst Mahmoud Saad, *Ahram Weekly*, 7 December 1995.

19 European Commission report, *International Herald Tribune*, *op. cit.*.

20 E. Mortimer, "European Attitudes Towards the Arabs Since the European Withdrawal from the Middle East", in *Arab Affairs*, Vol 1, No 1, 1983, p. 30.

21 E. Mortimer, "European Attitudes Towards the Arabs Since the European Withdrawal from the Middle East", in *Arab Affairs*, Vol 1, No 1, 1983, p. 30.

22 S. A. S. Hallaba, *Euro-Arab Dialogue*, Amana (Brattleboro 1984) pp. 2-3.

23 *Ibid*, p. 11.

24 Y. Sayigh, "Europeans and Arabs: Motives, Issues and Obstacles in a Dialogue": in *Euro-Arab Dialogue Lectures 1*, Lutfia Rabbani Foundation (The Hague 1985) p. 37.

25 Mortimer, *op. cit.*, p. 32.

26 F. Mansour, *The Arab World*, Zed (London 1992), p. 124.

27 Said, *op. cit.*, p. 328.

28 T. Hentsch, *Imagining the Middle East*, Black Rose (Montreal 1982), p. 211.

29 *Ibid*, p. 211.

30 European Commission, *The Barcelona Conference and the Euro-Mediterranean Association Agreements*, Memo 95/156 (London 1995).

31 See interview with Egyptian ambassador to the talks Muhammed Fathi El-Shazli, *Ahram Weekly*, 7 December 1996.

32 B. Khader, "The Role of Migrants in the Development of Their Country of Origin and the New Euro-Mediterranean Partnership", in *Merger*, Vol 3, No 2, 1996.

33 *Ibid.*

34 Parfitt, *op. cit.*, p. 868.

35 M. Lister, *The European Union and the South*, Routledge (London 1997) p. 71.

36 European Community, "Opinion on the Mediterranean Policy", para 2.3 (1989), quoted in Parfitt, *op. cit.*, p. 869.

37 *The Guardian*, 28 November 1995.

38 *The Guardian*, 25 November 1995.

39 *Ibid.*

40 *Ibid.*

41 *The Observer*, 20 October 1996.

42 More than 700 EU-backed projects worldwide were said to have been affected. Ibid.

43 *Ibid.*

44 *Ibid.*

45 *Ibid.*

46 Parfitt, *op. cit.*, p. 688.

47 European Commisssion, "The future of relations between the Community and the Maghreb: communication from the Commission to the Council, Parliament and the Economic and Social Committee," 1992, SEC (92) 401, p. 8.

48 *Bulletin of the European Union, op. cit.*, pp. 10-13.

49 *Ibid.*

50 *The Independent*, 8 February 1995.

51 *The Guardian*, 25 November 1995.

52 "Islam and the West," *The Economist*, August 6 1994.

53 *Ibid.*

54 Hentsch observes that construction of a knowledge of the Orient "is about us [the West]". Hentsch, op. cit., p. 212. In a similar vein, Schwarz refers to European construction of "powerful exclusions" which in the case of England, "were connected by an intimate set of relations to the workings of colonial rule". B. Schwarz, "The Expansion and Contraction of England", in B. Schwarz, (ed.), *The Expansion of England*, Routledge (London 1996) p. 5.

55 Esposito, *op. cit.*, p. 114.

56 P. Moya, NATO Sub-Committee on the Mediterranean Basin, *The Rise of Islamic Radicalism and the Future of Democracy in North Africa*, NATO 1994, p3.

57 A. Milward, *The European Rescue of the Nation State*, Routledge (London 1992). Also A. Callinicos, "Europe: the Mounting Crisis", *International Socialism* 2:75, 1997.

58 C. Harman, "The Common Market", *International Socialism* (first series) 49 (1971).

59 P. Hirst & G. Thompson, *Globalization in Question*, Polity (Cambridge 1996) p. 153.

60 Callinicos, *op. cit.*, p. 31.

61 B. Jenkins & S. A. Sofos, "Nation and nationalism in Contemporary Europe: a theoretical perspective", in B. Jenkins & S. A. Sofos, *Nation and Identity in Contemporary Europe*, Routledge (London 1996) p. 9.

62 M. Mitchell & D. Russell, "Immigration, Citizenship and the Nation-State in the New Europe", in B. Jenkins & S. Sofos, *op. cit.*, p. 75.

63 G. Knischewski, "Post-War National Identity in Germany", in B. Jenkins & S. Sofos, *op. cit.*, p. 145.

64 C. De Wenden, "North African Immigration and the French Political Imaginary", in M. Silverman (ed.), Race, Discourse and Power in France, Avebury (Aldershot 1991) p. 100.

65 M. Evans, "Languages of Racism within Contemporary Europe", in Jenkins & Sofos (eds.), *op. cit.*, p. 49.

66 *Ibid*, p. 50.

67 As REP leader Schonhuber argued: "We want to protect the German people's ecological [sic] living space against foreign infiltration", *Ibid*, p. 47.

68 One prominent German member of the European Parliament argued: "Europeans should understand that, like it or not, they have become a superpower, if only because of sheer economic circumstances. If a superpower wants to fulfill its role, it must have global political dimensions." Otto von Hapsburg quoted in Lister, *op. cit.*, p. 21.

69 *Financial Times*, 18 April 1989.

70 R. Cohen & D. Joly, "The 'New' Refugees of Europe", in R. Cohen, & D. Joly (eds.) *Reluctant Hosts: Europe and its Refugees*, Avebury (Aldershot 1989) p. 15.

71 *Ibid*, p. 17.

72 S. Castles & M. Miller, *The Age of Migration*, Macmillan (Basingstoke 1993) p. 125.

73 H. Overbeek, "Towards a new International Migration Regime: Globalisation, Migration and the Internationalisation of Labour", in S. Miles & D. Thranhardt, *Migration and European Integration*, Pinter (London 1993) p. 32.

74 For a summary of measures taken by the EU see A Burgess, *Divided Europe*, Pluto (London 1997) chapter 2.

75 *Ibid*, p. 58.

76 *Ibid*, p. 58.

77 *Ibid*, p. 58.

78 G. Delanty, *op. cit.*, p. 150.

79 Quoted in Collinson, S., *Shore to Shore: The Politics of Migration in Euro-Maghreb Relations*, RIIA (London 1996), p. 39.

80 B. Buzan & B.A. Roberson, "Europe and the Middle East: Drifting towards Societal Cold War?" in O. Waever, B. Buzan, M. Kelstrup & P. Lemaitre, *Identity, MIgration and the New Security Agenda in Europe*, Pinter (London 1993) p. 132.

81 Collinson, *op. cit.*, p. 40.

82 Lister, *op. cit.*, p. 101. Lister notes that these phrases "hark back to the influential 1968 book by Paul Ehrlichs, *The Population Bomb*". She adds, "it is worth recalling that this book had significant racist and sexist overtones and that its predictions that hundreds of millions of people would starve during the 1970s and 1980s proved wrong."

83 See Buzan & Roberson's account of media coverage in Britain, France and North America, Buzan & Roberson, *op. cit.*, pp. 131-132.

84 Reuter Information Service, 27 November 1995.

85 Lister, *op. cit.*, p. 101.

86 *The Guardian*, 16 November 1995.

87 Buzan & Roberson, *op. cit.*, p. 133.

88 A. Smith, "Mational Identity and the Idea of European Unity" *International Affairs*, 68: 1, 1992, p 74. *Ibid*, p. 67.

89 O. Waever, & M. Kelstrup, "Europe and its nations: political and cultural identities", in O. Waever *et al* (eds.) *op. cit.*, p. 66.

90 S. Panebianco, "European Citizenship and European Identity: from the Treat of Maastricht to public opinion attitudes", *Jean Monnet Working Papers in Comparative and International Politics*, December 1996, p. 9.

91 Quoted in *Ibid.*

92 C. Shore, "Inventing the 'People's Europe'? Critical Approaches to European Community 'Cultural Policy", *Man* 28, 4, 1993, p. 786.

93 *Ibid*, p. 793.

94 Martiniello, M. (1994) "Citizenship of the European Union: A Critical View", in Baubock, R. (ed.) *From Aliens to Citizens: Redefining the Status of Immigrants in Europe*, Avebury (Aldershot 1994), p. 40.

95 *Ibid*, p. 40.

96 *Ibid*, pp. 40-41.

97 *Ibid*, p. 39.

98 Delanty, *op. cit.*, p. 151.

99 A. al-Azmeh, *Islams and Modernities*, Verso (London 1993), p. 4.

100 S. Castles, "Migrations and Minorities in Europe. Perspectives for the 1990s: Eleven Hypotheses", in J. Wrench & J. Solomos (eds.) *Racism and Migration in Western Europe*, Berg (Oxford 1993), p. 27.

101 Speech to the conference on Islam in a Changing World: Europe and the Middle East, Copenhagen 1996, in Jerichow & Simonsen, *op. cit.*, p. 165.

102 *The Guardian*, 16 November 1991.

103 *Ibid.*

104 S. Huntington, "The Clash of Civilisations", in *Foreign Affairs*, Summer 1993, p23.

105 E. Mortimer, *Financial Times*, 3 April 1990, quoted in D. Morley & K. Robins, *Spaces of Identity*, Routledge (London 1995) p. 99.

106 *The Independent*, 8 February 1995. For an analysis of European policians increasing enthusiasm for Huntington's persepctives see P. Marfleet, "Europe's Civilizing Mission", in P. Cohen (ed.) *Frontlines, Backyards* Zed (London 1999).

107 Huntington, *op. cit.*, p. 42.

108 Huntington, *op. cit.*, p. 27.

109 S. Holmes 'In Search of New Enemies', *London Review of Books*, 24 April 1997.

110 In 1997, German foreign minister Klaus Kinkel, among others, promised the Turkish government that, "We are not going to close the door on Turkey. Turkey belongs within Europe". *Financial Times*, 16 December 1997.

111 *The Guardian*, 15 December 1997.

112 European Partnership and Regional Co-operation, Case Studies in the Middle East. Report in *Ahram Weekly*, 21 December 1995.

113 Quoted in S. Sobh, *op. cit.*.

114 *Ibid.*

115 *Ibid.*

116 Cecile Joly, "An Imaginary Mediterranean", *Arabies-Trends*, July-August 1998.

117 *The Independent*, October 1 9997.

118 European Commission, *Final Declaration*, *op. cit.*, p. 11.

119 *Ibid.*

120 For an analysis of this practice see N. Harris, *The New Untouchables: Immigration and the New World Worker*, I. B. Tauris (London 1995).

121 R. Miles, *Racism after Race Relations*, Routledge (London 1995) p. 18.

122 *The Guardian*, 15 May 1996.
123 *The Independent*, 23 August 1996.
124 *The Guardian*, 29 August 1998.
125 *The Guardian*, 27 November 1996.
126 *The Guardian*, 23 September 1997.
127 *The Guardian*, 28 July 1998.
128 B. Khader, *op. cit.*.
129 Parfitt, *op. cit.*, p. 877.
130 Lister, *op. cit.*, p. 71.
131 There was some evidence that the Union was switching its aid program away from North Africa. *The Guardian*, 21 April 1998, reported a new movement of EU development funds towards Eastern European states, intended to help them prepare for EU membership, which was likely to have an adverse effect on North Africa.
132 B. Axford, *The Global System: Economics, Politics and Culture*, Polity (Cambridge 1995), p. 192.
133 Y. Sakamoto, "Democratization, Social Movements and World Order", in R. Cox, et al. (eds.) *International Political Economy: Understanding Global Disorder*. Zed (London, 1995) p. 135.
134 J. Abu Lughod, *Before European Hegemony*, Oxford (Oxford UP 1989).
135 F. Braudel, *The Mediterranean and the Mediterranean world in the age of Philip II*, Collins (London 1972).
136 Collinson, *op. cit.*, p. 9.
137 *Ibid*, p. 41.
138 M. Mitchell & R. Russell, *op. cit.*, p. 75.
139 *The European*, 3-9 April 1997.
140 Delanty, *op. cit.*, p. 145.
141 F. Yachir (ed.), *The Mediterranean: Between Autonomy and Dependency*, Zed (London 1989), p. x.
142 J. Nielson, "Muslims in Europe into the Next Millennium", in S. Vertovic & C. Peach, *Islam in Europe: The Politics of Religion and Community*, Macmillan, (Basingstoker 1997), p. 272.

10 The American Shadow: U.S. Foreign Policy and the Middle East

JEFFREY W. HELSING[1]

Introduction: The American Shadow

In January and February 2000, an American president was once again working to bring about agreements between an Arab leader and an Israeli prime minister – first, mediating between Foreign Minister Farouk as-Sharaa of Syria and Israeli Prime Minister Ehud Barak in West Virginia, and then hosting Palestinian Authority Chairman Yasser Arafat in Washington. In the former case, President Bill Clinton was attempting to facilitate a peace agreement between Israel and Syria; in the latter case, he was hoping to instill confidence in Arafat so that negotiations between Israelis and Palestinians would continue. Earlier in January, there was a struggle at the United Nations over the naming of a new weapons inspector for Iraq. This was yet another chapter in the United States-Iraq confrontation, which has played out over the past nine years, and the American goal of ensuring the security of the vital Persian Gulf.

The future of the Middle East depends considerably on what next steps the United States takes with respect to Iraq as well as the peace processes between Israel and the Palestinian Authority, and between Israel and Syria. And, increasingly, it seems that President Clinton has attached his legacy (at least in foreign policy) as President to a hoped-for success in achieving a lasting peace between Israel and its remaining neighbors with whom it is in conflict. As a senior American official noted, "The end of Clinton's term creates a sense of urgency" for the United States to achieve peace in the Middle East. There is little question that President Clinton wants to ensure that his biographies in the future will read, "William Jefferson Clinton, 42nd President of the United States, who helped bring permanent peace to the Middle East" or better yet, "Winner of the Nobel Peace Prize for his role in facilitating a peace accord between Israel and Syria" and/or "between Israelis and Palestinians" – rather than references to his impeachment trial.

Because the stakes are high, including for Clinton, what happens in 2000 will ultimately play a major role in bringing long-lasting peace to the Middle East. As with the Camp David Accords in 1978, the Madrid Conference in 1991, and the Wye agreement in 1998, it is clear what a critical and powerful player the United States is in the region. The United States has established the process and framework within which Arabs and Israelis negotiate and even relate to each other. Through its roles as facilitator, mediator, and guarantor, the United States has shown that it is indispensable to the peace process, a fact that can be viewed either positively or negatively. And, as the worlds' sole remaining superpower, the United States clearly has a major impact on economic, political and even social issues throughout the world, including the Middle East.

To understand that impact, it is important to show how the various problems and conflicts in the Middle East are interlinked and how U.S. foreign policy overshadows almost all the critical issues in the region. Over the past nine years, U.S. foreign policy actions that do not match American rhetoric, inconsistencies in priorities and actions, raised and unfulfilled expectations among many in the Middle East, as well as weakening global U.S. leadership, have all combined to make U.S. foreign policy in the Middle East quite muddled. This makes the region more dangerous and the damage to the region as well as to U.S. interests, if there is conflict, is quite high.

On the verge of the 21st century, the Middle East continues to be a relatively unstable and volatile region of the world while remaining one of its key strategic areas, because the global economy depends heavily on Middle Eastern oil resources. After the expulsion of Iraq from Kuwait by an international coalition led by the United States, and with the end of the Cold War, Americans such as President George Bush talked of a "new world order" and many certainly envisioned a new order in the Middle East. Long-term peace between Israel and its Arab neighbors would blossom while those perceived to be threats to peace – Iraq, Iran, Sudan, and Libya – would be isolated and not allowed to share in the benefits of such significant changes. There was talk of a comprehensive and stable peace between Israel and its neighbors and a resolution to the status of the Palestinian people and the lands that Israel has occupied since 1967. Life-long enemies sat down together - Yitzhak Rabin and Yasser Arafat; Israelis and Syrians; Israelis and Gulf Arabs in the multilateral peace talks. Israel and Jordan made peace. Israel recognized the PLO, as was Israel's existence by Palestinians. The funeral of the murdered Israeli leader Yitzhak Rabin was attended by a number of Arab heads of state and high-level Arab delegations. Rabin's legacy, and that of his Palestinian counterpart Yasser Arafat, was a process and a timetable for the resolution of the status of the Palestinian people and Israeli-occupied lands. Significant changes had occurred, and significant expectations were raised.

But, by the end of the decade, in May of 1999, much had unraveled and expectations were quite low. To many in the Middle East and around the world, including most senior American policymakers and the President, the hopes for a comprehensive peace in the Middle East depended upon the Israeli elections held that May. Yet, by early 2000, the hopes of many, after Ehud Barak's election seemed to hold out the hope for peace, had been dashed. Polls taken in February 2000 showed that the numbers of Palestinians who supported renewed acts of violence against Israeli targets had risen to the same levels (between 45 and 50 per cent) they had been when Benjamin Netanyahu was Prime Minister of Israel. In spite of this, the United States remained optimistic, wedded to a peace process that it, more than any of the parties, believed in. One Israeli commentator, former Deputy Mayor of Jerusalem Meron Bevenisti cynically described the Americans as supercilious in their adherence to the peace process: "American spokesmen, who ceaselessly assign grades to their clients and ceaselessly hold pep talks and invent gimmicks drawn from the textbooks of 'conflict resolution'."[2]

Despite the treaties, interim peace agreements and establishment of official contacts with a number of Gulf and North African countries, the relationship between Israel and the Arab world has not really been transformed. And many areas of the region remain problematic. There is great internal strife within many Arab countries in the region. In some, like Algeria, Sudan, and Afghanistan, they have simply imploded. There are also significant internal cleavages in Israel and Turkey as well as sporadic unrest in Jordan and Egypt, and in some Gulf States. At the same time, the American military presence in the Persian Gulf is a thorny domestic issue for the states in the Gulf region and has done little to deter Saddam Hussein from thumbing his nose at the international community at the expense of the people of Iraq. Almost every Arab state is facing significant economic problems. The links between economic dislocation, failed economic expectations, continued high population growth and internal strife are clear, and growing. In addition, the region remains an arms bazaar and a huge recipient of arms sales. [3] While the likelihood of a major war in the region is not strong, the prospect of conflict and the perceived need for deterrence against potential military threats (and even internal threats) remains very high.

Amidst all of this is the United States. It is not that the United States simply has policy interests in the region; the United States is, in fact, a major player in the Middle East, perhaps the single most important and dominant player. The shadow of the United States permeates the region. American policies have a major impact on all of the countries in the region. The consequences of America's actions are not necessarily all good or all bad but they usually have a significant impact.

It is, therefore, important to understand the role of American foreign policy in the region, as well as its goals and how the policies are shaped and implemented. To begin, the collapse of the Soviet Union clearly had a major impact on the Middle East. It is doubtful that an international coalition against Iraq would have emerged or that significant steps toward peace between Israelis and Arabs would have occurred without the disintegration of the Soviet Union. That impact, however, was not sufficient ultimately to transform the region from one imbued with conflict to one of peace because the end of the Cold War did not wipe away the core problems between Israelis and Arabs nor make the region any less valuable strategically. America's fundamental interests in the region – oil, Israel and regional stability – have not altered either, even as the United States began to believe (or at least hope) that the region could be transformed. In judging American foreign policy toward the Middle East at the end of the 1990s, it has, in many important respects, failed. This is not just because the expectations in the early 1990s have not been met, but how America has pursued its objectives has damaged its credibility and leadership in the region, and possibly on a global scale. Securing America's three major interests have usually led to policies that are contradictory and very hard to coordinate.

The policy failures of today are grounded in the successes of a few years ago. The United States raised considerable expectations in the Middle East that there would be benefits from the defeat of Iraq and from peace between Arabs and Israelis. But these expectations have not been met and there is a growing tendency in the Arab world to blame the United States. This is due primarily to the fact that the United States has lost considerable support for its policies against Iraq and because the United States seeks to promote peace in the Middle East through a process that embodies an Israeli perspective of what peace will look like and how it will be achieved. It is a process that ultimately turns on whether Israel can live with its consequences. Given Israeli politics and Israel's military might as well as Israel's view of its place in the Middle East, that may well be the only way to achieve peace, but it is a process that is based on asymmetries and a bias against the Arab parties. It does not embrace the Arab demands for fairness and justice but instead reflects the role of power in international politics. Compounding this is that the United States does not truly understand, or at least care about, the Arab perspective and the linkage for Arabs between the Arab-Israeli conflict (and particularly Israel's actions) and what happens elsewhere in the region.

Support for the two main American foreign policy efforts, the Madrid peace process and Persian Gulf security, has eroded considerably among America's allies and moderate Arab states. There is a perception among most Middle Eastern countries that both are failures and simply serve to promote American (and Israeli) interests while not bringing about a just and comprehensive peace nor removing the potential threats of Iraq and Iran. Even as the Madrid process has been revived, with a meeting hosted by the United States and Russia in Moscow at the end of January 2000, there remains considerable skepticism throughout the Arab world about the American-initiated process of peace, dialogue, and cooperation. Does the mere fact that meetings of working groups on water, refugees, environment, and regional and economic development have been scheduled for the spring of 2000, mean that a process has been revived that will deliver peace and, as put forth by the United States, economic prosperity and regional cooperation? Or, is Israel, which benefits from this process of normalization, the only one to reap any rewards?

The two-tiered peace process launched by the United States at Madrid in 1991 grew out of the Gulf War victory. It was based on the need to link the states of the region to a common process that would help Israel and its neighbors deal bilaterally with their conflicts and most of the Middle East countries engage multilaterally on issues of concern throughout the region. The idea was bold and risky, but under Clinton it was not sustained with any consistency, primarily due to the changes in the Israeli government as well as domestic American politics, and because of the Clinton Administration's emphasis on both large-scale, often rhetorical, global goals and platitudes.

The key to the early success of American efforts to help the parties make peace has been to provide regional and international support and momentum for the hard choices necessary for peace. It was important to demonstrate that there were considerable benefits for those who took risks for peace. But, until the Wye Conference in the fall of 1998, when the United States feared that prospects for peace might be permanently damaged, particularly by an intransigent Israeli government, the Clinton administration had not been willing to risk or push others to take risks for peace, particularly Israel. The peace process became, for Netanyahu, little more than a deferential nod to peace and the need for negotiations and even concessions without, in fact, taking risks. A virtually meaningless process could not substitute for meaningful engagement between Israel and its neighbors. Even in the Wye talks, and in the subsequent Israeli-Palestinian negotiations and the revived talks between Syria and Israel, the pressure the United States put on Israel was to get the Israeli government to accept what is the most favorable arrangement for Israel if there is to be a permanent peace. With respect to the Palestinian track, much of America's efforts as a third party has been to get Israel to implement actions to which it has already agreed. Over the past three years, the lack of progress between Israel and the Palestinian Authority has been reflected in a decline throughout the Arab world and many other parts of the international community of support for the United States on both the peace process or containment of Iraq and Iran. This has been compounded by the continued U.S. military presence in the Persian Gulf, the hardships of most of the Iraqi civilian population due to the UN sanctions, and economic problems and dislocation in many areas of the Middle East, including the Gulf.

U.S. policy toward the Persian Gulf, particularly the "dual containment" policy directed against both Iraq and Iran, has created widespread concern among many in the Arab world that the United States views the potential threat of Iraq and Iran to the stability of the Persian Gulf and access to its oil resources as simply an excuse to maintain a large-scale military presence. This view was reinforced in Arab eyes when reports in the summer of 1998 indicated that the United States actually undercut the work of the UN inspectors in Iraq. At the same time, American military morale has deteriorated significantly because the U.S. armed forces are not happy about the permanent stationing of large numbers of men and equipment in the Gulf region.

There are a number of generalizations about U.S. foreign policy in the Middle East at the turn of the century that are important in explaining why American influence is in decline:

1. The general themes and goals of American foreign policy in the Middle East have been consistent from administration to administration. The implementation and tactics have differed.
2. The three major interests of the United States – oil, Israel and regional stability – are too often incompatible goals that make a consistent and coherent foreign policy almost impossible.
3. The United States has a tremendous credibility problem in the Middle East, even among its most staunch Arab allies, which is rooted in both its relations with Israel and its policy of "dual containment" towards Iraq and Iran.
4. The inconsistent promotion of lofty western goals of democratization and economic liberalism are too often inappropriate (or premature) for the region and too often ignored by the United States itself when political expedience is necessary for American strategic interests.
5. There exists a myopic devotion to a "Peace Process" that reflects the Israeli view of peace.
6. Domestic politics can never be ignored in understanding how American policies and decisions regarding the Middle East are shaped.
7. The lack of American vision and leadership in the global arena reinforces the status quo which has troubling consequences for a

region like the Middle East where change is feared and old patterns of conflict and hate are easier to sustain.

Themes of U.S. Foreign Policy

In the past decade, both Republican and Democratic administrations have espoused and promoted new internationalist thinking, if not exactly a new world order, that incorporates economic liberalism and free market capitalism as well as political principles such as democratization, human and minority rights, and the rule of law. Along with these ideas come American and/or western notions of civil liberties and civil rights, non-proliferation of weapons of mass destruction and reduction of conventional arms sales, no barriers to free trade, and multi-culturalism.

By the middle of the 1990s, with a strong international consensus arrayed against "rogue" aggressor states such as Iraq, and Israelis and Arabs seemingly on the road to making comprehensive peace amongst themselves, it appeared that the new thinking and the extension of America's vision of a more democratic, market-oriented world could be extended to the Middle East. In many ways, the peace process that emerged from the Madrid Conference in 1991 embodied that vision. However, the fact that most western states, and particularly the United States, do not necessarily practice what they preach or they stack the deck to favor their own interests, makes many countries of the world mistrust U.S. sincerity in places like the Middle East. Too often American actions and policies have been the result of narrow self-interest rather than some idealistic, long-range vision for a more democratic and economically prosperous world.

The past few years in the Middle East have demonstrated that this vision, this new thinking, was unrealistic. A few peace treaties and interim agreements did not transform the Middle East or change the conservative and often autocratic leadership in the region or transcend the historical distrust and competition between Israelis and Arabs. One could even argue that the past eight months of the Barak government in Israel has exacerbated this. The failed expectations amidst the hope that peace was on the horizon as a result of ousting Netanyahu and the Likud party from power, may actually increase the distrust between Israelis and Arabs, and thus make peace more unlikely. Arabs can either take the view that Barak is the best they will get and that this period is the most opportune moment to make peace, or that Barak exemplifies the fact that peace with Israel is impossible. The latter view would hold that "peace" will not be just and fair but dictated by Israel, and the results of a peace agreement will be the dominance by Israel, with American assistance, of the region.

Whether the United States is dominating the political landscape in the region or its influence is in decline, the shadow of the United States is hard to avoid. For policymakers in the Middle East, it is hard to predict just what direction the United States is heading and what its policy is with respect to the Middle East. An Egyptian diplomat noted that for the past few years, Egypt has been unsure what "the new American foreign policy paradigm is. It's unclear whether the Americans know." But in broad, general terms, what the American foreign policy paradigms are is fairly clear; but not necessarily how to achieve them. So America's strategic interests and its actions in the Middle East not only do not dovetail with the more general international paradigms but in fact often run counter to them. And, there is an inconsistency in the implementation. The United States pushes human rights on certain countries but not others, encourages adherence to the rule of law in some countries, and looks away from others.

What one might have referred to as a "new world order" at the beginning of this decade is now viewed as a world of disorder, one with increasing instability and political and economic disarray. But there are certain basic principles that have been articulated over and over by American policymakers and spokesmen. One may question how well these have been implemented but they are quite prevalent. The United States has also become much more selective in how and where it will become militarily and diplomatically engaged – whether in the Middle East or the Balkans, for example. And when America does become engaged or take action, it is usually with an eye toward domestic politics and public opinion.

What is clear about U.S. foreign policy is that the rhetoric has been fairly consistent and simple in articulating overall international goals and indicating the type of world the United States would ideally like to create. A sampling of statements by American officials in the State Department or on the White House staff over the years during the

Clinton Administration produces the following overall objectives or guidelines of American foreign policy:

1. Elevate the level of U.S. economic competitiveness overseas and promote economic liberalism. To U.S. officials, there is a clear emphasis that political and economic opportunities go hand-in-hand.
2. Promote and consolidate democratic values, in particular human rights, democracy, and the rule of law. Open societies do not go to war with each other nor support terrorism and do adhere to international agreements.
3. Adjust security arrangements to take into account the end of the Cold War. There is a new security agenda, one that emphasizes regional security arrangements, peacekeeping and non-proliferation.

These guidelines encompass three central themes of American foreign policy throughout the 20th century: Wilsonian idealism, the primacy of U.S. economic interests, and realism.[4] And just as these themes come into conflict, the pursuit of the three major foreign policy objectives will, inevitably, be incompatible at times and lead to the pursuit of one at the expense of another.

One of the most remarkable things about the end of the Cold War and the triumph of economic liberalism is that the United States essentially did more than any other country in designing and bringing about the current international system. However, while there is considerable American rhetoric and activity, there is little consistency and lots of hypocrisy, with a bottom line of narrow self-interest. In the words of a senior Asian diplomat that could just as easily have come from any number of developing world officials:

> Americans may say they simply want open markets and free trade, but what they mean is that we are supposed to become more like them. They want to change our distribution and retail system to suit their exporters, and change our finance system to suit their banks. They want us to swallow an American culture of CNN and Hollywood, insist that we welcome their rude and intrusive American media, while they lecture us on human rights. The cultural arrogance of a country with

> such problems of race and crime is breathtaking to people on our side of the Pacific. Frankly, there are times when rather more American isolation would be welcome. [5]

The United States influences much of the political debate and the parameters of much of the political action in the Middle East. American cultural norms are, for better or worse, something of a benchmark to gauge the nature and direction of societal change in many, if not most, developing countries. Many political and social movements, therefore, are often reactions to, or against, U.S. policies and ideas. And, too often, the United States is linked to forces of repression, inequality, and authoritarianism. As one liberal Israeli analyst has noted, "A foreign player like the United States who provides support for a local elite tends to create unfulfilled expectations and to become a symbol of evil in the eyes of opposition forces."[6] This is compounded when there is a great perception that the United States talks out of both sides of its mouth and its policies are hypocritical because an ally like Israel can act outside the bounds of international norms with impunity. For some, Israel is nothing more than an agent to push the American agenda in the Middle East so the United States does not have to dirty its hands, or, as a reporter paraphrasing Arab sentiments noted, "Israel is simply a neighborhood outpost of the U.S.-dominated global economy."[7] Even former U.S. President George Bush recently acknowledged that the United States has a real problem of perceptions in the Arab world and, rightly or wrongly, most Arabs believe there is an unjust double standard at work. [8]

The United States not only has an image problem but in the absence of strong leadership and little vision in a time of uncertainty and instability, foreign policy in the Middle East has become reactive and tactical at best. While the United States has never truly "controlled" events in the Middle East it has been a powerful force with often skillful uses of initiative and pressure to move parties in particular directions. No more. American weakness of leadership has great ramifications for the region, in large part because America rhetorically claims the mantle of leadership and has created significant expectations for such leadership. American foreign policy in the 20th century has been pulled between the twin pillars of Wilson's (and Carter's) moralism/idealism and Teddy Roosevelt's (and Kissinger's) realism. One path was visionary and grandiose, the other practical and powerful. Today,

American foreign policy is a muddle that is neither idealist nor realist. There appear to be no serious attempts at developing policies that marry a vision of the Middle East with specific strategies and tactics. American actions in the short term do not reflect what its long-term vision is. There are essentially four reasons for this: a lack of strong and sustained global leadership from the President; a decline in American power and credibility (which is somewhat related to and reflective of the first); the push and pull of domestic politics; and an inability to match lofty rhetoric and goals with facts on the ground and an inability to make hard choices. Examples abound from Kosovo to the Asian financial crisis or the nuclear testing in South Asia to the Middle East. With the conclusion of the Wye River Accord and the election of Ehud Barak, the Clinton Administration believed it had salvaged the peace process. But little was done to move forward on the key issues that divide Israelis and Palestinians. And, even as the United States has worked hard to facilitate an agreement between Israel and Syria, it may not have yet occurred to the Americans that Barak's election, while necessary to any peace, may not have been sufficient because the Israelis and Arabs may have very different conceptions of what peace is. The bottom line for Barak, as it was for Rabin, has been security. And the way to achieve that, particularly it seems for Barak, has been to separate Israel from Arabs, not to live in peace and cooperation with them. For all Israeli leaders, whether Barak or Rabin, Netanyahu or Begin, the peace process has been something of a zero-sum game: Israel is stronger when the Arabs, their neighbors, are weaker.

One of the largest failures of post cold war American policy has been, despite the rhetoric, the selective, politically motivated, application of the rule of law. It had appeared after the Gulf War that a new world order would be one in which the rule of law transcended the rule of the jungle, that law would replace naked aggression. But the United States has looked to international law selectively and only when it suited its purposes. The United States has resorted to military force both to uphold international law and subvert it. Such inconsistency does not endear the United States to many other countries in the world, whether ally or neutral. The United States wants greater pursuit of war criminals but eschews a permanent war crimes tribunal. The United States sponsors and upholds UN Security Council resolutions and actions aimed against Iraq while denouncing any aimed at Israel. The

United States condemns terrorist bombings and activities, yet responds in a way that smacks of cowboy diplomacy when it goes off half-cocked in attacking a so-called chemical weapons plant in the Sudan. Combined, such perceptions greatly erode U.S. credibility in the Middle East, particularly when there has been no delivery of the promised peace between Arabs and Israelis nor the realization of Palestinian self-determination. As George Bush noted, this greatly hampers U.S. credibility and effectiveness.

The United States consistently claims that it will oppose aggression everywhere but it becomes the arbiter of what is aggression and what is not. Thus, no matter what Israel's policies and actions are, they never seem to constitute aggression. Turkey's incursions against the Kurds are not acts of aggression that should be opposed. Even the Rwandan (and Ugandan)-backed aggression in support of guerrillas in former Zaire was not perceived as aggression by U.S. standards and thus was met with a lukewarm response at best. Nor does the United States respond consistently in those areas where it does see aggression. The Clinton Administration vehemently proclaims its opposition to Iraqi and Serbian aggression, for example, but even American responses under Clinton have not been consistent or effective, in part because of a fear of failure and a fear of risk as the air campaign in Kosovo demonstrated, and in part because of a perception that there is little domestic American support for opposing international aggression with military force. There may be good (and often self-interested) reasons for America's selectivity – acting against Serbian aggression in Kosovo, but not Russian aggression in Chechnya – but those reasons do not preclude other countries and peoples from expressing cynicism and anger at U.S. motives and actions, as well as questioning U.S. motives in its efforts at making peace in the Middle East.

U.S. Interests in the Middle East

Oil, Israel and regional stability are the three most important issues for U.S. policy in the Middle East. Regional stability or security in the Middle East used to refer to America's Cold War interests; now, stability is simply a necessary element for securing the first two priorities. The role of political Islam is not included because, while it is important, it is not a particular policy issue but a perceived threat that affects each of the three priority areas. There are also two specific security areas that are viewed as critical for regional stability: containing, if not eliminating, terrorism, and reducing the proliferation of weapons of mass destruction and increasingly sophisticated delivery systems.

United States foreign policy, therefore, concentrates on a few key issues in the Middle East: the Arab-Israeli peace process; military and security issues regarding the Persian Gulf; anti-terrorism; and, to a lesser extent, arms control. A sub-region such as North Africa is somewhat ignored because it is not considered of vital interest and because Europe, particularly France, is more heavily involved. Economic development and issues of democratization are in many ways peripheral issues because they are usually ignored if they are in conflict with the more critical interests and because many fewer resources are devoted to them. As an American State Department official noted, at high-level meetings between senior American and Egyptian officials, particularly at the level of Secretary of State and Foreign Minister, the American agenda is the Arab-Israeli, or Palestinian-Israeli, peace process. [9] Other issues are left to junior diplomats or organizations like the United States Agency for International Development (USAID). U.S. policy also focuses on other lesser policy goals, which are related to the main objectives, including the strengthening of economic and security ties with moderate Arab states and such trans-national challenges as combating cross-border terrorism and preventing the diffusion of more weapons of mass destruction. There are also internal challenges, particularly those posed by Islamists and the lack of economic and political reform in many Middle East countries. There are many unsettled societies with massive social and economic problems. In many of the countries the leadership is either weak (Lebanon, Algeria, Yemen, Kuwait) or old (Syria, Libya, Saudi Arabia), or in transition (Jordan, Morocco). The future is therefore greatly unsettled.

Security and the presence of American and British military forces in the Persian Gulf remain top considerations in relations between the United States and the Gulf Arab states. The primary reason is that the oil resources remain critical to the world economy, now and even more so for the future. The Middle East has the highest oil production (29.2% of the world's output in 1996) of any region in the world but more significantly has 65.3% of the world's proven oil reserves and 32.4% of its proven natural gas reserves. [10] Just as one must focus on the security of oil in the Middle East as a critical American interest in the region, one must also focus on the Arab-Israeli conflict and the peace process.

During the Cold War, the Middle East was significant for both the resources it held and for the role it played in the competition between the United States and Soviet Union. By the early 1970s Israel and the United States had forged a very strong strategic partnership, which would serve as a barrier to possible Soviet expansion in the region. At the same time, that relationship greatly complicated U.S. concerns for ensuring access to the vast resources of the Middle East.

Even with the end of the Cold War, many of the same problems have continued in the region or have actually gotten worse. Despite the turnover of a few leaders, little change has occurred politically within most Arab societies and their governmental systems. Religious fundamentalism remains strong within the region, often continuing its broad-based appeal to many disenfranchised or disaffected sectors of society. This reflects a growing divide between the haves and have-nots in society. In addition, the scarcity of natural resources such as water, arable land, and the pressures of high population growth increase the risks of conflict, both within countries and between them. Finally, on top of each of these issues, one must impose the fundamental conflict that still exists between Arab nationalism and Zionism as well as the competing claims for the same land among Palestinians and Israelis.

There is a fundamental and inherent contradiction between America's basic interests in the Middle East. Almost no post World War II American administration has been able to reconcile such basic goals of the United States: access to cheap and abundant sources of oil; the security of Israel; regional stability; and adherence to basic American principles of democratization, economic liberalism and the right of self-determination. While none of these objectives are strongly challenged within the American body politic, there is no consensus as to which of the goals is the most pre-eminent. But the pattern of U.S. actions over the past three decades is that the last objective is the least important and has usually been sacrificed in pursuit of the other three. Many have argued that Israeli security, particularly over the past 30 years, has often been allowed to overshadow the other vital American interests and objectives. But, at bottom, the security of Israel, Persian Gulf security, and regional stability ultimately means the preservation of the status quo – a region with a strong Israel and conservative, pro-U.S. Arab regimes – in the Middle East. The reason to resolve the Israeli-Palestinian dispute is that the conflict has undermined U.S. interests and challenged the status quo, not because of ideals of justice and self-determination.

In 1991, America used its power in a remarkable way. First, there was the creation of an unprecedented coalition of states in the Middle East and throughout the world that expelled Iraq from Kuwait and destroyed much of Iraq's military capability. Whether one agrees with the means or the ends, it was an impressive display of the power of military might and diplomatic and economic persuasion. Then came the almost equally extraordinary use of diplomatic power and creative vision which brought together Israel and the key Arab parties into the Madrid process, a process described by some Israelis, Arabs and Americans as brilliant even as they acknowledged that it was manipulative, overly ambitious and favored Israel.

There is a perception among many in the Arab world that the United States is biased against Islam. American credibility suffers because of the perceived double standard when Arabs point to U.S. actions against Iraq, Sudan and Afghanistan, while turning a blind eye to Israeli policies toward Palestinians and inaction for a long time against Serbian aggression in Bosnia and Kosovo, made up principally of Muslims. There is a lot of sentiment in the Arab world for Bosniaks and Kosovars, some of it rooted in a belief in Islam as the nation, not Egypt or Jordan or Morocco, etc. Often, appeals against U.S. foreign policy in Middle Eastern states are based on Islamic interests, not necessarily nationalist or state interests. Thus, the United States should not be surprised at the anger and doubts raised in the Islamic world about U.S. policy toward Iraq, even among those who have no use for someone like Saddam Hussein and are not necessarily anti-western. This is compounded when the United States violates state sovereignty (supposedly the very thing the United States urged the international community to punish after Iraq invaded Kuwait) and attacks an industrial plant in Sudan with cruise missiles on the flimsiest of evidence that it was producing components for chemical weapons.

The 1998 attack upon the factory in Sudan purported to be involved in the manufacture of chemical weapons was a classic example of how the United States either does not understand the Arab world or does not care at all how its actions are perceived by Arabs. For most Arabs and Muslims, this is both ignorant and arrogant, even among those in the Muslim world who are America's allies. As one anti-government Sudanese scholar who now works for the United Nations High Commissioner for Refugees (UNHCR) noted, the strikes there and in Afghanistan made the supposed target of those strikes, Osama bin Laden, "...a hero in Saudi Arabia, in Islamabad, in Cairo, in all capitals of the Muslim world ... this is a resurging Muslim world. You don't deal with it with cruise missiles you discuss it. You don't rub the entire Muslim world's nose in the dirt and make it kneel."[11] This is particularly problematic because the Sudanese government had, at that time, after considerable western pressure, closed most of the terrorists training camps in Sudan and had expelled Osama bin Laden. This serves to emphasize George Bush's point that the current administration needs to understand how American actions are perceived in the Arab countries. This credibility problem is at the heart of how U.S. actions in the peace process are perceived.

The American and Israeli Vision of Peace in the Middle East

The end of the Cold War and the defeat of Iraq were, for Americans, the defeat of extremism in the Middle East. Iraq had been humbled, Libya was isolated, the PLO severely weakened because it backed the wrong horse, and Syria, with nowhere else to turn, was humbled and joined the coalition. And, during this period, two internationalist-minded Presidents, and their Secretaries of State, directed American foreign policy in a new world in which the United States was the predominant power. George Bush and his Secretary of State, James Baker were more practical and had greater conviction in staying the course and seemed less concerned about the pressure of domestic politics (whether it was the reluctance of Congress to use military force in Kuwait or the challenges of pro-Israeli lobbying efforts when Bush suspended loan guarantees over the issue of settlements). Clinton and Warren Christopher, and later, Madeleine Albright, were more idealistic in some ways but were also more susceptible to domestic pressure. But both Presidents and their advisors were moralists, believing that the Middle

East could be re-made through an American-sponsored peace process into a peaceful, more democratic and more economically prosperous place. The region would be more integrated and the risks of deadly conflict reduced by making peace and reducing arms.

Such a vision needs to be understood because it helps explain American policy in the Middle East in the 1990s and the fact that the Americans have a long view of the situation which has kept them wedded to a process they believe will lead to the promised land of peace and a new Middle East. This is particularly true of the Clinton Administration because even as the Oslo process broke down completely for 18 months there was a persistent optimism that if only the parties could be brought back to the table, progress could be made. The process itself did not need to be revised or rethought.

To some degree, the framework and the intellectual basis for the American conception and development of the peace process is based on the American view of the rewards of regional cooperation. During the headiest post-Madrid and post-Oslo days some senior U.S. officials saw precedents with European history. They made comparisons between the Middle East and the CSCE (Conference on Security and Cooperation in Europe) process and also touted the cooperative economic networks created within the context of European integration, initially through the European Coal and Steel Community and then through the creation of the highly integrated European Union. In talking to many key American officials, these themes formed a substantial part of the long-term American vision for the Middle East. Ironically, this vision is neither shared by most Arab states or the Palestinians nor even by many Israelis. The Likud position, for example, has been that creation of peace between Israel and Palestinians, even Israel and Syria, still leaves the Middle East a dangerous place, an arena full of real and potential conflict. The American vision actually reflects much more a vision that Shimon Peres in particular, and some others in the Labor Party, has espoused and discussed as the payoff for trading land for peace.

How have these visionary goals been reflected in U.S. Middle East policy? In many ways, they have been very much at the heart of U.S. actions and ideas with respect to the Middle East since the military victory over Iraq. It is clear that the American priorities emphasize greater regional cooperation and integration. This idea was embedded in the Madrid peace process and has been a common vision shared by both

Peres and the Bush and Clinton Administrations. It is important to note that a number of key figures in American Middle East policy who have spanned both U.S. administrations - Dennis Ross, Aaron Miller, Daniel Kurtzer – have over the years strongly expressed ideas similar to those of Peres in discussing future Middle East cooperation and economic integration and institutionalization.

Israeli Deputy Foreign Minister under Rabin and current Justice Minister Yossi Beilin, emphasized in 1993 that, "The centrality of regional economic cooperation to the design of the New Middle East is clear...." He added, "We have a goal: The creation of a Middle East of cooperation and harmony with the chance to advance economic and societal goals on a shared infrastructure that will assure the prosperity of all the inhabitants of the region, of their peoples and of their states, and will bring about the hoped-for historic conciliation."[12] Israel under Rabin and Peres viewed economic cooperation as the linchpin for peace in the region. This may be less true with Barak, in part because Shimon Peres, Minister for Regional Cooperation, seems more marginalized from the decision-making process, and in part because Barak seems primarily focused on issues of military security. However, economic cooperation remains critical to President Clinton and his team of negotiators. As a recent study of the impact of U.S. economic aid on the peace process has noted: "U.S. officials sometimes act as if initiatives for prosperity and cooperation can be worked out even when political disagreements exist, because doing business together serves everyone's self-interest." [13]

Just as many in Israel see security as a zero-sum game, many Arabs view economics as a zero-sum game. As the study continued, "...the forces of old-fashioned protectionism and narrow economic nationalism are powerful everywhere in the Levant, in Israel as well as in Arab states. Syrian president Hafiz al-Asad and many other Arabs seem to see economic integration ... as a plot for Israel to dominate Arab economies." So, even though Israelis such as Beilin and Peres are considered in the "peace camp" in Israel, many Arabs were not thrilled at this agenda. Many view it as replacing military dominance by Israel in the region with economic dominance of its neighbors. Some believe this is simply a more subtle, yet nonetheless insidious, plot to undermine and dominate the Arab world. Israel's negotiator with Syria under the Rabin government, Itamar Rabinovich, has noted that Assad was more wary of

Shimon Peres' focus on economic ties than on Rabin's tough stance on security issues.[14]

One clear implication of this U.S.-Israeli vision reflects a key factor of a new world order for the United States: greater emphasis and reliance on regional responsibility and regional cooperation. Israel would be the linchpin for such a strategy in the Middle East but the United States clearly hoped that moderate Arab states could begin to accept Israel and engage in increased economic cooperation and perhaps some economic integration down the line. In part, this has been due to an American vision of a more interdependent world but also due to reluctance to be the world's policeman and a continuing decline of military resources necessary to allow the United States to be self-reliant in protecting its vast global interests. Whether in the Middle East or Europe, the United States has been pushing for a series of ever-tightening security, cultural and economic alliances that would link as many nations as possible in what President Clinton called a "web of institutions and arrangements" that protects and guides those within "while isolating those who challenge them from the outside."[15]

While the United States has a vision similar to that of Peres and other Israeli liberals, it was unwilling to put any pressure on the Netanyahu government in order to prevent it from wrecking the process – even when it seemed clear that the Netanyahu was not committed to the idea of "land for peace." As Ian Lustick noted, the Netanyahu government "treat[s] the agreements not as a basis for an evolving partnership, but as an array of legalistic and public relations weapons that can free Israel of its commitments, prevent further transfers of territory to Palestinian control, and delegitimize Arafat and the idea of a Palestinian state in the mind of Israeli public opinion."[16] Although the Likud government claimed that it was wedded to the Oslo Peace Process and the agreement with the Palestinians, it added a significant caveat that what Oslo means is what Israel interprets is written into the agreement, not what the Palestinians may have thought they had agreed to with the Rabin government.[17] As the failure of Israel and the Palestinians to agree on a document of principles to end the conflict on February 13, 2000, as agreed in the Sharm el Sheikh agreement of September 1999 indicated, that caveat appears to hold even with Barak. His government may have an interpretation of peace that is more favorable for the Palestinians, but it remains Israel's interpretation.

Part of Barak's problem is that in the months since his election, he has become weaker domestically and has been diverted by the increasing attacks on Israeli soldiers in southern Lebanon. Barak thought he had dealt with the problem of Lebanon by announcing that Israeli military forces would withdraw from there in July 2000, come what may. The Palestinians are incapable of making any further concession that might strengthen Barak's position and the Syrians will not do so because they want an Israeli commitment to withdraw from the Golan back to the 1967 border (even if Syria never recognized that border) as a sine qua non to any negotiations. Ultimately, the Israelis on one side and the Palestinians and Syrians on the other, have different conceptions of what is required to achieve peace, while Arafat and Barak, in early 2000, have been weakened.

At the heart of the U.S. vision of peace between Israel and its Arab neighbors has been "land for peace." Since the failed attempt to initiate the Rogers Plan in 1969, The United States has consistently followed the Israeli vision of peace. And, for both countries, United Nations Security Council Resolution 242, which embodies "land for peace," means that Israel should withdraw from land occupied after 1967, not withdraw from *the* land. Thus, from this viewpoint, the amount of land Israel can withdraw from while ensuring security is open to interpretation and must be determined by Israel's security needs. When the Americans promote "land for peace" they do not mean what most Arabs view as a "just" solution to the conflict: the return of all lands occupied in 1967. While the United States and Israel may disagree over how far Israel can go, there is agreement on the principle. On the other hand, the United States leadership rarely takes Arab considerations into account nor does it spend much time trying to understand the Arab perspective. A number of senior American officials, when asked about the peace process, felt free to articulate Israeli positions and interests but when asked about Arab positions and interests would reply, "you have to ask the Arabs." Most American policymakers sincerely believe that the peace process, as they envision it, will be good for the Arabs. From the American perspective, the Arab parties will not get everything they want and they will have to accept what is believed to be Israel's right to a homeland in the Middle East (as opposed to simply accepting Israel's existence, something most Arabs acknowledge that they cannot change).

But what the Americans, and many Israelis, do not seem to understand is that there is good peace and bad peace and for many Arabs no peace is better than an unjust peace, a bad peace. As many Arabs note, peace cannot exist if Israeli security comes at the expense of Arab security. The Arab parties do not buy into the peace process in the same way as the Americans. They don't necessarily see a significant payoff, particularly when it appears that the Israelis have benefited up front.

The main reason for this, and a significant reason why prospects for long-term peace remain problematic is that the United States has created a peace process, which favors the Israeli view of peace and Israel's view of what is necessary to ensure its security. A critical component of the American assumption is that Israel must remain the predominant power or even a regional hegemon in the Middle East. This is not just as a surrogate to protect U.S. interests but both the United States and Israel believe this is necessary to ensure Israel's security and existence. However, one of the reasons that the Bush and Clinton Administrations have favored the Labor Party over the Likud is that the Americans have little sympathy for those Israelis who promote a vision of "Eretz" or Greater Israel. The United States wants to see a secure and powerful Israel not one that must put more and more resources into territorial expansion and occupation, and control over Arab populations. That is one of the reasons why the Oslo process had appeal for both Rabin and Clinton. It gave back incrementally the populated areas of the West Bank so that Israel could divest itself of much of the Arab population while retaining as much land for security purposes (as opposed to expansion purposes). But Rabin, like Netanyahu and like Barak, put the onus for Israeli security on the Palestinians. Rabin believed that the Palestinians had to prove themselves capable of making Israelis more secure. He remarked shortly after the Gaza-Jericho agreement, "We will see to what extent [the Palestinians] can prevent terrorism against us" and ensure "security for Israelis in Israel, in the territories, and in the Gaza Strip."[18] Thus, whether Labor or Likud, Israel has retained the right to determine what security is, and what amount of land and what type of peace was necessary to achieve it. In July 1999, even when a senior Israel official acknowledged that Yasser Arafat had stepped up operations against terror, he noted that Israel still expected more.[19]

The Madrid Process

A key to the Madrid process was the creation of a framework that embodied the Israeli approach to negotiating Middle East peace: a series of bilateral negotiations, a series of separate Camp David Accords. Weaken the Arabs by dividing them, and there would be no common Arab delegation and no Israeli negotiation with a unified Arab coalition on comprehensive peace such that a final status was negotiated together. Israel would never have entered such a negotiation, so the Arabs were persuaded to come together for a series of bilateral talks under a common umbrella and also engage in a series of multilateral talks – that focused on more functional or technical, and less politically-charged, issues – in which Israel would have to face numerous Arab actors, and progress was measured by consensus.

At the end of the Cold War, the Arab world had to deal with the United States from a position of weakness since the two superpowers could not be played off each other. At the same time, the United States had to demonstrate greater balance and evenhandedness in its approaches to the region in order to show the Arabs that their vulnerability was not simply being exploited by the United States and Israel. The Palestinians had to be recognized as partners in the peace process and Israel could not afford to throw away the opportunity to attempt to make peace when its Arab adversaries were in such a vulnerable position. The process itself became critical because almost all the parties, including Israel, came to Madrid reluctantly and only to satisfy the United States. No one was prepared to negotiate or make concessions. As one analyst noted: "A process of 'playing to the United States' was begun. Israel did so to retain and sustain its special relationship with the United States while the more radical Arabs did so to acquire a relationship to supplant the one lost with the Soviet Union and its allies and the other Arab interlocutors did so to sustain, refurbish, expand or otherwise to enhance their relationship with the United States in an era of no alternative superpowers."[20] And, as James Baker has noted, no party wanted to be the one to turn the United States down: "One of our [the United States'] strongest points of leverage, with respect to all parties, was the threat to, as I found myself saying all too often, lay the dead cat on their doorstep. No one wanted to accept blame for scuttling the process."[21] Over time, and after the change of government in Israel in 1992, the parties began to develop faith in the process itself and not just participate because of pressure from the United States.

The United States did an exceptional job at getting the parties to the table and to participate in the process; it was not easy and Secretary of State Baker used considerable pressure and persuasion. But it must be understood that the U.S. role is not one of an "honest broker." The United States is neither neutral nor disinterested but is a broker nonetheless. For the Arab parties, the American-initiated peace process was the only option. It had to play by the American rules or stay outside the process.

The regional aspect to the peace process is clearly important to the United States. This reflects a broader, more long-term U.S. vision at work in the peace process. This ties in very much with America's broader global agenda and foreign policy goals. One of the major principles of the Madrid process that was emphasized by U.S. Secretary of State James Baker when he opened the January 1992 meeting in Moscow to establish the multilateral talks greatly reflected the U.S. view that peace between Arabs and Israelis was the key to peace and stability in the region: "multilateral negotiations on regional issues can begin to improve the lives of people and create a basis for greater stability in the area. As progress is made, as tangible benefits emerge, a vision of what real peace might mean will also begin to emerge."[22] As one analyst has noted, the premise behind the multilateral talks was "the functionalist thesis that the rewards of economic cooperation will drive the search and strengthen the foundations for political agreements...."[23] He added, "From progress in the multilaterals would emerge a vision of what real peace might entail and the benefits that would accrue to all parties, thereby facilitating progress in the bilateral talks. Functional cooperation would eventually spill over into regional peace."[24] Economic and technological interdependence would, therefore, create its own incentives for cooperation and the maintenance of stability in the region. The key to this type of thinking is that political agreements are not enough. Peace must be sustainable. It must be embedded in patterns of cooperation and all the parties must have a stake in the maintenance of peace because there are significant rewards from the cooperation and the absence of war.

These ideas came from two disparate sources, both from the European experience. The first was the CSCE process. [25] The CSCE was not a blueprint for the multilateral approach but the principle embedded in the Madrid process of building confidence and cooperation through meetings and workshops of experts on technical, lower-level and non-political issues was very much in the spirit of the CSCE.

A senior American official involved in the peace negotiations leading up to the Madrid conference noted that it was Eduard Shevardnadze, then Foreign Minister of the Soviet Union, who first proposed the CSCE model when he urged James Baker and Dennis Ross, then Director of Policy Planning in the State Department, to initiate a CSCE process for the Middle East. This was in June 1990 and the American response was that such a thing was premature. A year and a half later, however, the Americans purposely went back to Shevardnadze's idea. The only way such a multilateral approach would work was to develop two tracks of negotiation, not just one as with the CSCE (although one could argue that in the European context there was the CSCE multilateral level and then the U.S.-Soviet bilateral level). This was critical because Israel had rejected over the years any international forum that would serve only as an arena for the Arab states to gang up on Israel. So bilateral, face-to-face negotiations were critical for the Israelis. The multilateral track would provide a parallel arena, that was much less political and public, in which common solutions could be found to common problems, both local and regional. As conceived, these talks would include most of the states throughout the Middle East and many key countries from the rest of the world so that all would have a stake in creating peace in the Middle East.

A second precedent for the multilateral process was the experience of the European Union. Many in the west and Israel envisioned the ultimate institutionalization of cooperation and regional economic development. Others talked of a CSCME (Conference on Security and Cooperation in the Middle East) or other types of institutional frameworks. The Israeli-Jordanian peace treaty actually calls for a CSCME. If, as one senior American official noted, the Madrid process works, "why not institutionalize it?" Israeli Foreign Minister Shimon Peres talked of a "Middle East common market." And, clearly many of the ideas behind the American strategy for Madrid had been at the core of Jean Monnet's and Robert Schumann's thinking when proposing the European Coal and Steel Community. The functionalist premise of economic and technical cooperation spilling over into the political realm had been proven in the minds of many by the case of the great post-war cooperation between traditional enemies France and Germany.

In addition, it was felt that the multilateral talks might serve nicely as a way to develop and implement confidence-building measures and develop cooperative relationships and processes as well as ideas that might spill over into the more difficult and highly political bilateral negotiations. The multilateral talks would focus on ostensibly non-political issues, although most Israelis and Arabs would argue that the issues of arms control, water and refugees in particular had many political ramifications. Nevertheless, the key was perhaps less the issues themselves than the incorporation of many Middle East actors who were not the core states (Israel, Jordan, Egypt, the Palestinians, Syrian and Lebanon), most particularly those from North Africa and the Persian Gulf states into the peace process and discussions of issues critical to the future of the region. Thus, the level of the talks was such that the issues were being discussed in a regional context with a search for region-wide approaches and solutions. At the bilateral level, the focus was on the more immediate political issues of political acceptance, territory, borders, security, demographics, and the status of the Palestinian people. As one Israeli official noted, "In the bilaterals we are trying to overcome the past and in the multilaterals we have a forum to look to the future."

With the election of Netanyahu, Israel became much more intransigent on the bilateral level and was not committed to the same idea of peace as a broad-based, more cooperative vision as the Rabin-led Labour Party had been. After Rabin's death, the peace process was viewed by both Israelis and Palestinians as something that favored the other's interests, as a fig leaf for expansion and changing facts on the ground by the Israelis, or continuing to threaten the lives of Israeli Jews while not agreeing to Israel's right to a secure homeland by Palestinians. And, the United States did not put any real pressure on the parties, particularly not on the Israelis. That was not the case in 1991 when U.S. Secretary of State James Baker cajoled most of the parties who eventually came to Madrid to the table. It is important to note that there really has not been much of a change in policy or vision from the Bush to Clinton Administrations but rather a change in implementation. This is due in large measure to the fact that key policy makers on the peace process – Dennis Ross and Aaron Miller in particular – have not changed. They, along with current U.S. Ambassador to Egypt Daniel Kurtzer, had much to do with the early design and implementation of Madrid, and quickly moved to revive the multilateral talks after five years with a meeting in Moscow in January 2000. A more active and engaged President willing to take strong steps and risks has enhanced this. President Clinton has become much more involved in the peace process, particularly with the urgency of the end of his term in office.

Multilateralism in general and greater economic integration greatly benefits the Israelis. Many Arab countries chafed at that, yet most (excluding Syria and Lebanon which boycotted the multilaterals and Libya, Iraq and Sudan which were not invited) continued to participate in and actively embraced the process. But when there was no progress between Palestinians and Israelis after Netanyahu came to power, Arab parties gave up on the peace process and most boycotted the last multilateral meeting on economic issues in Doha, Qatar in November 1997. One of the primary reasons Syria has boycotted the multilateral talks is because Hafez el Assad believes that all rewards from such cooperation should only occur after a political peace has been achieved. Another concern of the Syrians was that too much progress in the multilateral talks would reduce Israel's incentive to negotiate with Syria. At the same time, Syria remained abreast of the talks and often asked to be briefed on their status and progress.

Regardless of the Syrian and Lebanese boycott and the skepticism of some Arab states, Israel, the United States, Russia, the Europeans, and Japan all believed that regional cooperation would help build peace. But there was suspicion in the region that the multilateral talks were also a stalking horse for greater economic penetration of the Middle East, by the United States, Europe and Japan, as well as Israel. All of these countries saw ways to advance their own economic interests because of the potential for regional peace and cooperation. One American official remarked that anyone who wanted to do a study undertook one. Through the multilateral process, France took the lead on transportation issues, railroads in particular, in part because the French want to make money by developing railroads in the Middle East. Uri Savir, co-chair of the Israeli delegation to the economic development talks remarked about a French presentation to one of the economic development workshops: "The French presented a very detailed paper on transportation and communication. It includes a map of a railway, an imaginary railway from Damascus to Beirut, Tel Aviv, Eilat, Riyadh, and Cairo. What may not have been anticipated was that experts from a French railroad company showed up a week later, taking measurements in the region and discussing the Beersheba-Eilat part of it, believing that whoever does this will get the rest of the pie." [26]

Many Arabs were suspicious that Israel was benefiting up front, particularly through economic cooperation, while the Arabs had to wait until the end of the process for Israel to give up land. One thing the United States tried to do to counter this was to use the multilateral talks as a vehicle for bringing aid and investment to Palestinians. But that was less extensive than hoped. Too often, the outside economic parties simply tried to enhance their economic foothold in the region, or had little faith in the ability of the Palestinian Authority to use outside aid and investment wisely and responsibly. Even so, there were a number of worthwhile projects developed and the United States encouraged the active involvement of European counties and Japan in the multilateral groups so that they had a stake in the peace process and helped establish the economic benefits the United States believed critical to spur confidence in the rewards of making peace. The most successful areas of cooperation and investment were in tourism, environmental protection, desertification, desalination and a few economic infrastructure projects. In the early stages of the multilateral talks, the Palestinian focus of the economic group became important because with the focus on the infrastructure of the occupied territories, the Palestinians were actually getting something tangible up front in the multilateral process. But the Arab delegations were somewhat nervous when Israeli Foreign Minister Shimon Peres began to advocate a region-wide economic community, one of economic cooperation and integration. The resistance to the idea of a regional development bank and the boycott of the Doha meeting highlights the fear that the west was working to integrate Israel into regional Arab economies through joint development projects.

Over time, many Arab states expressed disappointment in the whole process. It appeared to them that Israel got too many tangible benefits up front, including the removal of the second and third stages of the Arab economic boycott of Israel by the Gulf countries, as well as much greater recognition. As one senior Egyptian official remarked: "By definition, the multilaterals were unbalanced. From day one we knew Israel would get significant return up front. We didn't kid ourselves about that. That doesn't frustrate us. We had hoped that the imbalance would lead to Israeli movement on substance. We expected a much greater return by now." He added that even if the multilateral talks were a tool for the Israelis to achieve normalization that was not necessarily a bad thing for the Arabs - if it lead to Israel feeling more secure and then compromised on substantive issues. But for most Arab parties, that hope was dashed when Netanyahu came to power. It has yet to be truly revived, as Barak's actions have not matched his rhetoric.

One of the reasons the process becomes so important is that the United States does not want to prejudge the outcome of any peace negotiations. This has been essentially the U.S. strategy since the failure of the Rogers Plan in 1969, a clear attempt to define the outcome, something Israel has always refused to do, and refuses to allow the United States to do. As one analyst noted about the lessons of the failed Rogers Plan, the "Arabs should...learn that United States influence with Israel was conditional upon their restraint and moderation."[27] The United States would not pressure Israel simply for the sake of improving relations with other countries or adversaries and U.S. pressure was seen to work only with corresponding change in Arab behavior. This has held up through most of the past 31 years. But such an approach benefits Israel while frustrating the Arab parties, making it often harder for Arab leaders to gain popular support because there is no sense that their goals can necessarily be met. For Israel, the solidification and acceptance of the status quo that comes with a long, incremental process serves its needs. The competing approaches and logic is most starkly drawn in the two approaches to arms control in the Middle East. Israel argues that it cannot begin to discuss renouncing a nuclear deterrent unless there is full and comprehensive peace in the region. The Arabs, particularly Egypt, argue that there can be no true peace in the Middle East until Israel gives up its nuclear arms. It is easy for Israelis to fall back on a status quo that is not so bad for Israel.

The Madrid framework clearly incorporated a conceptualization of peace, security and a negotiation process that was more in line with Israeli thinking and needs. But, at the same time, the process was created in such a way as to provide rewards and benchmarks for the Arab parties as they continued to participate and progress was established, particularly because with the collapse of the Soviet Union, good relations with the sole remaining super power seemed, at that time anyway, paramount. This process was also risky for the Arabs because Israel could stop at any point in the negotiations, leaving the Arab side with little or nothing; it also meant that the negotiations could develop at a different pace on each negotiating track, allowing the Israelis to play one negotiation (or Arab party) off another. Many analysts argue that Rabin did this with respect to the separate Palestinian and Syrian negotiations. The prospect of a deal with Syria was viewed as a threat to the Palestinian cause because Israel could give up or put on hold the Palestinian track. Barak has revised this tactic as it became increasingly clear that with the suspension of talks with both the Syrians and Israelis in February 2000, Barak was considering playing one off the other.[28] In addition, the negotiations with Syria have made it harder for the United States and others to criticize Israel for delays in the negotiations with Palestinians or changing facts on the ground in the occupied territory of the West Bank—including the continuation of some settlements and house demolitions, although much less than the Netanyahu government – for fear of jeopardizing the critical Syrian track.

The United States has had to assure all the parties that there was a real possibility for a lasting peace and also help minimize the risks of pursuing peace. But the United States has perhaps relied too much on the argument that there is no alternative to the U.S.-brokered peace process. While it is true that there really is no other alternative process, or at least no other alternative broker, there is an alternative: no process, no peace. For many in the Arab world, and for a growing number of Palestinians, no peace is better than an unjust or bad peace. It is not altogether clear that successive American administrations have understood that. The American attitude on many of the key issues between Palestinians and Israelis has been that the United States will support what the parties (that is, the leaders of the two peoples) agree upon - regarding the final political status of a Palestinian entity, security arrangements, or Jerusalem. But that assumes that either the Palestinian or Israeli people will support what they perceive to be a "bad" agreement or an unfair, unjust or insecure peace. The United States cannot broker a sustainable, long-lasting peace if it is only concerned with the needs of one side or pressures the leaders to agree to something they cannot sell to their constituents. Both sides need something they can live with, now and in the future.

The Americans subscribe to the Israeli argument (embraced particularly by security-conscious Laborites) that under a "land for peace" formula, once Israel makes any territorial concessions it can only undo those concessions by going to war, whereas for the Arabs to go back on peace (which Israelis view as being comprehensive and normalized relations) would be much easier and less risky for them. Thus, in this light, Israel is viewed as taking greater risks, or making the greater sacrifice, for peace. Within this framework that incorporated the Israeli view, Israel under Rabin was clearly ready to use this process as a means to make peace with its neighbors, recognize Palestinian legitimacy, and establish some autonomous Palestinian entity. This was unlike Yitzhak Shamir who admitted that he used the peace process, as a way to stall so that Israel could create facts on the ground that would form the basis for a Greater Israel.

The Wye agreement brought the United States into the process as a much more active player. What changed at Wye was the dynamic of the negotiation relationship. In many ways, the talks at Wye were a negotiation between Israel and the United States. The 13% withdrawal was an American formulation. The Americans negotiated with Israel to accept the CIA as a third-party guarantor of Palestinian security efforts. And, Israel dragged into the talks the Jonathan Pollard issue, which is exclusively a dispute between Israel and the United States. All the Palestinians really did was to align themselves with everything the Americans were proposing. And the only way to explain the Palestinian position is that they are very weak or naive negotiators. They were effectively negotiating with Israel what had already been agreed to; the Israelis were demanding almost an airtight guarantee of Israeli security by the Palestinians while the Palestinians were no closer to statehood or agreements on Jerusalem, the settlements, and security arrangements on the ground (as opposed to security guarantees on paper).

In looking at the discussions between the United States and Israel at Wye it is not clear who had the upper hand. It could be argued that Israel would find it difficult to claim the Palestinians were not doing enough on security issues if the CIA maintains that they were in compliance. The CIA would lend credibility to Palestinian claims of compliance and that could give the United States cover domestically to pressure the Israelis. On the other hand, if the Israelis want the process to fail, they may have found a way to do so without taking the blame. Essentially, Israel has given hard-line Palestinian groups willing to use violence against Israeli civilians a veto on the peace process. Declaring the process a failure, Israel could settle for the status quo, ridding itself of Gaza and the Arab populations of the West Bank while retaining the necessary territory for resources and arable land and, ultimately, more expansion.

What has occurred in the relationship between the United States and Israel since the election of Barak has been quite interesting. Barak has wanted the United States much less involved on the Palestinian track, but quite involved on the Syrian track. This reflects the power relationship between Israel and its negotiating partners. The Palestinians are quite weak and significant U.S. involvement strengthens them. Too often, from the Israeli perspective, the Israelis were negotiating with the United States, not the Palestinians. That clearly occurred at Wye as Netanyahu had effectively pushed the United States and Arafat closer together. At Sharm el Sheikh in September 1999, the Israelis and Palestinians negotiated the Wye Implementation Agreement. Two months before, during his first visit to the United States as Prime Minister, Barak had made it clear that he wanted the United States to be less involved in the negotiations with the Palestinians and to cease acting as "arbitrator, policeman and judge."[29] At the Sharm el Sheikh signing, Secretary of State Albright stated that the United States wants "to help the negotiators succeed." But with such an asymmetrical power relationship between Israel and the Palestinians, what does that mean? What constitutes success? Will the United States simply sit by and wait until Israel bullies the Palestinians into agreeing to Israel's vision of peace?

The Syrian track is quite different. The Israelis want the United States involved. This reflects both the fact that the Syrians are a much more formidable negotiating adversary and the Syrian desire to improve relations with the United States, if not Israel. Israel has clearly accepted the U.S. role as facilitator and mediator. Barak made it clear on his first visit to Washington that Israel would expect significant financial aid for the sacrifices Israel makes in giving up the Golan and the costs to resettle the Israeli population from the Golan, the relocation of military bases, the loss of resources and crops, etc. In addition, Israel expects considerable U.S. security guarantees and possibly U.S. forces as a security buffer positioned in a demilitarized area of the Golan. Finally, in early 2000, the United States and Israel began to work out an official defense pact between the two countries. Such a pact has been pushed strongly by the United States. First, this would enhance regional security in American eyes and provide greater protection for U.S. interests in the Middle East. Second, it would provide the necessary guarantees of security and deterrence against the Arab countries in the region so that Israel would feel secure enough to withdraw from the Golan and make peace with Syria. This might also be a way of attracting more domestic support in Israel for such a withdrawal. One could argue that the Americans are hedging against the possibility that peace does not provide a great stimulus to greater regional cooperation, integration and prosperity. Or, this might be a way of pressuring the Arab world to realize that they have no alternative but to embrace peace on American (and Israeli) terms. Whether the Arab parties will view this as anything but a positive development is doubtful. Whether it enhances the will to make peace or not remains to be seen.

But even if the final outcome is not prejudged, as the Israelis favor, the nature of the negotiation process is strategic and will in many ways pre-determine what kind of peace will emerge. That is one reason why the United States emphasizes the process so much. The United States wanted Wye more than the Israelis, and not just because Clinton needed some successes on the foreign policy front. The United States almost seems to believe that it can get Israel the kind of peace that the U.S. leadership thinks it needs – namely, a peace unencumbered by religious attachment to a Greater Israel yet keeps Israel predominant and able to advance U.S. interests. It is the Labor version of peace, not the Likud one to date, and certainly not a Palestinian or Arab one.

Power and Security

It should be understood that it is not just the nature of the U.S.-Israeli relationship, which makes it hard to pressure the Israelis. Part of it is the nature of the conflict. An Israeli analyst noted at the time of the Israeli-PLO Accord, that, "The reality of the Israeli-Palestinian relationship means that any agreement is inherently asymmetrical: Israel will give up things it has; the Palestinians will give up claims to things they do not have and commit themselves to behave in ways consistent with the renunciation of those claims. Israel can subsequently rescind its material concessions only by full-scale war."[30] And Israel will only do the first if it is convinced that the Palestinians are doing or will do the second. The United States seems to agree and, as the Wye negotiations clearly showed, the burden is on the Palestinians. In fact, the day before the talks were to open in 1998, Israeli Ambassador to the United States Zalman Shoval outlined what each side must do. On his list, the Palestinians were to commit to security cooperation with Israel and catch and punish terrorists; destroy the terrorist organizational infrastructure; hand over all illegal arms; stop the incitement of violence emanating from state and religious institutions such as schools, the media and mosques; and abolition of the Palestinian charter or those articles in the covenant which call for Israel's destruction. Israel's commitment was simply the withdrawal from an additional 13% (or ten plus three to distinguish the land that is part of a nature preserve). [31] That equation remains true for the Barak government. The major difference is that Barak is more likely than Netanyahu to live up to his end, but it remains asymmetrical nonetheless – or, as many Palestinians feel, unequal and unjust.

What is critical to emphasize here is that the United States essentially supports the Israeli position although it is willing to help the Palestinians achieve the necessary security commitments (through intelligence and training by the CIA in particular). But those security measures are for the benefit of Israel, not the Palestinians. For Israel, security is everything. Peace is in fact secondary. What the United States is trying to broker in the peace process formula has changed from "land for peace" to "land for security." The former is much more long-term and comprehensive (and has a sense of permanence) while the latter is short-term and tied to specific acts. For the Likud government there could be no peace without security. The Labor governments have been broader in their conception, demanding certain Palestinian commitments to Israeli security as well but also noting that security could not truly be achieved without peace.

For many, if not most Palestinians, justice is a very important principle and many prefer justice to peace – the perceived injustices of expulsion in 1947 and 1948; the occupation of 1967; the expansion into

Arab lands; the destruction of property; the abuse of individual rights. A senior Jordanian official once decried the use of the term "security" by Israelis: "The Israelis define the term in its absolute sense to mean everything .... Security means nothing when defined as everything." [32] And, because the peace process almost exclusively emphasizes the need to guarantee Israel's security, it has lost sight of the necessary conditions for Palestinians to feel some hope that the process will lead to a realization of their aspirations and will lead to a betterment of their lives. There is no longer much hope, politically or economically. In fact, GDP per capita has declined considerably for Palestinians, particularly in Gaza, since the Oslo Agreement. Israel has put a tremendous burden on the Palestinians, a weak party essentially, by asking that they guarantee Israel's internal security. Yet, little corresponding good will or help on Israel's part is forthcoming to help alleviate the conditions, which create the seeds for terrorist acts. And just as security is in the eyes of the Israelis, so too is justice in the eyes of the Palestinians. This is why many Palestinians opposed the whole Oslo process, not necessarily for what was being negotiated but for how it was being negotiated – that is, a perceived dictation of terms by the Israeli government. The United States and Israel strongly emphasize process, with a goal of peace but not a pre-determined set of agreements as to what peace will look like. The Arab parties, on the other hand, want to know where the process will lead, that is, the specifics of what will be agreed to at the end of the road. That is true for the Palestinians, and true for the Syrians.

This will also be the case with arms control in the region. A nuclear free zone or weapons of mass destruction free zone will ultimately require the greatest concessions from Israel: giving up what it already has. But America ascribes to exceptionalism. That is the basis of the UN Security Council's five permanent members, the Nuclear Non-Proliferation agreement (only 5 countries are allowed the right to possess nuclear weapons), and even weighted voting rights in the World Bank and IMF. Some countries are more equal than others and there can also be circumstances that would legitimately call for an asymmetrical security arrangement. Whether the Arab parties agree with that is irrelevant because they will not convince the United States otherwise. The United States clearly agrees with Israel on that score.

In fact, the United States is wedded to the process of peace, almost regardless of who is in power in Israel. Most of the diplomatic efforts of the United States in the past couple of years have been targeted at saving the process and ensuring that it continues in the form of talks and contacts at some official level. No one was ready to declare officially that the Oslo process is dead and break off all contact or negotiations. Aaron Miller, Deputy Special Middle East Coordinator, summarized the U.S. attitude: "We've also seen the possibility ... of the beginning of the end of this conflict. A structure of negotiations has been created which has survived extreme rhetoric, terror and even some of the negotiating positions advanced by the parties themselves." [33] He talked about the survival of a negotiating structure and the "resiliency of the process." One of the issues to consider today is whether U.S. policy has become simply a strategy to keep the process alive, as opposed to having the process move forward or even resolve anything. But without progress the moderates begin to lose strength and hope and the extremists begin to step into the breach and begin to set the agenda. Miller has noted that the U.S. role with respect to the process has been to marshal economic and political support for the process and help "to defuse and insulate the process from crisis...."[34] Immediately after the Wye agreement, the United States called on other Arab parties to join in reviving the multilateral process and the Administration began to lobby Arab countries such as Saudi Arabia and Morocco to move ahead on normalizing relations with Israel. But the Arabs clearly did not trust Netanyahu or any American guarantee of Israeli behavior. Only when tangible changes in Israel occurred did Arabs move to join the process again.

The United States wants Israel to give up land for peace but in a way that conforms to whatever version of the formula Israel believes it can live with. Essentially, that means that Israel will not give up all the land it has occupied, simply that it will return occupied land. What land that will be is to be determined in negotiations that will lead to a solution that takes into account Israel's perceived special security needs. Thus, for Israel, no solution will include East Jerusalem while for Arabs a just solution must include East Jerusalem. Israel interprets United Nations Security Council resolution 242 to mean that Israel has a right to "secure" borders, however it chooses to define "secure." What is remarkable is that Israel, even under Likud, has ultimately come to accept a Palestinian state. But it will be a state defined by Israel, determined by Israel's good graces and, finally, at the mercy of Israel.

To what degree is that really self-determination for the Palestinian people? The United States has the power to push for something perhaps more equitable, but no Israeli government would go along and in all honesty any other kind of peace would not be in America's interest. A demasculated Palestinian state that Israel defines will be a symbolic, if pyrrhic, victory for moderate Arabs such that the Palestinian issue is no longer a rallying cry for forces of dissent within their countries and paves the way for integrating Israel more into the Middle East economy. The only true sticking point would be the disposition of Jerusalem, an issue that cannot in all probability be covered with a symbolic fig leaf of Palestinian statehood elsewhere.

But the United States created a problem in the post-Madrid era that is coming back to haunt it. The great success of Madrid was that the United States was able to invest considerable capital and time in convincing the Arab world that the peace process was good for the region and that they could all benefit from peace. High expectations were created. But the problem lies in the fact that when the process breaks down, it leads to a greater fear among rather insecure regimes. And, they are less likely to take a risk on the process again, which could thus spell its doom. For most Arabs the formula for peace that they think they have bought into is the formula of "land for peace." They are not inclined to accept a formula based on what Israel thinks is necessary for a secure peace unless they are so desperate and weak as Arafat appears to be. But can any agreement made by such a weak partner truly last?

One of the contradictions of the U.S.-sponsored process is that the right in Israel, the hard-liners, must be brought on board and given some consent to an agreement, if not the process itself; but the hard-line Palestinians must be isolated and kept out of the process. There seems a feeling that the Israeli radicals are rational, if fanatical, while Palestinian radicals are simply terrorists. Thus, a reason why the United States did not get particularly upset with Ariel Sharon's appointment as Minister of Foreign Affairs was the belief that the principle of the peace process is infallible and eventually Israel, even someone like Sharon, will come around to see the logic of peace, especially one which Israel can shape to meet its particular needs. Prior to Wye, Israeli settlers were briefed about a U.S. plan to have the CIA determine which 36 Palestinians Israel accused of acts of terrorism should be jailed and tried in Palestinian courts. After the briefing, Israel reversed its position, lending credence to the suspicion that the settlers had some veto power over Israeli positions. Yet these settlers, and hard-liners like Ariel Sharon, are still viewed as rational; the leaders of Hamas are not. One thing that neither the Israelis nor the Americans have understood is that many of the Palestinians trying to wreck the peace process are not dreaming of destroying Israel so much as they are fighting against what they feel is a humiliating process which is not based on equity or justice but simply on power. Again, what this does is take the Arabs for granted. The only Arab leader who really has never allowed that to happen is Hafez el Assad.

The Israeli approach puts an almost impossible burden on any peace process. Israel wants to approach everything incrementally. Even under Labor, every step is viewed as a concession that must test the other party; if the other side fulfills what Israel believes it should, then Israel will consider another small concession. There is no agreed-upon end-point. Israel holds the view that nothing can be given up until the end, until everything is guaranteed. And, Israel retains the right to halt the process at any time – even after it has gotten only a few payoffs. But for the Arab parties the process works in such a way that for the most part the Arabs only get the "payoff" at the end of the process, if they ever get that far. At the same time, it becomes harder for the Palestinians in particular to pull out of the process for fear of being the one accused of scuttling peace. The Israelis often adopt the attitude that all other parties must change their positions (and prove that the change is real and sincere) before Israel can alter its own. Israel trusts no one else ultimately – not its allies and certainly not its adversaries. Yitzhak Rabin and other Labor leaders never trusted the United States to guarantee Israel's existence and security while; in addition to that, Likud leaders did not trust the United States to help them secure their vision of a "greater Israel." Netanyahu did not so much trust the CIA to guarantee Palestinian compliance, but felt that Arafat was not capable of guaranteeing Israeli security. Barak also does not want to leave the fate of Israel's security in Palestinian hands so it appears that he wants the negotiations to leave most of the occupied territories with Israeli populations (primarily settlers) under Israeli control.

Overall, Palestinians and Israelis are more competitors than partners. Neither side is happy with the leadership of the other side. Israelis are disappointed with Palestinian Authority chairman Yasir

Arafat's leadership, but there is no enthusiasm for the only alternatives: to reinstate Israeli rule over the Palestinians; to accept chaos; or to find someone other than Arafat to lead the Palestinians. As for the leadership of Israeli Prime Minister Barak, he has not turned out to be much different than his predecessors in how he negotiates over Israeli security. Israel is counting on a process that Palestinians cannot retreat from, while at the same time, as a weak party, cannot achieve the required steps that would compel Israel to give up more, particularly if radical elements on both sides give Barak cause to leave any agreements unfulfilled, keeping him seemingly blameless for their failure. The Palestinian Authority has very little leverage other than saying "no" or walking away from the negotiating table. Palestinians have almost no concessions that they can make (except on things, like Jerusalem and refugees, that they do not have or do not control). They cannot reduce or redeploy military forces because they do not have any. Yet, the Palestinian Authority is being asked to take responsibility for people and events over which it has little if any control. The best leverage the Palestinians can hope for, as was demonstrated at Wye, is a strong relationship with the United States and having the Americans plead their case with the Israelis. But Barak has skillfully maneuvered the Americans away from the Palestinian track and toward the Syrian track. In addition, financial aid from donors like the United States, has not strengthened the Arafat government politically nor made the Palestinians feel more secure and confident in their dealings with Israel. This is due, in part, to the great needs of the Palestinian population but also because the Palestinian Authority has often squandered resources and has lacked a transparent and accountable political process and decision-making structure.

In a final conclusion about the peace process, it is not enough to reiterate that it favors Israel nor can one only conclude that it allows Israel to define what is acceptable for it and for the Palestinians in order to establish a modus vivendi that guarantees the security of Israeli citizens. One must add that this fact may be immutable if there is to be any peace. That may not be fair, but it seems most realistic. There is a tremendous power imbalance between the two parties and there are some clearly incompatible goals that cannot be mutually accommodated. The U.S. role has become in many ways one of pleading the Palestinian case to the Israelis. The United States does not ask for much for the

Palestinians but tries to persuade Israel that it can give a little more and still live in security. Rabin might have given the Palestinians more than Netanyahu or even Barak, but would not have gone anywhere near all of the pre-1967 land which is what is fair and just in the eyes of most Arabs.

One major difference between Rabin on the one hand and Netanyahu – as well as, to a lesser extent, Barak, based on the evidence of his first months in office – on the other, is that through the Oslo process Rabin did try in a limited fashion to empower Arafat, knowing that he could only make a deal with someone who had some power and authority to make what was agreed to stick. Netanyahu diminished Arafat at every turn and then complained that Arafat did not live up to the agreement. That is why the key to Wye was securing the American role of guarantor of Palestinian compliance. It was the only way to guarantee Arafat any measure of power. Again, it is not a fair process, and just as Israel is defining the parameters, Palestinians can say "no" to this process. Many Palestinians, particularly those affiliated with Hamas, already have. But the Palestinians have little leverage, and the United States will never tip the scales to make the negotiations more fair or equitable. However, in the negotiations between Israel and Syria, Assad plays the game very differently. He will not allow either the United States or Israel to set the agenda. He wants the end result agreed to up front so that negotiations are on details not final status and principles. Barak seems to see that full withdrawal is the only option for Israel and has worked hard to prepare the Israeli public as well as gain what he considers necessary financial and security guarantees from the United States in order to help Israel swallow the "bitter pill" of giving up the Golan.

The U.S.-Israeli Relationship

Israel and the Arab-Israeli peace process tend to consume American foreign policymakers and Presidents to the extent that, as former U.S. Secretary of State James Baker has noted, they "are inevitably sucked into the Middle East, where they expend an inordinate amount of time and effort...with few prospects for success and an enormous potential for disappointment." [35] The U.S. relationship with Israel has an impact on every other aspect of its policies toward the Middle East.

Ultimately, the reasons for unwavering American support for Israel and for America's overall pro-Israeli foreign policy orientation are rooted in both domestic and foreign policy reasons. It is important to note that while the influence of pro-Israeli organizations in the United States has a significant impact on American foreign policy in the Middle East, they do not control such policy. But the Middle East is such a thorny issue for most American members of Congress that they often take positions about issues related to the Middle East that run contrary to their positions on similar issues elsewhere in the world.[36] One of the major reasons is electoral politics. As one analyst has written: "There are no benefits to candidates taking an openly anti-Israel stance and considerable costs in both loss of campaign contributions and votes from Jews and non-Jews alike."[37] It is important to acknowledge that for Americans the issues of oil and religion (perceived to be at the heart of most conflicts in the Middle East) are seen as very important and often leads to passionate responses. More than any other foreign policy issue, Middle East policy is subject to domestic pressures. As a result, the foreign policy experts have less influence on Middle East policy than they do on policies toward other areas of the world.

Thus, the usually pro-Israeli nature of American foreign policy derives from a number of factors:

1. The influence of pro-Israeli organizations and lobbies during American elections for Congress and the presidency, and the continued influence on elected officials once in office.
2. The effectiveness of pro-Israeli groups to influence and become a critical factor for members of both political parties.
3. The identification of Israeli goals and interests in the Middle East with those of the United States.
4. An identification of Israel as representative of "western" or "American" values while Arabs are viewed as antithetical to such values and a negative image of Arabs is often reinforced through the media, entertainment, and public discourse.

Who makes such pro-Israeli policy? Many simplistically believe that the policy is simply shaped by interest groups. Such interest groups can and do have a large impact, but how much depends on a number of factors.

The most critical is the extent to which the President is engaged in Middle East policy. If he is disengaged, the influence of lobbyists and public groups, as well as Congress, expands. But even when the President is engaged, do interest groups have substantial influence on what the President does? The single most important factor remains the ability to influence the President because he is the most important player on foreign policy. As the issue of loan guarantees and the expansion of Jewish settlements on the West Bank demonstrated, the lack of presidential support by George Bush for the Israeli position went a long way toward undermining the influence of the pro-Israeli lobbies.

Although oversimplified, some would argue that the President and his top advisers are influenced from a pro-Israeli perspective by Congress and a strong pro-Israel lobby while influenced from a pro-Arab perspective from a business and executive bureaucratic perspective (particularly because of a long-standing group of Arabists in the State Department). Generally, if the State Department has greater influence on foreign policy, the President will hear a more pro-Arab, or at least less pro-Israel, perspective because those who have spent time in the region and analyzed it tend to be more even-handed in their sympathies. And the State Department diplomats will not usually be concerned with electoral politics. If the National Security Council has more clout, then the advice they give will be based more on domestic politics, which would favor a more pro-Israeli stance.

But even without the strong pro-Israeli lobby, there has been a coincidence of geostrategic interests that have helped cement the American-Israeli relationship. A strong and secure Israel is both an end and a means for the United States. First, because of domestic political factors, historical ties, and a soft spot for and identity with Israel, the United States is pledged to ensure Israel's survival. But Israel's survival is also viewed as critical to securing and furthering U.S. interests in the region. This is particularly true with the end of the Cold War and the decline of U.S. defense spending and military downsizing. The United States clearly wants to rely more on its strategic partners to help deal with regional conflict, whether that is Israel and Egypt in the Middle East or its NATO allies in the Balkans.

But Israel seems able to influence the terms of its relationship with the United States more strongly than almost any other American ally. One reason why there has never been a formal security pact between the United States and Israel (such as those with western Europe and Japan) is that Israelis have been very reluctant to put their faith in another's word or guarantee and because Israel has not been able to state what borders the United States would be asked to guarantee or secure. As soon as word emerged in February 2000 about the U.S.-proposed mutual defense pact, considerable opposition throughout Israeli society erupted. Even as Barak tried to weaken and limit the mutual commitments, particularly the role of the United States in providing military assistance to Israel, there was considerable concern that it would tie Israel's hands and erode Israel's history of self-reliance. Others were incensed that the United States seemed to be trying to bribe Israelis in to giving up the Golan. And most Israelis do not believe the United States will cut back its financial and military aid to Israel if there is no such pact.

For decades, the United States has cast its unwavering support for Israel in moral as well as strategic terms. Israel continues to be a strong ally of the United States on the global level but it is no longer clear, now that the Soviet Union is not a threat in the region and Israel's role in helping contain Soviet influence there is no longer needed, whether Israel's actions serve U.S. interests in the Middle East itself. Because Israel is so far superior militarily to its neighbors and because the possibility of a Middle East war is remote, Israel is clearly as secure now as it has been at any time in its fifty years of existence. Thus, the moral argument of protecting Israel's very existence seems no longer valid. Israel has effectively secured itself in the Middle East. Its military strength and reputation, as well as its nuclear capability, effectively ensures that.

Even though Israel continues to engage in some policies that many Americans clearly find unprincipled, the question of changing the nature of U.S.-Israeli relations or withdrawing military and financial support is inconceivable to most. At the same time, Israel is no longer the weak, embattled tiny nation and victim it used to portray itself as. It lost its "innocence" in Lebanon in the early 1980s and later during the Palestinian intifada. Nevertheless, Israel is perceived by most Americans as a friend, an ally, a country and a people "like us."

The United States certainly has close allies in the Arab world, but there is not the depth of the bond that exists between Israel and the United States. Arab-American relations have not been forged by historical or cultural ties, or even by a common view of the world. Rather, the American ties with countries such as Egypt, Saudi Arabia, Morocco, Jordan, and many others are ones of strong common interests in certain critical areas, which may or may not be long lasting. There is a mutual respect but no true bond. These countries will never be like Israel, not in fact and not in the minds of American policymakers and elites. Unlike Israel, Arab states will never be of the West – they may be tied to the West in many ways, but never a part of it. In many ways, these relations are coalitions of mutual interests rather than alliances. This could change in the future, but strong relations and friendships with Arab countries are not yet embedded in the American political process. The only factor that could change the nature of U.S.-Arab relations would be the emergence of a strong politically active Arab-American elite. Certainly, this is a fast-growing population in the United States as is the Muslim population in the United States overall. But there is little chance in the near future that the United States will act any differently. Only George Bush and James Baker ever put real pressure on Israel Σ and the reason why the Madrid meeting happened at all was because the United States put pressure on all the parties, from Israel to Saudi Arabia, to agree to a process that was in Israel's best interests.

The American Israel Public Affairs Committee (AIPAC), which began as the American Zionist Council in 1951 and was registered as a foreign agent for Israel, has had considerable success keeping issues of importance to Israel in the spotlight on Capitol Hill. The key to AIPAC's success has been less the money donated to campaigns by like-minded individuals and political action committees than the widespread campaign to convince members of Congress and the American public that support for Israel is in America's best national interests. One of the most effective ways of doing so has been to show that Israel and Israelis are "just like we are." In a superficial way, there is a similarity between both countries as immigrant societies and having tamed the frontier. There is a similarity of spirit between making the desert bloom and taming the Wild West. The histories of both often conveniently tended to ignore most of the native people who had been living on the land for centuries.[38] After the 1967 war, for many Americans there was some-thing attractive about this new power in the Middle East that had been created by survivors of World War II and built from the ashes of the Holocaust.

That may be simplistic history, but it was, and remains for many, a powerful and inspiring image.

Former head of AIPAC, Morris Amitay, estimated that in the early 1990s out of 100 senators and 435 members of the House, 99 and 350 respectively had visited Israel. Few of them also visited Arab countries.[39] Most of them, or members of their staffs, went on trips sponsored by pro-Israel groups such as B'Nai B'rith. In addition, there were close to 100 pro-Israel political action committees by the end of the 1980s.

Just as important as the ties to Congress is the tremendous access that Israeli policymakers have to the State Department, Pentagon, and even U.S. military headquarters. Intelligence is routinely shared and there is a liaison between the CIA and the Mossad, Israel's foreign intelligence service. Despite differences on issues such as settlements, there is strong agreement on a wide variety of issues. Prior to the Gulf War an Israeli official noted that, "The Americans let us know that the military, political and strategic interests of both countries were more or less identical."[40]

Just as significant has been the broadening of Israeli support within the American political spectrum. Pro-Israel advocates and American Jews are no longer tied mostly to the Democratic Party. One of Netanyahu's strengths was the support he had developed among American domestic constituencies, from traditional Jewish groups to evangelical conservatives. There has been a notable coincidence of interests between traditional liberals who support foreign aid (most of which goes to Israel and Egypt) but do not agree with many other Israeli policies on issues such as settlements and Jerusalem and evangelical conservatives who strongly support Israeli foreign policy but do not often vote for foreign aid. Israel benefits on both fronts as a result. The importance of Israel to the Christian right has grown over the past couple of decades. The leaders of the religious right not only support Israeli policies but also reinforce the image of Israel as defender of Christian interests in the Middle East. Americans often see religious values at stake in foreign conflicts and Israel is seen as representing the Judeo-Christian values held by most American Christians, but most particularly American evangelicals. Polls have shown that evangelicals are much more likely to support Israeli actions than mainstream Protestants and Catholics.[41] In addition, they are much more opposed to defense cutbacks and supportive of the use of force in the Middle East. Thus, there is a convergence of strategic and religious interests.

One irony to claims that Israel influences U.S. policies and that Israel and the pro-Israel American lobbies are in lock step is that there was a real divergence in the 1992 presidential elections. Many American Jewish leaders, lobbyists and financial backers of Israel strongly supported Clinton even though it had been made clear that the newly-elected Rabin government preferred the re-election of George Bush – in the belief that Clinton was more focused on domestic issues and his election would stall the peace process. As it turned out, Rabin bypassed the newly elected Clinton Administration and took advantage of direct talks with the PLO initiated by members of his government.

There is almost an overlapping political involvement by political elites in each country. The unstated American administration preference for Barak seemed to help his election prospects. The major Israeli political parties and candidates solicit major campaign contributions from the United States. Netanyahu and Barak are essentially American-style politicians who understand the modern-day campaign tools of media appeal, polling, interest groups and focus groups. In 1999, both major Israeli political parties and their candidates relied to a considerable degree on American campaign consultants.

The bottom line for Israel and its lobbyists and supporters in the United States is that there can be no "even-handed" treatment with respect to the Middle East. What many Americans might consider irrelevant – the religious and personal background of the President's key Middle East advisers – is watched very carefully in the Middle East. Arabs, diplomats and others, make it a point to note who is a Jew in American Administrations; but so do Israeli officials. Israeli officials ponder who is a "good Jew," one who is unwavering in his or her support for Israel.[42] An Egyptian official noted that after the appointment of Daniel Kurtzer, who is Jewish, as U.S. Ambassador to Egypt, some intellectuals and elites in Egypt remarked that Israel now had two ambassador in Egypt. A profile of Martin Indyk, U.S. Ambassador to Israel and former Assistant Secretary of State for Middle East Affairs, in *The New Republic* by the national editor of the Jewish weekly *Forward* claimed that Indyk, who was once an AIPAC staffer, was now "Israel's least favorite Clinton staffer." [43] Thus, positions and backgrounds are often oversimplified in a way that one is cast as pro-Israel or pro-Arab, making it hard to develop a more nuanced and equitable policy.

Often, the United States will indulge the domestic needs of the Israeli government (in a way it would not do for an Arab party) even if the lack of any U.S. pressure erodes its credibility in the Arab world. Thus, the United States did not try to pressure Israel to keep to the timetable agreed at Sharm el Sheikh to develop a framework for final status negotiations. And, on such occasions Israel benefits considerably from the usual public indifference in the United States over foreign policy issues. This leaves the field open to those, even if a minority viewpoint, which have great resources to dominate the debate over policy in the Middle East.

Regional Stability

The window of opportunity for the American vision of regional stability may be closing as fewer people in the Middle East are convinced that peace is either possible or that life will improve much even if it does materialize. There are significant problems in the region that cannot be ignored. Tremendous pressure from the population growth in most Arab countries strains the resources and the economy while also creating a whole generation of disaffected youth. For many, religion has become the only credible institution that provides some tangible assistance in the community and some answers to the problems many people face. Milton Viorst wrote that, "Arabs in the 20th century experimented with various secular doctrines Σ parliamentarianism, socialism, Arab nationalism – in the search for prosperity and power. They succeeded with none. Their failures, in turn, have invited the surge of fundamentalism."[44]

The uncertainty and instability in the region cannot be underestimated. Despite heavy crackdowns by authorities in many Arab countries, political Islam remains a potent force, one that is attractive for the poor and dispossessed and, even more importantly, the disaffected and often unemployed or underemployed young people of these countries. Economic problems are considerable. Egypt continues to have chronic unemployment and underemployment. Jordan has not realized much if any economic peace dividend from its treaty with Israel. Most of the Gulf oil producers have run up large deficits and Saudi Arabia has gone so far as to discuss allowing the return of seven American oil companies to the country. And, the leadership of many Middle Eastern countries is becoming older and older or is in a period of transition from one generation to the next.

The strain of the competition for resources in the region remains acute (water, land and minerals in particular). If the Arab world goes through any major transformation or transition it could be very bloody and could spill over throughout the region, jeopardizing all of America's interests there. Potential benefits of peace will be lost on the man in the street by that point. As one moderate Arab scholar noted in comparing western policies toward Arab radicals with what is going on in Israel: "They kick out Arab settlers, uproot their homes and nothing happens. I believe that almost all young Muslims are radicalized by the Israeli behavior."[45] As an American observer, who has spent considerable time in the Middle East, has observed: "The attraction of groups like Hamas is less religious than political ... Islamists remain hostage to the success or failure of the peace process. Their best allies are, in effect, right-wing Israelis who stand in the way of a just peace."[46] And, clearly, Israel has given Hamas the opportunity to remain relevant – although Arafat must take some credit because of the continued corruption, cronyism, and brutal tactics of the security forces.

It must be kept in mind, however, that Israelis (and most Americans in policymaking positions) are not interested in a just peace as most Arabs define justice; they want a secure, comprehensive and long-term peace. That will probably include a Palestinian state. Most Israelis are resigned to that. Many Americans, including such long-stalwart friends of Israel as Henry Kissinger make it clear that a state will have to be part of the final status. Even Netanyahu implied that a state was inevitable: "I know there is a majority of Israelis who believe a Palestinian state will exist...."[47] But the mere creation of a Palestinian state, particularly one that is very weak, resembles a block of Swiss cheese, and does not include some measure of autonomy over East Jerusalem, will not be the achievement of what most in the Arab world consider fair and just. Netanyahu noted that the only acceptable Palestinian state is one that would allow Israel to "restrict sovereign decisions such as an alliance with Saddam Hussein." That may be the only kind of peace possible given the power imbalance and the great divide and enmity between Israelis and Palestinians. Many Palestinians are concerned that a bad deal is worse than no deal and worry that

Yasser Arafat, weak politically and with signs of failing health, clutching to his small base of power, sees even a bad deal as better than no deal.

Countries in the Gulf are also increasingly nervous about their futures. They have had budget deficits for some time and governments, because of the cost of the 1991 war, have had to reduce services and subsidies and cut budgets. With the rapid increase in population and reliance on foreign workers, there is a growing disaffected population there. Per capita income has greatly declined in Saudi Arabia in the 1990s. In fact, the 1995 Unified Arab Economic Report, published by a consortium of Arab organizations reported that per capita income among Arab states has declined by more than 20 per cent since 1980.[48] In the Gulf states there is no place of recourse for the disaffected. With a declining economic base, arms sales to the Gulf region have declined, thus creating a greater dependence on the United States and the west for protection.

There will continue to be considerable pressure for economic reform and democratization, both from outside the country and inside. But the visions for such economic and political reforms may not be compatible at all. While the developed world may envision conversion to a market economy, others may simply push for a redistribution of wealth. Democratization may not mean the emergence of Madisonian democracy and a strong foundation of civil rights and a strong independent legal system, but a tyranny of the majority or the use of a democratic process simply to grab power. Many find the push for western-style democracy both antithetical to a region where communal interests and rights are often given more weight than those of the individual, and self-serving. As former Assistant Secretary of State for Near Eastern Affairs Richard W. Murphy has noted, there is a perceived "blatant hypocrisy" on the part of the United States regarding democracy in the Middle East. "There is a pervasive sense in the Middle East that the United States does not support democracy in the region, but rather, supports what is in its strategic interest and calls it democratic."[49]

Moreover, there is a growing perception in the region that the United States doesn't take action against Iraq because the continuing insecurity among the Gulf states forces them to continue to buy billions of dollars of American arms. The image of the United States has suffered because of its vacillating actions and policies in the Gulf; and it has suffered because it often does not practice the idealistic rhetoric it preaches. There is an additional problem for American credibility in the Middle East. This has to do with how the United States treats most of the countries of the Arab world. Too often, the Arab countries are viewed simply as a source of oil, vast individual wealth, markets for western goods and services, and terrorism. According to a number of U.S. officials who have dealt with the Middle East for many years, at the top levels of government the United States does not really consult and engage the Arab regimes. Too often, these "important allies" are viewed as military necessities and are treated as such, but not engaged politically much at all. This is particularly true in the Gulf, where too often it seems that the United States is not sympathetic to the costs, both financial and in terms of domestic political support, those regimes have to face. Former American Ambassador to the United Arab Emirates William A. Rugh wrote: "Although high-level political leaders from European and other countries, including prime ministers, frequently visit Gulf rulers to seek their advice and support, senior American officials rarely do so. When they visit the Gulf, American officials are often more interested in asking for money than in consultation."[50] Or they spend considerable time urging these countries to give stronger voice to support the peace process or expand their relations with Israel.

Nor does the United States put much effort into making the case for its policies; rather, it bulls its way ahead. Thus, there is a very negative image of the United States in the mind of the Arab man in the street. The leadership and political elites in these countries grudgingly go along with the United States because they have little alternative. At the same time, in the Arab world, Saddam Hussein is winning the public relations campaign, not America's alliance partners. He has exploited the suffering of the Iraqi people while the United States makes no effort to understand neither the Arab perspective nor the impact of its actions. Israeli actions (and U.S. bombings in Sudan and Afghanistan as well as the continued insistence on sanctions that hurt most Iraqis but not Saddam and his cronies one bit) tend to reinforce the negative image of the United States. For the United States there is a clear logic and rationale that peace between Arabs and Israelis is good, a weak Iraq is good, greater economic integration is good; but for the Arab world, that depends on the kind of peace and the costs involved in these objectives.

There is a resistance to buying into the American agenda: politically, economically, and even culturally.

And, as moderate Arab regimes from the Gulf to North Africa become weaker economically and domestic problems grow, they may become increasingly dependent on the United States, both economically and militarily, thus creating greater disenchantment at home. The heir to the Saudi throne, Crown Prince Abdullah, has asked top executives of seven major U.S. oil companies how his financially pressed country should be developing its vast oil and natural-gas reserves. Whether the Saudis are now prepared to shift policy and open their oil reserves and refining industry to investment by U.S. companies remains unclear. But the fact that such a review of its policies even exists seems a sign of desperation and the culmination of an erosion of any kind of singular and independent Saudi foreign policy.

Many senior American and Israeli officials note that one of the key components of the Madrid process was the presence of Saudi Arabia and the other Gulf Arab states and moderate Arab parties such as Morocco and Tunisia. Almost as much effort went into getting Saudi Arabia to Madrid as went into bringing Syria and Israel on board. Secretary of State Baker bluntly appealed to King Fahd by bluntly reminding him that his country owed the United States for repulsing the Iraqi aggression against Kuwait. [51] The United States continued to put pressure on the Gulf states to participate as full parties in the multilateral talks. They did so, and when junior diplomats initially headed many of the delegations, the United States pressed them to send more senior officials, which they eventually did. The United States pushed for ending the economic boycott of Israel (the secondary and tertiary boycotts were in fact ended) and after the first few rounds of multilateral meetings held outside the Middle East pushed for meetings in the region. Thus, in 1994 and 1995, high-level delegations of Israeli officials and technical experts went to Oman, Qatar and Bahrain. There was great talk of economic and technical cooperation from coordinated projects of tourism and desert development to linking electric grids and railways throughout the region. The United States and thousands of Middle East officials and businessmen met for the Middle East and North Africa Economic Summit (MENA) meetings in 1994, 1995, and 1996 in Casablanca, Amman and Cairo pushing for the establishment of a Middle East Development Bank.

But, by 1997 little of the cooperation and spirit of Madrid was left. The 1997 MENA conference held in Doha, Qatar, was a major failure as almost every Arab country, including Egypt and Saudi Arabia, despite considerable American pressure to attend, boycotted it. Then Oman and Qatar, the Gulf states who had gone the furthest to normalize with Israel, froze their relations with Israel. The comprehensive Madrid process was too costly, as was the American policy toward Iraq. The costs were both financial and political. Domestic groups were increasingly critical of the participation in a process that seemed to reward Israel even as it engaged in the building of more settlements, cracked down on Palestinians, and made no apparent effort to engage in peace negotiations. At the same time, budget deficits were mounting, unemployment rising, subsidies of some basic goods ending, and resources for domestic needs dwindling. There seemed little benefit to following the American path and too many costs, while at the same time the Arab countries in the Gulf and many elsewhere were becoming more and more dependent on the United States. Israel was being rewarded for its intransigence while it appeared that the Arabs were gaining little for their cooperation. Increasingly, as the United States did almost nothing to stand up to the Israelis it appeared that the Arabs were acquiescing in greater American and Israeli territorial expansion and dominance in the Middle East. Thus, the moderate Arab regimes were paying higher costs and getting fewer rewards for following the U.S. lead, with respect to Iraq and the Arab-Israeli peace process. Although the multilateral talks have recently reconvened, Arab parties are still very reluctant to move forward in discussions on cooperation on technical issues such as water, environment and tourism without progress on the bilateral tracks. Not only have they not benefited much from this process, there is a perception of considerable costs, some of which may make the status quo regimes less stable.

Iraq and Persian Gulf Security

The U.S. military presence in the Gulf has been problematic and has also led to even greater suspicions about U.S. motives now that it has a strategic foothold in the region. First, it has been very costly (both in terms of financial and military resources and in terms of eroding morale within the officer corps of the services). Second, the U.S. troop presence is not welcome among many sectors of society in the Gulf, or the Arab world at large. And while the American military presence may have deterred Iraq from repeating its aggression against a neighbor, Saddam Hussein continues to rule Iraq with an iron hand while defying the United States and United Nations in its attempts to prevent Iraq from developing weapons of mass destruction and the necessary delivery systems.

The United States has transformed the Persian Gulf into an American base with forward deployment of supplies and manpower. There are nearly 25,000 troops and the cost estimates (depending on budget lines, range from \$50 billion to \$70 billion annually, shared by the Gulf states and the United States). These include naval facilities in Bahrain and stationing of American soldiers in Saudi Arabia. The long-standing American presence has unsettled many in the region as well as many in the American armed forces and the Pentagon as well as on Capitol Hill. There is a major policy debate in the United States about American policy in Iraq. And it is increasingly difficult for much of the rest of the world to determine what American policy toward Iraq is.

It is important to understand that Gulf oil is critical not just for American dependence on it, but because the international economic system is highly dependent on easy access to this oil. If that were to change, the entire global economy would be affected, as would alliances and the post Cold War order. Disagreements on strategies and competition for scarce oil resources could split the developed world in a catastrophic way. At the center of the debate is the United States. It remains committed to a military presence in the Gulf, uncovering and destroying Iraq's potential for developing weapons of mass destruction and undermining Saddam Hussein's regime. The major force posture of the United States military, which underlies all its strategic military planning, is the need to be able to fight two regional wars simultaneously. The most important, and the one the United States will try to win first, is a war over the Persian Gulf.

But it is not clear what U.S. threats and actions are intended to accomplish. It is also not clear what the United States is committed to militarily against Iraq. U.S. Secretary of Defense William Cohen has often claimed that U.S. credibility is at stake. But since there is no plan "for the day after" as one analyst put it, there seems no clear strategy.

The United States understands that it has a credibility problem but seems to feel that the only available option is to use military force. That is neither persuasive nor indicative of real leadership. And, in the absence of force and a strong resolve to change the status quo in Iraq, either through the use of U.S. military force or supporting a successful opposition force, the international community can only fall back on sanctions. It must be noted, however, that the sanctions have hurt most Iraqi citizens considerably but have had no apparent impact on Saddam Hussein or those closest to him. Thus, to many, they appear, at best, simply punitive or, at worst, immoral – and in either case very ineffective.

While the argument could be made that Saddam, through his actions or inactions, is primarily responsible for the harsh consequences of the sanctions that is not, however, the common perception in the Arab world. Most blame the United States. This attitude comes from the perceptions of American intentions as well as capabilities. It is not enough to simply defend the sanctions by saying that it is Saddam Hussein who is responsible for the suffering of his people. While there may be a basis for that, it simply provides another tool for his dominance of the Iraqi political scene and his people, and makes the international community seem amoral if not immoral for providing him with the tool to starve his people. And, once again, there is no alternative if the sanctions have no effect on the man who makes the decision. There is no end game. Increasingly, many scholars who study the impact and effectiveness of sanctions believe that sanctions have little impact on non-democratic regimes or where there is little accountability on the part of the leadership.

Remarkably, the economic sanctions and arms embargo have remained in place and essentially complied with, for over nine years. To many, since the United States does not have a clear idea of what to do, the only apparent option is to retain some measure of flexibility by maintaining a strong military presence just in case a serious threat to U.S. interests re-emerges. But for many in the Arab world, maintaining sanctions, while not using force to change the regime, is an indication that the United States simply wants to keep the status quo in order to maintain a presence in the Gulf. This derives in part from the belief that the United States has the military power to depose Saddam and crush Iraq if it so desires. Most in the Arab world feel that the United States is so powerful that it can do whatever it wishes. To those who believe this, Saddam remains in power because the United States wishes that he do so; if Israel does not comply with UN resolutions it is because the United States does not wish to force it to do so.

In general, the policy debate seems to focus on whether to punish Saddam Hussein for his defiance of UN Security Council resolutions or force changes in Iraq, including the possibility of helping Iraqi opposition forces overthrow him. Congress has appropriated money for Iraqi opposition groups. And, while force has been used occasionally when Iraqi military forces have strayed into the "no-fly" zone that has been inconsistent. No direct U.S. military force has been offered in support of any anti-Saddam dissident groups to help them oust him (Congress has only offered money). And, the most likely sources of such opposition make the United States Government wary of backing a coup or revolt. They include: those in the circle of elite advisors around Saddam Hussein who may be no different than he is; Kurds in the North who pose a threat to Turkey, a key American ally; and Shi'ia in the South who may be strongly influenced by Iran. There is no good and logical opposition, in other words. And, since the United States sees no options to its liking, swinging between the status quo and punishing Saddam Hussein periodically seem the most appealing, if not only, options.

Over time, U.S. policy toward Iraq has lessened its credibility both in the Middle East and among its global allies. This is due partly to the fact that the U.S. has no clear-cut realizable objective, the achievement of which will lead to U.S. withdrawal from the Gulf. The United States works to maintain something of the old international coalition against Iraq yet often acts unilaterally. Finally, it does not follow through with many of its threats and even undermined the weapons inspection process that it claimed to be promoting. When does the United States "really mean it"? The United States never denied that it pressured the UN inspection teams to pull back on its own pressure on Iraq. Thus, the bottom line is that the status quo remains, which is frustrating to all, including the American military. The lack of credibility has also led Saddam Hussein to believe he can simply take a small blow or two and then wait out the United States and its leadership.

The sizable number of men and material required to be on alert in the Gulf have undercut readiness elsewhere in the military and eroded morale. In a series of articles in *The Washington Post* in the summer of 1998, the drop in military morale and an inability to retain top junior officers was blamed primarily on the long-standing military presence in the Balkans and the Persian Gulf, particularly the latter. [52] Key military officials note that the length of time for service in the Gulf is so long that it puts a great strain on the families of servicemen and officers because wives increasingly make re-enlistment decisions. Many are leaving the service in order to maintain family morale (there is also stiff competition from private businesses that can pay top dollar for well-trained military specialists and officers).

The cornerstone of U.S. policy in the Gulf region throughout the Clinton Administration has been "dual containment," aimed at containing both Iraqi and Iranian designs to expand their influence in the region. The premise was that both countries were, in the words of former National Security Advisor Anthony Lake, "rogue" states and needed to be isolated because they posed a threat to their neighborhoods and international norms. [53] In the words of Martin Indyk, "the U.S. needed to shift away from our earlier policy of relying on either Iraq or Iran to balance each other, a policy we had followed throughout the previous decade with disastrous results."[54] Dual containment is predicated on changing the regimes of the two countries. The United States would like to see a regime change in Iraq, although the United States has no clear idea as to how it can best bring that about, and would like to see a change in policies in Iran, if not an actual change in the regime, that are more moderate and less supportive of what the United States considers extremist positions and extremist forces. A key element of dual containment is the need for peace between Israel and its neighbors so that there is no incentive for the Gulf states to turn to Iran or Iraq or even sympathize with them. The logic of this policy would be to put pressure on Israel and its neighbors to make peace, which would further isolate countries like Iran and Iraq. Thus, the weak effort by the United States regarding Israel not only weakens the peace process but also undermine its policies in the Gulf. There is some evidence that the United States has used the argument with Tel Aviv that Israeli intransigence emboldens those it fears most, Iraq and Iran, but to little effect.[55] This is somewhat ironic because many claim that the policy of dual containment is a "made-in-Israel strategy."[56] American policy makers do make the point with Israel that a successful peace will do more to isolate Iraq and Iran than almost anything else. And, a peace that was embraced by most Arab states might help moderate the policies of both "rogue states." There were even rumors in Washington, and in much of the Arab world, about a purported U.S. plan to resettle Palestinian refugees in Iraq in return for the political rehabilitation of Baghdad.[57]

The problem is that dual containment seems to have accomplished little and is reactive at best. It has little support among developed countries and even little among the Gulf countries it is ostensibly designed to protect. Few countries see Iraq as a significant threat any longer, while they find the sanctions ineffective and immoral. Saddam Hussein, with little concern for his people, seems to believe he can absorb the short-term punishment meted out by the United States because it will not take more forceful action. Thus, U.S. credibility erodes further. Many of the Gulf countries also are finding the major military effort to contain Iraq quite costly at a time when their economic fortunes are in decline. With almost no support for dual containment among its friends and allies, and the United States not willing to risk unilateral action, the Clinton Administration simply holds on to the status quo: sanctions, some UN inspections, and occasional military strikes as punishment.

The U.S. has 3 concerns with respect to Iraq: 1) the development of weapons of mass destruction, contrary to Iraq's agreement with the United Nations; 2) the authoritarian nature of the government headed by Saddam Hussein; and 3) stability in the region that could be disrupted by the unpredictable aggressive behavior of the Saddam Hussein regime. It is also unclear whether military action against Iraq would have much utility. There is little agreement as to whether dropping many tons of bombs on Iraq would effectively reduce its military potential more than slightly. And, it would kill many innocent people in the process. If air attacks on weapons locations will only slightly hamper Iraq militarily, what is the point of doing it? If Iraq were the only nation with weapons of mass destruction, perhaps bombing could be justified. Many critics of the Clinton approach have argued that the focus should be on retaliation which should be massive, not military options which cannot guarantee success anyway and makes Saddam a martyr and hero in the eyes of many.

In effect, the United States has four options with respect to Iraq, and security in the Persian Gulf. Option 1 would be to oust the Saddam

Hussein regime. There are two alternatives within this possibility. The first is to target a particular opposition group, one that is more inclined to have views compatible with the west (this would most likely be opposition with a base in the North, either Kurds, Sunni or a more secular opposition). The second alternative is a more general support for any opposition against Saddam Hussein, whether from within the military or from the Shi'ia community in the south. While this may be more likely to succeed than the first option, from the American standpoint there is no guarantee – in fact, little likelihood – that such opposition would be sympathetic to the west, much less subject to any influence by the United States. Option 2 would be to ease off sanctions, and build up a potential defensive coalition against future Iraqi aggression (through the GCC, Turkey, Jordan, and possibly Israel). This would be a kind of cautious rehabilitation of Iraq.

A third option would be a U.S.-led retaliation against Iraq for violations of UN Security Council resolutions and evidence that Iraq was trying to continue its weapons programs. Such a military effort would have to be substantial enough to overturn the Saddam Hussein regime and the military order in the country. This has almost no appeal in Washington because it is unlikely that any other country, save perhaps Great Britain, would support such as strike, and because the United States would have no viable replacement for Saddam Hussein that would allow the U.S. military not to have to occupy Iraq. Anything less than a major military effort would be pointless since Saddam's survival would probably lead to a replay of the past few years. The fourth option is maintenance of the status quo. This remains the Clinton Administration policy because it finds none of the other options appealing or possible. But it also makes the United States appear weak. That was a major part of the reason Congress appropriated what amounted to a bounty in order to support any opposition group that would work to oust Saddam Hussein.[58] But that action undermines the efforts of UN inspection teams by giving ammunition to Saddam Hussein to accuse them of being a front for bringing down his government. It is hard not to argue that another agreement to allow UN weapons inspectors into Iraq would again be a pointless charade.

For the leaders of the Gulf countries, the status quo still seems the best option, although their populations are growing increasingly dissatisfied with it. The problem for the Gulf regimes is that while they are not happy with the U.S. presence in the region, an American withdrawal or reduced presence will most assuredly be accompanied by substantial U.S. pressure to increase the region's defensive efforts, which are already quite costly. In addition, many in the Gulf suspect that the United States will only withdraw when it sees that a Persian Gulf-Israeli-Turkish coalition is possible. And, that is impossible as long as the Israeli conflicts with its neighbors remain unresolved.

The great problem for the United States – the same one that existed for Bush as it does for Clinton – is a fear of attempting a policy that could fail. A strong U.S. military response against Saddam Hussein, support for weak or unknown opposition groups, would be risky or would carry costs the United States is not willing to pay, particularly because the United States paid so little ultimately to oust Iraq forces from Kuwait. Many analysts have recently pointed out that the United States government and U.S. military are more unwilling to take casualties or take risks in foreign policy. This permeates decision making from the Persian Gulf to the strategic decision to rely exclusively on air power in Kosovo.

The Continuing Arms Proliferation

In many ways, the United States puts too much emphasis on the Israeli-Palestinian issue to the exclusion of other important problems. Because a number of Middle Eastern states have internal conflicts or internal instability, there is a greater likelihood of external conflict arising. The likelihood of war increases because of the instability of many states and regimes in the region. Both, because of this factor, and as a result of this factor, arms continue to proliferate throughout the region. And, the prospects of some of these states securing or developing weapons of mass destruction cannot be discounted.

As the various states of the Middle East develop their capabilities with weapons of mass destruction as well as the ongoing proliferation of ballistic missiles, the region is becoming a more dangerous and deadly place. The United States continues to lead the world in arms sales, having sold 26.5 billion dollars worth of arms in 1998. That is 48.6% of the market (all of western Europe sold 40.2% of the market share). And, the Middle East and North Africa continued to be by far the recipient of the largest number of military weapons in the developing world. 16.7 billion dollars of arms were sold in the Middle East in 1998 (about 30% of all arms sold in the world; by contrast, all of NATO and western Europe took in 32.9% of all international deliveries while East Asia had 23% of market share).[59]

Israel has a tacitly acknowledged nuclear capability, while chemical and biological weapons are proliferating. U.S. government officials estimate that Egypt, Iran, Iraq, Israel, Libya and Syria either have or are developing (or acquiring) the capability for chemical and biological weapons. The proliferation of weapons of mass destruction, the increasingly sophisticated delivery systems, new anti-missile systems (such as the Arrow in Israel) and burgeoning conventional arms make the regional situation very serious. Will the continuing weapons proliferation undermine, or even negate, any eventual peace between Israelis and Arabs? There is undoubtedly a linkage as many analysts over the years have argued that the key to peace in the Middle East is a solution to the Arab-Israeli conflict and the heart of that conflict is the Palestinian problem. Can a solution to the Palestinian problem lead to peace in a region so well armed, with many possible fault lines for conflict? Without a lasting peace, the Middle East remains a potential tinderbox, where arms are abundant, populations are restive, and regimes are fragile.

The proliferation of conventional arms means that violent conflict is always a possibility. But, the potential development of weapons of mass destruction and Israel's nuclear capability greatly add to the risks if there is conflict. The mere presence of such weapons creates potential problems. Egyptian officials, for example, do not argue that Israel will initiate a nuclear conflict; rather, the thrust of the Egyptian concern is that Israel's nuclear posture provides an excuse for other states to develop and deploy weapons of mass destruction. Iraq was not deterred from attacking Israel with Scud missiles in 1991. Although some Israelis argue that Iraq refrained from the use of chemical weapons because it feared Israeli retaliation, there is no agreement whether Iraq had the delivery capability at that time. One can also add that Iraq's launching of Scuds was not actually an attack on Israel but an attempt at provoking Israel into the war, in the hopes of breaking apart the anti-Iraq coalition.

There can be no progress in controlling the spread of arms and the potential for weapons of mass destruction without progress in the peace process. Lack of progress in the negotiations has created greater incentives for the continuing arms buildup in the region. Thus, prospects for security arrangements and arms control and a settlement of the Israeli-Palestinian conflict are mutually reinforcing. The following points remain crucial: 1) security will not exist without peace; 2) land is neither a substitute for, nor a guarantee of peace or security; and 3) technological improvements and the increasing sophistication of weapons systems make distance much less important. For Israelis, the implications are clear: they feel a need for both a secure peace and a convincing deterrent. Thus, Israel will rely on its own guarantees. This exasperates many Arabs who believe that Israel wants to demilitarize the Arab world while retaining its own deterrent force - even in light of what Arabs perceive as a solid American guarantee of Israeli security.

The reason why arms control is so critical in the Middle East is not just that there are a number of regimes that are unstable and some that are developing weapons of mass destruction, but the manner in which a Middle East arms race might emerge holds frightening possibilities. Most significant is the likely scenario that none of the states with nuclear weapons or other weapons of mass destruction will have a second strike capability. Thus, there will be considerable incentives to strike first during a time of crisis, causing a situation where weapons of mass destruction have little deterrent value, thus creating tremendous instability in the region. This is one of the reasons the United States and Israel have long believed that it was necessary, in the case of Iraq for example, to destroy the potential for building weapons of mass destruction before they could ever be operationalized.

Even Israelis and Egyptians, who have lived in peace for almost two decades, remain wary of each other. Few believe the other would attack them, but they believe it may still be possible to find their countries at war, given the unsettled nature of the region. One cannot simply dismiss this, because war remains possible if only because it remains conceivable in the minds of those in the region. This is one of the failures of the Madrid process, particularly the multilateral talks on security issues. The use of military force against one's neighbors has not been eliminated as a policy option; the victory over Iraq did not settle that. Nor did the peace process succeed in its attempt to draw in most of the Arab states, along with Israel, in a common effort to create relationships of cooperation and mutual interest that could build confidence so that countries in the region, including Israel, could reduce their reliance on huge, deadly arsenals.

With respect to arms control, the notion of parity is important for Egypt and many other Arab states, but that attitude does not win it points with the United States, because American policymakers are convinced of the Israeli argument that ultimate arms control deals must come at the end of the peace process. The argument by Israelis and many Americans is that Israel can only give up its nuclear deterrent when, and if, it feels secure. Arabs argue that the presence of such a deterrent only adds to insecurity in the region, and many are convinced that Israel will use its military power as a means to coerce the Arab states and dominate the Middle East, economically and militarily. So any final or comprehensive settlement that leaves Israel well armed, while its neighbors must reduce their military arsenals and flexibility, may create more insecurity in the name of peace.

Conclusion: The Decline of U.S. Leadership

The United States continues to have a major impact on the region and international relations in the Middle East. Yet, in many respects, its leadership has declined. In large measure, this has arisen because the core of leadership is the ability to persuade others to follow your lead, your agenda. More and more, most of the American allies and moderate states in the region are less willing to follow the American lead blindly. In many respects, this is due to the dashed expectations of what would emerge from the end of the Cold War, the defeat of Iraq, and the Madrid peace process and Oslo Accords. Many of these countries were willing to take what they perceived as major risks at American urging but have found the payoff lacking. This includes Israel.

The United States faces a number of problematic issues in the Middle East but the single largest problem is that the United States no longer is confident about how to approach the region. The paradigms it touted and put its resources behind have failed due to a combination of declining international and domestic support as well as a significant change in events and players. The perception that there is a moral obligation to stand up to Saddam Hussein's aggression – his tyranny at home and continued subterfuge to develop the means to wage aggression with some weapons of mass destruction – is no longer valid for many in Europe and the Middle East because the effort does not seem to have had much impact and there are countervailing moral concerns about the impact of the international sanctions on Iraq. With respect to the Arab-Israeli peace process, the Clinton Administration has a vision of a new Middle East that may be unrealistic and perhaps even counterproductive. Expectations may have been set too high for regional cooperation and economic prosperity. Such unfulfilled expectations could poison any peace if not undermine the process before peace is created. And, in this region of conflict, does economic competition and greater political openness enhance or undermine stability, or simply create new insecurities about economic hegemony?

Many have suggested that the United States remains a critical player because it is the only actor capable of helping the parties resolve the conflict and provide necessary guarantees and credibility that will assure the parties that they can take on the risks of making peace. One scholar argued that the United States role must be that of an "honest broker with a clear view of the end result."[60] But this is not the U.S. role today. While the United States has never played an even-handed third-party role, today there is no longer any perception among the Arab parties that the United States is willing to be an honest broker. The United States has a vision of an end result that increasingly only Israel subscribes to – and even many Israelis are not in favor of a peace without some, if not most, of the occupied territories. It was nice when that vision had a broader regional focus and fit within the parameters of "land for peace," but at bottom, the peace process is about ensuring Israel's security.

The United States is strong and unchallenged now. So now is the time to use its capital and strength to forge a Middle East that is in its interests. Israel is strong and unchallenged now. So now is the time to make a deal from strength. The tide could turn; more radical regimes could emerge that have the wherewithal to get weapons of mass destruction. Israel may not always have the leverage and advantage. Working to create a safe and secure region is critical for that reason. For the United States to settle for a Middle East that reflects the status quo is very shortsighted and dangerous. Conflict may be aborted in the short term but the lack of any deep-rooted peace and stability will sow the seeds for violent conflict that is fueled by extremism, desperation born of poverty, economic dislocation and pressures on resources and infrastructure, failed expectations – both politically and economically – an increasing cultural backlash against overwhelming Americanization, and a belief that American leadership in the Middle East is hypocritical and unjust.

Notes

1 The views expressed here are solely the author's and do not necessarily reflect those of the United States Institute of Peace.

2 *Haaretz*, January 20, 2000, as quoted in *Mideast Mirror* (electronic version), 1/20/00, Israel section.

3 Recent figures show that the Middle east and North Africa took in 30% of all international arms deliveries in 1998. International Institute for Strategic Studies. *The Military Balance 1999/2000* (London: Oxford University Press, 1999), p. 283.

4 For a more detailed discussion of these themes in U.S. foreign policy see Haass, Richard N. "Paradigm Lost" in *Foreign Affairs* (January/February 1995) and chapter two from Kissinger, Henry, *Diplomacy*. (New York: Simon & Schuster, 1994).

5 As quoted in Walker, Martin. "The New American Hegemony" in *World Policy Journal* (Summer 1996), p. 19.

6 Hadar, Leon T. "Enduring Middle Eastern Quagmires" in Ted Galen Carpenter (ed.), *America Entangled: The Persian Gulf Crisis and Its Consequences* (Washington, DC: Cato Institute, 1991), p. 92.

7 *New York Times*, 10/26/98, p. A1

8 George Bush and Brent Scowcroft interview with Charlie Rose, Public Broadcasting System, 10/17/98.

9 Over the past 5 years, the author has interviewed senior American, Israeli, Egyptian, Jordanian and Palestinian officials, who have been intimately involved in the peace process, both at the bilateral and multilateral levels. The interviews were conducted on a not-for-attribution basis.

10 See International Institute for Strategic Studies. *Strategic Survey 1997/98*, (London: Oxford University Press, 1997), pp. 236-237.

11 Abdulrahman Abuzayd as quoted in the *New York Times*, 8/25/98, p. A14.

12 "A Vision of the Middle East" – Presentation of Dr. Yossi Beilin, Israeli Deputy Minister of Foreign Affairs, to the Steering Committee of the Multilateral Peace Talks. Tokyo, December 15, 1993, p. 8. Issued by Israeli Ministry of Foreign Affairs.

13 Clawson, Patrick and Zoe Danon Gedal. *Dollars and Diplomacy: The Impact of U.S. Economic Initiatives on Arab-Israeli Negotiations,* Policy Paper No. 49. (Washington, DC: The Washington Institute for Near East Policy, 1999), p. xi.

14 Itamar Rabinovich talk, Washington Institute for Near East Policy, September 16, 1998, as quoted in *Ibid*. p. 14.

15 As quoted in the *New York Times*, 5/1/98, p. A1.

16 Lustick, Ian. "The Oslo Agreement as an Obstacle to Peace" in *Journal of Palestine Studies* XXVII, No. 1 (Autumn 1997), p. 66.

17 Israeli Ambassador to the United States Zalman Shoval speaking at a United States Institute of Peace Current Issues Briefing, Washington, D.C., 10/14/98.

18 Interview with Yitzhak Rabin, 10/6/93 in *The Jerusalem Post*, p. 7.

19 *Yediot Aharnot*, July 15, 1999, as quoted in *Mideast Mirror* (electronic version), July 15, 1999, Israel section.

20 Reich, Bernard. "The United States and the Arab-Israeli Peace Process," in Ben-Dor, Gabriel and David B. Dewitt (eds.) *Confidence Building Measures in the Middle East,* (Boulder, Colorado: Westview Press, 1994), p. 226.

21 Baker, James A. III. "The Road to Madrid" in Crocker, Chester A., Fen Osler Hampson and Pamela Aall (eds.), *Herding Cats: Multiparty Mediation in a Complex World,* (Washington, DC: United States Institute of Peace, 1999), p. 188.

22 Speech by James Baker at Moscow Multilateral Meeting, January 29, 1992. In *US State Department Dispatch*, February 3, 1992, p. 79

23 Peters, Joel. *Building Bridges: The Arab-Israeli Multilateral Talks,* (London: Royal Institute of International Affairs, 1994), p. 27.

24 Peters, Joel. *Pathways to Peace,* (London: Oxford University Press, 1996), p. 6.

25 Begun in 1973 in Helsinki the CSCE was a multilateral process (conducted through a series of regular meetings) and later institutionalized in 1990 as the Organization of Security and Cooperation in Europe (OSCE). The premise was that the post-world war II borders would be finalized but there would be an attempt to transform the relationship between east and west from one of opposing alliances to one where common principles regarding self-determination, human rights and resolution of conflict could emerge.

26 As quoted in Twite, Robin and Tamar Herman (eds.) *The Arab-Israeli Negotiations: Political Positions and Conceptual Frameworks,* (Tel Aviv: Papyrus Publishing House, 1993), p. 121.

27 Quandt, William B. *Decade of Decisions: American Policy Toward the Arab-Israeli Conflict,* (Berkeley: University of California Press, 1977), p. 93.

28 See reports in *Maariv*, February 14, 2000, as quoted in *Mideast Mirror* (electronic version), February 14, 2000, Israel section.

29 *New York Times*, July 14, 1999, p. A1.

30 Heller, Mark A. "Palestinian Plebiscite" in *The Jerusalem Post* September 8, 1993, p. 6.

31 Zalman Shoval Briefing, 10/14/98, *op. cit.*

32 As quoted in Mroz, John Edwin. *Beyond Security, (*New York: Pergamon Press, 1982), p. 105.

33 Remarks by Aaron David Miller in "Arab-Israeli Negotiations and U.S. Interests in the Middle East: Second-Term Imperatives" (transcript of conference convened by the Middle East Policy Council, 11/21/96) in *Middle East Policy* Vol. V No. 1 (January 1997), p. 1.

34 *Ibid.* p. 4.

35 Baker James A. III. *The Politics of Peace: Revolution, War and Diplomacy, 1989 – 1992, (* New York: G. P. Putnam's Sons, 1995), p. 115.

36 For an interesting and more detailed discussion of this point, see Pipes, Daniel. *The Long Shadow: Culture and Politics in the Middle East, (*New Brunswick: Transaction Publishers, 1989), pp. 242-245.

37 Bard, Mitchell Geoffrey. *The Water's Edge and Beyond: Defining the Limits to Domestic Influence on United States Middle East Policy, (*New Brunswick: Transaction Publishers, 1991), p. 8.

38 That changed in the United States to some extent and is also changing in Israel with the rise of the group of "New Historians" such as Benny Morris and Sammy Smooha among others. One significant difference is that there have always been Jews living in the lands of Palestine and the state of Israel was created because of the return of Jews to their land of origin, whereas in America European settlers

colonized a newly discovered land and moved westward with a sense of "manifest destiny." But the link between land and destiny is certainly similar.

39 See Melman, Yossi and Dan Raviv. *Friends in Deed: Inside the U.S.-Israel Alliance,* (New York: Hyperion, 1994), p. 317.

40 *Ibid.* p. 382.

41 Wald, Kenneth D., James L. Guth, Cleveland R. Fraser, John C. Green, Corwin E. Smidt, Lyman A. Kellstedt. "Reclaiming Zion: How American Religious Groups View the Middle East." in Gabriel Sheffer (ed.) *U.S.-Israeli Relations at the Crossroads,* (London: Frank Cass & Co. Ltd, 1997), p. 159.

42 See Melman and Raviv, op cit, p. 445-446.

43 Gitell, Seth. "Martin's Move" in *The New Republic,* November 9, 1998. p. 14.

44 Viorst, Milton. "The Shackles on the Arab Mind" in *The Washington Quarterly* Spring 1998 21:2, pp. 172-173.

45 *New York Times,* August 25, 1998, p. A14.

46 Rodenbeck, Max. "Is Islamism Losing Its Thunder?" in *The Washington Quarterly* Spring 1998. p. 187.

47 As quoted in the *New York Times* 11/12/98, p. A1.

48 As quoted in *Ibid.*, p. 164.

49 Murphy, Richard W. and F. Gergory Gause, III. "Democracy and U.S. Policy in the Muslim Middle East" in *Middle East Policy* V(1) January 1997, p. 59.

50 Rugh, William A. "Time to Modify Our Gulf Policy" in *Middle East Policy* V(1) January 1997, p. 50.

51 Baker, *The Politics of Peace, op cit,* pp. 450-453.

52 See the *Washington Post,* June 16, 17, 18.

53 Lake, Anthony. "Confronting Backlash States" in *Foreign Affairs* March/April 1994.

54 Martin Indyk testimony before House International Relations Committee, June 8, 1999. As quoted in *Mideast Mirror* (electronic version) 6/9/99, Arab/Islamic World section, Part 1.

55 See Gitell, Seth, *op. cit.*, p. 15.

56 See Killgore, Andrew I. "Israel-Driven U.S. 'Containment' of Iran has Failed" in *Washington Report on Middle East Affairs* March 1997, p. 17.

57 See *Mideast Mirror* (electronic version), September 6, 1999, Arab/Islamic World Section.

58 See Cockburn, Patrick. "CIA Blamed for Saddam's Survival" in *The Independent,* 11/12/98, p. 1.

59 Institute for International Strategic Studies. *The Military Balance 1999/2000.* London: Oxford University Press, 1999. pp. 281-83. [Measured in constant 1997 $]

60 Reich, Bernard. "The United States and the Arab-Israeli Peace Process" in Ben-Dor, Gabriel and David B. Dewitt (eds.) *Confidence Building Measures in the Middle East,* (Boulder, CO: Westview Press, 1994), p. 243.

11 The United Nations and the Muslim World: Allies or Adversaries?

ALI A. MAZRUI

Islam and the United Nations were born out of competing concepts of universalism. Islam is a universalistic religion as it seeks to preach to the human race as a whole; the United Nations is a universalist organization as it has sought to represent the human race as a whole. Islam has envisaged a universalism of people, the *ummah*; the United Nations has envisaged the universalism of nation-states, the international community.

The universalism of Islam was to be based on a shared faith; the universalism of the United Nations was based on a joint contract. The faith of Islam consists of its five pillars, the Qur'an, and the Sunnah. The contract of the United Nations is its the Charter and subsequent conventions, declarations and resolutions. A universalism of faith expands by biological reproduction and religious conversion; a universalism of contract expands by signing up new states as members of the world organization.

Since there are fewer than 200 states in the world, and more than five billion people, a universalism of states is achieved more quickly than a universalism of people. At first glance it might therefore seem that the United Nations has achieved its universalism of states long before Islam has achieved its universalism of people. The UN already has 185 member states.[1]

Today one out of every five human beings is already a Muslim. In the 21st century the Muslim community will reach the mark of a quarter (i.e. 25%) of the human race. It will have become the largest concentration of believers in one religion in history. In terms of population, it is now one of the fastest-growing religions in the world.[2] But the United Nations seems to have already achieved a universalism of states. Or is it only pseudo-universalism? Is the UN universalism still a game of smoke and mirrors?

The "Clash of Civilizations"

In the summer of 1993, Professor Samuel P. Huntington of Harvard University unleashed a debate about the nature of conflict in the post-Cold War era. In an article in the influential American policy journal *Foreign Affairs*, Huntington argued that now that the Cold War was over, future conflicts would not be primarily between states or ideological blocs, but rather they would be between civilizations and cultural coalitions.[3] To use Huntington's own words:

> The fault lines between civilizations will be the battle lines of the future. Conflict between civilizations will be the latest phase in the evolution of conflict in the modern world.[4]

Huntington was at his best when he discussed how the West masquerades as "the world community", and uses the United Nations to give universalist credentials to Western interests. In Huntington's words:

> Global political and security issues are effectively settled by a directorate of the United States, Britain and France; world economic issues by a directorate of the United States, Germany and Japan, all of which maintain extraordinarily close relations with each other, to the exclusion of lesser and largely non-Western countries. Decisions made at the UN Security Council or in the International Monetary Fund that reflects the interests of the West are presented to the world as the desires of the world community. The very phrase "the world community" has become the euphemistic collective noun (replacing "the Free World") to give global legitimacy to actions reflecting the interests of the United States and other Western powers.[5]

We have here a situation where the universalism of the United Nations is far less than it seems. The United Nations has become the collective fig leaf for rapacious Western interests and actions.

On becoming a member of the *ummah*, a Muslim must recite the Shahadah, saying that "There is no God but Allah." It seems that to remain a member of the United Nations in good standing, all countries must acknowledge, "There is no political God but the West." Only the West has the ultimate right to determine when and how force should be used in world politics.

Huntington goes on to show how the West had used the UN Security Council to impose sanctions against Muslim countries or invoke the use of force. After Iraq occupied Kuwait, the West was faced with a choice between saving time and saving lives. The West chose to save time. In Huntington's words:

> Western domination of the UN Security Council and its decisions, tempered only by occasional abstention by China, produced UN legitimation of the West's use of force to drive Iraq out of Kuwait and its elimination of Iraq's sophisticated weapons and capacity to produce such weapons. It also produced the quite unprecedented action by the United States, Britain and France in getting the Security Council to demand that Libya hand over the Pan Am 103 bombing suspects and then to impose sanctions when Libya refused.[6]

In August 1998 the United States and Britain at last agreed to let the Libyan suspects be tried at the Hague instead of the U.S. or Scotland. Libya was still worried that they might not get a fair trial. In any case, there now seems to be evidence that Libya might not have been the culprit in the Pan American 103 disaster at Lockerbie, Scotland after all. Some other Middle Eastern country might have been implicated and not Libya at all. But the sanctions against Libya have not been lifted. Washington, London and Paris are reluctant to eat their own words even if injustice is being committed.[7] The arrogance of power is at work again.

Our own thesis in this essay concurs with Huntington that there is indeed a clash of civilizations, but disagrees with him about the nature of that clash and about how old it is. We believe that the clash of civilizations did not begin with the end of the Cold War but is much older. We also believe that the chief cultural transgressor has throughout been the Western world.

Following the formation of the United Nations in 1945, a strange thing happened. Quite unconsciously the West adopted an ancient and medieval Islamic view of the world. Not long after the creation of the United Nations the West appropriated for itself – almost unconsciously – the tripartite division of the world of ancient Islamic jurists.[8]

Ancient international Islamic law divided the world into Dar el Islam (the Abode of Islam); Dar el Harb (the Abode of War); and Dar el Ahd or Dar el Sulh (the Abode of Peaceful Co-Existence or Contractual Peace). Within Dar el Islam, amity and cooperation on Islamic principles were supposed to prevail. Pax Islamica was supposed to be triumphant. It included both Muslims and non-Muslims of the tolerated communities ("People of the Book" or Dhimmis), who enjoyed state protection against internal insecurity and external aggression.[9]

Dar el Harb, the Abode of War, was not necessarily an arena of direct military confrontation. These were the lands of non-Muslims, often hostile to Islam, constituting the sort of situation that Thomas Hobbes was to describe much later as a condition without a shared sovereign.[10] Centuries before Hobbes, Muslim jurists had evolved the concept of Dar el Harb, a state of war, for cognizance of authorities in countries which did not agree on the sovereignty of God. As Khadduri points out, this recognition was needed for the survival of mankind:

> Islam's cognizance of non-Islamic sovereignties merely meant that some form of authority was by nature necessary for the survival of mankind, even when men lived in territories in the state of nature, outside the pale of the Islamic public order.[11]

The third category of countries under ancient international Islamic law was the countries of Dar el Ahd or Dar el Sulh (the Abode of Contractual Peace or Peaceful Co-Existence). These were the non-Muslim countries which worked out a deal with the Muslim rulers for greater autonomy and peace in exchange for some kind of tribute or collective tax paid to the Muslim treasury. Most jurists did not universally recognize the last-mentioned area, as they felt that "if the inhabitants of the territory concluded a peace treaty and paid tribute, it became part of the dar al-Islam and its people were entitled to the protection of Islam.[12]

Following the formation of the United Nations the West appropriated this tripartite view of the world of ancient Islamic international law and simply substituted itself for Islam. For much of the second half of the 20th century, during the period of the Cold War, there were the following categories:

- Dar el Maghreb or Dar el Gharb (the Abode of the West) instead of Dar el Islam.
- Dar el Harb (the Abode of War - which was essentially the communist world).
- Dar el Ahd - or Dar el Sulh (the Abode of Peaceful Co-Existencewhich was the Third World). The Third World paid tribute to the West in the form of the debt-burden and other forms of

> economic exploitation. It was no different from the tribute paid by Dar el Sulh countries to medieval Muslim rulers.

But one major proviso needs to be emphasized in the second half of the 20th century. While doctrinally the Abode of War for the West was supposed to be the communist world, in practice the actual military fighting by the West in the second half of the 20th century has been almost entirely in the Third World, including the World of Islam.[13]

The Korean War was in the Third world but not the Muslim world. In the case of Korea and Vietnam it was not easy to draw a distinction between the communist world and the Third World. Several million people perished in the two American-led wars of Korea and Vietnam. Militarily no member of the Warsaw Pact was hurt directly. The Warsaw Pact and the North Atlantic Treaty Organization (NATO) were basically fighting each other through intermediaries. The doctrinal Abode of War was not necessarily the literal abode of war. The U.S. armed itself to the teeth to fight the communist Second World – and turned on the Third World instead. In Korea this Western onslaught appropriated the flag of the United Nations.[14]

While Korea and Vietnam might have been cases where it was difficult to determine where the communist second world ended and the Third world began, the Muslim world poses no such ambivalence. Muslim states have not been communist.[15] And yet since 1980 Western armaments have killed over 500,000 Muslims. These casualties have included Libyans, Iranians, Lebanese, Palestinians, and Iraqis. The West has been trigger-happy in responding to Muslim political challenges. In the Gulf War of 1991, the West used the flag of the United Nations to give its militarism a universalistic appeal and legitimacy.[16] The human toll in Iraq is still continuing as a result of the deprivations caused by the Anglo-American economic sanctions, given universalistic legitimacy by the UN Security Council.[17]

The rate of infant mortality in Iraq has doubled, even tripled, and death of ordinary people from preventable diseases has escalated.[18] On the other hand, while Iraq itself may have been physically and militarily emasculated, Saddam Hussein's hold on power appears to be unshakable.[19]

The ostensible reason is to make sure that Iraq does not rebuild weapons of mass destruction. And yet each of the permanent members of the Security Council is possessive about its own weapons of mass destruction. Unlike France, Iraq has not yet reached the arrogance of testing nuclear weapons thousands of miles away from its own core population – and endangering the population of other lands. Protests by the militarily weak Pacific nations have been manifested in the form of street demonstrations, diplomatic downgrading of relations, and boycotts of French goods such as wine.[20] Nor does Iraq have the equivalent of a permanent member of the Security Council to say to it "scratch my nuclear back – and I will scratch yours." Tony Blair scratching Jacques Chirac's back.

The West's doctrinal Dar el Harb, the Abode of War, was supposed to be the Communist world. The West's operational Dar el Harb has been the developing world and the islands of the seas. The United Nations has sometimes provided a universalist umbrella for the West's operations in the Third World.

The UN and the Cultural Counter-Revolution

The UN's universalism represents nation-states and world regions but does not try to represent civilizations. Six out of the last seven Secretaries-General of the UN have come from Christian traditions.[21] The Christian world is about one-fifth of the population of the world. There has been no Hindu, Muslim, or Confucian Secretary-General although together those populations outnumber Christians by more than two to one. There has been one Buddhist Secretary-General – the Burmese U Thant. One Buddhist, as against five Christians – although there are probably as many Buddhists as Christians in the world.[22] Should the UN system be more sensitive to civilizational representativeness?[23]

Should peacekeeping in the future be more sensitive to geo-cultural movements? International geo-cultural organizations like the Organization of the Islamic Conference (OIC) can be relevant in preventative diplomacy or in peacemaking – although the OIC efforts in trying to stop the Iraq-Iran conflict in the 1980s were less than successful.[24] On the other hand, patient efforts by the Economic Community of West African States' Monitoring Group (ECOMOG) in Liberia appear to have been more successful.[25]

Then there are intra-civilizational conflicts with extra-civilizational consequences – like movements of Islamic militancy in places like Algeria, Afghanistan and Egypt and potentially Saudi Arabia. Consultations have been taking place between officials of NATO, and some members of the

League of Arab States concerning Islamic militancy. Should the UN be involved?

For the time being, the United Nations' system is part of the cultural hegemony of the Western world. And when Director-General Amadou-Mahtar M'Bow of UNESCO tried to rebel against it, the United States and Great Britain withdrew from UNESCO – and M'Bow was consequently ousted.[26]

Primarily the victors of World War II formed the UN. Those victors belonged to one civilization-and-a-half: (Britain, USA, France, USSR.) They made themselves permanent members of the UN's powerful Security Council. They made one concession to another civilization – by also making pre-Communist China a permanent member.

Of the five original languages of the UN, four were in origin European languages: English, French, Spanish and Russian. A concession was made to another civilization – by recognizing the Chinese language.

A kind of bicameral legislature began to emerge – an upper house, which was the more powerful but less representative, called the Security Council – and a lower house which was less powerful but more representative called the General Assembly. This bicameral concept developed by practice rather than design and was in origin very Western. The upper house was the global "House of Lords" – warlords! The conception was basically from western civilization and history.

One of the major functions of the UN was to help keep the peace according to the principles of international law. The Law of Nations was itself a child of European diplomatic history and statecraft. It once used to be:

> The Law of Christian Nations, and then became,
> The Law of Civilized Nations, and then became,
> The Law of Developed Nations.[27]

That old International Law used to legitimize the colonization of other countries by Western countries. Intellectual ancestors of Western political thought were marked by an arrogant Eurocentrism. J.S. Mill distinguished between "barbarians and societies worthy of the Law of Nations." What was even more ironic was the approbation of colonialism by early socialists; Karl Marx applauded Britain's colonization of India.[28] Friedrich Engels applauded France's colonization of Algeria.[29] All these were civilizational criteria, accepted by almost the whole white world.

And then the UN began to admit not only more countries but also more cultures. These included the admission of Pakistan in 1947, Myanmar (Burma) and Sri Lanka (Ceylon) in 1948 and later Malaysia and Singapore. From the Arab world there later followed some additional countries: Morocco, Tunisia, Sudan, Algeria (Egypt was already a member), and subsequently newly independent Black African countries, beginning with Ghana in 1957. New values were trying to express themselves through a Eurocentric infrastructure.

Later, the UN became the channel through which other countries and cultures began to insist on changes in International Law. When India occupied Goa, thus liberating it from Portuguese rule, Krishna Menon enunciated the principle that "colonialism was permanent aggression" – thus delegitimizing colonialism.[30]

African struggles against apartheid led to the shrinkage of the principle of domestic jurisdiction as applied to South Africa's policy of apartheid. Eventually apartheid was regarded as a matter of relevance to international security and as virtually a "crime against humanity." The United Nations began to take a more active role in combating apartheid.[31]

In the post-Cold War era, is the UN likely to be used by the dominant civilization (the West) against other civilizations? Is that what happened during the Gulf War? Was the UN hijacked by the West to legitimize massacres in defence of its oil interests? In Bosnia, was the UN being used by the West to make sure there was no viable Muslim state in the middle of Europe? Were the Daton Accords a de facto partition of Bosnia?

The UN has sometimes been guilty of sins of omission. Such sins of omission include:

(a) Standing by while Patrice Lumumba was literally dragged to his death in 1961 in the Congo (Kinshasa).[32]
(b) Standing by while thousands of people were massacred in the bombing of Iraq – euphemistically termed "collateral damage" – during the Gulf War, and in the aftermath, continuing to ignore the privations of Iraqi individuals due to sanctions.
(c) Standing by while hundreds of thousands of Bosnians were maimed, murdered, mutilated, or raped in the early 1990s. Was this a clash of civilizations?

In an earlier work, we had raised the issue of the West, particularly the United States, becoming the defender of the holy places in Islam – Mecca and Medina – during the Gulf War.[33] In 1995 the United States emerged as the peacemaker acceptable to all parties in the Bosnian imbroglio – including Bosnian Muslims. Part of the Datan peace plan envisages reducing Serbian and Croatian armaments, while increasing Bosnian Muslim arms. The NATO peacekeeping forces will not be directly involved with this exercise, but the United States is apparently trying to get third parties to undertake the task of arming the Bosnian forces so that they will be able to repel any future challenge.[34]

It is striking to note that while the United Nations and the European allies, along with the Clinton administration, were reluctant to lift the arms embargo so as to allow the Bosnian Muslims to arm themselves, conservative Republicans (like Senator Bob Dole) had for long called for allowing Bosnia to arm itself.[35] In his *Clash of Civilizations* thesis, Samuel Huntington was concerned about an alliance between the world of Islam and the countries of the Confucian legacy. In our terms would this be a new Dar el Harb (Abode of War) for the West?

In the UN the temporary omen was in the 1970s. There was in 1971 the euphoric recognition of the People's Republic of China (PRC) by the United Nations.[36] There was also Yasser Arafat's address to the General Assembly in plenary session virtually as Head of State in the Fall of 1974.[37] Third was Algeria's launching of the campaign for a New International Economic Order (NIEO) also in 1974.[38] Fourth was the subsequent recognition of Arabic alongside Chinese as the only non-European languages accepted as official idioms of the world body for some occasions. Did these events portend a Muslim-Confucian coalition?

All these are modest even if significant achievements. On the whole the UN system, along with the Bretton Woods institutions (World Bank and the IMF), continue to be major disseminators of Western ideas, concepts and values. In conception, and in much of their operations, the institutions are rooted in the Western worldview (weltanschauung). Future Directors-General of UNESCO are unlikely to be as assertive as Amadou-Mahtar M'Bow.[39] And most developing countries have in any case been forced to toe the Western party line since the disintegration of the Soviet Union.

At the moment the UN Security Council is primarily a "White Man's Club" with non-white visitors. Four of the five permanent members are essentially white countries rooted in a Euro-Christian legacy (U.S.A.,

France, Britain, and Russia). Has the United Nations inevitably become a future arena for a clash of civilizations?

The different conflicts in the Muslim world dictate an agonizing reappraisal. The majority of the victims are Muslims, but there are conflicts where Muslims are the villains. Has the ancient Dar el Islam (the Abode of Islam) now become the modern Dar el Harb (the Abode of War)? In traditional Islamic international law, Dar el Islam was the land where Muslims were free and secure. But now Muslims are caught up in conflict in different lands.

In this regard we have three main categories of societies. First, those societies where Muslims are the victims of the violence of others. This has included the wars in Bosnia,Kosovo, Chechnya, Kashmir, southern Lebanon, and occupied Palestine. It once included Afghanistan under Soviet occupation. Second is the category where Muslims are at war with each other. This includes Afghanistan, Algeria, the city of Karachi in Pakistan, and to some extent Egypt. Third is the category where Muslims are more culprits than victims – where Muslims victimize others. Although the war in Sudan is not primarily a religious war, its net effect casts Muslims as the greater culprits in the conflict. What about the November 1995 terrorist act in Riyadh, Saudi Arabia against Americans?[40] Is that a case of Muslims against foreigners? Or is it the beginning of something comparable to Algeria and Egypt?

Within the ancient Abode of Islam, where conflict was not supposed to be the order of the day, we now have anguish and discord. The universalism of faith has yet to find a universality of peace. The United Nations is involved in some of these conflicts affecting Muslims, but not involved in others. There are UN resolutions about Kashmir, and many more UN resolutions about Palestine. The UN has sometimes attempted to help in the civil war in Afghanistan. The UN kept out of the war in Chechnya. What is heartrending for the Muslim world is how much fratricide, as well as victimization, there is.

While Muslims have failed in maintaining peace towards each other, Westerners have found it among themselves. A whole new body of literature is emerging based on the premise that "democracies do not go to war against each other."[41] The literature is not based on moral wishful thinking, but on what is presented as systemic and scientific analysis of the nature of the democratic process, especially in the liberal West. There is nothing in the democratic process to stop the United States from invading Panama, or to stop Britain and France joining a military coalition against Iraq in the Gulf War. But the new school of thought asserts that these democratic countries are systemically unlikely to go to war against each other. In Huntington's phrase, "Military conflict among Western states is unthinkable."[42] But how much of this peace is due to the presence of economic prosperity and nuclear weapons?

Instead of a situation in which Muslims do not go to war with each other (as the ancient doctrine expected), we have a situation in which Westerners do not go to war with each other (as the new political science asserts). Instead of Dar el Islam triumphant (the Abode of Islam in victory), we have Dar el Maghreb victorious (the Abode of the West in triumph). And the West controls the United Nations. Islam's universalism of faith has foundered because of the weakness of the Muslims. The United Nations' universalism of states has triumphed because of the power of the West.

Perhaps nowhere in the world was there such a stark confrontation between the universalism of faith and the universalism of nation-states as in Bosnia. The state called Yugoslavia disintegrated – and out of the fragments emerged several states including a country called Bosnia-Herzogovina with a plurality of Muslims. The idea of a Muslim-led government in the middle of Europe, however democratic, raised disturbing spectors in some circles. Muslim Turkey was a Middle Eastern country trying to be recognized as European. Muslim Albania was technologically the most backward country in Europe. But relatively advanced Bosnia in the middle of Christian Europe was a disconcerting prospect in a world where influential professors from Harvard University expected "a clash of civilizations."

Let us therefore look at Bosnia-Herzegovina as a case study involving the confluence of a number of factors. Bosnia was an intriguing case study pitting the universalism of faith against the universalism of statehood. It was a case study of the United Nations in opposition to the aspirations of most of the Muslim world. It was a case study of a clash of civilizations as Bosnia was gradually led towards de facto partition.

Bosnia-Herzegovina in the 1990s was originally invaded partly by troops from Serbia and partly by Bosnian Serbs armed by Serbia. The UN imposed an arms embargo on both sides. And yet the UN was wrong to impose the embargo on the Bosnian government. It was wrong for two main reasons:

(a) Because Bosnia had the right of self-defence under Article 51 of the UN charter.

(b) Because the Serbian side had inherited the bulk of the armory of the former Socialist Republic of Yugoslavia and thus came to acquire undue advantage

If the Muslims were humiliated and totally defeated, there might later have emerged new forms of Muslim guerrilla movements in the heart of Europe in the decades ahead. Humiliated Muslims have been known to haunt their tormentors for generations afterwards.

A Bosnian equivalent of the Palestine Liberation Organization and a Bosnian equivalent of the Irish Republic Army might have been unnecessarily created in the future by the humiliation of the Bosnian Muslims of today. A partition of Bosnia is indeed unfolding. Will it be as costly as the partition of Palestine?

The irony is that just when the Muslim world is, in spite of such acts as the Hebron mosque massacre perpetrated by a Jewish militant, learning to accept a Jewish state in the midst of a Muslim Middle East, Europeans are reluctant to countenance a Muslim state in a Christian Europe. Bosnia could have been a kind of Muslim Israel in the middle of Christian Europe. Had Europe the will to help it survive? Or was Europe behaving like Baruch Goldstein, shooting Muslims in prayer? Had the UN provided universalist legitimation to the occupation of Bosnia?

In Afghanistan the West armed the liberation of a Muslim society in order to frustrate Moscow. In Bosnia the West through the UN had disarmed a Muslim society, partly in order not to offend Moscow. In Afghanistan the West helped the Mujahiddeen throw out their Soviet invaders. In Bosnia the West and the UN had not been ready even to defend some of the UN protected zones like Srebrenica, Zepa, and Gorazde. At long last NATO's protection of Sarajevo helped to freeze Serbian territorial gains.

In Afghanistan the West did the right thing for the wrong reasons – it helped Muslims in order to checkmate the Soviets. In Bosnia the West did the wrong thing for the wrong reasons – appease the Serbian invaders partly because of sectarian indifference. One wished that the UN and the international community had the political will to do the right thing for the right reasons – help Bosnia survive as a united independent country instead of letting it slide into de facto partition.

The shadow of cultural prejudice persisted. Would the West and the UN have been slow to react in Bosnia if it was a case of Muslims slaughtering and raping Christians instead of the other way round? Would the U.S. administration and the Senate have been slow if the Serbian concentration camps were for Bosnian Jews rather than for Bosnian Muslims? Would the UN not have been forced to respond more robustly and energetically if Muslim men were raping Jewish women as an instrument of war, instead of Muslim women being raped by Orthodox Christian Serbs?

Indeed, there is reason to believe that if it were Jews who were being subjected to such unspeakable humiliation, Israel would not have waited for either the UN Security Council or the U.S. Senate.[43] Israel would have staged a major international spectacular event to grab the world's attention – even if it meant bombing Belgrade. And Israel would certainly have got the world's attention. Fifty Muslim governments, on the other hand, were content to timidly obey the demands of the Security Council, refrain from arming the Bosnian Muslims or even evacuate refugees. The tragedy of Bosnia illustrated that the universalism of states ostensibly achieved by the United Nations was still seriously flawed. The United Nations is still a creature of the Western World - and the West still views the world through the tripartite lenses of medieval Islam duly adapted (by the West).

What to medieval Muslim jurists was Dar el Islam (Abode of Islam) has now become Dar el Maghreb or Dar el Gharb, the Abode of the West. Westerners are the pre-eminent pioneers. Until the 1990s the Abode of War to Westerners were the lands of communism. Has the Abode of War now become the Muslim world in all its complexity?

To some medieval Islamists there was the Abode of Ahd and/or Sulh – the home of contractual co-existence in exchange for tribute. Tribute is what the Western world has been receiving from most of the Third world in profits, interest on the debt burden, and the returns on other forms of exploitation. And the United Nations has sometimes unwittingly provided an umbrella for this tripartite division of the world.

Conclusion

But when all is said and done, under what circumstances is the United Nations ever an *ally* of the Muslim world? First, the UN is an ally in the humanitarian role of the world body and its agencies – such as crises of refugees or international responses to famine, draught and other catastrophes. In such roles it does not matter whether the immediate beneficiaries are Muslims, as in Somalia and Bangladesh, or non-Muslims, as in Rwanda. The UN is supportive of all such efforts.

Second, the United Nations is an ally when it provides an umbrella for mediation for some of the quarrels between Muslims – as in the effort to resolve the destiny of Western Sahara. The UN in such instances helps the *Ummah* more directly. The UN helped in the quest for peace between Iran and Iraq in their conflict in the 1980s.[44]

Third, the United Nations is an ally to Muslims when the world body provides peacekeeping troops and peacekeeping auspices in conflicts between Muslims and non-Muslims. Over the years United Nations troops have often been involved in the often-thankless task of trying to keep the peace between the Arabs and the Israelis especially prior to the Oslo peace process. The UN's long-drawn role in Cyprus is another example of attempted mediation between Muslims and non-Muslims.

Fourth, the United Nations is allied to Muslims – when the Western world has been divided! The Muslim world has sometimes had the UN move decisively as an ally in such a situation – as during the Suez war of 1956 when, in spite of the veto by Britain and France in the Security Council, the mood of the world body was opposed to the invasion of Egypt by Britain, France and Israel.

When the Western world was divided, the United Nations was also able to play a major decolonizing role. This is the fifth positive role of the UN. The United States was historically opposed to some of the older varieties of European imperialism. By the second half of the 20th century the United States was often on the same side as the Soviet Union among the critics of old-style European colonialism.

Under these conditions it was indeed easier for the United Nations to become increasingly one of the great arenas for the anti-colonial struggle waged by the peoples of Asia, Africa and the scattered islands of the seas. The anti-colonial role of the United Nations encompassed not only the Trusteeship Council but also the General Assembly, especially from the late 1950s onwards. This anti-colonial role was often a great service to the Muslim world.

Sixth, the United Nations can be an ally of the Muslim world when it takes seriously the idea of prosecuting war criminals and those who have committed crimes against humanity. Especially relevant for the Muslim world would be the prosecution of war criminals in Bosnia and some Serbs in Serbia and many Serbs in Bosnia who have committed crimes against humanity as in the current proceedings at The Hague involving war crimes committed in Bosnia in the 1990s. The United Nations has done well to appoint the relevant tribunal for the task, but has fallen far short of providing the resources for this complicated task.

Seventh, the United Nations has been an ally when the Muslim world was united. It has at times been possible to pass through the General Assembly highly contentious points of principle. The state of Israel is based on an ideology which says that a Russian who claims to be descended from Jews, and whose family has had no connection with the Middle East for the last two thousand years, has more right to go and settle in Israel than a Palestinian who ran away from Israel during the 1948 war. Was such discrimination racist?

When Muslims were united in 1975, they managed to persuade the UN General Assembly to pass a resolution affirming that Zionism was a form of racism. But when Muslims were divided in 1991, an overwhelming majority repealed that resolution.[45]

When the Muslims were united they could persuade the General Assembly not only to defy the United States but move the Assembly itself out of New York in further defiance. Thus when in 1988 the United States refused to grant a visa to Yasser Arafat, thereby preventing him from coming to New York to address the UN General Assembly on his recent declaration of an independent Palestinian state, the General Assembly denounced Washington's action as a violation of the host country's legal obligations under the 1947 Headquarters Agreement. The General Assembly then shifted this December 13-15 session to Geneva, Switzerland, to make it possible to listen to Chairman Arafat. It was the first and only such move in the history of the United Nations. The unity of the Muslim members of the UN helped to persuade others to join their ranks.[46]

Finally, is the UN an ally or an adversary of Islamic values when the UN promotes such mega-conferences as the one in Beijing, China, in 1995 on the issue of women; the one in Copenhagen on the issues of poverty and development in 1994 and the one in Cairo, Egypt in 1994 on the issue of population? Muslims themselves are divided as to whether these UN mega-conferences lead on to the erosion of Islamic values or help Islamic values find a new historic setting in the 20th and 21st centuries. For example, are Muslim women being helped by new global standards of gender equity that are promoted at these conferences? These mega-conferences have of course been global and have been part of the United Nations' universalism of nation-states. Some tension has at times been created with Islam's universalism of faith.

But it is a tension that can itself be creative; it is a dialectic that can have a human face. At the very minimum, Islam and the UN have one paramount interest in common – to ensure that Dar el Harb, the Abode of War, shrinks further and further into the oblivion of history, and Planet Earth becomes a House of Peace at long last.

Notes

1 Arthur S. Banks, (ed.), *Political Handbook of the World, 1994-1995*, (Binghamton, NY: CSA Publications, 1995), p. 1107, reports 184 members; the updated figure is drawn from the Internet at http://www.un.org/overviews/unmember.html. This source also provides details on membership accession dates and other relevant details.

2 On population distribution and trends among Muslims, consult John Weeks, "The Demography of Islamic Nations," *Population Bulletin*, Vol. 43, No. 4 (1988), especially pp. 5-9.

3 See Samuel P. Huntington, "The Clash of Civilizations?" *Foreign Affairs*, Vol. 72, No. 3, (Summer 1993), pp. 22-49. Responses by Fouad Ajami, Kishore Mahbubani, Robert L. Bartley, Liu Binyan, and Jeane J. Kirkpatrick, among others, were published in the next issue of *Foreign Affairs,* Vol. 72, No. 4 (September/October 1993), pp. 2-22.

4 Huntington, "The Clash of Civilizations?" p. 22.

5 *Ibid*, p. 39.

6 *Ibid*, p. 40.

7 For one account of the Lockerbie investigation that casts a wider net of suspects than Libya alone, see David Leppard, *On The Trail of Terror: The Inside Story of the Lockerbie Investigation* (London: Jonathan Cape, 1991). While Leppard emphasizes the Libyan connection, he also points to Iranian and Syrian connections in his last chapter. On the sanctions, see footnote 15 in Vera Gowlland-Debbas, "The Relationship Between the International Court of Justice and the Security Council in the Light of the Lockerbie Case," *American Journal of International Law* Volume 88 (October 1994), p. 646; and *The New York Times*, (March 31, 1995), Section A, p. 3.

8 Our discussion here is based on Majid Khadduri's introduction to his translation of *The Islamic Law of Nations: Shaybani's Siyar*. (Baltimore, MD: Johns Hopkins Press, 1966), pp. 11-13, although he tends to emphasize the dual division.

9 *Ibid*, pp. 11-12.

10 Hobbes describes this condition in his seminal *Leviathan*; for one recent edition, see Edwin Curley, (ed.), *Leviathan; with Selected Variants from the Latin Edition of 1668/Thomas Hobbes*. (Indianapolis: Hackett Pub. Co., 1994).

11 Khadduri, *The Islamic Law of Nations*, p. 13.

12 As pointed out by Majid Khadduri, *Ibid*, p. 12-13. However, for our analysis, this distinction will prove useful.

13 Although international relations scholars concentrated on the US-Soviet connections, some have pointed out that the West, particularly the United States, has had its most problematic international relations headaches in practice in the Third World. See for example, Charles W. Maynes, "America's Third World Hang-Ups," *Foreign Policy*, No. 71 (Summer 1988), pp. 117-140, and Steven R. David, "Why the Third World Matters," *International Security*, Vol. 14, No. 1 (Summer 1989), pp. 50-85.

14 On the UN role in the Korean conflict, consult, for instance, Leon Gordenker, *The United Nations and the Peaceful Unification of Korea: The Politics of Field Operations, 1947-1950*. (The Hague: M. Nijhoff, 1959); and for a specific examination of the US moves in the UN regarding Korea, consult Leland M. Goodrich, *Korea: A Study of U. S. Policy in the United Nations*. (New York: Council on Foreign Relations, 1956).

15 Albania is demographically an Islamic country, but the communist authorities ruthlessly suppressed the religion.

16 See, for example, Burns H. Weston, "Security Council Resolution 678 and Persian Gulf Decision Making: Precarious Legitimacy," *American Journal of International Law*, Vol. 85 (July 1991), pp. 516-35.

17 For one recent analysis of the American stand on sanctions, see Eric Rouleau, "America's Unyielding Policy Toward Iraq," *Foreign Affairs*, Vol. 74 (Jan/Feb 1995), pp. 59-72.

18 In fact, according to one study, the infant mortality rate had increased fivefold since the end of the war in 1991, killing almost 576, 000 Iraqi children; see *The New York Times*, (December 1, 1995) Section A, p. 9.

19 For critical reports on the sanctions, see the analysis by Haris Gazdar and Jean Dreze, "Hunger and Poverty in Iraq, 1991," *World Development*, Vol. 20 (July 1992), pp. 921-945, and Eric Hoskins, "Killing is Killing – Not Kindness," *New Statesman & Society*, Vol. 5 (January 17, 1992), pp. 12-13. In spite of internal unrest and prominent defections, Saddam Hussein has not been hurt by the sanctions, as pointed out, for example by Steve Platt, "Sanctions Don't Harm Saddam," *New Statesman & Society*, Vol. 7 (November 4, 1994), p. 10.

20 French Beaujolais wine, according to one report in *The New York Times*, has lost many markets in a boycott of French products to protest against French nuclear tests in the Pacific. Markets lost include not only the Pacific nations of Japan, Australia, and New Zealand, but also the Netherlands, Scandinavia, and Germany. See *The New York Times*, (November 17, 1995) Section A, p. 10.

21 The Secretaries-General of the United Nations have been Trygve Lie (of Norway), Dag Hammarskjold (of Sweden), U Thant (of Burma (Myanmar), Kurt Waldheim (of Austria), Javier Perez de Cuellar (from Peru), and Boutros Boutros-Ghali (from Egypt).

22 See Evan Luard, *The United Nations: How it Works and What It Does*. (New York: St. Martin's Press, 1994) pp. 102-125.

23 Brian Urquhart, "Selecting the World's CEO," *Foreign Affairs*, Vol. 74, No. 3 (May/June 1995) pp. 21-6.

24 See John Bulloch and Harvey Morris, *The Gulf War: Its Origins, History and Consequences*. (London: Methuen, 1989), p. 117, p. 119.

25 On the peace plan and ECOMOG's role see the following news reports: "Peace is Accepted by Liberians,"*The New York Times*, (August 20, 1995), section A, p. 17; and "8 Nation African Force is Peacekeeping Model in war torn Liberia," *The Washington Post*, (April 1, 1994), section A p. 26.

26 For samples of attacks on M'bow in the Western Press, see *The Economist*, (October 3, 1987) p. 48, and *Nature*, (October 8, 1987), p. 472.

27 See, for example, Adam Watson, "European International Society and Its Expansion," in Hedley Bull and Adam Watson (eds.), *The Expansion of International Society*, (Oxford: Clarendon Press, 1985) pp. 13-32 and Ian Brownlie "The Expansion of International Society: The Consequences for the Law of Nations," in Hedley Bull and Adam Watson (eds.), *The Expansion of International Society*, pp. 357-369.

28 Consult, for example, Karl Marx, *On Colonialism: Articles from the New York Tribune and other Writings, by Karl Marx and Friedrich Engels*, (New York: International Publishers, 1972), pp. 81-87.

29 See Karl Marx and Friedrich Engels, *Collected Works*, Vol. 6, (New York: International Publishers, 1976, p. 471.

30 For a description of Menon's view of the Goa affair and Western reactions to the Indian action, see Michael Brecher, *India and World Politics: Krishna Menon's View of the World*, (New York: Praeger, 1968), pp. 121-136.

31 Guides to the UN's role in combating apartheid may be found in "The UN and Apartheid: A Chronology," *UN Chronicle*, Vol. 31 (September 1994), pp. 9-14; Newell M. Stultz, "Evolution of the United Nations Anti-apartheid Regime," *Human Rights Quarterly*, Vol. 13 (February 1991), pp. 1-23; and Ozdemir A. Ozgur, *Apartheid, the United Nations, & Peaceful Change in South Africa*. (Dobbs Ferry, NY: Transnational Publishers, 1982).

32 See, for example, Michael G. Schatzberg, *Mobutu or Chaos?: The United States and Zaire, 1960-1990*, (Lanham, MD: University Presses of America/Foreign Policy Institute, 1991).

33 See Ali A. Mazrui, "The Resurgence of Islam and the Decline of Communism," *Futures: The Journal of Forecasting and Planning*, Vol. 23 (April 1991), pp. 283-285.

34 As stated by Vice-President Al Gore on *Nightline*, December 1, 1995. Also see *The New York Times*, (December 5, 1995), Section A, p. 7.

35 See for example, Carroll J. Doherty, "Dole Takes a Political Riskin Crusade to aid Bosnia," *Congressional Quarterly Weekly Report*, Vol 53 (March 11, 1995), pp. 761-763.

36 See, Samuel S. Kim, *China, The United Nations, and World Order*, (Princeton, NJ: Princeton University Press, 1979).

37 UN, *Yearbook of the United Nations, 1974*, (New York: UN, 1977) pp. 189-251.

38 On the NIEO, consult, for example, Pradip K. Ghosh (ed.), *New International Economic Order: A Third World Perspective*, (Westport, CT: Greenwood Press, 1984).

39 See Lawrence S. Finkelstein, "The Political Role of the Director-General of UNESCO," in Finkelstein (ed.) *Politics in the United Nations System*, pp. 385-423.

40 On the bombing, see *The New York Times*, (Tuesday, November 14, 1995), Section A, p. 1.

41 A recent evaluation of the literature may be found in James Lee Ray, *Democracy and International Conflict: An Evaluation of the Democratic Peace Proposition*, (Columbia, SC: University of South Carolina Press, 1995). Also, several leading scholars on this subject, such as Bruce Russett, Christopher Layne, David Shapiro, and Michael W. Doyle, assess the state of the field in their contributions to the *International Security*, Vol. 19 (Spring 1995) issue on this topic.

42 Huntington, "The Clash of Civilizations?" p. 39.

43 Witness the airlift of the "Falasha Jews" from Ethiopia, detailed in Ruth Gruber, *Rescue: The Exodus of the Ethiopian Jews*, (New York: Athenuem, 1987).

44 For a critical account of the mediation, see Mohammed H. Malek and Mark F. Imber, "The Security Council and the Gulf War: A Case of Double Standard," Chapter 4 in Mohammed H. Malek (ed.), *International Mediation and the Gulf War*, (Glasgow, Scotland: Royston, 1991).

45 On the change, see "Zionism No Longer Equated With Racism," *UN Chronicle*, Vol. 29 (March 1992), p. 67.

46 For a report on this incident, see *The New York Times*, (December 3, 1988), Section A, p. 1.

12 The Global Ummah and the British Commonwealth: Four Ethical Revolutions

ALI A. MAZRUI

The United Nations was born out of the ravages of war. The British Commonwealth was born out of the ravages of imperialism. At one time Britain either ruled or controlled nearly two-thirds of the Muslim world. Both the UN and the Commonwealth have now become forces for globalization. The Commonwealth dropped the word "British" from its name, as its membership became more global.

Globalization consists of those trends in the world which are fostering, wittingly or unwittingly, such tendencies as economic interdependence on a global scale, cross-cultural awareness, and global institution-building to regulate both inter-human relations and the exploitation of the world's resources. Globalization does include international currency upheavals like the recent ones in Asia, but those will not be the focus of this paper.

The 20th century was the century when war went global. The human race fought two world wars. World War I gave birth to the League of Nations, which was primarily an European Club. Almost the whole of Africa, much of Asia and the Muslim world, and the United States were outside the League, though the reasons for their absence from the League differed. It was World War II which gave birth to a more credible world body – the United Nations – though it took two decades after its formation before its membership became truly universalized. One particular force was vital for the universalization of the United Nations and the global expansion of the Commonwealth – the force was decolonization. This particular push of history liberated more and more countries – and made the new states available for membership of the United Nations and for accession to the Commonwealth. Today more than a billion Muslims are represented in the United Nations and about half of those are also represented in the Commonwealth, including the Muslims of Pakistan, India, Bangladesh, Nigeria and Malaysia.

But behind these political trends have been equally fundamental ethical trends in the 20th century. These ethical transformations have changed the nature of the Commonwealth and of the world. Let us look at them more closely.

Towards Morally Accountable Economies

Four ethical revolutions have characterized the 20th century. In the first third of the 20th century we witnessed in the Northern hemisphere revolutions against laissez-faire economics and increasingly in favor of morally accountable economies. These trends ranged from socialism to the New Deal, from V.I. Lenin to John Maynard Keynes. The Trades Union Congress in Britain united with the small Independent Labour Party at the beginning of the century. By the end of World War I the Labour Party was large enough to become the official opposition. Muhammad Ali Jinnah, future founder of Pakistan, felt some of the Fabian influences of this period during his years in Britain.

In approximately the second third of the 20th century the dominant revolution was racial. It challenged white supremacy world wide, and undermined the legitimacy of European empires. The revolution galvanized anti-colonial struggles and energized human rights movements. The European Empires experienced wide-ranging struggles for greater racial justice. From Indonesia to Algeria colonized Muslims sometimes resorted to armed struggle.

In approximately the last third of the 20th century two revolutions have captured the imaginations of reformers – the green revolution in defense of the environment and the gender revolution in pursuit of the empowerment of women. Has the Muslim world kept pace with these latest revolutions as well? The 20th century has sought morally responsible economies (spearheaded in the first third), racially responsible societies (spearheaded in the second third) and a world attentive to the empowerment of women and the defense of the environment (spearheaded in the last third of the century). How has the Commonwealth been affected by these four revolutions in the 20th century? How has the Muslim world responded to them? Let us look at these momentous trends at both their global and Commonwealth levels more closely.

It is not often recognized that *laissez faire* economics was probably born out of religious pantheism in the same sense in which Marxian material dialectics were born out of Hegelian Idealist dialectics. Pantheism found in Alexander Pope a powerful poetic voice. In Pope's *An Essay on Man* we hear:

All are but parts of one stupendous whole,
Whose body Nature is and God the soul.
All nature is but art unknown to thee,
All chance direction which thou canst not see,
All discord harmony not understood,
All partial evil universal good.
Whatever is, is right.[1]

This philosophical complacency was repugnant to Islamic ethics, but became quite influential in parts of the West. Adam Smith took this optimism from the religious-philosophical universe and focused it on economics. If you let economic and market forces operate unimpeded, all discord would in reality be "harmony not understood," all "partial evil" would be "universal good." An invisible hand would see to that. While Muslim economies were subject to rules against *riba* and reckless profiteering, Western economies entered the era of *laissez-faire.*

To quote and paraphrase another thinker, "All is for the best in this best of all possible *economic* worlds" – provided the market had free reign. This optimism about the benevolent consequences of unimpeded market forces dominated economic thought in the West until approximately the first third of the 20th century. It may now be struggling to come back, to some extent.

The principle of *laissez-faire* at one time opposed the establishment of a minimum wage, or the regulation of the employment of children. The campaign to save English children from the grime and soot of chimneys did not come into law until much later. Even the formation of trade unions was once regarded as a conspiracy to sabotage the economy, punishable by terms of imprisonment. The most sustained theoretical challenge to laissez-faire philosophy did come in the 19th century with the rise of socialist thinkers, including Karl Marx. Many Muslim thinkers flirted with socialist ideas also. But it was in the first third of the 20th century that anti-laissez-faire economic and political thought began to have a direct influence on the fate of governments and their policies.

At one level it led to the most momentous revolution of the 20th century – the Russian communist revolution of 1917. This was a total rejection of laissez-faire market forces. Less drastic was the challenge posed to laissez-faire by Keynesian economics. The state could intervene in the economy and regulate it – but in order to save capitalism rather than to destroy it. John Maynard Keynes helped to give capitalist respectability to state participation in the economy. State intervention to create jobs and assist the unemployed was also calculated to alleviate the suffering of their children.

In the United States the divergence from laissez-faire came with Franklin D. Roosevelt's New Deal policies which were designed to help the poor and the unemployed during the Great Depression. Roosevelt faced considerable opposition from a more conservative Supreme Court. But the New Deal of the 1930s muted the philosophy of laissez-faire in the United States at least until the mid-1990s. Is the principle of a morally accountable economy about to be overthrown by Republicans in the United States? Or will their bark turn out to be harsher than their bite?

Towards Morally Accountable Imperialism

How did these trends in the wider world affect the future Commonwealth and the Muslim world? The nature and mission of European colonialism began to change. The evolution of the welfare state in the West gave birth to a kind of welfare imperialism for the colonies. Great Britain was later to establish the Colonial Development and Welfare Fund. The poorest Muslim countries under British rule were among the beneficiaries. The old mission of Pax Britannica that emphasized law and order in the colonies gave way to a greater commitment to the material welfare and development of the native peoples. Welfare imperialism abroad accompanied the British welfare state at home.

But all this was itself setting the stage for the great ethical revolution of the second third of the 20th century – the racial revolution. While Islam itself is doctrinally non-racial, most Muslims had been under European racist rule. This second major ethical revolution of the century intensified anti-colonial struggles in Asia and Africa, increased and deepened Afro-Asian nationalism world-wide, sparked off the civil rights movement in the United States, and created both white apartheid and its militant Black adversaries. Muslims in South-East Asia had to fight not only European imperialism but also Japanese.

Curiously enough, World War II played a direct and sometimes positive part in this second revolution of the 20th century – the racial revolution. If we blame the horrors of World War II on the Germans it is still amazing how beneficial some of the long-term consequences of that war were for the future Commonwealth. This is the silver lining of the cloud of the Third Reich.

There is no doubt that the Second World War played a decisive role in undermining the foundations of the old European empires in Asia, Africa and the Americas. The war accelerated the independence of the Asian part of the British Empire – resulting in the independence of India and Pakistan in 1947 within two years of the end of the war. The liberation of South Asia was an important precedent for the liberation of Africa a decade later. And South Asia had a huge concentration of Muslims.

The German military challenge undermined Britain's imperial will and impoverished the British exchequer. The Germans also humiliated France and undermined the myth of French grandeur and invincibility. After all, the Germans had defeated France with unexpected ease. The mythology surrounding France in Africa was never the same again. In less than a decade after the end of World War II Mujahiddeen in Algeria were fighting for their independence.

World War II had also knocked Western Europe (including Germany) out of the League of first-rank world powers – and revealed more clearly the temporary bipolar succession of the United States and the Soviet Union as the new superpowers on the world stage. Countries like Pakistan and Egypt learnt to exploit this superpower rivalry while it lasted.

World War II had been fought as a crusade against tyranny and dictatorship. This crusade carried anti-colonial implications. If German occupation of Poland or Belgium was wrong, what about British occupation of Nigeria, Malaya, Algeria, and India? The moral rhetoric against the Germans boomeranged against British and French imperialists.

The Atlantic Charter signed in 1941 by President Franklin D. Roosevelt and Prime Minister Winston Churchill was widely interpreted as the Magna Carta of self-determination for all societies (including the colonies) – in spite of Winston Churchill's attempt to exclude the British Empire from the liberating implications of the Atlantic Charter.

The war against Germany and its allies expanded the political horizons of the African and Muslim soldiers who had fought in it. These soldiers had seen more of the world, and had witnessed the human weakness of the white man's fear in war, sometimes cowardice in a white officer. The white man was cut-down to size from demi-God to fellow human being. So what gave him the right to dominate and exploit Arabs or Black folks? African and Arab veterans of World War II were some of the catalysts of nationalism in this phase of struggle.

Then there was the impact of World War II on the birth of the United Nations' Organization, which in turn played a role in the decolonization of Africa, Asia and the Caribbean. Some countries that were once colonies of Germany before the end of World War I became trusteeships of the UN after World War II. These countries included Tanganyika, Cameroon, Togo, Ruanda-Urundi and South-West Africa (now Namibia).

The UN was for a while a benign collective imperial power. But on the whole the over-all impact of the UN on Africa, Asia and the Caribbean was in the direction of greater decolonization. Most former British colonies joined the Commonwealth. Muslim members (with years of entry) include Malaysia (1957), Nigeria (1960), Pakistan (re-entered 1989) and, in a sense, India (1947).

With the disintegration of political apartheid in South Africa in the 1990s, a very important battle has been won. Canada played a big role against the apartheid regime. But the war against racial injustice in South Africa is surely not over. Political apartheid may be over, but economic apartheid is alive and well. As President, Nelson Mandela refused to turn his back on those Muslim leaders who had once supported him, such as Muammar Qaddafy of Libya and Yassir Arafat of the Palestine Liberation Organization (PLO).

The great wealth of that great country is still mal-distributed along racial lines. Whites in South Africa own the best land; whites own the mines and most of the mineral wealth; whites have disproportionately the best jobs in industry, commerce and the civil service. And whites still have the least unemployment and the best salaries and wages for the same kind of work.

Economic apartheid is still intact. With the peaceful formation of a multiracial government of national unity, political apartheid died in 1994. A major battle has been won; but the war is inconclusive. The Commonwealth as a whole fought to end political apartheid. Is there a role for the Commonwealth in the struggle against economic apartheid? Many Muslim governments helped in the crusade against white minority rule. Can Muslims still help in the new economic struggle?

Indeed, in South Africa, the anti-laissez-faire revolution may lie in the future rather than in the past. It may lie in the first third of the 21st century rather than the first third of the 20th century as it did in the West. The sequence of the four revolutions in South Africa was simply distorted by the aberration of racism, whose institutionalized form lasted longer in South Africa than anywhere else.

Outside South Africa the second ethical revolution of the twentieth century was indeed a racial revolution and was primarily in the second third of the century from the mid-1930s to the mid-1960s. For Africa and the Muslim world this revolution was, as we indicated, particularly wide-ranging. Armed struggle in Africa and the Arab world came to benefit considerably from the support of the Soviet Union and its allies at the time. What had happened in the anti-laissez-faire revolution of the first third of the 20th century fed into the racial struggles of the later part of the century.

In the United States the racial revolution included such momentous Supreme Court decisions as Brown versus the Board of Education in 1954, which ended the era of "Separate but Equal." The racial revolution in the African Diaspora also included the civil rights movement in the United States and the role of Dr. Martin Luther King Jr. in it. Did the anti-colonial movement in Africa in the second third of the 20th century help the civil rights movement in the USA? The symbiotic relationship between anti-racism and the anti-colonialism is still to be conclusively studied.

Another anomaly worth noting is that none of the Arab countries previously ruled or controlled by Great Britain applied to become members of the Commonwealth. While the Muslim world is well represented in the Commonwealth (nearly 500 million people) the Arab world is grossly under-represented. Countries like Egypt, Sudan and Iraq regarded Commonwealth membership as incompatible with Pan-Arabism. It would be ironic if in the 21st century the first Arab member of the Commonwealth became the new Palestinian state.

The Gender Revolution

As for last third of the 20th century, this has witnessed two other ethical revolutions – a concern for the rights of women and a concern for the ecology, including other living creatures. How has the Commonwealth been influenced by these latest twin revolutions – gender and ecology? Is the Muslim world a mere bystander?

The gender revolution in the West has helped African and Muslim children more than African and Muslim women. Liberated Western women have been an important additional lobby in support of the rights of children in Asia and Africa. Western influence in defense of African and Asian children is culturally less offensive than Western efforts in defense of African and Asian women. When the Nigerian Military Government of the late General Sani Abacha sent out feelers about outlawing female circumcision in November 1994, the regime did so in the context of the rights of children rather than the rights of women. Female circumcision was seen as a violation of the rights of children (since it was done in childhood) more than a transgression against the rights of women. Although General Abacha himself was a Muslim, both Muslims and non-Muslims practised female circumcision in Nigeria. It was more a "tribal" rite than a religious one. General Abacha's government was also considering outlawing scarification (tribal marks on the face). Again, if outlawed by his successors, the decree would be in the name of the rights of children who are scarred as minors.

In the phenomenon of women in top positions in politics, it is arguable that the Commonwealth has led the world. It did not begin with Margaret Thatcher as prime minister of Great Britain. It began in 1960 with Sirimavo Bandaranaike as Prime Minister of Ceylon (later Sri Lanka). Indeed, Mrs. Bandaranaike started the overwhelmingly Commonwealth phenomenon of female succession to male martyrdom. This is a situation where a woman attains ultimate political office but in succession to a heroic male relative, usually martyred. Mr. S.W.R.D. Bandaranaike was assassinated in 1959 – and his widow, Mrs. Bandaranaike, was swept into ultimate political prominence soon after.

Jawaharlal Nehru died in 1964 and in 1966 Indira Gandhi, his daughter, became prime minister of India. Zulfikar Ali Bhutto was executed in Pakistan in 1979 – and eventually Benazir Bhutto became prime minister for the first time in 1988. She has continued to be in and out of power. Pakistan is the first Muslim country in modern history to have a head of government who is a woman.[2] In Bangladesh Sheikh Mujibur Rahman of the nascent nation was assassinated with his wife and five of his children in August 1975, and eventually one of his surviving daughters became leader of the Awami League and finally Prime Minister in 1997.

Also in Bangladesh, President Ziaur Rahman was assassinated in May 1981. Ten years later his widow was sworn in as Prime Minister.

Bangladesh is the first Commonwealth country to have had two women prime ministers in succession, belonging to opposing parties. Bangladesh is also the first Muslim country to have achieved such female empowerment at the top.

Across the world is the only South American member of the Commonwealth – the Cooperative Republic of Guyana. Cheddi B. Jagan was sworn in on October 30, 1992, in succession to Hugh Desmond Hoyte. Cheddi Jagan died in March 1997. In December 1997 his widow Janet Jagan was elected president – amidst charges that since she was foreign-born, she was not qualified to be Head of State in Guyana. (Mrs. Jagan was born as a white American in Chicago.) Most Muslims in Guyana seem to have voted for Mrs. Jagan. The one remarkable Commonwealth female leader who was in no sense a successor to a heroic male relative was Britain's Margaret Thatcher, who became Prime Minister in May 1979, and maintained her top leadership for eleven years.

But Margaret Thatcher was a case where the two revolutions of the 20th century sometimes dramatically clashed – the struggle for gender equality and the struggle for racial equality. Although she herself symbolized the ultimate empowerment of a woman, and historians may well regard her as the most powerful single woman in any part of the 20th century, she was less than lukewarm in the struggle for racial equality. Within the Commonwealth she was sometimes isolated in her refusal to impose economic sanctions on the apartheid regime in South Africa. She would dig her high heels in – at once a symbol of female power and a symbol of refusal to fight apartheid.

A Commonwealth female leader who had reservations about the first ethical revolution of the 20th century was Dame Mary Eugenia Charles of Dominica in the West Indies. As a politically successful woman she signified the march of the gender revolution in the century. But as leader of the Dominica Freedom Party (DFP), she represented a right-wing alliance, which was associated with the propertied class at Rosenau. Mary Eugenia Charles was Prime Minister from July 1980 until 1994.

Eugenia Charles' right wing tendencies were a factor behind Dominica's enthusiastic participation in the multinational force, which, under U.S. leadership, invaded Grenada in October 1983. Once again, within the story of Eugenia Charles we find the gender revolution of female empowerment running counter to the earlier revolutions in defence of the economically and racially underprivileged. Grenada was at the time a country trying to create a morally accountable economy through socialism. It paid the price of a U.S.-led invasion.

Canada experimented briefly with a woman prime minister when Brian Mulroney resigned in favor of Kim Campbell in 1993. It was not a good time to have the first woman prime minister. Kim Campbell was confronted with an anti-Conservative tide, which she could neither contain nor reverse. Her Party (the Progressive Conservative Party) suffered the worst defeat to any ruling party in Canadian history – shrinking from 153 to 2 members in the House of Commons. She was Prime Minister for a mere 134 days. She resigned as party leader on December 13, 1993.

In spite of all this unevenness, the Commonwealth (including its Muslim members) has indeed been in the vanguard of the struggle for the political empowerment of women. Scandinavian countries have provided striking models of their own, and have set a good example to the rest of the world. But their international visibility is modest in comparison to the leading members of the Commonwealth. Within the Commonwealth at least one-fifth of the human race has been ruled by a woman at sometime or another in the last forty years. In South Asia over three hundred million Muslims have known rule by a woman. And if Sonia Gandhi – the widow of the assassinated Rajiv Gandhi – does eventually become India's second woman Prime Minister, the achievement will be both trans-gender and trans-racial. Sonia Gandhi is ethnically Italian, as well as being a remarkable woman. Her party (Congress) is widely regarded as Muslim-friendly.

Finally, we should remember that the Commonwealth might be the only male-dominated multinational club, which has had a woman for its Head for more than four decades. The Head is, of course, Queen Elizabeth II. The only reservation Muslims might have is that the Head of the Commonwealth is simultaneously the Head of the Church of England. The British monarch has to serve both roles. For once, it is the Muslims who might prefer a separation of church and state.

The Green Revolution

If the initial three ethical revolutions of the 20th century were socio-economic, racial and gender, what is the nature of the fourth revolution and how has it affected the Commonwealth?

The green revolution of the last third of the 20th century has sought to protect rivers and hills, air and water, Indian and Malaysian tigers and African elephants. Sometimes the struggle against environmental degradation and the struggle for morally accountable economies are inseparable. Particularly poignant in 1995 was the plight of the Oguni people of Nigeria and the brutal fate of Ken Saro-Wiwa in the full glare of a Commonwealth conference in New Zealand. The environment of the Oguni villagers was devastated by the oil industry in their area – and Ken Saro-Wiwa and eleven others were executed partly for protesting in ways which were unacceptable to the military in Nigeria. Because President Sani Abacha was a Muslim and the executed Ogoni activists were mainly Christian, the brutal incident had sectarian reverberations in Nigeria.

The green revolution has also sought to protect the dwindling legacy of wild animals against the greed of hunters, poachers and corrupt politicians. But is there also a danger that as far as Westerners are concerned, "one hippo is worth two Hutus!?" In other words, are the agricultural and pastoral needs of Africa's expanding populations being sacrificed to the whims of nature lovers? The rate of population growth among Sub-Saharan Muslims has been particularly high.

There is indeed a genuine dilemma. In many African countries, independence for African people (Muslim and non-Muslim) has meant less freedom for African animals. Widening political horizons for African people have coincided with narrowing physical horizons for African animals. Postcolonial African authorities have been far less effective in protecting African animals than the colonial authorities had been. What nature lovers sometimes forget is that post-colonial African authorities have been less effective in protecting African people too. The cost of learning how to govern ourselves has sometimes been high. But we do need to learn self-government in any case. It is a stage we have to go through.

On the other hand, the African animals have been lucky that the post-colonial era has coincided with the new ecological revolution. Post-coloniality has coincided with the rise of the green movements. While some human beings are indeed fast depleting the heritage of Planet Earth, other human beings are on greater ecological alert in the last third of the 20th century than ever before in history. However un-Islamic when taken literally, Alexander Pope's couplet has been given a new ecological meaning:

> All are but parts of one stupendous whole
> Whose body Nature is and God the Soul.

The environmental depletion is worse today than ever in history. But the environmental defenders are more active than ever before, in history. On balance the Asian and African environment has suffered because of independence but the Asian and African environment would have suffered even more if the era of independence had not coincided with the newly energized environmental consciousness worldwide. Indonesia under President Suharto was too permissive towards environmental degradation of the tropical rain forest. Fires have taken a high toll.

The ethical revolution of environmentalism is partly helping to discipline the earlier ethical revolution of race. The struggle for the rights of people of color is by no means over yet. But now there is concern for the rights of the leopard and the rhino, the rights of fish in the rivers and oceans, the green rights of valleys and hills.

Other environmentalists go further. There are even Muslim environmentalists who share William Wordsworth's belief that Nature's grand design is predicated on joy and wonderment. The discordant note in Nature's grand design is man. In Wordsworth's words:

> Through primrose tufts in that green bower,
> The periwinkle trailed its wreaths,
> And it's my faith that every flower,
> Enjoys the air it breathes.
>
> The birds around me hopped and played,
> Their thoughts I cannot measure,
> But the least motion which they made,
> It seemed a thrill of pleasure.
>
> The budding twigs spread out their fans,
> To catch the breezy air,
> And I must think, do all I can,
> That there was pleasure there.
>
> If this belief from heaven be sent,
> If such be nature's holy plan,
> Have I not reason to lament,
> What man has made of man?[3]

Yes, the grand design is for joy and wonderment. The discordant note is Man – including post-colonial elites of the Commonwealth and the Muslim world.

The environmental revolution and the gender revolution of the last third of the 20th century are interlinked at various points. But they are interconnected most poignantly through the issue of population and the whole culture of having and rearing children. It is to this area of convergence between gender, population and environment that we must now turn. After all, the Commonwealth includes among its members the second most populous country in the world (India). The Commonwealth also includes large parts of explosive Africa.

Many African countries have been witnessing their population double every 20 years. Children under 15 years of age probably account for 45% of the population of Africa - as compared with 37% in Asia and 40% in Latin America.

Infant mortality is still very high. In some years Africa accounts for 5 million out of 7 million annual infant deaths – although Africa has less than one-sixth of the population of the developing world and only about a tenth of the population of the world.

Africans have many children for a variety of reasons, including, on the one hand, children are an insurance for old age when parents will need to be looked after and, on the other hand, children are (in African tradition) a passport to immortality beyond the grave: We are not dead as long as our blood flows in the veins of the living. This is the phase of Sasa: The living dead still being remembered by their descendants. In the words of the English poet William Wordsworth:

> O Joy that in our embers
> Is something that doth live
> That Nature yet remembers
> What was so fugitive.[4]

Genes are a memory of ancestry. The duty of a Muslim father is to bring up good children (father as disciplinarian). The duty of a Muslim mother is to bring up happy children (mother as a fountain of sympathy). If children are an insurance for old age, mothers are greater beneficiaries. Women in the Muslim world and Africa live longer and are more likely to benefit from the children's care in old age. If children are a passport to immortality, *fathers* in Africa and the Muslim world have access to more passports. Polygamous fathers can have up to 50 children; whereas no woman is ever likely to be a biological mother to more than about 12 children. The role of children as insurance here on earth serves mothers better than fathers. The role of children as a heavenly insurance for immortality in African traditional religion gives fathers an edge – since per person African fathers have more children than African mothers.

For every human being there is an economically pre-productive age, which is followed by a productive age and which in turn is followed by a post-productive age. Clearly a newly-born baby is not economically productive. If it is being breast-fed, it is not even a direct economic consumer except in number of nappies or diapers it goes through.

In Western societies children below the age of about 7 are hardly ever economic producers. They are in the pre-productive age. In Nigeria and South Asia the pre-productive age may be children below the age of about 4 years old. After that they may be involved in serious economic activities on the farm or the household.

Although the productive age in Africa and South Asia begins early – perhaps at the age of four – the productive age also ends relatively early. Going into serious retirement at the age of about 55 is quite common in Asia and Africa. People are regarded as "old" in Nigeria and Pakistan earlier than they are in the United States and Western Europe. The post-productive age in Africa and Asia is allowed to start sooner than necessary.

But in addition the population of the elderly is in any case expanding much faster in the West than in South Asia and Africa – Western men and women live longer. And so the population of the post-productive sector is becoming a bigger percentage of the total Western community.

In Africa, on the other hand, fertility rates are much higher than they are in the West. As a region Africa has the fastest growing population rate in the world. Therefore the pre-productive sector of Africa's population is bigger than it is in the West – just as the post-productive sector in the West is bigger than it is in Africa. The West has a disproportionate number of elderly people, while Africa has a disproportionate number of children and minors.

In the 21st century the West has to solve a compelling dilemma – is it enough to delay death without delaying aging? People in the West live longer but the aging process continues relentlessly – until the elderly become decrepid and overwhelmingly dependent. The West has found the secret of living longer but not the secret of stopping the aging process. The Western world is not yet James Hilton's Shangri-La, where both death and aging are delayed.[5]

A Bridge Between Genders

But the quest for balance in the 21st century is not only between races, classes and generations. It is also between men and women. Politically how should Africa and the Muslim world respond to the gender revolution? Africa and Asia should work out institutions in the political process, which permit the following phases of parliamentary participation:

PHASE I: We should have gender reservation of seats under which both the candidates and the voters would be women. Some Muslim countries have made a start.

PHASE II: The seats would still be reserved for women candidates, but this time they would need to cultivate the support of both male and female voters. The electoral roll would now be universal. Iran is feeling its way towards such a system.

PHASE III: This would be a stage when there is confidence that female parliamentary candidates can compete without protection or reservation of seats. All parliamentary seats would therefore revert to a common electoral universal roll, free for all. Turkey believes it has reached such a stage. But although Turkey is another Muslim country, which has produced a woman Prime Minister [Tansu Cïller], women members of parliament are still few in Ankara.

India worked out a formula of reserving seats for women in the Lower House, but so far no government has followed through with required legislation. On the executive branch, the aim everywhere in the Commonwealth and the Muslim world should be to plan for at least a third of the cabinet and the bureaucracy to consist of women by the year 2025 or soon after. Gender revolution or not, Muslim and most Commonwealth women may never want to be as much as 50% of either the political or the military professions – 30% women in both professions could be optimum.

On the other hand, by way of compensation, women should own and control more than 50% of the economy before the middle of the 21st century. In some African countries, women already do the bulk of the agricultural work. What is needed is to give them greater rights of ownership of land and greater access to independent credit.

As for enhancing female participation in the judicial branch of government, this can best be achieved by encouraging and subsidizing more and more women to study the law – and help them establish themselves in the face of stiff masculine competition. From the wider legal profession women could then increase their numbers in the judicial system of judges and district attorneys and make a greater impact on the country's system of justice. New *fatwas* in the Shari'a may be needed to permit Muslim female judges. Can the legal testimony of a woman continue to have half the weight of a man's testimony in economic cases?

In September 1994, The United Nations Cairo Conference on Population was agonizing about how many new children would have been born thirty years from then. In Addis Ababa, at about the same time, another conference was agonizing about how many of those children would be born as refugees, either as children or as adults. Should the Ummah have a High Commissioner for Refugees of its own?

The Cairo conference was about new babies being born in normal circumstances. In Addis Ababa the UNHCR/OAU conference was in part about new babies born in refugee camps. What did reproductive health mean in refugee camps in Pakistan, Afghanistan or Tanzania? Is there a definition of refugee that would take into account whether the child is wanted or not? Perhaps every unwanted child, anywhere in the world, is a political refugee.

This applies to unwanted children of parents who are not themselves refugees. Unwanted new babies of Tutsi or Hutu in Tanzania are therefore refugees twice-over. Unwanted rape babies in Bosnia are refugees. International law and practice have tended to define a refugee in relation to whether a state tolerates him or her as a citizen. Should we include in the 21st century in the definition of a refugee the issue of whether the parents want the child as a member of a family? If the world is a global village, is it also to become a global cradle? When will every unwanted baby have global foster parents? Is the 21st century the relevant era? Should the Muslim world consider having a High Commissioner for Children and Orphans?

In response to both the gender and ecological revolutions, we need a global population policy, rather than just a policy for the growth rates of the Third World. Every child born in the United States is multiple times a greater threat to the Planet Earth than a child born in Nigeria, Bangladesh or Egypt.

The child born in the USA will consume a bigger share of the world's resources, generate more carbon dioxide into the atmosphere with his cars and gadgets, contribute more to the greenhouse effect, be a bigger threat to the ozone layer, generate more toxic and nuclear waste without adequate means of disposal, and perpetrate a continuing use of sophisticated military arsenals several times every decade.

The 1994 Cairo Conference on Population had many speakers who regretted population growth in countries of low gross national product like Pakistan and Nigeria. There were very few voices who regretted population growth in countries of high national consumption like the United States. According to Paul R. Ehrlich and Anne H. Ehrlich in their book *The Population Explosion:*

> ... a baby born in the United States represents twice the destructive impact on the Earth's ecosystems and the services they provide as one born in Sweden...35 times one born in India, 140 times one in Bangladesh or Kenya, and 280 times, one in Chad, Rwanda, Haiti or Nepal.[6]

While the global reformers should indeed champion reduced population growth in Asia and in the 21st century, they should also champion measures for minus-zero population growth in the industrialized world, and greater control of rates of consumption. But within that larger global policy on population, refugees and orphans the Ummah and Commonwealth should work out roles for themselves – sensitive to the four ethical revolutions of the 20th century.

Conclusion

Early in 1998 I was attending the World Economic Forum in Davos, Switzerland, the largest and in some ways most important economic conference of its kind. The theme for this 1998 World Economic Forum was based on a consciousness of the new century, and the new millennium. The forces of globalization were in the Davos air.

From Commonwealth Africa the Davos Forum invited some of the men who represented a new generation of leadership, fit to prepare Africa for the new millennium. The Forum was addressed by President Yoweri Museveni of Uganda, who defended his vision of an economy without the state, and a state without political parties – Uganda as a no-state economy and a no-party state. President Jerry Rawlings of Ghana, a former military ruler who had been creatively recycled into a democratic ruler, addressed the

Forum. Is this a new wave into the 21st century? Is Jerry Rawlings the second Kwame Nkrumah of Ghana's history?

The World Economic Forum was also addressed by Thabo Mbeki, President of the African National Congress in South Africa. This Deputy President of South Africa discussed the pitfalls as well as the promise of globalization for the 21st century.

Representation from the Arab world included the distinguished Palestinian woman activist, Hanan Ashrawi, as well senior ambassadors from diverse countries. Nawaz Shariff was the most senior statesman from the Muslim world at the World Economic Forum. The Prime Minister of Pakistan called upon international investors to distinguish between short-term political problems in South Asia and long-term economic opportunities. They should rise to the challenge of long-term optimism. Iran was represented by the woman Vice-President, Masoumeh Ebtekar, Vice-President of the Islamic Republic of Iran and Head of the Organization for the Protection of the Environment and Kamal Kharrazi, Minister of Foreign Affairs of the Islamic Republic of Iran.

In this paper our longer term perspective concerns four ethical revolutions which have unfolded in the 20th century – the revolution of moral accountability; the revolution of racial equality; the revolution of gender equality; the revolution of ecological balance.

In the first revolution of morally accountable economies, thinkers within the Commonwealth provided some of the best answers to the challenge of morally accountable capitalism. The most influential of the thinkers in the Commonwealth was perhaps John Maynard Keynes whose theories helped capitalism find in its own enlightened self-interest, a formula for its survival. It was in the interest of capitalism to avert abject poverty and prevent class-polarization. But capitalism can only do so with the help of the state. Selective state intervention became a lifeboat for the survival of capitalism during the Depression. Most of the Muslim world was already under capitalist direction. Keynsian theories later resulted in major developments in the construction of welfare states in the Commonwealth – helped by the landslide victory of the British Labour Party after World War II. Muslim thinkers were influenced by such Western schools of socialism.

Canada later blazed the trail in morally accountable economies in the Americas, capping it with the most responsible National Health Scheme in North America. In the British Empire morally accountable power resulted in such innovations as the Colonial Development and Welfare Fund and other experiments that sought to tame colonial exploitation with colonial development and imperial responsibility. It also helped to speed up the process of turning the British Empire into the Commonwealth.

As we enter the new millennium we know that the process of creating morally accountable power is reversible. There has been a partial dismantling of the welfare state in some Commonwealth and Muslim countries. We are unlikely to relapse ever again into laissez-faire – but nevertheless, capitalism has sought to free itself recently from some of the moral fetters of social democracy in a number of countries in the Commonwealth. The question for the Third millennium is which tendency is more enduring – the pull towards a social democratic order and a morally accountable economy or the pull towards the sovereignty of the market and reduced moral accountability.

In the second ethical revolution of the 20th century (the struggle against racism), the Commonwealth has also been in the vanguard. Some of the greatest fighters against racism have emerged out of the womb of the Commonwealth. They have ranged from Mohandas Gandhi in South Africa to Muhammad Ali Jinnah in British India; from Barbara Castle in Britain to Winnie Mandela in apartheid South Africa; from General Abdel Nasser in Egypt to Shridath Ramphal of Guyana; from Mahathir Mohammad of Malaysia to Robert Mugabe of Zimbabwe. Mahatma Gandhi and Nelson Mandela are widely regarded as the moral giants of them all – whose ethical message has resonated and resounded around the world. Most Muslims will accept the choice of Mandela; but some Muslims may have reservations about Mohandas Gandhi. Will the 20th century hand over to the 21st century a world with little or no racism? Or will the second millennium hand over to the third a different kind of racism instead? We are beginning to suspect that a classless society in the 21st century is most unlikely. But is a raceless society in the 21st century at least conceivable?

The four revolutions themselves will continue to be needed. Economies need to be socially accountable. Societies need to be racially equitable. The world needs to be gender egalitarian. And the human race needs to be ecologically responsible. The Commonwealth and the religion of Islam itself are bound to play a part. The Commonwealth is caught in the vortex of those four revolutions of the 20th century as we approach the new millennium. Islam is bound to be one of the most influential sets of values unfolding upon the new configuration.

Is there a fifth revolution waiting to be born in the 21st century? The world needs to be culturally more balanced – restoring validity to traditions that have been marginalized, cultures, which have been eclipsed, and languages that have been diminished by the aggressive expansionism of Western civilization. W.E.B. Du Bois once argued that the ultimate problem of the 20th century was the problem of the color line. Perhaps the ultimate problem of the 21st century will be the problem of the culture line. The Commonwealth and the Muslim world are bound to be in the middle of it all. But that is a subject for another study.

Notes

1 Alexander Pope, *An Essay on Man*, (1733-34).

2 Pakistan pulled out of the Commonwealth in 1971 in protest against international recognition of the independence of Bangladesh (formerly East Pakistan). The new Pakistan was readmitted to the Commonwealth in 1989.

3 William Wordsworth, *Lines Written in Early Spring*, (1798).

4 William Wordsworth, *Ode on Intimations of Immortality*, (1807).

5 See James Hilton's novel *Lost Horizon*, (London, 1944 edition).

6 Paul R. Ehrlich and Anne H. Ehrlich, *The Population Explosion*, (New York, NY: Simon & Schuster, 1990) p. 134.